The Candy Men

The Rollicking Life and Times of the Notorious Novel *Candy*

Nile Southern

Arcade Publishing • New York

Visit the author's sites at www.terrysouthern.com and www.dadstrangelove.com

10 9 8 7 6 5 4 3 2 1

Library of Congress Cataloging-in-Publication Data is available on file.

Cover design by Charlotte Strick

Print ISBN: 978-1-62872-419-6
Ebook ISBN: 978-1-62872-458-5

Printed in the United States of America

For Carol

If there are two, ahem, interesting minds at work . . . it's like two friends telling each other jokes—there's a built-in incentive to do it . . . and of course if you're a better writer than you are a talker, then there's also a nice strong incentive to actually get it down on paper. I would say it's the purest form of writing there is, like a letter to your best friend, because it's writing to an audience of one, and that one is a reflection of yourself. I mean you do have to have that sort of regard for the other person.

—Terry Southern, on collaborating with
Mason Hoffenberg on *Candy*
The Realist, May 1964

Contents

"In *Candy* we set about to do something that had never been done before. Romantic sex. It's usually made ugly, like 'I stuck my finger in her bunghole.' We made it a romantic treatment. Ultimately funny, but erotic."

—Terry Southern to *The Realist*

"It's as if you vomit in the gutter and everybody starts saying it's the greatest new art form, so you go back to see it and, by God, you have to agree."

—Mason Hoffenberg to *Playboy*

Paul Krassner: *Does Candy Christian represent an actual contemporary prototype?*

Terry Southern: *Yes, it's one of the most common and disturbing phenomena going. You see a groovy chick, and she's with some kind of nut, creep, or crackpot. "What the devil do you see in him?" you ask. "Oh, you don't understand!" she says. And then, when really pressed, it comes down to "He needs me." Beauty and the beast, simple as that, Paul.*

Preface to the Paperback Edition on the 50th Anniversary of *Candy's* American Publication

A few years ago, I was asked by my daughter's middle school in Boulder to give a presentation on *The CANDY Men* — which had won the Colorado Book Award for Creative Nonfiction. Since Banned Books Week was upon us, the school librarian thought it also a good idea to present something on *Candy*, since the novel, cowritten by my father, Terry Southern, and his friend, the poet Mason Hoffenberg, had a unique and volatile publishing history — which is what *The CANDY Men* is all about. Upon its publication in 1958, *Candy* was formally banned in France and tacitly in the United States through a series of sporadic police actions and community ordinances. Librarians across the U.S. came to *Candy*'s defense and fought for the right of their adult patrons to read the book. This was doubly ironic, since the novel had become the most brazenly pirated book of its time, with various editions literally flooding the drugstores, airports, and train stations of America — wherever books were sold.

At the school, I addressed a group of advanced "Language Arts" students (my father would have lampooned that phrase) in metal folding chairs with the Rocky Mountains towering in huge windows behind me. Since the kids had navigated Sex Ed, I thought it would be fun to compare their understanding of intercourse with Guru Grindle's "instruction" of Candy, while also pointing out that there were no obscenities in the following text:

> "Now I'm going to put this member into you," said Grindle judiciously, "and in that way can the sensation of the so-called 'sexual act' be approximated and surveyed to advantage." . . .
>
> "Now I am inserting the member," he explained. . . .
>
> "I shall presently demonstrate still another mastery of glandular functions," claimed Great Grindle, "that of the so-called *orgasm*, or *ejaculation."*

As the teachers hid their faces, I reminded the students that the Guru was in a position of authority over Candy — and that today he'd probably wind up in jail for even saying such a thing to a student. As for Candy's concerns about getting pregnant, Guru Grindle, all charm and oiliness, had some pious advice:

> "Don't be absurd. . . . naturally, in willing the chemistry of the semen, I would eliminate the impregnating agent, spermatozoa, as a constituent — for it would be of no use to our purposes here you see."

Many of the kids were gobsmacked, not so much for the "bad science" on display as the clinical rape described. My point was that books of the past were often banned not for their "curse words" alone, but for their *ideas* and the "offensiveness" of their depictions. In this case, the grotesque abuse of Candy is depraved and disgusting; and the language, dialogue, etc., *reflects* that depravity. "The book itself is not obscene — the *characters* are," I ventured. *Candy* may not be in many school libraries, but it is in most public libraries these days — perhaps still on the higher shelves and out of the reach of children, which is where librarians used to keep the so-called "dirty books" of literature.

In his witch hunt for the obscene, J. Edgar Hoover identified *Candy* in 1965 as a "suitable vehicle for prosecution." In a cryptic but enlightened memo, the FBI reviewed the book, determining it was "obviously a work of satire," presumably because they found it had, as per the Supreme Court's new guidelines, "redeeming social or literary value." Also, the book's language was not vulgar, but rather charming and clearly comic. The George Carlin–like flood of obscenities Candy screams at the height of her hunchback pleasure —"Fuck! Shit! Piss! Cunt! Cock! Crap! Prick! Kike! Nigger! Wop! *Hump!*"— is visually overpowered by her shout (in caps): "GIVE ME YOUR HUMP!" Perhaps the most distinctive stylistic choice is how that obscure object of desire — Candy's "vage"— is longingly hyperbolized with enticing, fluffy food-stuff references like "honey-pot," "fur-pie," "lamb-pit," "hot puss," "honey cloister," "ever-sweetening-pudding-pie," and the volcanic pièce de résistance, her "seething thermal pudding." Besides being funny, the effect subverts our expectations of the porn mechanics; instead of finding obscenity at the "main event" (intercourse, etc.), we find it in the situation between the characters: their obsessions, beliefs, and ultimate corruption. The use of these euphemisms may also have helped *Candy* stay alive on the streets of Paris (as *Lollipop*), where her porn nature wasn't detected.

When *Candy* was first published in America, fifty years ago, the nexus between sexuality and media was radically different than it is in 2014. It is almost impossible to imagine a bookseller today, or a librarian or regular customer, being threatened with jail time for buying, selling, or mailing a potentially "indecent" book like *Candy*. Back then, before the Supreme Court decisions on obscenity, your harassment depended on the town you lived in, and its "community standards of decency."

Candy plays with the notion of decency and the social tensions between what can be said in public and what was, and often still is, impermissible:

> "I'm in the mood for cock and plenty of it!" cried Liv gaily. "About ten pounds, please, thick and fast!" . . .
>
> "Now, Liv," said Uncle Jack, laying down his menu gently, "You *will* go too far."
>
> "Who's talking about 'go'?" demanded Liv. "The girls want to *come*! Am I right, Can?"

Though the book had been banned in France since 1958, *Candy*'s much-anticipated American debut in the spring of 1964 was seen by many intellectuals as a chance for the public debate over "decency" in literature to finally catch up with the Supreme Court victories won for Grove by publisher Barney Rosset and his attorney, Charles Rembar. *Candy*'s use of humor, social lampoon, and a hip knowingness mimetically siphoned the anarchic, playful riffing going on in the cafés and jazz clubs of Paris and Greenwich Village, making it a reflection of its times. Terry and Mason captured the spirit of the "put on"— inserting flies-in-the-ointment on the various American dreams being sold uptown by the Mad Men of "Mad Ave." *Candy*'s excellence became a rallying cry for such prominent figures as Nelson Algren, William Styron, Joe Heller, and Malcolm Cowley to help America get over what Lenny Bruce was calling its "dirty word problem."

The book's American publisher, Putnam, maximized the critical attention and ran multiple ad campaigns, one of which I recently unearthed in agent Sterling Lord's archives in New York:

> In just a few short weeks America has made an unprecedented best seller out of this unique comedy. Why? Because CANDY is a refreshing breeze in America's house of hearts, a comic chop at all our false totems, and a veritable earthquake in the underground literature of our time.

The frenzy around *Candy*'s publication in 1964 coincided with the arrival of other cultural tastes from abroad, namely the British Invasion by the Beatles *and* the Rolling Stones. African American culture was transforming America musically and politically; Martin Luther King and Malcolm X were leading a nationwide movement; the Civil Rights Bill was passed. The "sexual revolution" was exploding in music, pop art, advertising, and fashion, reflecting a passionate, nonconformist youth culture awakened to pleasure and mind-expansion. It was also a time of great turbulence and growing confusion for young men — with Kennedy's assassination the year before and the Gulf of Tonkin "Incident" spuriously igniting America's total involvement in Vietnam.

Pressure was building on boys to become young men. The transformative and therapeutic power of masturbation, a Wilhelm Reich–inspired theme Terry and Mason explore in *Candy,* ironically came to pass when Candy (the character *and* the book) became the objects of intense, masturbatory focus for many. With its nonstop sex — a requirement for Girodias' *Traveller's Companion* series — its fine prose style, outrageous humor, and propensity for *escalation* — a technique perfected in Terry's books and Mason's bull sessions — the novel became a salve for many a frustrated teen at the time, including the artist Richard Prince, who recently reflected on *Candy* as a rite-of-passage in his online blog *Birdtalk*:

> I read *Candy* one summer just before turning fifteen living in a tent with seven other pre-teen boys. The tent was part of a camp out on the back nine of the Hyannis Port Golf Club. We were all caddies, living there before going into the tenth grade trying to make tips to pay our own way. We'd all been dropped off at the beginning of the summer. Most of us were there because parents felt the experience of working and paying for your room and board would provide a life lesson. Discipline we were told was what we all needed. The place was run like a military camp for junior cadets. Golf was beside the point. Survival of the fittest was the way things worked. We were all masturbating like mad and *Candy* helped get the spanking going. We took turns with the book, passing it around with a flashlight to read it under the sheets. Sometimes we would hand-job each other. Sometimes we would sit around in a circle and "circle jerk." Whoever could shoot their cum the farthest got an extra ten minutes with the book. By the end of the summer you could hardly open the book. The pages were glued together with so much cum.

Richard Prince paid homage to *Candy*'s role in America's (and presumably his own) psychosexual development by including an Olympia Press first edition of *Candy* in his exhibition "American Prayer," alongside other "hi and lo" sexual-cultural artifacts, including *Lolita*, *Playboy* (Marilyn Monroe cover), bunny regalia (including ears and pod-like hostess bodice), and a variety of pulp-novel French erotica/porn. Prince named the section "*Lolita* and *Lollipop*"— after the confectionary title employed by Girodias to mask *Candy*'s true identity.

After *The CANDY Men* was published in 2004, I began making a documentary film about my father, *DAD STRANGELOVE*. The process (still ongoing) has provided a tremendous opportunity to revisit the important eras profiled in this book that shaped so many artists, including me. When I interviewed Dick Seaver and asked why he decided to publish *The CANDY Men*, he said, "I thought the *Candy* story was one of the more facsinating literary stories of recent history"— this coming from a man who was at the center of perhaps *the* most interesting literary histories, including the secret authorship of the *Story of O*, and Seaver's discovery of Samuel Beckett. I'm honored to have known Dick, and to have had him as my editor. When asked why Terry was not taught in colleges more often, he said with a wistful smile:

> For somebody who is a meddler; who has *Strangelove* as one of his mindsets — satire as one of his chief assets, which Terry did — it takes longer for him to be absorbed into the culture. But there's no question in my mind that he will be. And he will be taught in academe in years to come. He is his generation's Jonathan Swift.

As *Candy* celebrates her fiftieth anniversary, *The CANDY Men* it's tenth, and Terry his ninetieth birthday, I say . . . *Bon Voyage, and many happy returns!*

Boulder, Colorado
May 2014

Addendum to the Acknowledgments

It's been ten years since *The CANDY Men* was first published, and in that time, we've had some sad passings. First, Richard Seaver, true grandee of publishing, without whom this book would never have received the love, attention, and consummate professionalism it did. Dick was the only publisher in New York who could *relate* to this story so intimately — for he not only personally knew each of the protagonists (Southern, Hoffenberg, and their wily publisher, Girodias) but, having done business with Southern and Girodias, he knew their habits and mindset inside out and saw the best and worst of both. And as this is a cautionary publishing tale, who better than Dick, who was there at the beginning, to help tell it?

The passing of my mother, Carol Southern, in the summer of 2011 was a shock, especially to me, Jeannette Seaver, and Carol's other close friends who were with her until the end. Besides being my lifelong emotional rock, she was my editor; and how incredibly fortunate I was to have her at my beck and call, helping me weave the myriad events, characters, and stakes in this tale — making them "track," as she used to put it. She lives in this book, as a character, editor, and the wonderful person who nurtured my father and me; she was, in heart and deed, a consummate creator.

Gail Gerber, Terry's longtime companion, died last spring. Though she's not a character in this tale, she was Terry's muse — hitching up with him for the wild ride and dizzying celebrity that *Candy*'s success brought into Terry's life, which, in combination with the phenomenal impact of *Dr. Strangelove,* prompted Victor Bockris to declare: "In 1965, Terry Southern was the most famous writer in America."

This past spring, Peter Matthiessen passed away. One thing I learned from him (besides constant wise wryness) was that he had a powerful unseen hand in Terry's emergence as a literary talent worthy of attention. For "Bushmaster Math," as my father later called him, had (with Doc Humes) published a bewitching story of Terry's, "The Sun and the Still-Born Stars," in the magazine he edited with Humes, the *Paris News Post* in 1951. As Matthiessen described in a letter to Dick Seaver shortly after *The CANDY Men*'s publication:

> I persuaded Doc that we should quickly abandon the *Paris News Post* . . . and start a new literary mag in which we would reprint Terry's story in a more auspicious ambience . . . one might fairly say that Terry was an important factor in the founding of *The Paris Review* (even before I invited George P[limpton] from Cambridge to Paris). . . . At the extreme risk of self-promotion, unbecoming in a Zen student, it might also be fair to say that as fiction editor of both *Paris News Post* and *Paris Review*, it was no less a person that P. Matthiessen who "discovered" T. Southern.

Thank you, Peter!

Marilyn Meeske-Sorel, one of the great hipster Olympian writers, has been a good sport about the often sophomoric depictions of her in Terry and Mason's letters, and I'd like to thank her for her patience. As a writer today who remembers Joe's Dinette, the Bonaparte, and the San Remo like it was yesterday, she reminded me recently that: "With all those crazy junkies and characters in the Village what united us all, because I didn't do junk — was the *music*. Jazz was such an important part of the scene — bebop — and it can't be overstated. It was the thing that made everything interesting for everybody."

I'd like to once again acknowledge the Hoffenbergs, and Mason, without whom this story of the making of *Candy,* and indeed *Candy* itself, would not exist. One of the joys of this project was discovering what a fine, funny, tortured, and wickedly brilliant guy Mason was. My father was attracted to New York Jews (artist Larry Rivers was his best friend) with "giant brains"— and surely Mason took the cake. It was also Mason who introduced my parents in Washington Square Park — smart move! After *The CANDY Men* was published, there was a resurgence of interest in Mason — and his poetry appeared in *Evergreen Review*. Additionally, his papers, which include correspondence, poetry, and notebooks, were acquired by the Berg Collection at the New York Public Library, which also houses Terry's papers.

Last but not least, I'd like to thank Jeannette Seaver, my original publisher along with Dick, who has given me such support and love over the years, and who, despite Terry's at times "impossible" behavior, never turned her back on him, neither as friend nor author — no doubt because he was, as she would say, "such a *damn* good writer, and so *funny!*" And to Cal Barksdale, part of the original hard-hitting Arcade publishing team. It's great to be back in the saddle with you all — as *The CANDY Men* rollicks on!

Author's Note

Throughout this book, many pieces of correspondence, both personal and legal, are quoted. These original documents contain idiosyncratic spellings and grammatical usage, as well as some typographical errors and misspellings. I have made no effort to correct or alter these documents, nor have I signaled any uncommon or erroneous words or phrases with the bracketed *[sic]*. Instead, I have presented all excerpted correspondence exactly as it appears in the original documents, except for some omitted passages, which are all signaled by ellipses, and underlined words or phrases, which appear in italics.

The story of the publishing history of the novel *Candy* takes its setting in part in France of the 1950s and 1960s, and details a number of business dealings that occurred in that milieu. In some places where amounts are discussed in French francs in excerpted correspondence, I have provided the reader with a rough dollar equivalent in brackets, for clarification.

Between 1950 and 1958, the exchange rate was more or less five hundred francs to the dollar. In 1958, President Charles de Gaulle devalued the franc, after which the exchange rate became five francs to the dollar. For years after the devaluation, however, many if not most of the French — including the central personalities of this narrative — continued to make their calculations in old francs. Therefore, when old francs are referred to, before *and* after 1958, I have used the exchange rate of five hundred francs to the dollar, which is fairly accurate. When new francs are specifically referred to, I have used the exchange rate of five francs to the dollar.

Introduction

When I was in grade school in 1967, one of my six-year-old classmates, Daisy Friedman (now a writer), turned to me and said, "Your father is a *dirty old man!*" I asked how she knew that, and she said, "He wrote a book called *Candy*— and it's a dirty, *dirty* book!" Again, I asked how she knew all this, and she said, "Because my parents told me — they have it on their bookshelf." Not knowing what a "dirty old man" was, I came away with the impression that whatever my father was, he was a great Upsetter. I would later learn that young, literate New Yorkers had no issue about having a copy of *Candy* in their libraries, but this was certainly not the case across the country — censorship and prudishness were in fact still alive and well, not only in the United States but abroad.

I first got the idea for *The Candy Men* after reading a letter in Terry's files from a British barrister advising how (even in 1968) the only way *Candy* could appear in England would be to undergo a "pornectomy" — eliminating about eighty instances of what was considered "indecency," which the barrister had handily indexed in a kind of blueprint for the operation. The assessment featured page after page of cryptic references to offending words and passages to be excised or modified: *Page 60 line 7 "COME" amend to "come to you" without capitals; Line 15 "jack-off" amend to "liberate"; Page 93 line 2 "exactly like an erection." Delete.*

The legal advice appeared to me to be a kind of alchemical prescription for transforming the lively into the dead. I imagined the shoddy, disjunctive product such a procedure would have created — the spontaneous, irresistibly effervescent Candy Christian, her thoughts, feelings, and train wrecks of sexual experience becoming a clerical series of truncations and awkward *politesse.* She would be disfigured for eternity — or at least, ironically, for the

British reading public — only because of the arbitrary mores and laws of the day, now long gone. By the 1980s, I understood that Terry's friend Lenny Bruce had essentially died so that (at best) George Carlin and (at worst) Andrew Dice Clay could say "cocksucker" on HBO — and that the road to where we are now (i.e., anything goes) is paved not only with breakthrough books, but with broken lives.

There were three men responsible for bringing the erotic fantasy *Candy* to fruition — and they could not have been more different.

The first, Maurice Girodias, was Europe's most infamous publisher and indefatigable survivalist. Girodias put out otherwise unpublishable works of (mostly) erotic literature in English when the English-speaking world needed them most: *Lolita, Naked Lunch,* Henry Miller's *The Tropics,* the Marquis de Sade. As Girodias wrote of himself, "The connecting link is clear enough: anything that shocks because it comes before its time, anything that is liable to be banned by the censors because they cannot accept its honesty." Girodias was also a seasoned gambler. "A day out of court is a day wasted," he used to quip.

Mason Hoffenberg, the second of the three, was one of the smartest, hippest, most undisciplined poets on the scene — whether it be Joe's Dinette, the Riviera bar in the Village, or the Old Navy on the Left Bank of Paris. A "permanently kicking junkie" as William Burroughs once described him, Mason the writer never really got started — though Terry, his best friend, described him as a "Nobel Prize–type genius."

And Terry Southern, a writer with a destiny and a killer ear for dialogue. Terry's mandate was to take things as far out as they could go — with absolute *credibility.* A prose stylist gone Hollywood — his Texan, Irish, and Native American roots made him Trickster and Taurus bull — oblivious to the rules of the Game.

Growing up around Terry's work in Canaan, Connecticut, and later helping him organize his papers, I was often struck by the fragile carbon-paper pages of correspondence preserved in one of the few manila files he labeled himself with such headers as "Grand Guy

Hoffer," "Candy Legal," and "Gid." The letters within these files were written on white onionskin, sometimes on blue one-piece aerograms — each typed manually and with great care for language and punctuation. They were light as air, as international mail was expensive, especially for writers. I noticed that a whole slew of these letters were addressed to Terry as "Master Maxwell Kent" and were sent from a joker who never signed his real name, using "Yolanda," "Leslie," "Jessica," or any name other than his own: Mason Hoffenberg. Terry also kept carbon copies of many of the letters he had sent to Mason, some dating back to the mid-1950s. The letters were entertaining — about people, hipsters, junkies, chicks, who was "balling" whom, and what the latest "news" was. Some were written on a barge in the Hudson, others on West 11th Street, others in Switzerland. Mason's were from Paris, Spain, and the Dordogne. I got the sense that Terry kept these letters as evidence of a life he had consciously lived — before fame blurred what life was all about.

This story also tracks the transformation of Terry and Mason as artists, and what happens to their ideals when commerce begins to grip their lives and the culture around them. Terry used to write to Mason for the exuberance of engaging his friend in a kind of debauched pranksterism unwittingly ennobled by the Swiss, French, and Lower Manhattan mail services. As he wrote in 1956, "The question of whether or not to open the packet at risk of ruse is sure to confond* and annoy you, and to cause interesting imagery to form in your huge brain. I'll be grooving on the speculation of it all, you see. . . ."

They both drew out the best in each other. With Terry, Mason explored his craft and artistic approach without embarrassment — as he does in a letter from 1957, offering a glimpse into his unique "methodology":

> I've gotten all set up to answer your recent letter and find that I've mislaid it. . . . I've just gone through all my papers — and I've got

* French for confound

> plenty — but it's not with the clippings containing Chinese characters, not in the specimens, not in the aborted poems envelope, not in the noteworthy language phenomena specimens, or lists-of-groovy-words sheaf and not in the folder (thin) of poems in their "heavy" and definitive versions (where it couldn't possibly have been forgotten — you know how insanely careful I am of what goes in there, and a letter of yours, no matter how welcome, cannot and does not pretend, for that matter, to meet the brutal standards I've set for myself for what gets in to that elite company).

Similarly, Mason enabled Terry to tap into his feelings — even if expressed through a feigned earnestness, as in a letter from the spring of 1957, when Terry lauds Mason's "warmth, goodness and affection":

> It is of course your possession in such abundance of those very qualities which has so sustained the very real and high esteem it has over the years been my pleasure to feel for you. And, if, in your past difficulty [with drugs], my clumsy good-intentions were of help to you — let it stand in simple testimony to . . . the power of true-love.

Shortly after Terry died in 1995, Leon Friedman, who was Maurice Girodias's lawyer, sent me his entire *Candy* file. The letters, organized chronologically, provided snapshots of the growing misunderstandings, temper tantrums, paranoid fixations, jealousies, dreams, and utter despair that each of these men went through as they tried to regain control over their bestselling book lost in a miasma of cloudy copyright. Many of these documents had capital letters (*A, B, C,* etc.) written on them, vestiges of their use as evidence in the *Candy* trials. When I phoned him, Leon explained, somewhat apologetically, that he had been Girodias's attorney during the fight over *Candy.* I sensed that he felt a little ashamed for having served "on the other side" but also wanted me to know that these papers he had given me were an important part of literary history — the keys not only to one of the *grands scandales* of publishing but to these incredibly enigmatic figures themselves.

Candy was arguably the first (if not the only) "dirty book" to take hold of mainstream America (and its bestseller list) for so long. As a kind of literary confection, it was lighter than *Lolita* and never took itself too seriously. After all, the book had been under siege for five years in France, yet had been celebrated in Greenwich Village as fun contraband. Whereas *My Secret Life* and other underground, "anonymous" sex odysseys immersed the reader in the wholesale transgression of Victorian puritanism, *Candy* was swinging with the *Now.* It sold millions of copies in the United States, from its release in May 1964 through the summer of 1965 and beyond. Another reason the book infected so many so quickly was because it was so widely available across the country. Printing *Candy* was like printing money — the pirates had smelled the festering copyright problem like a pack of wolves, and sold millions without having to account to any authors or agents.

The wild success of *Candy* can be attributed to America suddenly growing up after the relaxation of the "decency laws" that had kept such works as *Lady Chatterley's Lover, Howl,* and *Last Exit to Brooklyn* from sullying America's Doris Day–hallucination of cheerful, neutered perfection. The release and embrace of *Candy* in some ways symbolized America's heralding of its own sexual transformation: out of the repressive Styx of (Eisenhower's) sleepy Wisconsin and into the happening hipness of (Ginsberg's) Village. Sex and humor were anathema to the Eisenhower era, and in "heavy combo," as Terry would say, they were its knockout punch. On the front lines of thawing the '50s ice was an army of adolescent readers — male and female — who were consuming the book urgently with one hand by night, and reading it aloud to the uninitiated by day.

Some of these letters are hilarious — others incredibly revealing. I have organized them in an attempt to tell the story — indeed, the saga — of *Candy:* its writing, publication, banning, piracy, bestsellerdom, and silver screen debacle. It is one of the legendary tales of winners, losers, and suckers, in what Terry used to call "the writing game."

— N.S.

Part I

BEYOND THE BEAT

She dreamed that she and her father were together in a great wide field of wild flowers on a beautiful summery day. He was reciting poems of Mallarmé, but it was as if he himself had written them; and Candy was much younger, and she ran about the fields picking flowers, and though she would sometimes be at quite a distance from her father, she could hear every line he spoke. He spoke the lines perfectly, with exactly the right intonation and feeling for each word. Sometimes when he finished a poem, he would say: "That wasn't a bad poem. Now here's another — this is one I wrote for you, sweetheart; it came to me in a *flash* — in a terrible, beautiful flash just as I was releasing the sweet powerful seed from my testis that made you!"

— *Candy*

Chapter 1

Paris: 1947–1953

Terry Southern and Mason Hoffenberg met in Paris in 1948. Both had come on the GI Bill and were — ostensibly — studying at the Sorbonne. Exchanging glances at the Café Royal on St. Germain, they must have immediately recognized each other as kindred spirits. They were an odd pair. Mason's Peter Lorre–like, hunched, bug-eyed demeanor (very New York) was in sharp contrast to Terry's Presbyterian, Texas-bred, hawklike features and reserved manner. At times they were like a comedy team — entertaining each other and those around them.

They shared a similar extreme distaste for the clichéd or hackneyed — the two of them could be very dismissive — and very funny.

Hoffenberg had large blue eyes that protruded, which his future publisher Maurice Girodias described as "full of false promise." As Girodias recalled:

> When people saw him, they would start laughing convulsively without knowing why. He became a master of the minimalist approach: it was enough to look at someone in a certain way, to stare at a girl . . . with a haggard grimace, to suggest a whole story.

Mason's delivery was Brooklynesque and nasal. While he spoke the raw truth as he saw it, often in harsh, uncompromising terms, Terry was a master of understatement, preferring to deflect the obvious via a surprising remix of clichés.

"Old values are crumbling" was an expression that brought particular satisfaction and mirth to them both — indeed, they relished it, for they were on the front lines of late '40s–'50s hipster iconoclasm, sending up and smashing down smugness wherever they found it. From their vantage points in Paris, and later Greenwich Village, they regarded the straight world as populated by Paleolithic squares, while the world of arts and letters offered an urgent creative antidote to a culture increasingly paranoid and conservative. Terry developed a pointed lexicon of nuance: a birdlike tilt of the head, a quick wince of the eyes, a click of the tongue against the roof of the mouth, lips frozen in a pained half-smile, smoke rising from a Gauloise — peppered with hash, no doubt. Mason's style, on the other hand, was more straightforward and confrontational — a nonstop commentary of brilliantly relevant non sequiturs, delivered in a kind of hipster whine. On Pernod-soaked evenings, when they could afford it, Mason and Terry could both be seen leaning toward each other at a café table, heavy with Sartre's "iron in the soul" — their attitude: bemused detachment, cutting insight, or outright stoned hilarity. As Terry recalled of those days in an interview with Mike Golden:

> From '48 to '52, the cafés were such great places to hang out — you could smoke hash at the tables if you were fairly discreet. There was the expatriate crowd, which was more or less comprised of interesting people, creatively inclined. So we would fall out there at one of the cafés, sip Pernod until dinner, then afterwards go to a jazz club. . . .
>
> That . . . was a golden era for Americans in Paris. All the great black musicians — Bird, Diz, Thelonius, Bud Powell, Miles, Kenny Clarke, etc., etc. — were first appreciated there, so it was a very swinging scene musically. Also, there is a large Arab quarter in Paris, and hashish was an acceptable (to the French authorities) part of the Arab culture — so the thing to do was to get stoned and listen to this fantastic music. That was the most important aspect of life in Paris in those days.

Terry and Mason embraced the notion of the Absurd as championed by Camus, who wrote, in *The Myth of Sisyphus,* "The absurd is not in man nor in the world, but in their presence together." Existentialism struck a deep chord in Terry, one which lasted throughout his life. "You do what you do," he once said, "I don't think intentions, opinions, expressions of attitude . . . count for anything at all."

Many in the *Paris Review* crowd regarded Southern, photographer (future filmmaker) and jazz enthusiast Aram "Al" Avakian, and Hoffenberg as ultra-cool vets on the expatriate scene. The Southern-Avakian-Hoffenberg preference for pot and hash over booze also put them in a class of their own. John Phillips Marquand, son of the well-known novelist and a writer himself, found them intimidating. Southern seemed a "silent, inscrutable presence" who was, as described by Terry Southern biographer Lee Hill, "often seen in an attitude of enigmatic conspiracy with Avakian," who also frequented the Old Navy, a Left Bank hangout on the Boulevard St. Germain. At the Hotel Bar Américain in Pigalle one night, Southern told the more solvent Marquand it was bad form to buy a girl a drink: "You ruin it for the rest of us if you pay for her beer." On another occasion, Marquand recalled how he returned to a café to retrieve some papers he had left under a chair. Terry was there, and said with mock sympathy, "Forget it, man — it wasn't any good." Later, they became best of friends.

Their favorite hangouts, like the Café Flore in Paris and the White Horse Tavern in Greenwich Village, were once described by Terry as places "where the whole point was not to write a book but to talk one." Actually getting published was often an afterthought:

> It was sort of an embarrassment like you had sold out or something. If it was corny enough and square enough and bourgeois enough to get accepted by some of these asshole editors, how could it be worth anything? . . . [The literary scene] was all about reading and turning people on to things you had read like Mallarmé, Malaparte, and Canetti. . . . And then showing people stuff you had written and then there were those things where people would read aloud, which seemed a little suspect and too social for me.

As Henry Allen wrote of that era in the *Washington Post:*

> The essence of hip was being in on the joke, aware of the irony and facetiousness of even your compadres in hipness. . . . Hipness was a constant struggle over information and who controlled it: you, the government, the newspapers, the guy drinking coffee at the next table. If you put him on, you controlled it. Terry Southern [and Mason Hoffenberg] took this grim doctrine and made it funny, satirizing both hip and square in a style of spectacular grace, clarity and modulation through all the realities you could bite into like a napoleon, all the flaky layers.

Put-on as reality check was a key foil to the "moldy figs" who threatened to dampen everything with their stodginess. And "sense derangement" neutralized all. Besides hashish (whiz), marijuana (boo, bush), and Pernod, there was the music, the girls, and the *put-on.* Pulling off a put-on provided a contact high, one which Terry strove to replicate in his writing. Mason did it live — in real time. *Shock* — and something more — was what they were after in both their writing and their repartee with each other. Terry recalled the "Laurel and Hardy" aspect of their relationship:

> Back in the late forties, when I was living in Paris on $75 a month from the GI Bill, Mason and I used to eat at this student restaurant, and it was really pretty bad — the kind of place where every now and then you get a piece of meat with the hair still on it. So it wasn't a scene that was too easy to make, but there was this very cute chick who also ate there, and I used to try to sit where we could see her eating this crap, because I felt, well, if she can do it, so can I. I had this image of her being so delicate and fastidious that nothing could possibly touch her lips unless it was perfect. And so one day I mentioned it to Hoff, and he stopped eating, turned towards me and said:
>
> "Are you kidding? She's probably been *sucking cock* all day!"

They kidded each other constantly about getting laid, though both had very different ideas about the art of seduction. Terry played it cool and, when warmed up, was a consummate gentleman and teaser. Although Terry loved to kid around, and Mason played the role of agent provocateur and tough cynic, at heart they were both romantics. They became fluent in the French culture and the language. Terry's patois was put to service to bed French girls who sometimes resembled his Candy Christian. In an interview with Lee Server in 1986, he describes his techniques for picking up American college girls in Paris:

> 1) pay a French person to annoy her at a café, then go to her "rescue," dispatching him with rapier thrusts of Parisian argot.
> 2) hang around the American Express mail line until the girl with perfect American derriere and nips arrives, then get behind her in the mail line, concealing your appearance with a newspaper; and in that way learn her name (when she asks for her mail); then follow her to a hotel or to a café — and when opportune, approach her. . . . It can help if you are able to see where the letter she gets is from, then you can get some regional rapport at ID going ("Say, didn't you used to be a cheerleader in Racine, Wisconsin?").
>
> The third surefire way is to go to the Louvre and sit on a bench in front of a large El Greco, studying it. . . . Then, when the time is right . . . you make your move ("I know this is going to sound, well, sort of forward or silly even — but I couldn't help noticing how much your hands are like those of the women in El Greco's paintings.") Never fails . . . Poon city!

Despite Terry's elaborate pickup fantasies, Mason was the one who managed to "score" in a serious way with the charming young Frenchwoman he would eventually marry, Couquite Matignon. When they met, Couquite was having an affair with Mel Sabre, who had written a novel about his time as a paratrooper during the war. Couquite recalls:

> Mason started having eyes only for me, and decided to seduce this girl Mel had. My guess is that he was more interested in irking Mel, whom he was making fun of constantly, than actually starting something serious. Anyway, in no time he succeeded. When I told Mel, in

The Old Navy, of this development, I found myself lying in the sawdust on the floor with a bloody nose and stars moving in front of my eyes: Mel had hit me with his huge paratrooper fist right in the middle of my face. Mason quite enjoyed his winning and picked up the debris.

Couquite's family was an interesting one. Her father was an oil prospector who died in a plane crash over Russia; her grandfather was Elie Faure, a writer and well-known art critic whose writing was favored by Henry Miller and Ezra Pound. Mason met Couquite at one of their favorite spots, the Royal, on the corner of rue de Rennes and boulevard St. Germain. Couquite recalls:

> Mason was a "bad boy," and we had a lot of fun. Mason knew everybody. Jack Kerouac wanted to come live with us, which I wouldn't have minded — he was so handsome at the time — but when he suggested it, Mason kicked me hard under the table. Terry was so handsome and distinguished looking, always with tall, extremely elegant skinny girls. Doris Lessing [the novelist] was one of them and became my friend. Al Avakian, Johnny Welch [a light-skinned black Sorbonne student and jazz fan], Terry, they all lived in this little hotel in the 5th arrondissement — there was a stove in every room — to visit with your friends there — it was like going to a fabulous café.

One of Terry's friends, William Styron, was in another little hotel not far away, the Libéria, awaiting the publication of his first novel *Lie Down in Darkness*. He wrote in a memoir:

> I was living then in a room that Doc Humes had found for me. . . .* The hotel was on the little rue de la Grande Chaumière, famous for its painters' *ateliers;* my room cost the equivalent of eight dollars a week or eight dollars and a half if you paid extra to get the henna-dyed Gorgon who ran the place to change the sheets weekly.

---

*Harold "Doc" Humes was one of the founders of the *Paris Review,* having already published the *Paris-News Post.*

Another of Terry and Mason's pastimes was cultivating grand eccentrics, among them "Hadj" and "Zoon." One hangout was the Café Soleil du Maroc on rue des Rosiers in the Jewish quarter, where lemon tea was served with pipes of hashish. The two Americans adept in the French argot became friendly with the café's owner, a Moroccan named Hadj. As Couquite recalled:

> It was a time when Jews and Arabs lived peacefully together in the 4th arrondissement. Mr. Hadj, so-called because he had done the Mecca pilgrimage — or pretended so — was jointly selling grass and changing dollars at the black market with a huge profit for both the GI Bill boys and himself.

Terry and Mason later dedicated *Candy* to Hadj, and also to Zoon — who, if you asked him for a light, would oblige "by focusing sunlight on your cigarette with a magnifying glass." According to Terry:

> He was really Mr. Soun . . . a grand old man with a snow-white beard that came down to the middle of his chest. He was from Mongolia, and one of his IDs said he was eighty-nine. His story was that he had walked to France. He had no abode and slept on benches. He'd go into a trance and get several hours' rest that way. He hung out on the boulevards and wore a loose-fitting cloak with big pockets full of books, booklets, and clippings. He'd come to the Soleil du Maroc, and when you mentioned something, he'd pull out the relevant document from his cloak. If he phoned you, he'd say: "Ici *Zoon!*"

Mason and Terry grooved for years on characters like this in both the Village and Paris.

And then, of course, there was the writing. Early on, Terry developed the habits for composition that remained with him for the rest of his life. "Let discipline be my touchstone," he wrote in his journal of the early '50s, and later, toward fulfilling his minimum "page a day," he would say, "Get up, no matter what time, have coffee and go to the desk. Chain yourself to the chair." In his writing, Terry relished Edgar Allen Poe's technique of "taking things further." Terry's tales began combining a Beat sensibility with a refined narrative prose style. He seemed to attempt to "one up" the stylings of the top scribes of the '30s and '40s — Flannery O'Connor, Hemingway, Faulkner, O'Henry — while introducing contemporary themes: race, drug use, politics. He was trying to make beautiful prose do something new and relevant.

Despite their cynicism about publishers, both Terry and Mason were eager to appear in print, and the burgeoning small presses springing up at the time offered possibilities. One of the first magazines to showcase new writers on the European scene in English was David Burnett's *New Story.* Its cutting-edge aspirations attracted Terry and Mason, Mordechai Richler, James Baldwin, and others. Mason had published in *Botteghe Obscura* and *Janus,* a literary magazine edited by Daniel Maroc, a translator of Melville and Rilke, who published French and American writing.

Another group, more well heeled, emerged in 1953, revolving around George Plimpton. William Styron was also involved. Plimpton later noted that Terry was partly responsible for the birth of *The Paris Review:*

> In the early stages of publishing a Paris-based *New Yorker* imitation entitled *The Paris News-Post,* its editors, Peter Matthiessen and Harold L. Humes, were so impressed by the strength of a story ["The Accident"] that they decided to scrap the *New Yorker* imitation and start a literary magazine.

Merlin, a more edgy literary magazine, was founded in 1952 by Alexander Trocchi, a Scottish poet with tremendous energy and wit. Shortly after the first issue, he was joined by Richard Seaver, a handsome, intense young man studying literature at the Sorbonne, who would soon marry the beautiful young Frenchwoman he met at the Paris Conservatory, Jeannette Medina, a budding violinist. Terry became especially friendly with this group, whom Beckett would later refer to as the *Merlin* "juveniles." Aside from Terry and

Mason, the Merlin group was the poorest of the expat lot. One future Merlin editor, Austryn Wainhouse, had toured Europe on a motor scooter before settling in Paris. Austryn spoke in a fluent but decidedly archaic eighteenth-century French and often wrote with a quill pen. Trocchi's girlfriend Jane Lougee, a banker's daughter from Maine, financed the magazine, at least in its early stages.

Terry found he had much in common with the Merlinois: he favored pot and hash as did Trocchi — as opposed to the scotch and schnapps of the *Paris Review* set — and they, like he, never seemed to require sleep. Terry was particularly taken by Trocchi and Christopher Logue, a British poet who exuded a kind of regal debauched enchantment. The two men, highly educated and decadent, their Olympian good looks and charm transcending their dire straits, were in stark contrast to the junkies and weirdos of the Village, who often seemed a bit cagey and somewhat dangerous.

It was Dick Seaver who gave *Merlin* its big break. In 1952 he was living on rue du Sabot — Street of the Wooden Shoe — just behind boulevard St. Germain and intersecting with rue Bernard-Palissy, home to the fledgling publisher Editions de Minuit. Passing that publisher's window one day, Seaver noted that two of the titles displayed were novels in French by Samuel Beckett, *Molloy* and *Malone meurt (Malone Dies)*. A Joyce fanatic, Seaver remembered that Beckett, himself a fervent Joycean, had written an article about *Finnegan's Wake* in Eugene Jolas's magazine *Transition* before the war. Intrigued, and curious about how this Irishman had moved from Joyce's inner circle to novel writing in French, he entered Minuit (which had once been the local bordello), mounted the rickety stairs, and bought both volumes. He read *Molloy* overnight and was stunned. Ditto *Malone Dies,* which he read a day or two later. Bringing them to Trocchi et al., he said in essence that this was the kind of author *Merlin* must publish. He recalls that the rarely-uttered word *genius* was mentioned. In any case, Seaver wrote an essay on Beckett in the second issue of *Merlin*. Then the director of Minuit, Jérôme Lindon, revealed that when Beckett was a member of the Resistance, he had written a novel in English called *Watt,* which had never been published. Seaver wrote to the author, asking to see it for a possible excerpt in *Merlin*. For weeks there was no reply.

As Seaver recounts in the introduction to his anthology of Beckett's work, *I Can't Go On, I'll Go On*, published by Grove Press in 1976:

> We had all but given up when one rainy afternoon, at the rue du Sabot banana-drying *depot*, a knock came at the door and a tall, gaunt figure in a raincoat handed in a manuscript in a black imitation-leather binding, and left almost without a word. That night, half a dozen of us — Trocchi; Jane Lougee, *Merlin's* publisher; English poet Christopher Logue and South African Patrick Bowles; a Canadian writer, Charles Hatcher; and I — sat up half the night and read *Watt* aloud, taking turns till our voices gave out. If it took many more hours than it should have, it was because we kept pausing to wait for the laughter to subside.
>
> We never had a real editorial discussion about which section we would use in the issue: Beckett had seen to that. He had specified which section we could use. . . . I suspect Beckett was testing the artistic fiber of *Merlin* in so specifying, for, taken out of context, that passage might well have been considered boring or pedantic, waggish or wearily experimental-for-experimental's-sake, by any literary review less dedicated to berating and attacking the Philistines without mercy.

Subsequently, Seaver, Trocchi, and the other editors decided to publish the book in its entirety. But for *Merlin* to publish books legally in Paris, it needed to demonstrate to the French authorities that they had a French business manager. Through Austryn Wainhouse they approached Maurice Girodias, who had just started a new publishing house, Olympia Press, and had a reputation for breaking ground where others feared to tread. Girodias was receptive, and he and *Merlin* agreed to publish *Watt* under a newly formed Olympia imprint, *Collection Merlin*.

The marriage of *Merlin* and Olympia was fortuitous for the young Americans, as it was for Girodias, for his previous publishing house, Editions du Chêne, a relic from another era, had been ignominiously taken over by the giant publisher Hachette, leaving him angry and bruised. The appearance of these intense young people marked a new dawn, not only for Girodias, who was looking for new opportunities, but for a postwar world that was desperate for new expression.

Chapter 2

A Booklegger's Son

At the time the Merlinois approached Girodias, working out of his rue Jacob bookshop, he had already created quite a foment of his own. He had turned to the publishing model his father had established before the war with his Obelisk Press — bringing out books in French and English that pushed the boundaries of French "decency."

The direction of the Obelisk Press was set in the 1930s, when Girodias's father, Jack Kahane, a classic English Edwardian dandy (his son would become a French version of the same), wrote and published in Paris a risqué novel, *Daffodil*. Like his earlier work, *Laugh and Grow Rich* (written in a sanatorium while recovering from tuberculosis), it had become highly successful after lending libraries had banned it and controversies arose. Kahane concluded that "spice between the covers invoked censorship, which triggered protest, which produced sales." As Maurice Girodias later recalled, his father's techniques for acquiring novels became an essential tool in his own bag of tricks:

> These were the novels published in England or in America that had been subjected to prosecution under the obscenity laws, and condemned. Each publisher not only had to pay a fine and court expenses, but also lost all the money he had already invested in the book. That [was] the point at which my father was usually able to get the publishing rights for very little money, and sometimes even to buy the printed sheets. . . .* Each one of those books, having

*The raw pages of a book before it is bound.

been subjected to intense publicity during the court hearings in New York or London, would be sure to attract the English-speaking tourists when visiting Paris. The sales were therefore always easy.

A literary man at heart, Kahane found no shortage of innovative authors who could fit the *scandale* bill, and published many under his Obelisk Press imprint, all of a respectably debauched nature: Henry Miller, *Tropic of Cancer;* Frank Harris, *My Life and Loves* (in two volumes); James Joyce, Kahane's idol, *Haveth Childers Everywhere;* Bataille, Apollinaire, Sade, and later Lawrence Durrell, Chester Himes, and Anaïs Nin. It was these authors, and these legacies, along with an assortment of printing plates, artwork, and rights, that became Girodias's literary inheritance when his father died on September 2, 1939, the day after war was declared.

Maurice Girodias's history and tenacity was the stuff of legend, bringing to mind Jean Gabin in *Pepe le Moko* or Bogart in *Casablanca.* His determination to start a publishing house during the German occupation — printing for both the Germans and the Resistance — was only the beginning of an audacious career. All his life he would be skirting the authorities while maintaining an elegant, often glamorous lifestyle.

Girodias began working for his father as a teenager. One of his first paid assignments was to illustrate the cover of Henry Miller's *Tropic of Cancer* in 1934. As a jack-of-all trades, he quickly became indispensable to the operation. "I worked like the devil, my duties including storage, packing, shipping, billing . . . talking to many strange people, running errands, secretarial work, and typing with two fingers. My father was as flabbergasted as I was myself by the efficiency I revealed, and he presented me to his callers as his general manager, with a restrained pride." Girodias thus learned the ins-and-outs of publishing. "Our small scale made it easier to understand the workings of it," he later recalled. "For example, the fact that we dealt with only about twenty retailers in different countries gave me a personalized image of the book dealer, more true to life than any I could have gathered."

Girodias also had the job of proofreading the racy Obelisk

titles for his father, which included three more Miller titles: *Black Spring*, *Max and the White Phagocytes*, and *Tropic of Capricorn*. About sex, which was described in detail throughout most of the books, Girodias later wrote that he had "learned enough to became a professor of erotic technology," though he remained a virgin well into his twenties. Even as a teenager, he was full of contradictions. He joined an ashram in Paris at the age of sixteen — after falling in love with one of the young girl disciples there — and for what seemed an eternity, lived a student's life of quasi-Hindu asceticism and abstinence.

After his father died, Girodias wrote, "I learned to present the image of a thoughtful, well-organized young man, equal parts idealist and realist, and wise beyond his years." One of the first things he did was to go see a tailor, Sazarin, "who received millionaires in his quarters at Place Vendôme, and dressed them like billionaires." Girodias's sense of style was decidedly French and upscale:

> My hats, of ultralight nutria, made to order, of course, came from Gélot's; my shirts were custom-made at Charvet's. . . . As for shoes, I ordered them, for a small fortune, from M. Ghazérian, a conscientious bootmaker who worked alone in a small austere shop on the rue Richepanse. . . . Naturally, all this vestiary luxury was in perfect taste. Nothing ostentatious. On that point, my father had exercised the best possible influence on my sartorial education . . . one thing he once said to me was, "It's better not to be too well dressed."

In 1938, Girodias inherited the publishing rights of a great lineage of literary properties, but he also gained many personal relationships that his father had cultivated over the years — not only with authors, but with powerful players in the publishing business. One such figure, who became a godfather to him, was Michel Bogouslawsky. "Bogous," as he was known, worked with Hachette, which still controls a great deal of the book and newspaper distribution throughout France today. As Kahane's silent partner, Bogous made sure Girodias got off to the right start. "Because of his role within the Hachette group," Girodias later recalled, "Bogous had a sort of monopoly over the distribution of foreign books in France. He could not only block the sale of [other publishers'] books . . . but also help a rival line to come to life."

Immediately after the death of Kahane, Bogous gave Girodias the idea to wind down Obelisk and take up publishing inexpensive pocket editions, in English, of books that were selling well in London and New York. Advising Girodias as to what was to become of his father's business (and himself), Bogous told him, "You will have an exclusive contract for distribution with Hachette, and you'll receive an advance of fifty percent upon delivery, for each book."

As Girodias later reflected, "It was incredible! [Bogous] was constructing a business, financing it, and turning it over to me as a gift. He was treating me like an equal, like an experienced businessman."

During the occupation of France, Girodias developed talents for survival and control that few after the war could match. "My only capital was my blissful ignorance," he later recalled. Half Jewish, he took his mother's name (Girodias) to avoid suspicion by the Nazis and acquired a fake passport and ID. As he told Mike Golden, in an interview published in *New York Writer* in 1989, "I spent the entire four years of Occupation straight in the middle of the German operations." He continued:

> I created . . . this French art book publishing house, *Les Editions du Chêne* which was very successful. . . . It was a bit of a miracle. Of course, the biggest miracle was that I went through the four years of occupation and nothing happened to me. So I know that I was lucky, I was a lucky man, I could do anything I wanted, I just had to decide.

With the encouragement of Monsieur Bogous, Girodias decided to expand his operations and publish novels, fiction, and political books and discontinue the expensive art books. What he later called his "enlarged activities" after the war included publishing Henry Miller's *Sexus.* He also brought out new editions of John Cleland's eighteenth-century classic *The Memoirs of a Woman of Pleasure (Fanny Hill)* and an English translation of Nikos Kazantzakis's

Alexis Zorba (Zorba the Greek). While these books raised a few eyebrows, it was *The Bread of Corruption* — a book attacking the government — that landed Girodias in the French courts, since a government minister sued him. As he recalled, "I published a pamphlet denouncing the economy. I had a huge court case where the government came in as a witness against me. . . . I won that lawsuit, which was very bad for my future. . . . I was marked." Girodias was targeted again by the authorities when they banned his reissue of Miller's *The Tropic of Capricorn*. Girodias biographer John de St. Jorre described this as a historic moment, the first time the French government had moved to ban a book since Flaubert's *Madame Bovary* and Baudelaire's *Fleurs du Mal* in the nineteenth century. Writers, intellectuals, and critics rose up in protest and the government abandoned the prosecution. But, as would be the case throughout his life, Girodias fell into financial troubles, and in 1942, Editions du Chêne was taken over by Hachette. The Olympia Press would rise from its ashes.

And so, in the early 1950s, Girodias adjusted his father's "literary bootlegger" tactics for the new breed of young hungry expatriate writers and the more judicially minded Parisian authority. One brilliant solution to the censorship problem was that he began to publish exclusively in English — thereby lessening his apparent "threat" to local standards of decency, and confounding the authorities with inscrutability. Girodias's knowledge of how to outmaneuver the law was so intricate and potentially debilitating for his authors (in terms of their rights and royalties) that he never explained his business practices to any of them. As Girodias recalled about the expat group:

> These people had come to Paris in the belief that it was still Paris in the thirties. They had heard all the stories of the wonderful life in the thirties, but when they got here they didn't find any trace of the city. The war had changed it completely. And there were absolutely no English or American writers except them. Those kids, you see, had never written anything, but they all had talent . . . they were all very interesting. They had gotten together because of a similar taste

for literature. I mean, they were the first English-speaking people to discover Samuel Beckett.

Muffie Wainhouse, then wife of Austryn Wainhouse, remembered Girodias taking them to dinner:

> One evening Maurice packed Alex Trocchi, Jane Lougee, Dick Seaver, Pat Bowles*, Christopher Logue, Austryn and me into his big Citroën and drove us to a restaurant. Here we all had our first escargots, then trout with Sancerre, *boeuf bourguignon* with Nuits St. Georges, cheese, *poires belles Helene* and finally cognac. (At that time we were eating for about $1.50 a day; Christopher Logue for less.) Slightly avuncular, Maurice was a wonderful host and storyteller. A convivial group; a merry evening. We also saw the possibilities of earning money. And Maurice must have seen the possibility of launching the Traveller's Companion Series.

Indeed Girodias *was* thinking along those lines. Gallimard had launched a successful detective imprint, The Black Series, so surely an erotic series was what the world was ready for. There was enough talent in the group to produce books for years. Girodias presented the idea to them, suggesting that one way the impoverished Merlinois could make money writing, and fund the magazine, would be to supply him with original erotic novels. The idea was enthusiastically received. Girodias recalled: "I usually printed five thousand copies of each book, and paid a flat fee for the manuscripts which, although modest, formed the substance of many an expatriate budget."

Muffie Wainhouse continues:

> Afterward, we talked of little else in our café gatherings: the excitement, the danger, was it prostitution or not? There were enough members from McCarthyite America to be paranoid, and the British, with their tourist visas, were worried. Code words were needed, lest we be overheard by FBI spies or by the French secret

*A poet, writer, and editor of *Merlin*.

> police. The group around the table would throw out ideas: How about "Gid" for Girodias and "DB" for dirty book? It's hard to believe how clever we were. Or how young.

Gregory Corso, a friend of Terry and Mason's, wrote *American Express* with no illusions about the proposition Girodias was making — it was a kind of mutual obligation with trust (and trepedation) on both sides. Writing to his future publisher James Laughlin in 1960, Corso reports: "Girodias of Olympia Press here, gives me fifteen thousand francs [$30] a week on which to live, and in return I promised him a book. . . . Contract with Girodias is for one year, and so I am sure that by the end of that year, if I keep working like I am, he . . . will be kept by my faith." While Trocchi and others (especially the poets) understood well that their work for Olympia was disposable — and would probably never be republished elsewhere — many novelists would come to resent (and litigate) the wholesale license Girodias took over their material.

He paid in dribs and drabs, but the fee, between $300 and $500 per book in the mid-'50s was quite decent for what was essentially experimental writing. "Our backgrounds, and where we were coming from — we didn't know how to handle him businesswise, but there was this tremendous resource available to Girodias of educated, funny, eager, English-speaking writers who would do anything to stay in Paris," recalls Marilyn Meeske, one of the first women authors to write a book for Girodias. "It was a great arrangement." As Girodias recollected:

> With most of the writers I worked that way [paying piecemeal] because that was the only way to get the pages, you see. To the end. The contract was that I was to protect their anonymity completely because they were taking big risks doing what they were doing. They would have been kicked out of the country immediately if they had been found out. So I was supposed to have been the author of all those books. A set of them. Twenty books a year. When I went to court, I had to claim that I made them. Very simple — and they would threaten me with three months in prison for every book.

Despite his brushes with the law, Girodias seemed immune to prosecution:

> Twice I was caught, and I thought I'd had it, since I carried this total of so many sentences over my head. If I was in prison by the end of the day, then I was there for six years, you see. It was quite serious. But I managed to get out by the end of the day by the one telephone call allowed me. I had a very good lawyer in those days.

Girodias made a great impression on Terry, as he recalled in an interview with Lee Server:

> He was able to entice impressionable young American expatriates . . . by convincing us we were writing *quality Lit!* Not only did the Hemingway types succumb to his wily persuasions, but . . . *young American girl-authors* as well!

As Marilyn Meeske, one of those "girl-authors," recalls:

> The anti-censorship aspect is a reason why we were doing all this. We were escaping from McCarthyism, a lack of First Amendments — a lack of exploration, lack of ideas in the States — it offered an opportunity to fool around with language and situations. You could also get him to publish things which were not about sex. . . .
>
> The main thing about this whole epoch is that we were not judgmental. The people who were, would let it come out in whimsy or wisecracks — like Mason.

Iris Owens, whom Terry called "Gid's great love," was one of the most prolific Olympia women authors, penning, under the name Harriet Daimler, *The Woman Thing, Innocence, Darling, The Organization,* and, with Meeske, *The Pleasure Thieves.* As Terry wrote of Owens, "Aside from her Junoesque beauty, she had rapier wit and devastating logic. She was a pre-Sontag Sontag, and [Girodias] was determined to get the best of her."

"We were natural DB writers," she told John de St. Jorre.

"Sexual revolutionaries with a need to shock. There was a streak of anarchism in all of us."

Girodias quickly became "Uncle Gid." To many a writer searching for extra francs to sustain the basics of Parisian life — cigarettes, coffee, *le cinema,* and an occasional bistro meal. Terry captured Girodias's "boss charm" and "what at first appeared to be an extraordinary generosity," again in his article "Flashing on Gid":

> He seemed to fancy himself one of the last of the grands seigneurs and tried to act like one. . . . He was a sort of *arriviste extraordinaire.* . . .
>
> Very early in our relationship, I detected in Girodias a marked disapproval of the style of dress of Alex [Trocchi] and myself — a style that might best have been described as modest, if not indeed occasionally threadbare.
>
> "In France," he said, "literary men dress correctly. Look at Camus and Sartre. You won't see them without a necktie or proper shirt."
>
> "Beckett and Genet don't wear ties," I reminded him. "And neither does the great Hank Miller."
>
> He half closed his eyes and wearily tilted his head. "My dear boy," he lisped, "you have just named three of the most n'er-do-well *non gratas* in all Paris." . . .
>
> On that very first day of our acquaintance . . . a friend of mine, H. L. "Doc" Humes, one of the founders of *The Paris Review* and a grand eccentric in his own right, pulled up alongside us, riding a Vespa. After a brief exchange he went on his way.
>
> *"Moi, je n'aime pas le velo,"* said Gid in a tone of absolute disdain. "I would not wish to be seen on one. Your friend just now, is he a student?"
>
> "No," I explained, "he's a grand eccentric."
>
> Gid shook his head gravely. "He will not be taken seriously if he rides a *velo.*"

Despite Terry's interest in Girodias, his own work took precedence, and he did not sign up for a DB until several years later. Mason began developing Faustino Perez, his DB alias, in 1955, when he first signed on with Girodias to write *Until She Screams.*

Chapter 3

Greenwich Village: 1952–1955

Not unlike her sister province, the Left Bank of Paris, Greenwich Village fifty years ago was indeed a village — an insular hamlet of bohemian and artistic possibilities. From the late '40s to the mid-'50s, Terry and Mason moved from there to Paris and back.

Sometime in the early '50s, in either Paris or the Village, Terry met and married a fashion model, Pud Gadiot. She was a slender, stunning, statuesque brunette from Georgia, who would become known for her dramatic Merry Widow ads in *Vogue* magazine, appearing in a black bustier, eyes concealed behind a feathered mask. Part of Terry's appeal (she was the breadwinner) was his connection to Paris: she loved to travel and they lived for periods in both Paris and Ibiza. Terry returned to New York with her in '54 and they moved into an apartment on West 11th Street in the Village. Pud's rather glamorous career and perhaps high-maintenance lifestyle would seem to be antithetical to Terry's milieu, and this may be the reason the marriage dissolved soon after.

Mason spent much of 1953 in the Village. He signed up for the New School under the GI Bill and took a furnished room on MacDougal Street. Around this time, he met James Baldwin:

> I'm walking home from school to do my homework after the first night of classes, and I'm carrying my notebooks and all this bullshit, and I decide to stop into Minetta's for a few drinks. There were only two bars in the Village, Minetta's and the San Remo. So I'm drinking and talking to this spade cat and he says, "Why don't you come

> and live with me? I'm bisexual, but that don't apply to you." And that was Jimmy Baldwin. So we lived together and it was just what I needed. A lot of people, a lot of women. There was a tremendous ferment going on in the Village, and Jimmy's place was one of the centers of it. Paris was like that, too.

During his New York sojourn, Mason corresponded with Couquite, and when he moved back to Paris in '54 they began living together with her daughter Zeline in her mother's Montparnasse apartment. They were married soon after. Iconoclastic as he was, Mason enjoyed the bourgeois accoutrements of his in-laws — the rambling top-floor apartment with *balcon* just off the rue de Rennes and the country place in the Dordogne where they spent summers.

On one of his trips back to the States in 1952, Terry visited his parents in Dallas and received a letter from old "Zoon." Writing in block capital letters concerning a "Persian miniature" painting from Tehran that Terry had undertaken to sell for him, he reminds Terry to "BRING SOME PEYOTE WITH YOU," as well as an eclectic collection of books, including a translation of the Chinese classic *The Monky Wife, Hatha-Yoga,* and Engels's *Origins of Family and Private Property.* The notion that Terry could have found any of these items in Dallas is amusing.

Terry returned from Dallas to Paris by way of the Village, where he updated Mason regularly on goings-on there. Light blue onionskin pages were ideally suited for letters since they traveled light and the carbons produced a serviceable author copy — helpful in boosting morale in the absence of a book in progress.

In those years, the two primary gathering places in the Village, in addition to Minetta's, A Kettle of Fish, and the San Remo on MacDougal Street, were Joe's Dinette at the corner of Fourth Street and Jones, and the Riviera on Seventh and West 10th. Fugazi's farther down Sixth Avenue was another option.

Joe's Dinette attracted junkies, who often came there to score. The group included Stanley Gould, a smart, wiry, fast-talking quintessential New York junkie; Mel Sabre, a brashly handsome New York "can do" type; Chuck and Harriet Katz-Nelson, who were married and both into heroin; and the great piano player Joe Albany — to name a few. As Marilyn Meeske recalls:

> This was the first wave of artists and people doing drugs. There was a demarcation between people who smoked pot and people who did hard drugs. . . . The "in" group were people who were smoking grass everyday. . . . Getting high, looking at things — you had a kind of snobbism — where you didn't talk to everyone — you ignored many people . . . it was a clique or a little gang. We sat at the Remo — that was our job and people came in and out and a few were part of our group, but they had to be funny, or have an insight — or be epigrammatic — it all had a certain beat.

Mason and Terry swung with that beat. Lovers of jazz, surrealism, "sense derangement," and wiggy people, they dug the improvisational nature of the scene. For Terry especially, who studied the way people *talk*, the cafés and bars were incubation centers for a vibrant, new kind of fiction. As Marilyn Meeske said of Joe's:

> It was café society — and I think that's what made the transition to Paris so natural. . . . It was the River Styx, and the ferry men were Stanley [Gould] and Mason. . . . You crossed that line into this alternate world. Joe's was one of the first places — on West Fourth Street . . . where scenes like this were happening. Larry Rivers came by with his sax, and Auden would pad around in bedroom slippers coming from upstairs to get milk for his tea.

Many of the downtown characters were given names, such as Jimmy "the Greek," Dorothy "the Shoebox Girl" (because she kept her marijuana in a shoebox), and Jimmy O'Hara, whose real name was Earl Smith. Jimmy was a book thief who was one of the first persons on the scene to wear a leather jacket. He had done jail time for theft, which may be why he used an alias. He was also a close friend of Gregory Corso's.

Though Mason would soon become an addict, in the Village of the early- to mid-'50s, Mason and Terry were fascinated by, but ultimately wary of, the heroin scene, and saw the goings-on around

Joe's Dinette as a kind of theater of the absurd. In a letter to Mason of February 4, 1954, Terry creates an elaborate prank (shades of *Magic Christian*) in which a heroin-shooting session goes awry when a homemade siren sounds and the floor opens up. He riffs:

> And everybody is plunged into a tremendous vat — of something incongruous, like honey, or cotton-candy (cotton-candy would be good because, by the nature of it, retrospective accounts would have interesting discrepancies as to what it actually was; for example, later at Fugazi's, Chuck is telling Harriet (while Charlie Lear opposite is so cross he is black), "And, dig, baby, we fell into like a kind of pit, you know? Full of cotton-candy. But deep, you know what I mean?"
>
> Harriet (in disbelief): Ah!
>
> Chuck: Yeah, man, ask Charlie. Isn't that right, man, it was cotton-candy?
>
> Charlie: What!
>
> Chuck: Cotton-candy, man, you know, that jive they sell at Coney Island, for kids. Cotton-candy.
>
> Charlie: Man, will you come down?
>
> Chuck: Yeah, man, that's what it was. Cotton-candy. I tasted it.
>
> Charlie: Oh, man!
>
> . . . Later, at Joe's Dinette, Stan [Gould] would tell Anton [Rosenberg, who owned a frame shop], "That's the LAST time I get involved with Jimmy O'Hara, I can tell you that! For any reason, man, ANY reason!

Terry continues his letter with an update on the Village scene, commenting on the bizarre murder of poet Max Bodenheim and his wife:

> Harold* was an odd person, even for the Waldorf, where he was often the focus of curiosity and attention, because he had, as Max himself noted shortly before his demise, "the eyes of a cobra." . . .

---

*Harold Weinberg, a dishwasher at the Waldorf Cafeteria, killed poet Max Bodenheim.

> There is a bit of sad news which you may have already heard — the death of Jimmy the Greek*, about 3 weeks ago, in Baltimore, of pneumonia. He had started south because of the cold here. Dylan Thomas died here recently, in equally ironic straits — an overdose of M [morphine] or more precisely, a sizable dose of M when he was very lushed.

Terry took great relish in recounting the myriad romantic triangles among the revolving cast of characters with whom Mason was intimately familiar — but far away from — in Paris.

> About 3 weeks before the Bodenheim slayings, Bob ("I'll ball and suck you til you bleed") Hanlon fell off a bar stool at the White Horse and fractured his skull. Bob is back on the scene now, however, and is more or less fully recovered. "My head is all right now," Bob will say of an evening down at the Horse. He holds his head in both hands when he says it. "My head is all right now." Standard hipster repartee to this is "Well, give me a little then! Haw!" No one puts down Bob quite so hard as do Chuck [Katz-Nelson] and Harriet. The simple fact of their getting involved at all is not unlike something out of Henry Green, and to my mind a gas and groove. Imagine then the situation of Bob, having heard about the "freeze" quality of C[cocaine], scoring for some horse through Chuck and Harriet, to rub on his cock, and their trying to get him to "shoot it!" Chuck was very cross, and Harriet was actually ill, the poor darling. Bob stood fast.

As the hipsters and artists of the Village began experimenting with heroin, so did Mason, particularly during one visit to Paris, in which he befriended jazz trumpeter Chet Baker. Mason was now exploring the world of music and drugs on a different level than Terry — one that would bug Mason out for the rest of his life.

---

*A toothless junkie friend (and connection) of Mason's who had been on the Village scene for years.

Chapter 4

Enter Candy Christian

It was sometime between 1954 and 1955 that Terry wrote a story about an American girl from the Midwest, quite different from the hip chicks on the New York scene, named Candy Christian. Pert, bright-eyed, and in love with the whole world, she heals suffering through the act of "giving herself" fully to whoever needs her most. The story as first conceived contains her encounter with a weirdo hunchback on Grove Street, which remains one of the novel's most fully developed (and uproarious) episodes.

> Wasn't it just too much, she thought joyfully, standing here in the rain, in Greenwich Village, talking to a hunchback — when she *should* have been at her job ten minutes ago! . . . She considered the explanation she would have to give, the attempt to make them understand, and she was so happy and proud of herself she could have wept.
>
> "That's *my* tree, you know," she said instead, smiling like a mischievous child, then laughing gaily at her own foolishness. "I pretend that it is," she admitted, almost shyly. "The *only* tree on Grove Street! Oh, I do love it so!" She leaned forward and touched it gently, half closing her eyes, and then she gave the hunchback another tender smile.
>
> The shop on this corner of Grove was a man's underwear shop, and the hunchback's eyes devoured another crotch or two before he looked up. He was also smiling. He supposed she was a policewoman. "Rubatubdub!" he said, agitating his hump vigorously against the tree. Getting run in was part of his kick.

Terry showed the story to many of his friends, for whom it became a source of great amusement. As Terry recalled later in *Grand Street:*

> Everyone who read the story, *loved* the girl — all the guys wanted to *fuck* her, and the girls wanted to *be* her . . . Alex Trocchi . . . wanted to publish it in *Merlin* for nil recompense. I told him no thanks. . . .
>
> "Well, in any case," said Trocchi, "this spunky heroine of yours should have more adventures! I would like very much . . . like to see her involved with the Roman Catholic Church!"
>
> Mason . . . read it and said, "Why don't you have her get involved with a Jewish shrink?"

Candy Christian is from the Midwest, but she was inspired by girls like her in the Village and Paris. In the following letter, Terry, observing the Village scene in 1954, seemed to be developing the Candy character based on certain girls looking for their "freedom and independence":

> Mazor Hoff!
>
> Dear Mace. Well, Mace, now that you have given up all pretense to art and letters, it is a little difficult to know what to say to you, what common ground we have to meet upon, so to speak. Dope and pussy, I suppose. Well, as you may have guessed, my thick bit sees plenty of action here in the Village. There are any number of attractive girls, wanting to assert their independence by coolly entering into the sexual-act with someone. Naturally, I get first nod, being somewhat more respectable than Stan [Gould] and the others — especially the spades — the spades get them last, their graduation, so to speak. Most of these girls are young Catholic-girls-in-revolt who want to enter into the sex-act for the freedom and independence of taboo it represents. Within that framework though, they move cautiously . . . down-the-ladder, one might say, towards . . . [Jimmy] O'Hara . . . Stan Gould, and the others, down to the very bottom which is Fats Edwards, monster spade-faggot. It is generally agreed that nothing is more indepen-

> dent, more finally symbolic-of-emancipation, and "farther from home," so to speak, than one of these young girls taking Fat's 17 inch cock in the ass and mouth. Naturally, I get plenty of Jewish puss as well. These young Jewish girls are warm and passionate, a fact I attribute to the role of food and father in the Jewish home, and to the strong welcome of security (in an anti-semitic world) which they imagine these momentary embraces to represent. Also the fact that I am a white protestant does excite them (I suppose they think they are fucking Christ) and makes them come like the dickens.

Terry alerts Mason to two very dynamic women who were heading for Paris, Marilyn Meeske (who would later work for Girodias) and Eleanore "Nori" Hickox:

> A couple of nifties are headed your way, Hoff. I won't mention their names, because the very thought of them might make your wire-like bit shoot off wildly all over Zeline [Mason's young stepdaughter] and the others. Anyway, they are two young hipstress from the Village. Initials, MM, and NH! I can give you this hint: you've had your teeny bit and head up to the proverbial cervix of each, trying to shoot-off there. These are two nifties, Hoff, and will be calling for organ thick and fast. To get the best out of one of them (by way of another hint) you'll be wanting to don a beard and say, repeatedly during the act: "I'm your old dad! I'm your old dad!" and the child will spasm like a veritable machine-gun. As for the other, give her a cool look and a quick crack in the mouth. This will make her come out of pure respect. Then wipe away the blood with your pencil bit, and soothe her wonderously. The poor child can't understand gentleness until after her vulva's been chewed to a pulp.
>
> [Joe] Fineman took a crippling bust the other day and Mel [Sabre] is plenty cross as this gives Joe an edge in their running battle for King of the Junk scene. Mel and hot Dorothy swing Joe's Dinette beginning at two pm each day waiting for the connection and making phone-calls. Mel has been busted eight times now, but nothing ever comes of it because one of his uncles is a highly placed magistrate. Mel has to weigh his eight hollow busts against Joe's Lexington rap and is insecure about it. He feels, however, that he will ultimately exhaust his uncle's patience. Mean-

while, of course, he is his usual groove and gas self, coining new words, etc. . . .

Bob Hanlon has an interesting dodge now, whereby he comes on as a John to a junkie chick, offering her a fix in exchange for puss, shoots off in the darling girl then sends her packing. "You little fool," he says, "I'm Ace Crane of Narco! Clear out or you'll be cold turkey in the Tombs!" These junkie chicks are so embarrassed at having been conned by a John that they don't hip the others, so Bob continues to swing. About three in the morning you'll see Bob in Jim Atkins flashing a BC* and saying: "It's dynamite! baby, how about some puss."

Well, I'll be pointing for France, Hoff, if things break right. I can tell you, you needn't bother coming back here. It's the same old six and seven, here. Pussy and dope. It'll be a groove to see you. Meanwhile, let's keep in touch.

T.

Terry did return to France — and to nights spent hanging out with Mason. The two of them, paragons of existential cool, had a disdain for a kind of inauthenticity that was invading the writing life and literature in both Paris and New York and producing what Terry called "artistes manqués." As William Styron recalled:

> You could stroll from the hotel in less than two minutes to La Coupole or to the terrace of Le Dôme, Hemingway's old hangout, which also reeked of pot or hash and featured many young American men sitting at tables with manuscripts while affecting the leonine look of Hemingway, right down to the moustache and hirsute chest. I even overheard one of those guys address his girl companion as "Daughter." Terry and I would sit after lunch on the terrace, drinking coffee and smirking at these poseurs.

Terry and Mason were interested in a new kind of fiction, a fiction that used stylistic juxtapositions, Hemingway's clarity, and Faulkner's precision, overlaid with the Beat irony and existential

*Sodium bicarbonate, i.e., baking powder.

Now. They both knew that some of the people in their crowd were too outré to resist literary treatment. In the following letter, Mason, on a visit to the States, revives a book idea he and Terry had talked about, involving a "cultural tourist," self-consciously determined to master the Hemingway mystique.

Milford, Conn., Winter 1954

Dear Terry,

> . . . I don't know how strong this should be, but picture a guy, an American, picking up on *Farewell to Arms,* wanting to be the cynical connoisseur, to know his way around Paris, order drinks with funny names and be on intimate terms with whores and so on. Instead he is exposed to a barrage of tourist experiences — tries to catch the street names from a taxi at night — has to ask the names of the statues and can't understand the answers, in short, a kind of a parody on Hemingway where the guy is trying to have his life look like that, collecting experiences that would look good in print but it never comes off and finally getting his just desserts in the bull stampede. Mel [Sabre] is the model, of course. I should think we could think up some pretty grotesque bits involving misunderstandings and wild fiascos of this kind, aside from what we might actually remember. Some of Joe Feinman's trips might serve too. This line could all be subordinated to some conventional plot of course, and should be, I guess. The guy could have a wife and the part about fancying himself a Hemingway hero be something which has to take place within the confines of a colorless domestic setup. However the wife is lost in Paris, not to the guillotine but a masculine embodiment of it, at which point, actually on his own, and feeling very upset he cuts to Spain. At any rate, there could be this contrast thing running through it — the difference between the Hemingway habitué and what would be likely to happen to a tourist who makes a pilgrimage because of it.
>
> Fifty pages doesn't sound impossible. We're leaving the first of May, but I think we could get enough to show by then.

Nothing came of their proposed collaboration, but later that winter, Terry, who also saw the dynamic, Ivy League junkie Mel

Sabre as the perfect model for a contemporary comeuppance tale, wrote "The Night the Bird Blew for Doctor Warner." It concerns a musicologist who is writing *The History of Music: From Bach to Be-Bop,* and his final chapter to research and complete is: "Jazz." As a top-drawer academic, he consults a sycophantic group of colleagues. The story begins like this:

> "I'll have to be a *hipster,*" Dr. Warner said leaning toward them from out of billowing dark leather while behind this great chair, where study lamplight softened to haze on a thousand grains of dullest panel, there danced in points of twos the refracted amber of glassed cubed-ice in the hands of his two friends opposite — danced, it seemed, on an opaque screen which could measure the wildness of thought and the tedium of conversation.
>
> "A very *hip* hipster," he continued genially, and withdrew himself slightly, for emphasis, "if not, indeed, something *more.*"
>
> "Something *more?*" said professor Thomas, stressing his mock surprise with a sickly smile. He loathed strange jargon. "Don't tell me there's anything *more,* Ralph, than being a hipster!"
>
> Dr. Warner allowed his own gaze to grow sober and formulative, staring down at the drink in his hand.
>
> "Yes," he said evenly, "you might say that a *junky* is something more than a hipster."

Terry had already fully developed this "cultural tourist" theme in 1952 in Paris when he wrote "Thriving on a Riff" (later called "You're Too Hip, Baby"). It revealed, with unflinching detail, the painful aspects of sycophantic white American stoners digging the primarily black (American) Paris jazz scene:

> Later, in the evening, when the place was jumping, Murray kept himself slightly apart from the rest of the crowd — the tourists, the students, the professional beats, and the French *bonne famille* — who all came to listen to the great new music. And always during the evening there would be at least one incident, like the famous tenorman's casually bumming a cigarette from him, which would prove Murray's intimacy with the group to those who observed. Old acquaintances from Yale, who happened in, found Murray changed;

they detected in his attitude toward them, their plans, and their expressed or implied values a sort of bemused tolerance — as though he were in possession of a secret knowledge.

By December of '54, Terry was back in the Village, where he moved in with his Paris pal, Aram Avakian, who had a floor-through on Sixth Avenue. Almost immediately, Terry got his first big break. *Harper's Bazaar* signed three stories, two of which debuted in their July 1955 issue. The Editor's Guestbook began with an announcement:

> This month, in an issue devoted to the younger American writers, the *Bazaar* breaks precedence by publishing two stories by the same author. . . . Last December he appeared in New York with a fresh batch of stories and the completed novel, *Flash and Filigree*. When his work came to the attention of our editors, they were so impressed with his range and individuality, and the clarity of his prose, that they bought three stories within a week.*

Despite the prominent plug for *Flash and Filigree* (a darkly satirical look at a Los Angeles dermatologist and his prankster alter-ego), Terry's literary agent at Curtis Brown was not getting any interest in the manuscript from publishers. Over the next year Terry plastered the bathroom wall with dozens of rejection letters.

But in that summer of '55 Terry was the talk of the Village, which was just now discovering "The Sun and the Stillborn Stars," a haunting and enigmatic story of a sharecropper-couple in Texas. The story first appeared in H. L. Hume's *Paris New Post* in 1952. *Paris Review* editor Peter Matthiessen spotted it and insisted it appear in *The Paris Review*, which it did in 1953. Finally, *Harper's Bazaar* was bringing it to the United States, and thereby introducing American readers to Terry Southern.

---

* "The Sun and the Stillborn Stars," "The Panthers," and "The Night the Bird Blew for Doctor Warner," published six months later.

* * *

Mason was enjoying a summer of a different kind. The following letter was written in the Dordogne, where he was spending August in the Faure country house with Couquite and her relatives.

Early September, 1954, the Dordogne

Dear Terrio,

I was so glad to hear from you you delightful old crackpot and hasten to reply. Marilyn Kantoman married to Harold Meeske is a fine person and I trust you don't have any ideas of sticking your skinny bit in her mouth. Harold is a gas too and let me know if they're still planning to point out here. I've been here all summer and been playing tennis a lot aujourdhui j'ai joué comme un dieu and split sets with Couquite's cousin, Jean-Louis Faure. I haven't seen anybody but her family all summer except for one week I was in Paris. I've been boating a lot too in the river down here in a rowboat.

My sister saw you in *Harper's* and sent it to me — she has hot nuts for you after looking at that photo and this may be your chance to break into a rich Jewish crowd.

Anyhow I haven't been giving a thought about writing and realized I was really happy like that. Now the summer is done and we're leaving for Paris on September 19 so I got out the old charge the other day and sat down to give it a whirl. As a result I was terribly depressed for a day or so and fucked up my tennis and underwater swimming and everything. However I still feel that as soon as I feel like I want to show somebody something I'll send it to you.

Perhaps to take the edge off what Terry imagined would be Mason's irritation that Terry had taken the updated Hemingway cultural tourist theme and run with it alone (with "Dr. Warner"), Terry encouraged Mason to go on writing. "The style you suggested in your letter was excellent," he wrote, "and provocative. Let's have more of the same. . . . You'll want to read my story in the January *Harper's Bazaar,* Mace. It is based on Mel's character as we have often discussed it, and caused lots of talk. I know you are doing plenty of your own work and am anxious to see it."

Chapter 5

Giving the Old Head a Breather

In the fall of 1955, both Mason and Terry were in New York, and Carol Kauffman, an art student and jazz aficionado who had met Mason in Joe's Dinette, encountered the two one day in Washington Square Park. Mason introduced her to Terry, who was looking down, too hip to make eye contact. She recalls:

> They were sitting together on the circle. I thought Terry quite handsome and the essence of cool — but the whole time he was looking away as if I wasn't there. I wasn't sure he actually saw me! A few weeks later, we met again. Robert Frank had won a Guggenheim and Mary gave a huge costume-party bash in their loft. I arrived very late, about 2 A.M., dressed in my idea of a Parisian Apache dancer. Terry came over and said, "Mason speaks very highly of you," a joke really, since Mason was a known junkie. On a date at the Riviera Bar, his first words were, "Do you know the work of Henry Green?" I found him funny and incredibly touching.

By spring 1956, Terry and Carol were living together in a studio on Charles Street and making plans to go to Europe. In June, a fan of Terry's, painter Madeline Bernard, invited them to her mother's Adirondack camp. They were married there on Bastille Day — the day before Terry started this letter:

Tupper Lake, July 15, 1956

Dear Mace-eo,

Giving the old head a breather here in the lake country of the Adirondacks and it just occurred to me what an *au fond* groove and gas you are. It was fun hearing from you again, Mace, and so good to know that you and yours are enjoying the pleasures of a summer holiday in Garonne (Garches?). What, down for a fortnight or so, that the idea? You didn't go into much detail about your plans . . . keeping them flexible, I suppose, eh? Too much fun just living-in-the-present, so to speak, just letting-things-happen, as it were. Well, your 'easy-going' attitude towards life, many say, is your greatest charm, and I'm not sure I don't agree. One thing I do know, it was more than generous of you to offer me the run of your Paris flat while you and the family are on holiday. I would have thought you could sublet it for a few thou, but I guess some people are less opportunistic than others; then, too, I imagine you get more than enough money from your folks in New York City, so you are in a position to extend these favors. Please believe me when I say I don't interpret this move on your part as an attempt to ingratiate yourself with me so that I will continue the poetry-critiques, etc. No, I think I take it on its face-value: a natural impulse of a generous and darned swell guy. Thanks again, Mace, you're a groover, and you will not regret this move.

Terry liked to find people's hot buttons and push them repeatedly. In Mason's case, keeping his drug habit secret from his family was a subject he explored with Terry humorously and with self-deprecation. Sometimes he questioned his own sanity. The following passage from the same "breather" letter refers to Mason's stepdaughter, Zeline, age six, and her great grandmother Faure. When it came to put-ons about sex, Terry and Mason clearly thought you could never go too far:

I won't say I was not disturbed by your letter in part — namely, where you really get going about how you are always "fucking Zeline and dry Granny Faure," and again where you say you wonder if you are not losing your mind. Actually, though, this set the stage for some rather nice irony, when, a day later, I received a hastily written note,

> evidently from Zeline herself. In contrast to your more dramatic interpretation of the set-up there, her letter was all lightness and caprice. She seemed particularly amused by the visual incongruity of your thick hams and heavy bottom, and the fine, whippet-like darts of your little "bamboo shoot" against her tiny damp. "Comme c'est mignon!" she squealed. "Naturellement, c'est ne marche pas! C'est fantastiquement trop mince, tu sais! Mais quand meme, comme c'est mignon!"

Terry had heard via the grapevine that Mason had attacked Sinbad Vail, the son of Peggy Guggenheim, who started a literary magazine called *Points* and was well known to the Paris gang. Terry continues:

> The idea that you may be "really going insane" never occurred to me before, at least not with the forceful seriousness you seem to want to give it; frankly, I think it is an error (and a rather morbid one) to harp on it the way you do. On the other hand, since you did choose to bring it out into the open, so to speak, I think I should tell you that there is a story being circulated here about your cruel attack on Sindra Gale. As for myself, I don't put much stock in hearsay (though may not one truly say: "ou on trouve la fumee, par la, aussi, sera un peu de feu peut-etre, ne'st ce pas Mistor Masor Hoff!!") hehe! Well, the story (going the rounds like the proverbial wild fire) is that poor Sindra was just out of his sick-bed on a winter's day, and had gone to Luxembourg Gardens with a few crumbs of bread he had saved to give the pigeons there, and was, in fact, in that very attitude, leaning forward giving these dear birds food, when out you rushed (in some sort of narcotic frenzy) and gave poor Sindra good pummelling on his abcessed kidney with one of your vicious little barbells. Now, no one knows better than I how these stories get all twisted and distort, and as I say, I don't give them too much credence. Still in all, fumme de feu, etc., eh Mace? So you had better give me the proper account of it and maybe I can straighten out this mess. Naturally, Tony, Georgia, Greg, Stan, Bob, Iris, Cookie, Shadow, and the others are hurt and confused by the story. . . .

Mason never did explain, but Couquite Hoffenberg remembers:

> Sinbad Vail at the time was having an affair with Iris Owens, but also was dating me in his charming apartment on the Luxembourg Gar-

dens where I was seeing him in the afternoons. "Well," you may think, "this Sinbad must have been quite good looking, clever, funny, etc., to be having all these wonderful girls." Just the contrary. He had ordinary looks, was a bore and a poor lover. But think of this mountain of gold. . . . That's what started us poor girls dreaming.

Anyway, I got home late one afternoon. Mason was angry and suspicious, and I looked so guilty and felt so ashamed, I actually fell down on my knees and asked him to forgive me. When I confessed it was Sinbad, he slapped me around, mercifully with the flat of his hand. The next morning, early, he waited in the Luxembourg for Sinbad, and attacked him — which was a great shock to him, as he was a very mild man. . . .

Terry's letter from Tupper Lake continues:

Well, Mace, things are pretty much the same in the Village — or rather, you wouldn't know your old Greenwich Village, Mace. The *I Ching* has been remaindered for $2.95 and your old master, Doctor Billy-Bob Reich, just took a two-year fall for peddling his useless device [the orgone box]. Well, maybe 'Orgone' can cure a two year jail sentence, too! Eh? He-he! Otherwise, its dope and pussy, and lots of it! Mel still dominates the scene, having won out a number of contenders for Dorothy's erotic puss (she will bear him a manchild in December) and manages to keep hip-talk alive and poignant ("B.J. cut out on an O.D." etc) even to the point of saying things that aren't actually true but have a nice ring to them.

You're mistaken, Mace, if you don't think I get my share of Jewish damp. As a matter of fact, though, I never approach it in that sort of ethnic way (that is to say, Jewish or non-Jewish puss), so that your attitude of initial discrimination is a curious one, though I don't say I am too surprised by it. In fact, I was particularly impressed by that very implication when I first considered your relationship with MM [Marilyn Meeske]. As you may recall, you had taken her to your parents' sumptuous flat, in the hope that the combined weight of drug and wealth would be enough to get your head in (and, in fact, had succeeded, when your good Mom Hoff arrived). Quickly stuffing the darling's entrails back in her, you put on a show of gentility, which ***may*** or ***may not*** have fooled Mom Hoff.

In any event, she said: "All right, it's matzoh and gevelt for all!" then added, by way of a feeler: "But, perhaps your friend does not care for Jewish food?" and gave you both a searching look, whereupon you said: "Gosh, Mom, Marel's as Jewish as they *come!*" which proved to be a classic error in the choice of words, for then, at that very moment, the darling girl, with the honey-thick mid-eastern slime of her vulva still seething, actually *did* come, spewing the hot juice (or, as you seem to prefer, "jewse") all over the handsome appointments of the room, Mom Hoff's new frock, the video screen, and everything else — the bitter fruit of group-identification, Mace, and your hand was shown again! . . . Well, we've discussed it more than once, and I know you're keen. Still in all, it does seem strange to me. And now there is something about all Jewish people having the same finger-prints; I suppose you'll make capital of that as well.

En tout cas, I'm pointing for Paris (with my new bride, Carol Cooper.* You may remember suggesting her to me one night when you were trying to come between me and groovy Harriet). Well, Carol is a darling, Mace. . . .

Sue Schwertly [also] is pointing your way, Mace, her loins heavy with the desire of you. She asked me what I thought her chances of getting some of your teencie. I gave you a boost, Mace, by allowing a wan smile fleet past my impassive aquiline features, as I slowly ground out my half-finished butt, and said softly: "Mickey's got his price, Sue." So clean off the old broom-straw, Hoff, I've set you up again! Not that I can't afford to, the way the chicks around the Rive and the Dinette, keep hitting on me for organ. "How about a length of that Texas iron, big boy?" They ask, referring in this way to my great derrick-joint. Sometimes I give them a taste of the old granite, but mostly they have "contact-orgasms" from just thinking about it there at the Dinette, so I'm spared the time of stripping down, etc. . . .

Now, how about some news. You're mistaken if you think I want to hit Paris cold. Give a guy a break, Hoffer.

While Terry and Mason often joked about "making it" with "chicks" — whether in Paris or the Village — many women ex-

*Terry had nicknames for everyone.

ploring the scene were escaping the Eisenhower conformity and McCarthyism of America through a kind of life improvisation involving spontaneity, verve, and risk taking. Marilyn Kanterman (Meeske) hardly fit into the "innocent abroad" category. About *Candy,* she commented that Terry and Mason may have missed out on the complex emancipation that many women were undergoing at the time. Meeske, who moved to Paris in her twenties, became an Olympia author, writing as Henry Crannach, and met Iris Owens. Meeske recalls her adventures with Nori Hickox — a beauty from an upper-class Connecticut family, whose great love was bebop jazz legend Alan Eager:

> I first went to Europe with Nori. . . . We were so crazy . . . Nori was very beautiful, black eyes, Celtic tiny features, perfect teeth, seemingly widthdrawn. . . . She was the perfect Woman Thing* — she had this milkmaid face. . . . She did wind up being with Anton Rosenberg, who was very much in love with her. That's when I became aware of her. . . .
>
> So I got her into the national maritime union — and sure enough she became a waitress on the South American run. We got her to take in a huge haul of Columbian Gold grass — can you imagine anything so dangerous? and obviously that run was one they were all watching because they must have been bringing in cocaine — all the Cuban bellboys were on cocaine — we were all high. That's something that Terry was missing — the experimentation and the neuroses of women at that time.

Earlier in the summer of 1956, Terry had asked Alex Trocchi, who by then had migrated from Paris to New York and was working as a barge captain for the Trap Rock Company, to help him get the same kind of job, which he did. And so, a few days after their wedding, Terry and Carol, with minimal belongings, reported to the flats of Far Rockaway where Terry took command of his "craft." As Terry later wrote:

---

* *The Woman Thing* was Iris Owens's most famous Olympia book, about a woman as love/sex object.

> We were Barge Captains, as they called themselves — rather euphemistically, since it was a job so lowly that it was ordinarily held by guys who had been kicked out of the Longshoreman's Union; old winos and the like, being replaced now by this new breed, the dope-head writer. . . . It was one of those classic writer's jobs, like hotel clerk, night watchman, fire-tower guy, etc., with practically no duties ('Just keep her tied up and pumped out. . . .') Alex found it by chance, wandering around the West Side docks after a few hours at the White Horse. The guy who did the hiring happened to be Scottish. So he took a fancy to Alex, Alex being a Ludgate scholar from Glasgow, and boss-charm besides. 'Have ye had any experience at sea, lad?' 'Only with small craft, sir — punting on the Clyde and the like.' 'Good enough, lad, I like the cut of yer jib.'

The barge job would bring in enough money to get to Europe and stay for a while. Terry continues his letter to Mason, on the Royal portable as they are towed up the Hudson:

> August, 1956, Aboard the barge
>
> I began this letter to you sometime ago (when I was giving the old head a breather). Now, I'm writing from a scow in the East River, a sinecure post I've taken for the moment. Captain of the Barge, sir! I'll be telling you more about it later. It's another frontier opened by the old unwitting pioneer, Mel Sabre. Similar posts are held now by Jim Kolb, Big Mike, and Alex Trocchi.
>
> Meanwhile, our plans have taken a more tangible form, so to speak. We leave on the 28th of September, on a freighter, arriving at Antwerp, 7 or 8 days later. We have some money and plan to travel about a little as it is Carol's first time abroad, but what I'm wondering, of course, is if you will be in Paris at that time and/or if we could stay at your flat for a few days while getting straight for a room. As a matter of fact, we will probably get a room that very day (of arrival) but it would be nice to "check in", so to speak, with you first, leaving the bags there, etc. while I leg it about the quarter to find decent lodging. (I suppose Hotel Etats-Unis is a good bet . . . get a nice double there for about 190 francs [$.38], I guess, eh Mace?) No, I ran into Dick Fremit the other day and he said Paris was plenty ex-

pensive. I guess one has to figure about 500 [$1.00] for a decent room. Or is it 750? I would appreciate knowing the rates of a typical groover hotel in your quarter. Maybe you could stop in the next time about the rates (without bath). Also, could you let me know about the dollar exchange? Is it worthwhile to bring (at risk) currency instead of traveller's checks? What's shakin', Hoff? Groove me, you hep. I'll be bringing the Utermeyer discs you wanted, also rough bush if its shakin'. Let me know if there is anything else you need. Nescafé? Nylons for the little lady? Jan Kindler? . . .

There is a good possibility that Carol may get a teaching job at the U. N. Ecole Enfantine in Geneva. This would begin in December, and if this happens we will be there for a while. Otherwise, after traveling a bit, we may go to Ibiza or similar for the winter. I know you're keeping your plans flexible, Mickey, but do let me hear from you soon.

Take care.

T.

Mason responded:

Paris, Sept 8, 1956

Cher copain,

I received your letter, and understand very well your desire to insinuate yourself and your chick into this groovy pad during the awkward first week of arrival. I've discussed the thing with the family and wrestled with the idea myself late at night, praying jewishly and the rest of it, and the answer, as you must have slyly guessed it would be when you asked, is "pourquoi pas".

I assume you are going to go thru with your part of it — records, bush, tongue-bath for the concierge, and now, a new item: you are to call my mother, who will have a few articles of clothing to send along to me in your care, such as dacron shorties and the like which you can't get here.

You'd be lucky to find a double room for 750 — a mille [$2.00] would be more like it, unless you care to live in The Slimy Sheet Hotel, rue Mouffetard [where Terry lived in previous years]. I guess you mention Les Etats-Unis from having heard that it was a center of rottenness and corruption and that there was plenty of black cock there. This is no longer true. The club part ceased to exist several months ago and, as far as I know, nothing is happening there. Montparnasse generally is rather dead with all the merrymakers seeking the truth at St. Germaine which has begun to wail and shake with their victorious shootings off.

I started this a few days ago but have been goofing. I notice it's already the 11th so I'm going to mail it of without delay.

So long

Mason

By November, with enough money set by, Terry decided to ditch the barge at the 79th Street boat basin and flagged a guy in a passing speedboat to take them ashore. Not long after, they were boarding a freighter bound for Antwerp.

With no steady income, but a handful of stories published, one novel written, and another novel, *The Hipsters,* begun — Terry spent the twelve-day Atlantic crossing writing a Guggenheim grant application. He had already received endorsement from many writers, including Henry Green, Malcolm Cowley, James Purdy, George Plimpton, and Nelson Algren, who wrote: "I think 'The Sun and the Still-born Stars' is a classic. . . . 'The Night the Bird Blew' has style, is your own all the way. . . . Being older than yourself, I feel a bit of twinge when reflecting how lightly I took my own talent, and how wasteful I've been with it. You have a true talent, as well as a tendency to dissipate it. That is why I hope the coming year is the hardest you ever had. And the rest of the way is by the stars." Although fortified with letters of recommendation, Terry did not submit his application for another two years.

Despite financial uncertainty, life was good for Terry that fall of 1956. He and Carol arrived in Paris as planned, stayed for a week or so with Mason and Couquite in their roomy Paris apartment on the rue Henri Barbusse in Montparnasse, then moved to the Hotel Etats-Unis on the rue Jacob, minutes from the Deux Magots.

Chapter 6

Our Poets Love It So

While Terry was tending his barge on the Hudson, writing to his pals by the light of a kerosene lamp, Maurice Girodias was making literary history. Girodias published Nabokov's *Lolita* in 1956 in the well-distributed Traveller's Companion series. As Girodias later recalled:

> The publication of *Lolita* in fifty-six was *the* event. I had my biggest litigation with the French government over that. And once again, I won the case — but it really finished me completely. After that they harassed me until I was forced out of business. But in the meantime I had made a fortune with *Lolita*. It was the only book I ever published which made me temporarily rich, because it was the only book I had a solid contract which the author couldn't break when he became famous. He had to live up to the contract, which gave me one-third of the income of the reprint in English or sale of foreign rights.

Terry met Girodias for the first time that fall in Paris through Alex Trocchi, who was writing a book for him and was en route to his office.

> [Trocchi] was going to collect some money from Girodias . . . and he had some pages to turn in, so we stopped by there and he introduced me. . . . Girodias asked, "Would you be interested in doing some work, doing one of these . . . short novels?" And I said that I would think about it.

Terry was enthusiastic about the prospect of developing *Candy* for Olympia, but explained that he had a number of other projects on the fire, and that since his intention was to become known as a novelist, writing anonymous sex books would not help achieve that goal. Mason, on the other hand, had already become a part of Girodias's stable of expatriate writers and had completed *Until She Screams* under the name Faustino Perez. Still, Terry took the opportunity to have lunch with Girodias, an event he later wrote about:

> It was one of those . . . French restaurants that has a prix-fixe lunch — a kind of Boul' Mich mom-and-pop operation. It was certainly not a restaurant where you would send back the wine — or so I presumed until he did it, twice, each time with a show of annoyance charmingly tempered with a saintly forbearance. Noblesse oblige personified. "It is only when I have to deal with French waiters," he said, half closing his eyes with his eternal ultra-ennui, "that I began to understand the phrase 'white man's burden'." And, having said that, he ordered absinthe — somewhat to my surprise, since it had been outlawed in France for about two decades. "I like to keep a cache at different restaurants," he explained. "Our poets love it so."

Girodias and Terry intended to meet again before Terry left Paris, but the rendezvous never happened. Having purchased a black 1938 Citroën convertible for $100, Terry and Carol set off for Geneva, oblivious to the gasoline shortage created by the Suez Canal crisis.

> Geneva, 28 November 1956
>
> Hoff, you old Grand:
>
> Well, settled at last, Hoff, and I know you are eager to hear about our motor-trip down. I can tell you it was a gasser.
>
> You may remember my saying I had the tank filled. Well, I had done this on the day I got the car and hadn't bothered about more up until our departure. On that day, after leaving your good flat, we had some minor mechanical trouble and had to spend a couple of

hours in a garage on the Blvd Raspail. As we were about to pull out for Geneve, it occurred to me that I might as well get the old bus filled up then and there.

"Cinq cents balles d'essence, pas plus!" was the attendant's surly retort.

"Why, you poor dumbo," I said, "I'm thinking in terms of full tanks and full jerry-cans, and you talk of half a mille balles d'essence. Forget it! I'll take my trade to Esso Extra! We're off for Geneve and the old bus needs plenty of gas! Cinq balles wouldn't wet the bottom of *this* powerhouse!"

Lashed into speechlessness by my caustic tirade, the poor attendant shrugged, and we slammed out in high gear for the open road.

As we turned into the Blvd Raspail, I happened to notice that there was a line of cars outside the station about a block long waiting their turn at the pumps. "Why, those poor dumbos," I said, "why don't they hit the open road! On the outskirts of the city, there'll be petrol enough to float a van-cat chevaux in!"

All along the way to Porte d'Italie, there were these outlandish queues waiting for the essence. I had to laugh. "These poor dumbos!" I said, "guess they've never heard of supply and demand! Out Fontainebleau way there'll be gas enough for an army!" We didn't bother to look anymore, had group-singing until Fountainebleau, then decided to pull in and get the old bus filled up. It was an annoyance to see that all the stations were closed, due I supposed, to some sort of local fete.

"These local fetes are a nuisance," I remarked to Carol, "we'll be needing gas soon and I don't know whether the trucking stations farther along carry Super or not. Also, their service is sloppy. Tant pis! We'll have to shoot on down the line."

Well, Hoff, the stretch of road from Fontainebleau to Corbeil would make your old negative heart thump wildly. Pump after pump unmaned, most of them hung with impromptu cardboard on which was scrawled (with, seemingly, a gleeful defiance) "Vide" "Sec!" "Foutu" "Kaput!" "US Go Home" etc, etc. "Why, those poor boobies!" I said to Carol, "here we're off to Geneve and they're fucking around like that! What a nuisance!"

It was getting near dark and the register showed sec. Fortunately, at just about that time, we had a rather serious breakdown, had to call a garage and be towed in. We had come about an all-night batterie charge and some dynamo repair before getting the old show on the road again. We passed a pleasant night however in an old inn, and were up bright and early to hit the road. The repair bill put me in the position of being one of the garage's most favored clients so they could hardly refuse to fill up the old bus with Esso Extra, and we roared out of the garage and onto the highroad.

About the time the tank was empty again, more trouble, another night's waiting, and another full tank. This time, they had to send to Paris for the piece detache, had it sent down colis express, and we slammed out of there bright and early for the open road. Because of fucking around, leaving the main road for out of the way ceramic factories, old churches, groovy restaurants, etc. we were still only about halfway there. There began to be more open pumps however, so I felt we had no worries.

As we approached Dijon we passed countless open pumps, and though I knew we would need about 20 litres to get from Dijon to Geneve, I didn't bother to stop. "Get the old bus filled and serviced in Dijon," I said, "after we've had a nice meal at the Marmite D'or."

Well, by the time we finished dinner, it was about nine o'clock and all the stations appeared to be closed. "This early closing of Dijon stations is a bother," I said, "I don't like hitting the Alps with only a couple of litres in the tank."

After cruising around the city for about an hour, we went in to the Prefecture and showed him our autorization. He let us fill the tank from his private pump and we slammed out of there and up the hill. It's 200 kilometeres from Dijon to Geneve, and by the time we reached the last 50, it was 3:00 AM. The last fifty is down an extremely steep mountain and, as it happened, there came a sudden drop in temperature so that the very heavy fog turned into something else.

Just as we were entering into the descent the car began to handle oddly. "Say, feel that smooth gliding," I said to Carol, "now the old bus is plenty smooth." The fog was so thick that we could only see the shoulder of the road. Suddenly the car came to an abrupt sideways stop and a sign loomed up out of the fog.

"May be a directional indicator," I said to Carol, "I'd better have a look." I got out to see the sign even though it was about two feet directly in front of the car. The words were "Verglass Formidable" and then beneath it "DANGER DU MORT." Getting back to the car I stepped out into the road for a minute and almost at once fell on my ass. The road was covered with a thick sheet of ice. There were also signs of increasing cold and possibly even of mountain storm. Nothing to do but push on, I decided. If we stop here we'll freeze to death.

As soon as we were back on the road we began to careen wildly down the hill and came to another abrupt stop on the opposite side of the road, about half a foot from a bottomless pit. About half the length of this road has no guard rail whatever. We got out of the car to have a look, then I got back in to try to ease it back on the road. Perversely enough however, it began slipping the other way until the back wheel on that side was half over the precipice. It was the weight of the trunk etc., I suppose, that made it behave so oddly on the verglass. It scared the fucking shit out of me, I can tell you that. I was afraid to try to get out of the car then, for it did appear that any agitation at all would send it sailing over. Finally I gave orders for rocks etc. to be placed (gently) beneath all the wheels for a last try before attempting my escape (I had decided I would have to go out the other door as that was the side fartherest from the abyss.) Anyway, this did the trick and sent us careening down again this time to the other side, against the wall of the mountain and in a ditch.

By the time we got it out of the ditch, it was incredibly cold. I had a scheme whereby we could lay down lengths of clothing to form a carpet over which we could proceed at about three feet an hour, but it was too cold, etc., so we started walking back up the mountain, soon reached a house (about 4:30 AM) and woke them up. It was exactly as in a movie. I was going to ask if we could sleep in the barn until first-light, but couldn't think of the word for barn. Anyway, the good woman gave us hot drink and a warm bed for the night. The next day, men came and put gravel on the road. She said it was the second time in six years she'd been there that such verglass had occurred. So, after a more or less leisurely trip, we pulled in at the enfant school on Friday (having left Paris Tues.)

Despite the harrowing trip, they were soon settled in a room above the school, which was housed in an elegant seventeenth century villa with garden across from the United Nations in Geneva. Carol reported to the British headmistress and began work as teacher for a group of international pre-schoolers.

"The job was fun," Carol remembered, "but the best part was the vacations. Before each one, we would pack up the Citroën and Terry would be at the school door waiting, so we could take off for Paris or Spain, or wherever, the minute I was free."

Though Carol's salary of $500 a month, a small amount even then, kept them strapped, they were able to find a comfortable apartment quite in contrast to their one-room studio on Charles Street. Life in Geneva was ordered and pleasant and an ideal place to write. A very fertile period of work for Terry began.

Unlike Terry, who wrote every day unless he was traveling, Mason almost always found something of greater interest to do. Although he was supposed to be writing another book for Girodias, *Sin for Breakfast,* his writer's block, wide-ranging obsessions, and drug addiction were seriously interfering with his ability to focus. Mason opens and closes this letter by making a mock issue of Terry's request for a loan, alluding to Terry's use of Mel Sabre and others in the stories he published the previous year.

Paris, December 15, 1956

Dear Mr. T.

I'm getting very selfish, T., which you will have observed perhaps with your cold-hearted watch you mount on your friends in order to cash in on them literarily. . . .

I'm having a hell of a time getting the old book going [*Sin for Breakfast*]. Haven't written a word in over a week and, of course, the more this sickening interval elongates the harder it gets to interrupt it. In the meantime, it is a positive delight to do anything else. Thus I'm buying books frantically. Here are some of the titles: Langenscheidt's German-Eng. Dict.; *The Greek Myths* (2 volumes) by

Robert Graves; Marlborough's *Latin Self-Taught* and Marlborough's *Chinese Self-Taught; The Burl Ives Song Book* (115 American folk songs, containing the guitar chords); *L'Etat D'Israel* by Andre Chouraqui; *Specimens of English Literature, A.D. 1394–A.D. 1579* by Walter W. Skeat; *Teach Yourself Hebrew* by R. K. Harrison; *Hebraische Grammatik* by George Beer; *A Dictionary of World Literary Terms* edited by J. T. Shipley; Jarrold's *Dictionary of Difficult Words.*

As you can see, each one of these requires many many hours of perusal and I frequently spend white nights studying *all* of them at once. I'm making good headway with Hebrew and the guitar chords, only fair headway with Latin, Chinese, and the Greek myths. I'm working steadily however, and as soon as I've mastered these various subjects I'll get back to writing the book which will, consequently, be more erudite than if I'd simply tackled it cold.

Mason playfully berated Terry on a number of issues, including Terry's criticizing Mason for his desire to "write for money." He continues:

You say you're sure that being attracted to a cold woman is an "aberration" whereas it's universally recognized that a woman's failure to respond has the effect of intensifying a man's eyes, and the opposite case — where she naively shows that she wants it — tends to diminish her desirability. Isn't that the great feminine tactic — deliberately concealing their positive feelings, being "mysterious"?

No, old boy. I'm afraid there's a bit of dishonest bullshit in your argument and so I won't be able to lend you the money. All fooling aside, a hundred smackeroos? Are you kidding?

Spater

Mason

Chapter 7

A Clean, Well-Lighted Place

Geneva, 1956–1958

From their base in Geneva, Terry found the solitude and isolation he needed to write. It was also an opportunity to commit to print some of the brilliantly subversive routines which he, David Burnett, Mason, and others had riffed on in their many drug-and-booze-soaked evenings at Riviera, the Remo, wherever they gathered. With no social scene, Terry could break the pattern that made those evenings at the Flore and the Riviera so exhilarating — yet so frustrating, for Terry now had little else to do but write.

The Southerns were delighted to be invited to spend their first Christmas with Henry Green in London. Terry had discovered the English novelist many years earlier through an article in *The Partisan Review* that defined Green, who wrote his books almost entirely in dialogue, as "a terrorist of language." Reading Green's books during and shortly after the war, Terry found them "so extraordinary that I wrote Green a fan letter. I just wanted to express my appreciation of his work. Surprisingly enough, he wrote back. So we got into a correspondence, and through that developed a curious friendship."

And so, a few days before Christmas, Terry and Carol drove the indomitable Citroën to Calais and then on to London via channel boat and train. Upon meeting the eccentric aristocratic Green and his beautiful, birdlike wife, Dig, in Belgrave Square, they were also introduced to friends Francis Wyndham (who would later review *Candy*), Arthur Koestler, and Kitty Freud, married to Lucien Freud. Green would become Terry's great supporter. Theirs became an important friendship, which would help them both: Terry would interview Green for *The Paris Review*, and Green would soon endorse Terry as a serious novelist.

But before leaving, Terry wrote to Girodias. With no hope in sight for the publication of *Flash and Filigree*, and increasingly in need of money to supplement Carol's $500 a month salary, Terry proposed that he write a book anonymously for the Traveller's Companion (TC) series to be called *Candy*. Setting the book up to be as open-ended as possible, Terry emphasized the episodic nature of her adventures:

Geneva, 10 December, 1956 VIA AMERICAN EXPRESS

Dear Mr. Girodias,

Sorry I didn't get to see you before leaving Paris, but the proverbial press of last minute affairs, etc. did not allow for it. I trust however, that Mason H. may have told you of my sustained interest in doing a book for your Traveller's Companion Series. I have decided to use a pseudonym though, this at the request of my agent in New York who is trying to sell a novel of mine there now, she feels that the explanation required would complicate things at this particular moment, and that, on the other hand, the fact of it could not fairly be withheld. This does not mean however, that my interest in the 'literary possibilities' of the TC medium has in any way lessened since our talk. I would, of course, stand by the book, that is to say, would claim it as my own and would be prepared to defend it as something seriously done; naturally too, I would do it with as great care as any other of my writing. To put it another way, I would want the book to be generally *known* as mine (or so become) but would not want it be blatantly *proclaimed* so at this time.

The story I have in mind is in the tradition of *Candide*, with a contemporary setting, the protagonist an attractive American girl, Candy, an only child of a father of whose love she was never quite sure, a sensitive progressive-school humanist who comes from Wisconsin to New York's lower-east side to be an art student, social worker, etc. and to find (unlike her father) 'beauty in mean places.' She has an especially romantic notion about 'Minorities,' and, of course, gets raped by Negroes, robbed by Jews, knocked-up by Puerto Ricans, etc. — though her feeling of "being needed" sustains her for quite a while, through a devouring gauntlet of freaks, faggots, psychiatrists, and aesthetic cults — until, wearied and misunderstood, she joins a religious order, where she finds fatherly rapport at last in the gentle priest, who, at the right moment of confidence, is stricken with a severe chill, has Candy cover him for warmth with her body, and slips it to her. Almost disillusioned, she moves another step towards the mystical, to the Far East to become a Buddhist. Alone, in the ancient temple, before the great stone God, she begins to achieve the solace she seeks. In her house of contemplation, she has found the point of fixation for her attention to be the nose of the Buddha — and there is some emphasis given here to the almost incandescent beauty and devotional qualities which that object (the Buddha's nose) takes on for her, as her spiritual self rises nearer nirvana. She senses, increasingly, and with increasing satisfaction, her great need of the Buddha, but this culminates in a transport of child-like Blakean joy with the ultimate realization that the Buddha too, *needs her!* (something, you see, she had never been quite sure of with her father) and her state of pure grace is attained. The book ends then, with an incident of war which destroys the temple, killing everyone, including Candy, on whom the Buddha has toppled, its nose burying itself (ironically enough) in her vagina — it is not a sad ending however, for there is, on the face of the prostrate girl, a smile of simple wonder, while below, from the lifted hem of her austere sack-cloth garment, her white, well-rounded legs arch out gracefully, raised ever so slightly, to facilitate this last great need and entry of her.

This kind of description, of course, does injustice to the story, and is intended rather to indicate to you that I have given thought to the thing in its entirety. The title would be *Candy* (by Maxwell Kenton) and it would be in a novella format (150 pages). I have already done some writing on it and will send you the sequence I feel to be most finished. If this is satisfactory to you, you could send me some money, and I could devote full-time to it and finish it in two months. I would do it for 150,000 francs [$300], which, I believe, would be at the regular page-rate, if I could have a large amount now.

We just spent an extraordinary sum getting an apartment here; and it has, in view of our plans for going to England for Christmas, left us short. Anyway, I would like to have 50,000 francs [$100] if possible. We have money coming in after the first of the year, and I would not have to press you for more until the manuscript is delivered, completed. I realize this may be an unusual advance, but I feel you can trust me to come through with something of interest.

You should have the sequence [Candy and the Hunchback scene] I speak of a couple of days after you receive this. Please let me know your decision, at your earliest convenience, as, if you cannot do it, I will want to make other arrangements.

With all best wishes,

Terry Southern

Girodias received the letter the next day, and wrote back immediately:

My Dear Southern,

Thank you for your letter of the 10th. Indeed, I was wondering whether you were still considering the project we discussed, and I am very glad to see that it has not been abandoned.

However, I find the form you want to give to this volume rather embarrassing for use in the TC, as we tend to have books of exactly the same length, or at least an average of 190 pages. I wouldn't mind a longer book, eventually, but a shorter one raises very difficult problems of pricing, etc.

This may seem silly, but it is really an essential point. Is there no means of inflating the novella format to a full-size book, or adding to the story you want to write another shorter one?

As to the problem of money, it is unfortunately a rather difficult period for me in that respect. If we could reach some understanding on the afore-mentioned problem, I could let you have the 50,000 you mention *in England*. Would that suit you?

As to the story itself, it is rather difficult to judge from the outline you gave me, but I am quite certain I can rely on your skill. I am looking forward to the sequence you are to send to me.

Yours,

Maurice Girodias

Receiving payment in England and in British pounds was great news. Although Terry was concerned about his ability to sustain the "gag" of Candy and keep it interesting, he agreed to a longer book.

Geneva, December 18th 1956

Dear Mr. G:

Thanks for your quick reply to my inquiry; sorry I could not be equally prompt with mine, but the news that you could not use the format I had in mind gave me pause — to try to work it out in that new light (that is, 190–200 pages of 250 words) though now, having duly achieved the 'inflation' (being hardly, good sir, the kindest term, nor yet the most exact) I am prepared to do it.

As for getting the money I requested in England, that would be fine. How can it be managed?

There will be a slight delay in my getting the section I promised to you, since, in working the story out again, I started making changes in it and finally re-writing it altogether, so that it must now be typed over in full.

With all best wishes,

Terry Southern

As Terry was just beginning his professional relationship with Girodias, J. P. Donleavy, an Irish writer, was desperate to end his. Donleavy had not forgiven Girodias for the shock he had given him in 1955, in a Fulham pub in London. At last holding the first copy of his great work *The Ginger Man,* Donleavy discovered on the back cover that it was being promoted as one of many in an unknown series called Traveller's Companion, which included such patently lascivious titles as *School for Sin, Rape, The Loins of Amon,* and *The Sexual Life of Robinson Crusoe.* "When I saw that I realized it was a total disaster," he said later, particularly since Scribner's in the United States had been keen on publishing it. Perhaps almost as bad, Donleavy had received no royalties for his Olympia book and had been trying unsuccessfully for the past two years to reclaim the only copy of his highly annotated manuscript from Girodias and his secretary, Miriam Worms. Finally, he went back to his carbon pages and was able to get a publishing deal with a London publisher. He had done this based on the much-contested notion that Girodias had given him verbal permission to do so at a party. The evening in question — Girodias's *grande soirée* for Donleavy in his Paris apartment above the restaurant La Boucherie — was in fact Girodias's last chance to make a deal with the reticent writer, who was returning to Ireland the next day. Girodias had laid out the finest of wines and invited many Olympians to come by. As Girodias recalled, "Those were the days when the greatest vintage years, 1947 and 1949, had reached their full splendour, when a single sip of Clos-Vougeot or Romanée Conti would turn you into a god." As Terry later wrote in *Grand Street* about the evening, his friend Hadj's hash was also put to service:

> The soirée itself proved to be quite a gala affair. . . . Girodias's generally low opinion of Monsieur Hadj (and, indeed, Arabs by any other name) seemed much ameliorated, perhaps because his M.O. for the evening, I soon began to discern, was to get Donleavy so blotto that he could have his way with him, in terms of contracts, royalties, or whatever else might relate to *The Ginger Man.* And in that regard it was apparent that a bit of hashish would be a welcome addition to his arsenal of derangements. "Baudelaire," I heard him confide to our hapless guest of honor, "used to have it in his confiture."
>
> At one point in the evening I fell into consort with Trocchi and the English publisher John Calder — a deadly combo, derangement-wise — and so failed to follow the complete dismantling of J. P. Donleavy; suffice to say I recall him being bundled out the door and into the Paris night by Gid and his brother Eric.

When *The Ginger Man* went to press in England, Donleavy came to Paris to try to finally straighten things out with Girodias. As he told John de St. Jorre, "This was the lowest point in my entire life. There was this book waiting to come out in England and saving my whole future as an author. . . . I arrived in Paris in [a state] of some desperation. . . . It was like walking down to your execution, and I walked that road."

Girodias told him unequivocally that he was not permitted to publish in England, and that any royalties were to be shared with him. Donleavy announced, "I'll see you in court."

Publication went ahead in England as planned, and eventually in the United States. Girodias and Donleavy would sue each other over the next decade, ironically, both men financing the suits from earnings on *The Ginger Man*.

Before the close of 1956, Terry sent a note to Mason trying to determine whether Girodias's deadlines were serious and how to get more money out of him. Mason wrote back explaining that he himself was overdue with *Sin for Breakfast,* and not to worry. Gid, he said, has "a way of making cracks about wanting a book 'soon,' but it's just his way of spurring you on, since, in the long run, he *does* want the book of course, and is mainly worried about someone not doing it at all." Mason also observed that because of the bans on his books, that "there seems a chance that he's going to discontinue the operation"; however, "the stores continue to sell them (discreetly), and there has even been a boom in business as a result." Mason signs off with a useful tip: "As for the loot, you can certainly ask for more when you've written what's been paid for; I try to keep him a little bit ahead of me."

In January, Terry set up his office in the new rue Schaub apartment in Geneva and began work on *Candy* in earnest. The novel opens in Racine, Wisconsin, where Candy Christian lives and attends college. Terry knew Girodias would be looking for immediate sex and perversion — but Terry would make him wait a few pages — setting the tone with a rich prose style and precise character development. Establishing Candy's classic naïveté, Terry introduces the absurd bravado of the provocative Professor Mephesto, *in medias res* of another spellbinding lecture — this time on "human ethics."

After class, Mephesto offers Candy the proverbial glass of sherry in his office. "This sherry was sent to me by Lucci Locco, the Portugese humanist-symbolist poet — now living in Paris, of course — I think you'll find it rather good." The reason for their private conference is Candy's thesis, "Contemporary Human Love," developing the idea, encouraged by Mephesto, that "to give of oneself — fully . . . is a beautiful and *thrilling* privilege!"

> He sat down again, and put a hand out to the girl, as though in an effort to express some extremely abstract feeling, but then finding it ineffable, let it drop, as though it were useless to try, onto her knee. "And the burdens — the needs of man," he said with soft directness to her, "are so *deep* and so — *aching*."

After discussing her paper, his intentions are clear:

> As he spoke he gradually slipped his hand around her neck, along her throat and toward her breast, and Candy dropped her glass of sherry.
>
> "Oh, my goodness," she wailed, going forward at once from her chair to pick the pieces off the floor, for the glass had broken and scattered. She was so embarrassed she could scarcely speak for the moment.
>
> "Oh, I'm sorry, I —"
>
> "Never mind about that," said Professor Mephesto huskily, coming down beside her, "it's nothing, only a material object — the merest chimera of existence!"
>
> On the floor next to her, he put his face to the back of her neck and one hand under her sweater.
>
> "You won't deny me," he pleaded, "I know you are too wise and too good to be selfish. . . . Surely you meant what you wrote." And he began to quote urgently "'. . . the beautiful, thrilling privilege of giving fully,'" meanwhile pressing forward against her. But as he did, Candy sprang to her feet again and the professor lost his

balance and fell sideways, rolling in the spilled sherry, trying to soften his fall with one hand and to pull the girl down with the other, but he failed in both these efforts; and now, having taken a nasty bump in the fall and, perhaps too, because of his unwieldy bulk, he merely lay for the moment in the pool of sherry, wallowing and groaning.

Candy soon decides she must give herself to Mephesto, and there her erotic adventures begin. Terry was off and running.

Meanwhile, Henry Green's fondness for *Flash and Filigree* led him to recommend it to a publisher in London, Andre Deutsch. In January, Mordechai Richler, who had published his first novel, *The Acrobats,* with Deutsch, reported that Deutsch was seriously considering the book. Greatly encouraged, Terry started working on another idea he had been thinking about. It involved an eccentric billionaire prankster, Guy Grand, who spends his millions "making it hot for them." Terry would work on Guy and Candy simultaneously over the next two years. Of the two competing for his attention, *The Magic Christian* (as he soon called it) was far more compelling. However, Terry had promised Girodias, and needed the money. "I see the clock moves on," he wrote in early February, "and I think it better to send you this* now, as it is — by way of assurance that the work is in progress." Girodias wrote back:

Paris, February 8, 1957

Dear Terry Southern,

The piece you sent me, and which I am returning enclosed, is most excellent, and I liked the ingenuosity very much.

Never mind about the delay — but I have to have the book within 4 or 5 weeks at most. Is that possible? Please be kind enough as to let me know precisely what your plans are by return.

Have we discussed the question of the title?† We need one urgently, as we are now working on a new catalogue. And also a blurb

*Probably the expanded Hunchback sequence.

†Terry had suggested *Candy* in his proposal of 10 December 1956.

for same, about ten lines, more if you can, giving a good enough notion of what the book is about.

You may have heard of the trouble we have run into here. 25 books published by us in English have been banned in France by the French minister of Home Affairs. An absolutely ridiculous business, with no doubt more profit in it than trouble, in the long run. Only we have to put a terrible fight in order to have the ban cancelled, which we will obtain within 3 months from now. Also, it does make things a little more embarrassing for this year's program; still, we are bringing out the books as we planned, with a short delay.

I would also like to know what you intend to do regarding the name under which the book will be published. It would really be of considerable help to us if we could have your name appear on the book; it would substantiate our claim that most of our writers are genuine authentic legitimate authors. I swear that it would involve no actual legal risk for you except in the worst of cases a slight fine (which I would be happy to pay), if things came to the worst, which is unthinkable. Please think it over, because the problem is now of much greatest importance to us than when we first discussed the book.

Yours sincerely,

Maurice Girodias

Chapter 8

Publishers and Other Criminals

In 1957 Paris, Girodias was fighting a pitched battle on the front lines of censorship. The Olympia Press had been under attack since Christmas. Girodias later recalled, "One day a police inspector of the Vice Squad . . . visited me. . . . He wanted some reading copies of a number of books listed in our latest catalog . . . explaining that the British government had requested information about the Olympia Press, and that it was his job to build up a file on us."

Days later, all the books the police inspector had taken were banned by an official decree of the Minister of the Interior. Ironically, the distinguished French publisher Gallimard was intending to publish *Lolita* in Girodias's brother Eric's French translation. Girodias had planned to leverage the Gallimard publication for *Lolita*'s publication in the United States, where pornography laws were finally loosening up due to a Supreme Court decision protecting "controversial writings" under the First Amendment. Now all these hopes and more seemed dashed — but only for the moment, because Girodias rose from defeat like the perennial phoenix. Girodias had to prove that his publishing house produced books of some redeeming social value. Terry, with his respectable publishing history in the magazines, would add some credibility to his list — which, lately, seemed largely composed of drug-crazed Brits, Scots, and New Yorkers.

Geneva, 15 February 1957

Dear Mr. G:

Thanks for your letter of the 8th. I am especially glad you liked the piece I sent (you forgot to enclose it in your return letter).

I had heard only vaguely about your troubles, and am sorry to learn that they are as grave as they are. I am confident, however, that it will work out all right. The poor devils, they are simply trying to turn back the clock!

As I mentioned earlier, I took up the matter of name or pseudonym with my agent, and she was against my using my name (or at least the name she is handling) at this point. I must respect her wishes in this. The name, Maxwell Kenton, however, is a legitimate pen-name which I have used for detective fiction, and I would readily acknowledge anything appearing under it as my own. If the book could be listed under the same series as Nabakov's, I am pretty sure she would agree to it, but then I would want to do it without any deadline pressure at all.

It does seem to me that you would do well at this point to consolidate your listings, that is, all in *one* list, since your current catalogue is no doubt the one on which you could be judged. Perhaps you imagine this would greatly inconvenience buyers and present distribution problems otherwise, but I daresay it would not to the extent you may think. Those who buy at shops invariably look through the book first, to see whether or not it is brutally frank, etc, and as for mail-order, I should think it would be quite easy to judge which buyers, regardless of what they order, want the brutally frank, and substitution is easy enough. Finally, as to the book-sellers themselves, a separate index, or the regular index with asterisks to designate brutally frank, would suffice, or a standard phrase within the usual descriptive passage, at the end, such as "A great favourite with servicemen, etc.", or better, simply, "Best-Seller." In other words the distinction between those series (of pornography and non-pornography) should be a *trade* distinction, and not a *public* one — otherwise, it is self-condemnatory.

I continue with the work and I hope it goes fast enough to meet your catalogue promises, though I don't want to embarrass you on this. Working under deadline pressure is bad for me and I admit, with deepest apology, the mistake I made in contracting to do so. The schedule I have been able to achieve so far would put it as finished on March 31st. I know this is slow, and I try, as I have in the past, to better it, but it would be misleading and unrealistic for me to promise it before then.

Perhaps it would be better to wait for the next batch. If you consolidate your list and, for example, bring in Trocchi as the author of a couple of them — which I'm sure he would do. If you would pay any fines involved — I feel sure you won't have any trouble. Alex is short of money now, and was mentioning this to me in a letter just a couple of days ago, and wondering about writing another book for you, etc. I give you his address here in case you do not have it: Alexander Trocchi, c/o Lougee. 333 West 11th Street. New York City, N.Y.

Candy is a very good title, for it has in English many sweet sexual sucking connotations, as well as brutally frank ones, "as easy as taking candy from a baby," being an old cliché, referring to seduction.

Here are a few lines as requested:

> *Candy* by Maxwell Kenton
>
> *Candy,* the bitter-sweet story of a beautiful young girl's undoing . . . and of the men and boys who do. Or perhaps it was the darling girl's own fault, for being . . . *irresistible.* You can decide, in nine [here the word *thrilling* is crossed out by hand] exciting chapters: Candy and the Professor of Philosophy, Candy and the Italian Painter, Candy and the Jewish Writer, Candy and the Giant Negro, Candy and the Porto Rican Drug Fiend, Candy and the Mad Hunchback, Candy and Her Father's Twin, Candy and the Psycho-analyst, Candy and the Gentle Priest, Candy and . . . Buddha!
>
> A masterful satire, with something for every taste — except perhaps the prudish. Sure to be a Best Seller.

I don't know whether or not that is what you had in mind, but you can work it out from that.

All best wishes,

Terry Southern

As 1957 wore on and Terry missed his deadline with Girodias, he found himself increasingly absorbed with *The Magic Christian*. Like *Candy,* it was to be an episodic book, but Guy Grand's adventures were wildly original and surreal — as opposed to a send-up of Voltaire — and the project engaged him completely. Carol recalls:

> I think the idea of *Candy* initially amused Terry a lot, but he got bored with the execution. He set himself a quota of two typed pages a day. He would write longhand, I would type, and sometimes the longhand pages didn't fill the two pages of typescript and he would groan and come up with a few more sentences. He really was forcing it out. That's why he decided to ask Mason for help.

Asking Mason flat-out was dangerous, as it might preemptively launch his famous writer's block. There was also the matter of Mason's addiction, which was sending his family into a tailspin.

At some point that spring, Terry began sending *Candy* bits to Mason, and offered to share the rest of the money with him if Mason would help him finish the book. Terry recalled:

> When Mason first came in, he wrote a scene about Candy meeting a Jewish psychiatrist. . . . That was great because he was very much into the Jewish ambience, and that's how that collaboration began. We'd do a chapter each, I'd do one and show it to him and he'd do one and show it to me — like two people telling each other jokes; each time you were motivated to surprise the other person. We had the same idea of where it was going. It was like *The Perils of Pauline,* putting the girl in different erotic situations.

Terry credits Mason for the conception of Candy's Aunt Livia — the boisterous, lusty foil to Candy's innocence. Terry loved Livia as a character, and although Mason hadn't written anything featuring her yet, Terry introduced her in the Wisconsin chapter. Here she is:

> "Have any of the boys gotten into those little white pants of yours yet?" Aunt Livia asked, as though she were speaking of the weather.

"*Really,* Liv," said Uncle Jack, coughing, "this hardly seems the appro —"

"But, isn't she *lovely?*" his wife persisted, turning to Jack Christian, "a ripe little piece she's getting to be, I'd say. It seems to me that's the first question that would occur to anyone . . . oh god, haven't we come far enough," she went on then in a change of mood, "let's have a drink." . . .

"Right," said Liv, "out of these wet pants and into a dry martini! Eh, 'Can'?" And she gave the blushing girl a suggestive wink.

"Liv's in one of her moods," Uncle Jack explained as he helped her out of the car.

"I'll say," said Candy.

"I'm in the mood for cock and plenty of it!" cried Liv gaily. "About ten pounds, please, thick and fast!"

Wanting to include more about Livia, Terry devised a pre–Dr. Krankeit scene in the hospital waiting room. In the following "TV pitch" monologue, one can tell that *The Magic Christian* was on his mind, for Livia's description of sabotaging a daytime soap opera is the same sort of prank Guy Grand will pull. Here is Livia, full throttle:

> "The opening scene, after the break, is in a smart rest clinic in the French Alps. For the furnishings of this set no expense should be spared, no detail overlooked, to authenticate the desired mood — gracious living. The room is light and airy, the appointments exquisitely delicate. A very large picture-window affords a mountain panorama, a vista of rose-white snow, and sky the color of blue smoke.
>
> "On the bed, clad in peignoir of topaz Chantilly, lies a girl patient. As the scene opens, her physician has just entered:
>
> DR HERSHOLT:
>
> *(pleasantly)*
>
> Well, Bambi! And how do we feel this morning, eh?
>
> BAMBI:
>
> *(frowning)*
>
> What?

DR HERSHOLT:

(tentatively)

Well, I mean . . . uh . . . you know . . . how . . . do . . .

BAMBI

(interrupting)

Doctor, I had a dream last night — it's been puzzling me ever since. (*She looks puzzled, cute*) I mean, dreams *do* have secret meanings . . . *don't* they?

DR HERSHOLT:

(seriously)

Yes, child, very often they do. (*Then in genuine interest*) Now, why don't you tell us about it?

BAMBI:

(after a sigh)

Well, I dreamed I was in a big place — it reminded me somehow of my house . . . at home, in Glendale. And my father was there with me . . . always . . . we were together . . . alone. And I . . . I kept sucking him off. (*She looks puzzled, cute*) What does the dream *mean*, Doctor? . . .

"Of course, it wants more work," [Aunt Livia] said, a few wrinkles to be ironed out, some tightening up, brightening up, et cetera, but the first question is *capital* — how about it, Eddie, can I put you down for a few thousand?"

In *The Magic Christian*, Guy Grand makes this kind of exploration of the limits to which people will go his central occupation. Around this time, Terry sent along an outline and the first chapter of *The Magic Christian* to Andre Deutsch for consideration, and began sharing it with friends.

Chapter 9

Essentially More Warm Than You

On March 9, 1957, Mordechai Richler wired Terry with congratulations:

> YOU ARE NOW ENTITLED TO KNOW THE SECRET HANDSHAKE, THE STABLE CHEERS AND — SOON ENOUGH — YOU GET YR. ANDRE DEUTSCH SWEATSHIRT TO WEAR.

Not only was Deutsch preparing for the publication of *Flash and Filigree*, but *The Magic Christian* had also been accepted. Meanwhile, Girodias was waiting for his *Candy*, which Terry had promised for March 31. In mid-April, he wrote: "I am anxious to know where we stand now? When do you think your ms will be completed?"

Geneva, 24th April, 1957

Dear M. Girodias:

Sorry to keep you waiting, but I have been both sick and out of town.

I will send you about half of the book, completed, in a few days. I have been re-writing it at the rate of two pages a day, which would put it finished the middle of June. Is there still no possibility of a 150-page format?

Don't worry about the advance; I will of course return that if I don't deliver the book.

Best,

S.

A few days later, Henry Green telegrammed out of the blue: "UTTERLY EXHAUSTED STOP CAN YOU PUT ME UP SEVEN DAYS REPLY BY TELEPHONE HENRY GREEN." Terry wired back "COME AT ONCE."

Green arrived in Geneva and instantly made himself at home both in the apartment and at the nearby café, where he would go (as was his wont in London) to eavesdrop and observe. At the end of his visit, the three squeezed into the Citroën and headed for Mont Blanc. Terry was anxious for Henry to take the téléphérique to the top — an awesome and somewhat hair-raising ride. "Alarming" was to be the key word throughout the trip. Carol reports, "Driving Henry on to the airport in Nice, we were caught in a blizzard. As I turned the windshield wiper knob by hand, Henry, head out the window, called out the number of feet we were from the edge. Henry, who always relished things going wrong, was not disappointed."

Terry returned to Geneva to find another anxious letter from Girodias.

Paris, 26 April, 1957

Dear Terry Southern,

Thank you for your note. I am relieved to learn that you haven't abandoned the book altogether, and I look forward to receiving the promised first half.

In the same time, I am really not feeling too good about your news: the middle of June would be too late for us, really, and would probably make it impossible for us to bring out the book this year. On the other hand, in order to plan our publicity in advance, we have to be absolutely *certain* of the date of publication, and therefore of the date of delivery of the MS. I therefore offer you the following alternative:

- Either we postpone the book until next year, and you deliver the MS in January '58;
- Or you undertake to give me a 170 pages manuscript by May 15: provided of course that in that time you can guarantee a good job, I mean, not the sort of weak disorderly and

inconsequential last third I usually obtain in such circumstances.

In any case, I need your answer BY RETURN OF MAIL. I really have to take a final decision right away now.

Yours,

mg

There was a sigh of relief at the new deadline of January, but even so, Terry was hoping that Mason was putting some work into *Candy*. But in fact Mason had fallen more deeply into drugs. Terry apparently knew he was back on the stuff through the reporting of friends — and had sent Mason a note of admonishment, saying something to the effect that as they were all to be together for holiday that summer, Mason had better get his act together. Mason replied, looking for sympathy for the hellish withdrawal he had suffered throughout the fall:

Paris, May 10th, 1957

Dear Terryo,

I can't help getting the impression that I am, in my normal composed state, a kindlier, more essentially warm person than you; for, writing at a time when you had reason to believe I was slipping ineluctably into the slimy slough of poor tortured wretches, all hooked and marked and perforated, you adapt a lousy, sneering, callous tone concerning my misfortune, instead of one of aroused concern and compassion, and strongly hint that the next time you lay eyes on me (assuming probably that I would by then be in a state of extreme feebleness) you would do physical violence to me. . . .

You have seen me out-of-my-skull nuts before and know very well that it's worth it to put up with a bit of harmless crankiness with a guy that can be as sweet and warm most of the rest of the time. Look at this letter for an example — I'm excusing you for lousy things you said and how you brought me down at a time when what I needed most was a pal's love and good concern instead of a lot of

> cheap, and stincking fucking sly remarks and ill-disguised menaces to my person you dirty rat-bastard and doublecrossing anti-sem.

In a previous letter, Terry had asked Mason whether he enjoyed his parents visiting him in Paris. Mason continues his letter, answering that the highlight of their trip was "riding by the Notre Dame cath.[edral] with boxes of our Jewish matzohs in our laps which we'd picked up on rue des Rosiers (it being our holiday of Pessach) and not giving the venerable cath. a glance." About his parents' subsequent trip to England, Mason was embarrassed by his father's stinginess with their affable old Paris buddy Charlie Sinclair, who had generously agreed to show them around:

> I got a letter from my Mom describing how [Charlie Sinclair] spent a whole afternoon taking them around London, answering their dumb questions, chuckling at their corny jokes, agreeing with their tedious impressions . . . after which my Dad slipped him an envelope with *two* pounds in it — a nice round figure — which represents a 65% reduction from the amount I'd stipulated (pointing out that I really owed it to Charlie for the many times he'd put me up in his pad). That's the kind of gracious, social flare that has gotten Dad where he is today.

Mason signs off reporting that Gregory Corso had come to Paris and gone to Tangiers, adding, "He's a horrible scumbag and I'm not sorry he left." Mason fretted about not being able to come to Geneva "as there isn't enough gas," referring to the lingering Suez crisis. Couquite, entering into the spirit of their jokes, added a handwritten postscript to Carol and Terry, also alluding to Mason's drug bout:

> As you know, Mason has been a sick man for the last 4 months. Well, dear Mom and Dad, he has been recovering his health quite nicely, and god bless him, I'm getting some of that delicious fat Jewish cock as much as I want again. I want to thank you personally for your kind invitation to stay for a few days with you in Geneva. It

seems a little hard for us to leave Paris, so it doesn't look like we can make it right now. But some other time you can be sure. Maybe we'll meet some place this summer along the line between Geneva and Tangiers. I send you my kindest regards,

Couquite "Velvet Pussy" Hoffenberg

Terry responded almost at once, chiding Mason for not coming to Geneva on account of the gas rations. Taking the moral high ground on money matters, as he often did, Terry mockingly psychoanalyzes his friend:

Geneva, 19 May 1957

Dear Mace,

. . . Those gasoline-coupons (which you name as the obstacle for our being together for first hand gas, etc.) are on the counter in the rue de Rosier for a few wretched franken? Good Lord, Hoff! Come down! Wise up! Play the game! What the fuck! I see this blind-spot of yours, Hoff, and I can tell you now, with all due respect, how it happened. Let's say it first began when you realized, as a small child, (and you told me this once yourself) that certain of your friends liked you more for your money than for your *true-self,* so this gave you an odd feeling about it (money); then you had to pay your way into the hippy group like the other initiates, springing for the privilege of sitting at the same table, etc., and then, with your full membership, developing a contempt for cornball novices and easy marks, such as Stanley [Gould] and Bob Vaughn prey upon. Now you've identified tightness with loot as a sound principle because you think it is necessarily a part of being hip, and it is comfortable for you to hold on to this because it makes that trait in your grand old Dad Hoff seem cool and realistic, rather than foolish, naïve, and petty. . . .

[It] is a blind spot, Mace, and, as such, will affect or retard your development in other areas. So now that you see how wrong you were in that, you can, all smiles, lay out *plenty* for those black-market coupons and drive like the wind here for good holiday. Don't forget, there is not rationing here; you can tank-up all you like, and also you can take a jerry-can (20 litres) back into France with you.

Well, Hoff, get cracking and come here for a visit (it will be a savings for you in the long run because of the food you will get here, hee-hee) Bring sun-trunks, smoked-glasses, and your own velvet pussy; everything else is free (at least, for the first 10 days). No, seriously, can you come to us for two-weeks (no cost, except outdoor things such as movies, etc.)? Let me know your conditions; I am not unreasonable.

Best love to you both from us,

Al Grosberg

Chapter 10

I to the Hunchback, and Thou Therefrom

In 1957, there were few publishers in France or America bold enough to test the limits of free speech. Many of Girodias's books — Miller's *Tropics* series, Burroughs's *Naked Lunch,* and Nabokov's *Lolita* — remained unpublishable in America, and now, to add insult to injury, under France's new conservative government, these titles would be banned where Girodias had inaugurated them and had kept them quietly available for years — the streets of Paris.

In his fight to get *Lolita* off the banned list, Girodias asked Nabokov to join his suit against the French government. Nabokov was not so sure. The Cornell professor had not been issued a royalty check or statement from Girodias on *Lolita* since the book's publication in 1955. As Nabokov began to retreat from Girodias, *Lolita*'s reputation as a work of art attracted the attention of Putnam's publisher, Walter Minton. Within the next seven years, Minton would save *Lolita,* and also bring *Candy* to America. Meanwhile, back in Paris, Girodias wrote to Terry in mid-June, again inquiring about *Candy,* requesting pages and telling him about a new idea:

> I am beginning to work on a new project: an enormous magazine in English entirely devoted to the artistic & scientific aspects of sexuality and eroticism. A luxurious arch serious production, with the appearance of Vogue, or Verve. Quite a bit of an enterprise, don't you think? The idea is not quite clear yet but I would like to know what you think about it.

Terry compiled all the Wisconsin chapters he had and sent them to Girodias, hoping to elicit another payment later that summer. He included a revised version of the Hunchback scene — which was considered the centerpiece.

> "Rubatubdub!" he said.
>
> Candy laughed. She heard a wisdom and complex symbology in the hunchback's simple phrases. It was as though she were behind the scenes of something like the Dadaist movement, even creatively a part of it. This was the way things happened, she thought, the really big things, things that ten years later change the course of history, just this way, on the street corners of the Village; and here she was, a part of it. How incredibly ironic that her father would have thought she was "wasting her time"! The notion made her throat tighten and her heart rise up in sorrow for him.
>
> "You got quarter, lady?" asked the hunchback then, nodding his head in anticipation. He held out his hand, but Candy was already shaking her curls defensively and fumbling in her purse.
>
> "No, I don't think I have a *cent,* darn it! Here's an Athenean florin," she said, holding up a lump of silver, then dropping it back into the purse, "550 B.C . . . *that* won't do us any good, will it? Not unless we're Sappho and Pythagoras and don't know it!" And she looked up, closing her purse and shaking her head, happily, as though not having any money herself would actually make them closer.

Terry knew that the hunchback bed scene — involving a wire hanger and thousands of black snakes — could never have been published in *The Paris Review* or any other journal fearful of the ever-watchful customs officials, ready to scan for obscenity and impound. But Terry was hopeful that Girodias could get this climax of all climaxes through:

> The hunchback . . . lunged headlong toward her, burying his hump between Candy's legs as she hunched wildly, pulling open her little labias in an absurd effort to get it in her.
>
> "Your hump! Your hump!" she kept crying, scratching and clawing at it now.

"Fuck! Shit! Piss!" she screamed. "Cunt! Cock! Crap! Prick! Kike! Nigger! Wop! *Hump!* HUMP!" and she teetered on the blazing peak of pure madness for an instant. . . . and then dropped down, slowly, through gray and grayer clouds into a deep, soft, black, night.

A week before Carol and Terry left for their summer travels, Terry delivered fifty pages to Girodias, and described an additional twenty-six pages (heavily marked up) as "two amorous adventures of the girl and take the story up to the Hunchback episode."

Geneva, 20 June, 1957

Dear Maurice Girodias:

Thanks for your letter of June 14th.

I am sending along to you under separate cover some of the work in question. . . .

I would like to have the work back as soon as possible for more deliberation on it. If . . . you should see Mason Hoffenberg, you could give the work to him as I will be seeing him in the south of France, and he could bring it to me there.

Your magazine project seems sound and worthwhile, and I am sure it will have every success. Will it carry any short fiction? Under the guise of "Examples of (something or other)" you might be able to reprint a series of seduction scenes from various works past and present. You could take a moral or indignant tone in their presentation (the 'Look at this! What are we coming to!' sort of attitude) though at the same time relatively detached, as in merely observing certain phenomena.

I don't know about a name for the magazine. "Priestess," wouldn't be bad, nor would something blatant, like "Fucking Without Kissing" — but of course these are things which have to be thought out with some care.

Anyway, all the best.

K.*

---

*Kenton.

Terry and Carol had accepted Green's invitation to stay at his rented villa on the Costa Brava and were planning to spend the rest of the summer touring Spain, returning via Tourettes sur Loup to see Mordechai Richler. Terry suggested that they meet in either Tourettes or Deya, Spain. Mason tried to coordinate something at the last minute:

Paris, 29 May, 1957

Dear T.

Now you write (possibility 2.) of Alston in Deya. That sounds great! If he could come up with something — a large house or 2 small for August — that would be greater than Les Tourrettes. . . .

Get Alston [Anderson] on the ball, man! Get that worthless, black son of a bitch moving! If that doesn't work, then we can go ahead on making the best of Les Tourets and philosophically ignoring its manifest disadvantages. . . . God, we could even be making the bullfights Sundays in Palma!

Cynthia

Alston Anderson was a lively and erudite Jamaican poet and jazz critic who had lived in France and was now living permanently in Mallorca. Terry became friendly with him in Paris, and in 1955 they did a joint interview with Nelson Algren for *Paris Review* no. 11. Terry could not resist turning Mason's throwaway racist joke into a full-blown routine.

Geneva, June, 1957

Alston drowses sprawling in the half-shade of an adobe wall in Deya, clad only in a pair of faded dungarees secured at the waist by a length of frayed cotton rope, the sweat of pure sloth slithering on the black bulk of his shoulders and across his animal brow. According to best account, he hardly stirs, only occasionally lifting a hand against the swarm of afternoon flies, or again to languish a gentle, reassuring caress on the heavy potent coil which pulses lazily between his sinewy loins. 'Who da . . ." he murmurs, closed-eyed, half cocking his head, insolent even in sleep, nostrils quivering — for it is not from a physical presence that he stirs, but in response to the sticky waft of deep-frying catfish or turgid white-monthly which has drifted near and hangs like pools in the heat of the island afternoon.

"You black son of a bitch!" I shout, *"GET MOVING!!!"*

But there's only one language these fellows understand; you've guessed it, Mason, the *boot!* According to all account, he must actually be flogged to his feet, but then once set to ambling, he has a loyalty and perseverance which is truly touching. I have hopes that he can find us something of first account.

So, you're cutting out or splitting from Paris on/about June 15. where to, Mace? Why, in the name of good God Almighty, don't you come here for dang good gas and gabfest?

Schwertly

After spending a few weeks with Henry Green and Dig in Spain — where Terry finished his interview with Green for *The Paris Review*'s Writers at Work series — they went on to Mallorca. In late August they stopped in Tourettes where Mason and family were ensconced, and Terry and Mason were finally able to work together (when they could find a moment) on *Candy*. Lee Hill recounted:

> [Ted] Kotcheff recalls Hoffenberg and Southern trying to finish up a bunch of pages so they could join a poker game. The book was still far from done. . . . Charismatic and talkative, Hoffenberg was a Roman candle of ideas, but he had little stamina for the day-in, day-out regimen of writing.

Terry showed Mason the fifty pages of *Candy* he had sent to Girodias. He made it clear to Mason that he needed him to write his sequences. To emphasize the point, he again offered him half the fee, which he suggested Mason immediately renegotiate with Girodias. After all, the novel was well planned out, there were now more pages to show, and most important, there were two writers on the job, instead of just one.

During the few days of partying with Mordecai and his lot,

Terry and Mason planned how to finish the novel — down to the number of pages each would need to write. Mason introduced some intricate plotting for the hospital sequence, exactly the kind of thing that was lacking in Terry's episodic approach. They used the original Greenwich Village hunchback story as the keystone around which the other scenes were arranged, following Terry's original outline closely. Riffing through the hijinks of each scene, no doubt outdoing each other with lines of dialogue and voice characterizations, they soon realized they had their work cut out for them:

Candy's Professor	Terry — written
Candy's Father	Terry — written
Candy's Gardener	Terry — written
Uncle Jack and Livia	Terry — written
Aunt Livia's TV Show Idea	Terry — written
Hospital: Daddy and Candy	Mason—to write
Telegram Boy	Terry — to write
Hospital: the Doctors and Candy	Mason — to write
Humpback on Grove Street	Terry — written
Riviera examination	Terry — written
Police Car and Crackers	Terry — to write
Cracker Camp	Terry — to write
Guru gets Candy	Terry — to write
Calcutta/Holyman	Terry — to write

When he returned to Paris Mason met with Girodias and made the case for the new advance, and immediately wrote back to Terry with the good news:

Paris, 27 Sept 57

Cher Vieux:

I went to see G this morning and explained matters to him. He got sore, calling you a "lousy mumzer", a "two-faced", and a "leaky tit."

I cut him short: "Terry says you can take it or leave it."

He smiled anemically. He was in a bad jam and he knew it. "What about the sucks?" he asked. "Did you tell him about the sucks?"

"No, but I will," I said. . . .

Result, I sewed it up and the deal is *in the bag*!!! The figure of 300 G's [$300] was mentioned (also as a result of my foxy operating).

So we go ahead as planned — I to the hunchback and thou therefrom. I intend to get cracking on this in the next few days and will drop you a line letting you know how it shapes up.

Before we actually get paid, of course, there is the question of the sucks. Briefly, this means you'll have to come up to Paris for a few days and let him shoot off . . . all over your face a few times. . . . After that, it should be clear sailing right through to publication.

As ever

Leslie

Chapter 11

Mason Gets Cooking

By October 1957, Mason had conceived the bizarre working relationship between the psychiatrist Dr. Krankeit and his protégé, Dr. Dunlap. Before getting to the fun of Terry's orgasm clinic, Mason also took charge of refining a plot complexity that Terry had mentioned in the blurb but not worked out: Uncle Jack and Candy's dad were to be *identical twins*. In the climax of Mason's hospital sequence, Candy is found "copulating on the floor" with Uncle Jack — whom everyone in the hospital thinks is actually her brain-dead father — adding to the scandalous nature of the incident. In the scene, Mason amuses Terry by echoing the "give me your hump!" refrain as drunken Uncle Jack snuggles into her:

> "Yes, give me your warmth," he said, in hushed urgency, "how I need your warmth! Liv is so cold."
>
> "Oh, my poor darling," said Candy as he nestled his head between her breasts and pressed her closer.
>
> "Give me your true warmth," he said, raising her sweater and her brassiere and taking her breast in his mouth.
>
> In the lamplight her Uncle Jack's face was just like that of her father's, a fact which could hardly have escaped Candy as she watched him, nursing, stroking his head and sighing, "Oh my poor darling, oh my poor baby."
>
> Meanwhile, Uncle Jack's hands were not idle, but had found their way beneath her skirt and along her legs into the sweetening damp.
>
> "Give me all your true warmth," he said, one hand fondling her tiny clitoris, the other pulling down her white panties.

"All my true warmth," breathed Candy, "oh how you need my warmth, my baby," and she lay very still while he undressed her and then himself; but when he thrust himself into her, forgetting her taut hymen, the girl cried out, and apparently this was overheard by the nurse in the corridor — because she rushed in at that moment, flinging the door open wide and shrieking in horror at the sight of these two, stark naked, hunching wildly half beneath the sickbed.

"Great God!" she screamed. "Have you no *shame!* Have you no *shame!*"

A husky woman, quite six feel tall and heavily built, the nurse threw herself against the pair who were writhing in oblivion.

Now that Mason was onboard, Terry felt obliged to get him half the money Girodias had already advanced. Since Mason was in Paris, he would have the "donkey work" of collecting future monies from Girodias himself. As Terry feared, Mason's writer's block, junk, socializing (or all three) would soon interfere with his ability to deliver. Mason to Terry:

Paris, 21 Oct. 57

God bless you, boy, there's no need at all for you to be concerned about the 28 mille [$56] you owe me — I'd all but forgotten the matter.

As you suggest, the most expeditious way to handle this would be for me to simply deduct these funds from Uncle Gid's "Candy" payments — a consummate solution. I'm surprised I didn't think of it myself. I'm to visit him tomorrow, by the way, for this very purpose of being paid. He's supposed to give me 40, having already given 10, and is pledged to give monthly sums of 50 thereafter till the total has passed into our hands. I will then owe *you* a tidy packet (78 mille) [$156] which I shall slip to you at our next meeting.

Now for some less cheerful news. I am having an unusually severe case of writer's jam and simply haven't been able to really get cracking on the thing as yet. Caught up in the sickening coil-spin of lewd Paris times; the waiting in bistrots; the feigning; the bone dry, jacked off emptiness; political anxiety; chill Autumn fall of sodden givings in; instability of the state apparatus, strikes, slayings and riots — hardly the conditions to put one in a mood to write a frothy cockybook. Oh, never fear. I'll accomplish the job — no doubt by X-mas — with a nightmare grimace of hilarity frozen onto my heartbreak . . . but neither you nor anyone else will ever know what this is costing me. . . .

I think it would help if we could correspond more frequently, discuss the book, inform each other of the plot's development. I'm sure this added contact would serve to make a *reality* of liberalizing our financial agreement a bit too. I can't impress you enough with the need I have for these sorts of encouragements, reassurances, signs that you *believe* in me.

Here's a summary of the few pages I *did* manage to write before my block squared in.

You'll recall that a large nurse had just entered "Daddy's" sickroom, alerted by "Candy's" hymen-shout, and had tumbled patient and bed on the writhing lovers.

I've developed this scene a bit more — nurse and frigging couple are all inextricably tangled and covered by bedclothes and mattress. "Daddy" watches this heaving mass a second, then picks up "Uncle Jack's" discarded clothing and exits. Next, "Candy" herself emerges and she too flees this impossibly embarrassing situation. Nurse and "Uncle Jack" remain under the mattress since he clutches her (thinking she's "Candy" in the confusion) and is jaying off on her arm. She finally frees herself by smashing him on the head repeatedly with a bedpan. He's unconscious when she uncovers him and she assumes that he is "Daddy" (his twin, n'est-ce pas) and puts him back in the bed. His head is bleeding badly and he now has the same fatuous expression as "Daddy" — another accidental lobotomy in short.

Anyhow, it strikes me that this is the sort of thing you should know about. After all, this switch of "Dad" and "Jack' may conflict with some theme you're introducing. I think you'll allow that it (the switch) can lead to some fun — comedy of errors. I had in mind that "Candy" and "Livia" would continue to believe "Jack" was "Daddy" even when he returns from hospital in wheelchair, permanently deranged, liable to behave shockingly — expose his erection during Aunt Ida's visit and so on. . . .

By the same token, I think you should let me know what you're cooking up on *your* side of the hunchback since that might be of use to me in creating, and also since I shall then take care, naturally, not to snag things up for you by destroying, or irremediably altering some person or thing or theme that you might be intending to make use of.

I must admit that the first part of this proposition is of more importance to me than the second. Frankly, I'm terribly jammed at this point and can think of absolutely no idea with which to get cracking. So if you can think of any twist, situation, intrigue, anecdote, argument or device that might serve, for God sake rush it along by return post and the devil take the hindmost.

I realize this is pretty disgusting on my part — it amounts to shirking and whimpering and asking you to do *my* part of the task — but if you *could* somehow see your way to liberalizing the financial agreement it seems to me that that would go a long ways towards mitigating *that* part of the problem at least. . . .

Ira

Mason had not yet developed his greatest contribution to *Candy* — Dr. Irving Krankeit. Trying to spur Mason on, Terry suggested a bit of homosexual hijinks occur between the as yet unnamed doctor and his colleague.

Geneva, 24 Oct '57

It seems to me that a long chapter on a psychiatrist would be good fun and easy in that it could have a lengthy build-up of quite ordinary dialogue (dialogue, I am sure you've found, fills a page quickly) in which he is holding forth (dream interpretations, etc.) like Mel Sabre or Bob Hanlon (pompously and with a fair sprinkling of vernacular). Gradually (after he has impressed Candy and the reader) he begins to act strange and, in the end, is seen to be hideously gay and insane. One of his funny eccentricities could be that he keeps a huge heavy-duty rubber diaphragm at the back of his throat (that's how fecund and lushly feminine he thinks he is) and in his growing excitement (which reaches a veritable prancing frenzy) he keeps disgorging this big diaphram and wildly stuffing it back in! This chapter could sound the note of irony, in that he has been talking a lot about "mental health," etc. Candy leaves with the feeling that *he* needs help himself!

His flipping could reasonably occur when he tries to put Candy into hypnosis (to relax her) and instead hypnotises himself. (He had previously, and in his cool, self-sufficient way, mentioned self-hypnosis, and that he occasionally uses it at night to go to sleep instantaneously.)

In the end, after the water cooler is upset on him, he thinks that the spigot is trying to find its way into his juicy bun and he puts up a scratch and flurry of resistance, turning this way and that to avoid the consummation, saying, "No, Jim! Oh God, no! No! Please, Jim!" Etc. but it is apparent that his own excitement is raging against him and at last he seizes the water spigot, and begins sucking it with abandon, intermittently disgorging the diaphragm and crying, "Not yet, Jim! Not yet!" But finally with a press of his finger the spigot begins to spurt, all over his face, etc. at a moment before he can get the diaphragm back in, "Oh God, Jim, what have we done!" he beseeches (he thinks he is pregnant). Candy rushes into the street. "Good grief," she says, he's the one who needs help if you ask me!"

Dr. Krankeit makes his first appearance in the hospital hallway, where his colleague, Dr. Dunlap, humiliates Candy about the apparent incest incident with her father:

"Last night, Miss Christian, at a time when your father was hovering so closely to death that the slightest disturbance might have sealed his fate, one of our nurses, hearing a noise, entered the room and found you . . . *stark naked, writhing, wallowing,* and — and — and — COPULATING ON THE FLOOR OF THAT SICK-ROOM!"

A gasp of triumph — almost of relief — burst from the crowd at this revelation. The girl with the goiter slapped herself on the thigh as if she had somehow guessed what was coming all along.

Dr. Dunlap had actually shouted the last few words of his terrible accusation and now stood with his jowls trembling from the intensity of his emotions.

Mrs. Prippet, the receptionist, smiled proudly, and as for poor Candy, her knees suddenly sagged and she felt as though she were going to swoon.

"No," she moaned. "No . . . no . . ."

Terry often added his own flourishes to Mason's material, and with his near-trademark use of exclamation marks, added the following rejoinder;

> "*What!*" the director demanded indignantly. "I say that you were *seen,* you and some man, having wanton intercourse on the floor under your father's bed! *Seen* — do you hear me? Seen going at it like a pair of HOT WART HOGS!!!

In a letter from late October, Mason updates Terry on the "hot wart hogs" sequence and Girodias:

> Paris, Oct. 27, 1957
>
> Dear T. —
>
> I can't resist interrupting the clocklike progression of "Candy" sheets as they go curling round the platen of my Underwood and plop into two piles (one for me, and the light, carbon copy for thee) to sneak this message to you. . . .
>
> Here is the real "meat" of this letter. Savor it in cupped hands for the rare and aromatic tidings it doth bring.
>
> When I saw G. several days ago (24th?) he asked when he could expect the ms. "About a month" I said, feeling not the least guilty. It will be another month before he terminates payment and the agreement *is,* or can be interpreted as being that the books are paid for cash on the line like in the Old West. Well he didn't seem too perturbed although this was advancing the deadline a good bit further than it had been your impression that it was . . . So you've time and to spare and can polish the book until it becomes practically blinding.
>
> I had hoped to send you a chapter which I've about completed but there are two places where I want to change and I'm still not

sure whether I'll take the trouble to re-type three pages or make the changes in the form of inserts.

One of these changes is that at the point where Candy faints from the emotional stress of Dunlap, the director's frenetic revilings, I have Mrs Pippet, the receptionist hurry to her aid with a bottle of "smelling salts." Candy has already begun to come to — eyes fluttering open, chest heaving, etc., and then as Dr. Krankeit holds her head against his shoulder, Mrs. Pippet passes her vial beneath her nose saying, "thaaat's right, darling, breathe it in nice and deeply . . ." Candy takes a couple of strong snorts as ordered and her eyes click shut definitively, head lolls limp. . . . Krankeit snatches Mrs. Pippet's vial and smells it, then hands it back, says icily, "This is *ether* in this bottle, Mrs. Pippet, not smelling salts . . . you've *anesthetized* her!" I do this because a good bit of dialog and action are to occur while C's out and it wouldn't seem that mere fainting would last that long.

As Ever

Andy

The "action while C is out" reveals Krankeit, a kind of Machiavellian Dr. Kinsey, egging on Dunlap toward the holy grail of sexuality, which lies unconscious before them. Krankeit, the author of *Masturbation Now!* encourages Dunlap to act on his sexual impulses with the sleeping Candy — and also enables Mason to both celebrate and satirize the simplicity of Willhelm Reich's ideas:

> "You have an ocean of drowned impulses to *jack off!* All your life, something's been preventing you . . . deep down you're a veritable sewer of bestiality and lust!" . . .
>
> "This mechanism you've contrived to keep your sexual lust a secret from the world, and from you yourself, is causing you more trouble than you realize. That's why I decided it was all right for you to look at Miss Christian's legs — it's exactly what you need."
>
> "Exactly what I need," echoed Dr. Dunlap like a zombie, and moved a few inches closer to the luscious form on the couch with his fingertips twitching spasmodically . . . "Dunlap . . . I say, DUNLAP!!"
>
> Dr. Dunlap had quickly stepped to Candy and he was wrestling

off her panties in a veritable frenzy. "I thought you said it was 'exactly what I needed,'" he mumbled, confounded now.

"Ah yes, but only up to the point where it doesn't interfere with some *other* party. That's an important distinction."

Dr. Dunlap finished pulling Candy's panties over her shoes and flung them over his shoulder, where they settled like a silken butterfly on Krankeit's typewriter. Candy was now delightfully nude from the waist down and lying on her back. Unhesitatingly, the hospital doctor put his hands on her legs and drew them apart. . . .

"DUNLAP!!"

Dr. Dunlap hastily placed his hand on the pulsating jellybox he'd exposed, with the air of a little boy caught doing wrong and wishing to hide the evidence . . .

"If you don't take your finger out of Miss Christian this very instant, and replace her undergarment, I shall report what you're doing *in detail* to the board of trustees."

Mason's fixation on his own Jewishness was comical, even to himself, and Terry encouraged him to project as much of it as possible into his prototypically Jewish characters: Dr. Irving Krankeit and Krankeit's mother, Mrs. Semite. Mason breaking into Yiddish at the climax of the doctors' involvement with the unconscious Candy added an unexpected touch of verisimilitude he knew Terry would like:

"Good Lord!" said Krankeit, exasperated. "If you're going to poke your finger into that girl every three minutes, you could at least put a p.c. on." (p.c., standing for pinky cheater, was hospital slang for the rubber fingers gynaecologists wear during digital examinations.) . . .

Dr. Dunlap fingered his goatee in meditation. "Let's examine her," he said brightly.

Krankeit, with revulsion, pictured the two of them poring over the naked girl like a couple of scholars with a rare manuscript.

"What the hell, she's only a shicker," Dunlop said with a conniving wink.

"Only a *what?*"

> "A shicksy? I'm not sure I'm pronouncing it right — it's Jewish, means a Gentile girl . . ."
>
> "I wouldn't know," said Krankeit coldly.
>
> Dunlap's vernacularism — intended to invoke a hot gush of friendship — had the contrary result. And there had been that remark about the ghetto. Krankeit thought Dunlap was beginning to harp on the subject.
>
> *Subject* was hardly the word to describe Krankeit's feelings about his Jewmanship — a muscle with the outer skin flayed off, twitching violently in the air, gives a more accurate idea. For someone to say something to him — as Dunlap had just done — which referred in any way to Jewishness, was like poking a finger in his eye.
>
> This time it had come in mirthful form, which was the most familiar pattern — the Gentile, in a mood of alcoholic joviality, shows off the Jewish term (usually vulgar) which he has learned. To his mind, this ought to please and flatter the Jew, witnessing as it does his knowledge and appreciation of the latter's culture. Instead, the Jew — jumpy as an eyeball — feels such a remark is patronizing and disrespectful.

Very pleased with Mason's work, and keen to amuse, then shock him — Terry set some of *Candy*'s action at their old haunt, the Riviera in Greenwich Village. The scene opens with Candy sitting at the bar, lost in thought as she replayed the day's sex-filled events. Her undoing begins immediately, with the lascivious barman pitching one of the most bizarre come-ons ever:

> "Somehow, from the gamut of emotions which crossed your face, I had the idea that the stool had slipped up into your *damp*."
>
> "I beg your pardon?" said Candy, not comprehending, but even so not too keen on the fellow's tone.
>
> "*You* know . . . your puss, your jelly-box . . . I thought the stool had somehow slipped up into your jelly-box. It happened the other night, a hefty babe was sitting here at the bar . . . not on the stool you're on, but the next one, and I was watching her. Well, she seemed to gradually *sink down* toward the floor, you know, as though the stool itself were going right through the floor, and . . .

what *had* happened was that somehow the stool had slipped or pushed up into her jelly-box, right up inside it, taking all the clothes with it, skirt, slip, panties and all, right up into her *thing* . . . the whole seat of the stool and about a foot of the legs. Christ, I never saw anything like it before!"

The scene proceeds with Candy talking to a gynecologist who does an impromptu examination of Candy in the Riviera john — much to dismay of the owners and, eventually, the police.

Chapter 12

This Souped-Up Correspondence

In November of 1957, as the cold of winter set in, a flurry of letters were exchanged between Terry and Mason, who began taking the lead in handling their business affairs with Girodias. He wrote:

Paris, 7 Nov. 1957

If you'll excuse my tardy answering then I shall try to do the same for your yipping and nipping. I was away for All Saints weekend. I was confined to my bed with a murderous attack of flu and depression (from sputnik). Each of your letters sends a cruel nail of remorse and anguish into the base of my spiny column. (I was about to arise from my sickbed yesterday when one of them arrived and sent me diving back into the sheets with a splitting diarrhea.) Arose cautiously this day, noted thankfully that you'd accorded me 24hrs respite and am pecking this off to you with frail, spasmodic jabs of my diehard index boys.

To put you at ease let me say that I was forced to laugh aloud at Candy in the Riviera. That was really excellent. I received the other [squad car] section safely too and have no doubts that it is equally witty. I'm waiting to read it at the not far distant time when I awake one morning feeling reasonably steady and optimistic. I figure it will help put me in the mood to write. I shall, as you suggest, send you a carbon of same, but, until I do it please have the good taste to not niggle at me since this has the opposite effect and sends me off into one of my great big Hebrew depressions. Lord knows I'm angry enough at myself that I didn't clean up the whole thing in Oct. as I'd intended. Son cosas de la vida.

> My immediate reason for not giving Candy a top priority amongst my activities was that Gid appeared in no hurry whatsoever. Let me restate the outcome of that meeting I had with him in which we settled the particulars of loot and time.

Mason's attention to financial details was in stark contrast to Terry's disinterest in procedure and business matters. After confirming that "the overall loot is 300 [dollars], he suggests a payment schedule:

> 50 [dollars] on the 20th [of] each month . . . for 5 months. Now, I see that you would have preferred faster money to finance your high living. Let me know what your needs are and we can work it out by giving you a larger proportion of those next two payments. . . .
>
> Lazybones

Terry was relieved about having more time, as he was now working exclusively on *The Magic Christian.*

> Geneva, November, 1957
>
> Dear Mister Sloth:
>
> Thanks for your letter of November 7.
>
> In my own small corner of that garden of perennial wonder and delight we call Life I daresay no single flower has burned so brightly nor again with such terrible beauty as have those occasional moments of realization that you after all are capable of getting off a really straightforward letter, free from all semantic high-jinks and *Zoon-dialetic.* Such was your last, and a vote of thanks its due.
>
> First, I think you're wise to suggest a policy of take-it-easy for getting this work out. I myself had hoped for as much, but didn't feel it my place to bring the point forward before now. Plenty of sleep and bed-rest are the thing, of course, with a movie now and then perhaps, a quiet bottle of lush (while abed) and a leisurely s. or jay o. But mostly just lolling about I should think. In fact it reminds me of a scene in the novel I'm working on (*The Magic Christian*) about a billionaire who stages immense practical jokes—one of

which is this swank one-class passenger ship (*The Magic Christian*) he has outfitted to include life-jackets which inflate in an extraordinary way (apparently the very act of donning the jacket sets off some device which causes them to inflate to colossal dimensions — *about 12 feet in diameter*) — so that during the first life-boat drill this happens and these passengers (the elite of international gentry) are either hopelessly stuck in the corridors, or else, if they are in an open space, like their cabins or the lounge, they just "loll about: quite obscured within their balloon-like jackets."

My idea of pure sloth would be to weigh so much (say about 5000 pounds) that one couldn't move and also to have sleeping sickness. As it is now I get up later and later each day. About four in the afternoon usually, don't bother to wash or dress, or even eat really — just a bottle of milk with a couple of raw eggs in it, go to the bathroom, then get the Herald-Trib (we have it delivered to the door) and back into the old bed I go. Try to read between the lines of Scamp, then have a snooze till dinner. After dinner, I may listen to one of the AFN [American Forces Network] programs, write a few lines in my novel, or a letter to you, then turn in early with a couple of ambutals under my belt.

Decency vies with cunning in your restatement of terms, Mace. My understanding was that we were going 50-50 on the overall figure, and it seems to me rather cruel bait to suggest otherwise. If, in view of your general slack, being carried, fed ideas like the veritable piranna, etc., etc., you think that it would be bad for you morally to put down such an outlandish hyp, then certainly I wouldn't hold you to it. The new time factor does of course put the thing in a somewhat different light and it may be that you have taken that into consideration, independent of the original agreement. Do know though that above all I want to be assured of your own satisfaction in this matter, and look forward to harmonious collaboration in the future. Certainly you were top-drawer in your suggestion about my drawing a bit heavily on the first payments (perhaps you could hold off on your extra fifty until the end, that would do it.)

By now the deadline for Candy was an afterthought — but getting paid regularly by Girodias wasn't. Mason responded:

Paris, November, 1957

. . . As you say, there's no sense in burning ourselves out on this project. I am presently going at the urbane tempo of one, to-be-discarded-later page a day. Nothing whatever comes to mind and I write meaningless sentences describing furniture and recording Candy's displacements in space — "She crossed the room. She sat down and crossed her legs." — not too interesting I'm afraid, but my present theory is to keep the typewriter keys crackling no matter what and hope that something will come out of the work itself, instead of mooning around like Samuel Coleridge.

I called G. to remind him that the 20th was at hand and he sounded very surprised and hurt, eventually grumbled to come in Monday (25th). So don't expect anything till then. I'll send a mandat for 35 to Annemasse, *poste restante*, on the 25th or 26th but wait till I confirm it before making that trip.

Judy Cowflop

Mason finally had a breakthrough writing spurt, which allowed him to nearly finish his part.

Paris, 15 November, 1957

Hi, there,

Since 5:30 A.M., 14th of Nov. I have got crackling. That is to say I suddenly stopped futzing around (which had been going on for two months) and began whacking a path to the hunchback.

I accomplished this by staying up all night of the 13/14th. Around 5:30 that morning I heard — and felt — a distinct "crack" and one whole side of my writing-block split off and slid into the toilet with a resinous "boom."

I lost no time in exploiting this advantage — remember, this is one time in two months that so much as a ray of ingress and a beam of penetration had gotten through my non-filterable, tough writing-plug.

By dint of whacking assiduously on the filthy keyboard of my Underwood I soon had cracked my block in a number of places and it was with the pieces of this latter, as they broke off, that I fashioned the soaring Candy-chapter of how she now receives a wire from Dr. Krankheit, resident "therapist" at the Municipal Hospital.

That, I'm afraid, will be the sequence involving psychiatry. Hands off, therefore.

Saw G. again and I could maybe get him to give an extra fifty for yuletime. At any rate I'll send you a mandat at Annemasse soon when he springs.

. . . Before I forget, I couldn't help noticing that the pages that result from my having gotten cracking are of an objectively stinky quality. Good to be garbage-flushed. Still, I was so happy from the "cracking" itself, for its minimum value as the merest portent, that I'm in a much better state. I hope too that, cracking along, the quality would eventually cease stinking and I could then discard places where it did. Should this not happen then I still would have provided padding before the hunchback but will have failed in helping it to be a book; will have failed again; will have helped it, actually, to become something other than a book — a sodden, bloated lump for instance.

Quite good idea, the colossal life-jackets. I can see this letter is keeping me from Candy so I'm going to break off now and say goodby.

That was untrue; it's Life magazine it's keeping me from. Don't feel like crackling very much I'm afraid. Christ, I hope *that* isn't going to start again — big turdy chunks of my block wedging into place all the time while I'm writing this letter . . . find myself all clogged and stuck again . . . What an ordeal!

Your fellow American

Clyde Fingerstall

Geneva, 21 Nov 1957

Thanks for yours of 15 Nov., Mace — another tiny-perfect; Christ, but you've got an eye for the well-turned phrase! You signed the letter "Clyde Fingerstall," and I take it as an oblique reference to the difficulty you've had in getting crack on this project, that is, actually getting down to the writing itself. When I have a peevish pinkie that sulks or plays the little donkey at key-board time, I chop it right off — yes, with a small ax I keep in my desk. You can bet *that* keeps those little misters in line! Now when we sit down to the machine you ought to see them stir and bustle, even before I've got the paper in! It's the associational thing that does it of course — the very nearness of the machine sets them (the six of them) thumping and pecking like a little nest of trip-hammers! It's the best disciplinary gimmick I've come across, though naturally you have to be fairly carefull, or you'll chop your way right out of the darn writing game altogether, eh? (Up shit-creek without a pinkie-paddle, eh?) it's mighty "white" of you, I suppose, to shoot that mandat [a money order] to me in Annecy (Ht. Savoie) France. Natch you will want to drop me a line saying you've done so' — that way I won't be legging it all over the place for no reason, storing up hateful resentment against your neg and inconsideratch. There was a marvelous, I think that is the word, head-line in the Herald Tribune the other day, I'm wondering if you saw it:

EISENHOWER SAYS HIS FAITH
IN GOD HAS KEPT HIM SANE

With Christmas but a month away, Mason made an extra effort to try to get more pages together so he could ask for another payment.

Paris, Nov 25, 1957

Greer dear,

I have your letter at hand suggesting that we accelerate this already souped-up correspondence and answer each other by 'return of post'. You realize of course, that this will take up time and mental energy that could have gone to *Candy*.

I've got a chapter's worth of your recent letters clipped in with the ms. which pads it out well but the readers are going to resent the break in the narrative; are going to be puzzled and possibly irate when they understand that a second-rate, loony correspondence has been foisted on them taking up valuable shoot-off time and lowering value of their porno buck.

I'm pointing over to G's now for crisp, and then I'll go to post a mandat to Annecy. I'll mail this at the same time and I daresay they'll arrive together.

Herb

Terry to Mason:

Geneva, 26 November 1957

Dear Herb:

Thanks for yours of the 25th.

It's biting cold here today in tiny Switzerland, and while I've got the car motor running for warm-up before pointing for Annecy, I'll just rap this out and get it in return of post.

If you knew how very much your letters mean to me, I *don't* think you'd begrudge my desire to step-up our correspondence. Also, there seems to me to be a fair amount of irony in the possibility that two chaps engaged in a job-of-work could spend all their time exchanging letters frantically about it, complex and lengthy letters always just skirting the periphery of the subject, and never actually getting a word done of the work itself. I don't know. Perhaps I'm wrong, but it does strike me as hilarious.

As for the correspondence itself, you'll see that in my turn I am doing what I can to rule out more botch-ups like the other day (the loss of your wet letter — where is it?). Already I use the most expensive paper I can get (thin paper) and I have taken to using a seal and sealing-wax. I think this is a pretty good idea. These waxes come in plenty of colors are fun to use (or is it *waxi*?). I don't actually have a *seal,* properly speaking, as yet, so simply use an old coin. It is a Greek coin, silver, from the time of Plato, which I gave Carol as a present, but now I have had to take it back to use on my letters. Actually it doesn't work too well on the thin paper, and I have set fire to a number of envelopes using it — I may have to switch to *thick* envelopes soon, so be on the lookout.

You're tops to get that mandat in the poste so quickly, Mace — thank God you didn't run into Zoon or someone who might say (as a trick) that they would bring it along to me! Also it was quick thinking to write that letter before going to G. and the poste. You have a real talent for organization when you put your mind to it, Mason, and I certainly think we can establish some sort of orderly work arrangement for bringing loot through collaborative writing for the future — *if* you'll get cracking on your letters (never mind about the work itself for the moment).

Nothing was simple for Mason — and his tortuous mission at the bureau de poste to send money had to be shared in detail with Terry.

Paris, November 29th, 1957

Man!

This part about having to send you mandats turns out, as I suspected, to be the most irksome aspect of our collaboration. There was a small queue — three or four people — so there was a slight delay before I was able to see one of the postal employees and explain that I wished to send a "mandat."

Where is it?" he said.

"I haven't filled it out yet. I want a blank one."

"Over there," he said pointing to a shelf on the wall.

I went to the shelf feeling a little sore that I'd had to sweat out a line for such an obvious *renseignement*, and chose, from one of the numerous compartments, a yellow form resembling every mandat I have ever received or seen anyone else ever receive. I had stupidly forgotten to bring a pen and had to use one of the public ones (three of the public ones I should say, because the first two were so impossible that I had to discard the form each time. The third one wasn't any better either, but there weren't any more). By painstakingly repeating each stroke of the pen six or seven times I finally got down your name and address and my name and address and the sum in figures and the sum in letters, and then, in another place, your name and address again and my name and address again and the sum in figures only, again, and then went back and got on the little line.

After a short delay I was once again facing the clerk and handed him the form. He stamped it, wrote something in a ledger and said, "Where is the postal check?"

"No postal check. I just want to send this money to someone." (I showed him the money.)

"This isn't the right form then," he said. "You want the form for sending a mandat to *domicile* — the *brown* one."

I returned to the shelf, took a brown one, repeated the intricate filling-out process, got back on the end of the line etc., and this time it went off without a hitch. The whole thing couldn't have taken more than three quarters of an hour, yet I felt spiritless and frail afterwards and almost got run over on the way home.

I sort of expected you wouldn't receive it either and that I would have lost the 35 mille [$70] but I got your letter acknowledging receipt this morning so I suppose you'd have to say that the thing went off okay. Yet, I should like to point out that I'm never gong to do it again because it leaves me in a nasty mood. We'll see one another during yuletide, London holidays, or summer vacation, or Sun will be going to Geneve . . . I much prefer to do it on the warm, human level . . .

Dawnballs

During the winter of 1957, Terry asked writer and poet Alston Anderson for feedback on early drafts of *Red Dirt Marijuana* and *Razor Fight*. Finding his comments useful, he then sent him advance proofs of *Flash and Filigree* along with a letter asking for his take on J.D. Salinger — whose writing Terry admired. Alston responded:

December 13th, 1957

Dear Terry,

Thanks for the fine letter, and the book.

I *hated* Salinger. In fact, I was so infuriated after reading "A Fine Day for Bananafish," that I flung the book clear across the room (without damage, however, either to the room of the book.) I think the parts of "Flash & Filigree" that I've read are so *far* superior to Salinger that I wonder why you bother to read him at all — and, even more why you like him.

Terry wrote back, intrigued about what Anderson disliked so intensely about Salinger's work. He responded a week later:

> He infuriated me precisely because he *is* a good writer. There are very few of us, after all, and our faults are usually glaring ones. And in Salinger's case they are so glaring that if he were present I would have tried to choke him. His dialogue is good — very good — but I don't think good dialogue is enough. The idea behind it has to mean something, or one might as well write for the Sat. Eve. Post. One can present life as it is, without comment, and make it equally good fiction. But I do not think there is a middle road, and this is the one it seems to me that Salinger has taken. The suicide at the end of whatever that story was — perhaps it was "A Fine Day for Bananafish," but I'm not sure — was completely unnecessary, and reflected more on the author's personal problems than on the problem of Life itself, which it seems to me is the point of fiction. One doesn't always have to — or even EVER have to — tromp on the thing with eight-league boots, but it's always there.
>
> A

Chapter 13

"... 3 ... 2 ... 1 ... Jack Off!"

Terry and Carol accepted Mason's offer to spend a few days in Paris over Christmas at the Faure apartment. Carol recalls, "Mason and Couquite were away and I cooked duck à l'orange for Christmas dinner; Allen Ginsberg was there and demolished every morsel down to the orange rinds. He was very excited about William Burroughs' new manuscript, *Naked Lunch,* had a copy with him and showed it to Terry."

Decades later, Terry, writing about this time in Paris, melded several memories together to create a set piece describing Girodias's introduction to the work:

> Our most frequented café in those days was the Café Saint-Germain des Prés, opposite the Flore. It was there one winter's morn, while Mason and I were having our customary *grande tasse,* that a certain Greg E. Corso, author of the epic poems "Bomb" and "Gasoline" and the novel *American Express,* presented himself at the table. He plopped a manuscript down and said in his usual gross manner, "Now dig this . . ."
>
> It turned out that the ms. was, of all things, *Naked Lunch.* It seems that Burroughs had given it to Allen Ginsberg and he had given it to Gregory. Mason and I set out to convince Gid that it was worthy of his distinguished imprimatur.
>
> His first response was to leaf through it impatiently. "There is no fucking in the book," he said. "No sex at all in the book."
>
> We pointed out something on page seventeen.
>
> "Ah, yes!" he said triumphantly. "All the way to page seventeen! And still it's only a blow job!"

He got up from his desk and turned to an old wooden filing cabinet. His offices had a Dickensian mustiness and clutter, which he seemed to believe lent his operation a degree of respectability. He took out a couple of letters.

"Let me show you what our readership requires," he said, bringing them over. If memory serves, they were from a couple of Indians in the British Army, and they pleaded for books that were "brutally frank" and "frankly explicit," phrases they had picked up from porn advertisements.

"Could we truly recommend such a work as this to these readers? And the title is no good. What does it mean, this 'Naked Lunch'?"

I told him that Jack Kerouac had suggested the title, hoping that might impress him. But Mason had the right idea: he said that it was American slang for sex in the afternoon.

Gid brightened somewhat. *"Ah, comme notre cinq-à-sept!"* he declared, referring to the cherished French tradition of having sex (with a mistress, of course) every day from five to seven P.M.

"No, this is more like an *orgy*," he was told.

And eventually he came around.

Back at their respective desks after the Christmas holiday, Mason updated Terry on *Candy* — which was sliding into the new year.

Paris, January 21st, 1958

Dear Terry,

Today, according to pre-arrangement on the phone, I was to collect from Gid. He came on like he'd forgotten all about it as has happened before and it is now agreed that I should come on Friday and it will be there without fail.

I am coming along slowly (as usual), but plugging doggily. I can't think of anything in what I'm doing that you might need to know about for your part, but I'm making you a carbon copy and will send it as soon as I've got a ten-fifteen page chapter.

Ginsberg is hopping mad with you. Somehow he got wind of your [*Howl*] parody (certainly not thru me), and he swears to calumniate you with his powerful San Francisco group. Worst of all, somebody actually sent a copy to the states and it's going to be printed in the first issue of a new Negro quarterly called "Eight Ball." This will teach you to be more prudent in the future as alienating the west coast will serve you in ill stead.

I may not be able to write as often as in the past as I don't want to go and get myself compromised in this thing.*

As ever

Mary Ellen

*(please burn this)

Throughout the fall and winter of 1958, Terry was deep into *The Magic Christian.* Terry and Carol's penurious circumstances probably fueled his fantasies — and the public pranks orchestrated by Guy Grand became ever-more outrageous and expensive. Candy Christian's perilous adventures were now supplanted by the Magic Christian's infiltrations of corporate America. The feedback of both outrage and glee that Terry received from the chapters he shared with his friends added to the great momentum *The Magic Christian* was taking. John Marquand wrote, describing how passages filled their novelist friend and critic Anthony West with "vast . . . anxiety," and that certain scenes were "unrelievably disgusting" — but in a postscript, he says:

> PS: Tonight, before a merry group . . . I took the liberty of reading aloud the Movie House, Steamship and TV sequences. There was not a dry eye nor unbruised (from slapping) thigh in the room by the time I'd finished. The effect of your prose was hilarious and you are to be congratulated for that. It is an extremely funny conception and everybody wanted to see the complete book. (I'll tell Brownie Reid about this, one chap remarked. We'll serialize it in the Herald Trib, for sure.) It was, in fact, such an accolade that I am almost willing to write off my strictures phrased above as being more pompous, jealous cavils. Bravo. Finish the job.

By mid-February, Mason had completed nearly twenty pages of *Candy,* covering the entire hospital sequence and Krankeit's "digital examination" of the nude sleeping girl. Terry and Mason were both concerned with every detail of the writing. Terry critiqued and edited Mason's pages, his comments ranging from overuse of the word pussy, to consternation about the metaphorical pun — Dr. Krankeit "stiffening" like an erection. Mason complained that Terry was getting "carried away playing English Prof." Mason wrote:

Paris, February 24th, 1958

Howdy.

Far from striking me as cavil or picayune I find that your suggestions are mostly excellent. (Remarkably, they touched on many of the points with which I myself was dissatisfied, and usually cleared them up.) And surely no one has more right than you, bless you! . . . to work the bugs out of this MS.

However, when letter #2 (with #3, #4, #5 coming up presumably) arrived, the passing thought *did* strike me that you perhaps might be in danger of getting a wee bit involuted about this thing like the morbid crackpot you are. Let's bear in mind that we've adapted an attitude of gentlemanly insouciance for this job, and that this precludes dwelling indefinitely on Dunlap's little jerks, much as this might appeal to your librarianism.

I find most of your points well-taken then, and propose that you make the necessary corrections, if you haven't already done so, in your copy of my section, since that's the one we'll submit, n'est-ce pas?

p.10, line 5 . . . Yes, I don't like "pussy" in this context and it would be well to change it for one of those synthetic inventions like "syrup dipper" or, simply "crotch." However, in calling it "slangy, tired and . . . *tiresome*" you really got a bit carried away playing Eng. Prof.

p. 3, line 14 . . . can't say I like "precise signal" What would an *im*precise signal be? "forthwith" can go — perhaps replaced by "immediately" (saving the 6 francs [1 cent])

p. 4 line 20 . . . One thing with which I *wasn't* dissatisfied was my one-s spelling of "focused" which is an accepted form (preferred, in my dict., to two-s) whereas "focussed" looks anomalous. Same goes for "Zeline."

p. 17, "too banal . . . (too) vulgar even" has an unfortunate Polish immigrant ring considering the refined sentiment involved. ". . . she decided it would be too banal . . . even too vulgar." sounds better, or ". . . too banal, too — too *vulgar.*" . . .

I agree ". . . . slump he'd been standing in" is not so hot. How about ". . . began to straighten in little jerks from its slump of despondency." I'm sorry you don't dig the erection image though. I might say that's the one case where your suggestion seems unjustified. Criticizing it as 'obscene' indicates a *frightening* lapse of judgement. For one thing, "Candy" lacks obscenity (the hunchback passage is the only one so far which compares obscenely with much longer and more frequent similar passages in other books of the series). So that, apart from its obvious merit in other senses, "Candy" barely squeezes under the line as pornographic, a fact which can hardly escape G. and the readers I'm afraid. I remember, for that matter, that at the moment I created the erection image I found it felicitous for this very reason — furthering the porno ambience — and decided it would be well to spot *the narration* with others like it.

Furthermore, dicks do erect in little jerks as you've no doubt observed, and this strikes me as being a *superior* sort of symbol (faithful visually and philosophically) for the transition a man goes [as he rises] from shriveled despair to 'cocky' self-respect.

What you've got in #2 — ". . . his spine . . . in little jerks (exactly as though it were being '*jerked off*' K. thought . . ." confuses me on 2 counts.

1) It sounds as if there's a play intended between 'jerks' of "little jerks," and 'jerked' of "*jerked off*" but, after 5 minutes of concentrated observation, I fail to see a connection. This is because a spine, or a rod going up jerkily, i.e. spasmodically, has nothing in common with the up-down, quite unjerky jerking of "jerking off."

2) I can't picture a man's spine, his back or torso that is, being jayed — would never fit in a fist, all those ribs and shoulders. Also, man's member doesn't straighten in little jerks *while* being jacked — the first process has concluded before the second begins. Try it sometime. Unless of course you're referring to some sterile, senile, limp and wrinkled old organ being madly jounced in the vain hope

that it will once again get up in little jerks as it did (unassisted) in days of yore.

I've just finished this section and rush to you before forging on anew. I must say, even I did not expect it would take this long. I appreciate how patient you're being and what an effort it must be for you not to give vent to your natural impulse to be bitchy and cranky. Perhaps we will again be lazing on some summer beach discussing "Candy" before all this is finished. . . .

I received Richler's powerful novel of our times — thanks.*

Terry found an elegant solution to the "erection image" conundrum by making it a *thought* of Krankeit's rather than a heavy-handed metaphor. Not to be outdone by Mason's poker-faced defense of the bookish boner, Terry offered his analysis — which, as usual, was geared toward sustaining a level of storytelling credibility. That the two argued these intricate points of word usage and expression would surely have amazed their readers — especially those only looking to get off.

Geneva, 26 February 1958

You *are* an odd duck. Perhaps my remark on "obscenity" was misleading and ill-chosen thereby. Certainly the erection-image is clever and apt, and (having failed to extend it with the "jerking off" image) I'm certainly all for using it. My point was simply this, that here is a beautifully written scene, where the reader feels he is invisibly present, alone with these two men, getting a nifty earful, etc., when suddenly some wise-acre (from God knows where — behind the water-cooler?) shouts out: "Look, he's straightening up like an erection,)" destroying the magic of the private and very personal eavesdropping which the reader thought he had fully covered. The point is that it is such a *striking* (strikingly good) image that it is intrusive, suddenly confronting the reader with a personality perhaps more incisive and interesting than either of those on the scene, so that the emphasis is shifted, distractingly so. I do fail to see how you

*Probably an advance copy of *The Apprenticeship of Duddy Kravitz.*

can object to having it occur in Krankeit's mind; certainly his interest in such matters is known and it would hardly be an unlikely thought of him to have, but on the contrary would strengthen and intensify him as an interesting personality . . . whatever truth or outrage the reader may find in his observations is gravy. . . .

I had restored the image in question, as follows: ". . . little jerks — 'like an erection,' thought Krankeit, and he took a step or two, almost involuntarily it seemed, toward Dunlap . . ." I had only gotten this far. Now then, you say (and quite right I think) that "jerks" here has nothing to do with "jerking off," that you could not jay a man's entire body o[ff] with your hand, that it would not fit into the fist, etc. What about the organ of an elephant? Would that not require both hands to give good jay-o? And where you have the image "like an erection" applied to a man's body (or the little jerking movements made by it) then surely that body is being seen either directly or indirectly as an organ, and a fairly large one at that. After all, the word "erection" does either apply to, or invoke image of, the organ. Right? Why then would it be so outlandish for Krankeit to start forward, hands poised to jay Dunlap (his upper trunk). And then to stop, or possibly to even attempt it, massaging him wildly, etc. for a minute before coming to his right senses.

While playing "English Prof," Terry deconstructs Mason's notes to a Kafkaesque level of absurdity — combining double-consonants with panties, syntax, and Mason's "telling" (and supposedly contradictory) intentions in naming things. It was this degree of precision literary demolition-work and a stubborn determination to ride out the gag, that Mason loved about Terry — and no doubt often hated the most.

I found your observation about "vulgar even." to be excellent, as well as your remarks about the anomaly of spelling *focused* with two s. (I don't see that it applies to "Zeline" however, since non-functional, or purely decorative things — lace-trim on panties, etc. — is very much a part of girls, though you might want to take this up again in your next letter — the way it was phrased in your last, you seemed to have lumped both cases under the one objection, "anomalous," though I doubt that you did intend it, etc.

Certainly that objection is sharply pertinent to "focused," since the double-s merely contradicts the precision-sense meaning of the word, diluting it, etc. How this would apply to the word "Zeline" which is a girl's name, I don't quite, as I say, see. It would not, presuming it is the non-functional presence of the extra-l you refer to, in any case be "anomalous," for the reasons given above — that decor, and useless frills are not in contradiction here, but highly telling. However, I don't want to spend any more time on that now. Perhaps you can start clearing it up in your next.)

Well, I guess you're sitting on a fat packet for us about now. Am I right, Mace? Want to divvy up? Want to send mine to me Poste Restante, Annamasse, Hte. Savoy, France, with my last name in caps? Or just pop the bills in a couple envelopes and send them here poste ordinaire? Use a fairly thick (such as your last) for this purpose.

Jeanne

Mason responds:

Paris, March 11th 1958

Gentlemen:

Now, as Ike Eisenhower often says, I will say that in the 26 Feb. letter you develop a darn good argument, and one I hadn't seen, concerning the problem of how much "author" is showing in a passage which had been running on a no-intrusion tone. Still, in the case of the hardon image, I'm really not aware of a marked violation of this kind: I think it could get by easily and doesn't ring me in. In matters of this kind however, feel free to amputate wherever you notice this fault for, as I say, it's a worthy point and one I'd never noticed. Furthermore, the idea of Krankeit having the image — and starting over involuntarily with joined hands is a scream and should go in.

Now, going over letter #2, I note that you've decided there are lots of author intrusions in the MS and have decided to let them stand. Very well. As you will. It's a fairly subtle point in most specific cases I daresay but valid and very much something to bear in mind during the rest of the book. . . .

I've about finished a rough draft of a short chapter wherein Candy and Krankeit examine Uncle Jack to determine the exact nature of his disability. Then comes my final bit which will be a sort of general bruhaha at Candy's house centered on "Daddy's" homecoming and containing Candy, Krankeit, Uncle Jack, Livia, Aunt Ida, Luther, her husband, "Dawn," their snotty 13-year-old daughter and what have you.* Candy will become disenchanted with Krankeit (whom she'd been thinking of as her grand amour) when surprising him as he sticks the old Chinese needles into Livia's derriere. She'll then decide to leave Racine and hit for NY in order to lose herself in the big-town anonymity or something. I'll send you the whole thing just as soon as it's ready which I hope will be soon as I intend to get down to hard grind and cease this forever dawdling and dallying. What should I do with the pages you've already seen and which need a bit of finishing? Do carbons and send them? I'd like to avoid this if possible as it's just another chore. Perhaps I could simply fix them up, then add them to the MS whenever you send it and bring the complete thing to G. What do you think?

As you surmise, I haven't come on with him for the final 50 since I'm a bit embarrassed as to how long it's taking. I've been hoping we could finish her and that I could have it with me next time I ask for crack.

Here's a bonus of late Paris news to make up for my tardiness. . . . Gregory Corso, crappy-personality poet of the sentimental Grandson Moses school, has landed the Guggenheim account! Fabulously loaded, sixtyish Peggy has fallen like a ton of lasagna for him and openly signified willingness to have him share her silken *quatro cento* featherbed. Despite the enormous stakes, Corso found it impossible to clamber into this heavily trafficked piece of furniture (he can't even do it with winsome *young* chicks) and thereby proved a big flop in his chosen role of avantgarde, non-objective loverwop. Mrs Guggenheim's poor heart broke at the news that Greg would be unable to mate with her, but is apparently going to be a good enough sport to continue springing for his chow and basic survival expenses. . . .

André

---

*This scene was never written.

In the pages Mason sent Terry, Candy emerges from Krankeit's office in a daze, and happens on Mrs. Semite, Krankeit's jealous cleaning-lady mother, who shrieks at her, "LEAVE MINE BOY ALONE!" Mason ends the scene abruptly with a setup for Terry to complete: Mrs. Semite urges Candy to look through a portal and watch her son, the "genius," at work in his lab. It was up to Terry to invent what kind of deliciously bizarre orgasmic experiment the doctor would conduct.

Although he appreciated the setup, the resulting masturbation "countdown passage" also was a way for Terry to fill up a page or two quickly — which was his object at this point — as his heart was in *The Magic Christian*. Candy sees Dunlap in the laboratory chair with "a device of some sort clamped to his head" and electrodes leading to a monitor that Krankeit is observing:

> On the screen danced a jagged pattern of lines — wave lengths of the electrical impulses of his brain, apparently — and the distinguished-looking doctor, leaning forward slightly, stared wide-eyed at them as if hypnotized.
>
> "Can you give me an 'all-clear'?" called Krankeit tersely, a small megaphone raised to his mouth.
>
> "All clear!" replied Dunlap, tight-lipped.
>
> "Ready for you little *standby?*" demanded Krankeit.
>
> "Ready for little *standby!*" snapped Dunlap . . .
>
> "Ready for you little *countdown?*"
>
> "Ready for little *countdown!*"
>
> Krankeit regarded his wristwatch, stared at the sweeping second-hand.
>
> "8 . . . 7 . . . stand by for standby . . . 6 ready for ready . . . 5 . . . 4 . . . *stand by!* . . . 3 . . . 2 . . . 1! Ready for your big *standby?*" He was practically shouting now, and both men had the intensity of children at a game of magic.
>
> *"Ready for big standby!"*
>
> *"Ready for your big countdown?"*
>
> "Ready for big countdown!"
>
> "Stand by!" shouted Krankeit, and, as he continued, his voice took on an odd metallic quality as though it were coming through a

large public-address system: "100 . . . 98 . . . 97 . . . 96 . . . 95 . . . 94 . . . 93 . . . 92 . . . 91 . . . 90 . . . 89 . . . 88 . . . 87 . . . 86 . . . 85 . . . 84 . . . 83 . . . 82 . . . 81 . . . 80 . . . 79 . . . 78 . . . 77 . . . 76 . . . 75 . . . 74 . . . 73 . . . 72 . . . 71 . . . 70 . . . 69 . . . 68 . . . 67 . . . 66 . . . 65 . . . 64 . . . 63 . . . 62 . . . 61 . . . 60 . . . 59 . . . 58 . . . 57 . . . 56 . . . 55 . . . 54 . . . 53 . . . 52 . . . 51 . . . 50 . . . 49 . . . 48 . . . 47 . . . 46 . . . 45 . . . 44 . . . 43 . . . 42 . . . 41 . . . 40 . . . 39 . . . 38 . . . 37 . . . 36 . . . 35 . . . 34 . . . 33 . . . 32 . . . 31 . . . 29 . . . 28 . . . 27 . . . 26 . . . 25 . . . 24 . . . 23 . . . 22 . . . 21 . . . 20 . . . 19 . . . 18 . . . 17 . . . 16 . . . 15 . . . 14 . . . 13 . . . 12 . . . 11 . . . 10 . . . 9 . . . 8 . . . 7 . . . 6 . . . 5 . . . 4 . . . 3 . . . 2 . . . 1 . . . JACK OFF!"

Mason was delighted with the scene and responded with news as well about visiting the "Beat Hotel" on rue Gît-le-Coeur. Ginsberg's *Howl* had been banned in the States and was only available through City Lights Bookshop in San Francisco.

Paris, April 26th, 1958

Dear T.

Your "countdown" episode reached me yesterday. It's a gasser and fits in nicely. I'm making good progress now on the work and should be set for final typing in a few days. I trust I'll be able to send the finished copy in about a week. How's your end? When do you suppose you'll be able to send on the definitive MS? . . .

And last night I paid a call on the San Francisco wild men. They're all in the same hotel — Ginsberg, Corso and Burroughs and an astounding number of seedy, angry young men that keep falling by at all hours. Very stimulating and I must say I envy them their freedom and allnight talking and writing. Ginsberg is getting published like a pig (lots and lots) after "Howl's" big splash. I have an idea he's living in Europe cause he's likely to get lynched if he goes home before his *scandale* has blown over.

I'm not sure but that we may be going back ourselves this summer — looks like Couquite is going to have a baby in the fall and Milford [Connecticut, the Hoffenberg country house] might be the easiest place to have it happen. On the other hand we've gotten deplorably rooted here and I shudder to think of all the bullshit entailed in such a major move.

Are you planning to stay on in Geneva another year? What about trying one of those Caribbean islands where you can sprawl on the beach all year round and swim in the green water?

Shalom

Mason

By the way, does "Daddy" have a first name? I've needed one down here on this part of the job and have been using "Sidney" for want of a better one.

I've been looking over the work and strongly agree now that it was a real error to say "pussy" and "nooky" like I did. This comes from the careless smuttiness I'd adapted in my previous work. Delete them at any rate and put "sugar-dripper" "jelly-scoop" "butter-pouch" "Dixiecup" "spice-box" "lamb-pit" or "stink-tank."

By the way, could you let me know what I've sent you so far — where the passages begin and end? I'm a trifle uncertain. Did you get a little insert where C is given ether instead of smelling salts when she faints?

Chapter 14

Flashpoint: 1958

The year 1958 was a great success for Terry. *Flash and Filigree* was published in the U.K. in March — to an extremely favorable review by Henry Green, who voted it the "novel of the year" in the *Observer.* Green appeared on BBC radio's *Book Talk* to introduce the British audience to the writer he felt he'd discovered. The host (Mr. Robson) described *Flash and Filigree* as "a mad, deft book, subject to the rules of poetry."

> **ROBSON:** I wonder, Green, if you could tell us how this curious dreamlike quality of the book is created. Because I agree . . . that it has a very odd, distinctive flavor — which doesn't really seem to be a particularly American flavor. It isn't quite like anything else that I know, and I wondered what devices he'd used in order to create this peculiar quality of a dream.
> **GREEN:** Well, I know the man, I think it's just like him. It's a very, very good expression of his personality.

Many of Terry's poet friends didn't understand the book or its intentions. Allen Ginsberg shared Mason's bewilderment. As he wrote to Terry in 1958, "I asked Mason then, he said [*Flash and Filigree*] was purposely pointless, a form of wit, is that so, is that it? I was not sure, if so too Dada for me, tho perhaps inevitable if you want to destroy that form of novel, that's one way of doing it."

The divide between the Beats and other poets was sometimes

severe. Terry was a bridge between both camps. One of Terry's correspondents on the New York scene was poet Michael McClure. In this letter from early 1958, McClure provides a crotchety update on the Beat clique in New York, where San Francisco poet Kenneth Rexroth was doing spoken-word riffing to jazz:

> Gregory Corso's book, "Gasoline," was published and the "White Horse" set has once more set out patting each other on the back over their great movement to free American verse. What a bunch of bums! Actually, I don't think that some of Gregory's poems are bad at all, but after Ginsberg gets through praising him, Kerouac praising Ginsberg, and everybody bowing to Rexroth, there is very little left to say but fuck them all. Rexroth is due to read at the Five Spot [a jazz bar on the Bowery] for two weeks, sometime soon; another revolting development, this poetry and jazz business. Kenneth Koch and I decided that we would start a movement of Poetry and Baseball.
>
> I read, barber-chair style, your story in the Nov. Esquire ["Sea Change"] and liked it very much.

Meanwhile Girodias wrote an imploring letter to Terry:

> Rue St. Severin, Paris, March 1958
>
> Dear Terry Southern:
>
> Mason is not quite clear about when your part of the book will be finished. The writing of that book will soon enter its third year, and now that there are two of you on the job, I hope it is going to reach the final phase soon?
>
> Please let me know what the prospects are.
>
> All the best.
>
> Yours sincerely,
>
> Maurice

Mason's hanging of *Candy*'s delay on Terry apparently elicited a cutting letter. Mason responded in ironical self-defense:

Paris, March 29th, 1958

I'd intended writing you from the Austrian Mts . . . calmly, but I can see that you're beginning to snap your wig there and nothing will do but a speedy reply.

In answer to your particularly crotchety letter about Gid's note I did tell him by phone that I wasn't clear about when your part would be finished because that is the simple truth of the matter. Have you finished? Would I know you had without you're having told me so, you simple s.o.b.?

Bear in mind that I've been getting the brunt of Gid's angry impatience; shielding you, sparing you the insult and heartache and naturally the thanks I get from a so-called good pal is to get a letter which reviles me. . . .

O.K. Now I feel there is nothing to be gained in an unseemly argument between us as to who's dumber or lazier. I can also see that you're probably in a hot state of tension wondering what I thought of "Flash and Filigree." There you can put your mind at ease as I thought it a damn fine job . . . showing plenty of sensitivity, talent, and very funny too. Some of the prose "stuck in my craw" a bit, but I'm not sure if it wasn't my fault. At any rate, the story soon got moving again and that cleared things up. So, I'd certainly call that an impressive first book and something to be happy about.

For "Candy," my plan's to take it to the mts. and clean it off/up.

I don't see how I can send you any of it therefore, since I need it to work on. Should have it all set to final-type when I return to Paris April 13 and, after that (2-3 day's typing) I can send you the final carbon.

This shouldn't hold you up. Can't you go ahead, as planned, with the final chapters? It's not as if there's anything to be integrated; it's better, for that matter, for the parts to be distinct and having nothing to do with each other — refreshing.

I feel it's time to clear up this work and move on to something else. Now let's forget petty partisan quarrelling and outbreaks of temperamental, "prima donna" sulking and nipping in the interest of getting on with this job.

Truly yours

Rex

On Terry's thirty-fourth birthday, an unexpected present arrived from Mason — word that he had finished. Although Mason's part was only forty pages long, they were the most complex, as they involved the most characters and subplots.

Paris, 1 May 1958

Dear T.S.

In sending the wrapup on this job I'd like to say that I consider it an honor to have worked with you on this job — I can't answer for you of course, but for me, these have been a very fruitful two years and I know I shall often look back on them as a *happy* two years come what may.

I know we haven't always seen eye to eye on this thing, that you don't agree with some of my methods of running the hospital and so forth, but nonetheless we have stuck together on this thing, getting the job done through teamwork and — often's the time — through sheer nerve and inertia.

Ar revor then, but *not* goodby.

David Selznick

P.S. I'm writing a letter pointing out several slight changes in my part which you may have already noticed.

Three days later, Mason sent Terry his last corrections — making small but important changes here and there, which he indicated with surprising precision:

1.) p. 10 of my 1st chapter (C. has just rushed from K's office and is talking to nurse.)
"Dr. Krankeit," nurse cut in
"Dr. Krankeit," C. repeated . . .
should change to Dr. Irving Krankeit,"
"Dr. Irving Krankeit," C. repeated . . . so that later when K's mother says: "mine Irving," C will know who she is.

2.) p. 19, 1st chap; Dunlap says, "TROLLOP! SLUT! LECHEROUS FLOOSIE!"
I think it should be 'FLOOZY.' . . .
3.) p.10, 2nd chap.; . . . "Krankeit's expressive black eyes flashed . . ." should be "brown" since they were brown in initial description.
4.) p.15, 2nd chap.; "I was just using a bit of acupuncture . . . I couldn't bring you back to consciousness, and it worked, he said. Delete "and it worked" Can't think why I wrote that — it sounds moronic.
5.) "It might be a good idea to add a line during Krankeit-Dunlap dialog (in the scene where C. is unconscious), whereby K would make an appointment with D., for that afternoon, for a 1/2 hour session of K's "therapy." Or don't you think such a tie-in is necessary? As it stands, there is an incongruity twixt their parting on bad terms (K. kicks D. out of his office), and their being seen next in the countdown scene where the feeling is that they're scientists collaborating. On the other hand, such a small discrepancy might pass unperceived in the general wackiness.

Such a line could go . . . where Dunlap compliments Krankeit on his book — ". . . defy all the conventional sex mores." Better still, at the end of this scene . . . (K. fussing with packet of papers at his desk), K. could say, "I wonder if you could drop back this afternoon — I'll demonstrate some of the techniques I mention in my book, which are, I think, what are indicated in your case — but right now you'll have to excuse me: I've got some work here I'd like to jack off — I mean knock off."*

I hope this will hold you, you monster, for a bit, till I send on the final chapter in fo-fahv days (give or take 2 weeks, eh Terryo).

---

*Terry modified the passage to read:

Fussing with a packet of papers, he said: "I wonder if you could drop back this afternoon, Doctor, I've got some work here I'd like to wrench off."

We are each to do approximately 60 pages. If that results in something less than 200 in the book I say toughshit as we are being fantastically underpaid considering that this job has taken two years to date and isn't in the clear yet.

The 'insert' I referred to has nothing to do with panties! It's where Mrs. Prippet gives Candy ether for smelling-salts and is on the first page of the chapter you have beginning "As Candy fell." It's ten lines that go between ". . . simply *astonishing*" and "Dr. Dunlap was quite silent now."

Please advise if I haven't sent this as it's structurally important and also brings up my contribution to 19 [and] 4/13 pages!

I don't doubt but that my whole section will be unrecognizable by the time you get through going over it with your microscopic cootie-pincers; but, for the sake of the record, I conceived my part as 3 chapters — I don't know how they treat this problem on the big glamour mags you *used* to be able to publish in, whether they haggle about 8/17's of a page & so on — but I consider the blank half-pages where one chapter ends and another opens as *full pages*. That, at any rate, is the way we regard this point here at Oilympia. You have, therefore, 20, and with this, 40 pages of my section!

Terry was finally able to revise and complete the entire manuscript by mid-May. Mason wrote back after receiving the news:

Paris, May, 1958

Dear T.

I've just phoned Gid who was tickled pink with the good news and the upshot was that you should send the MS. to me & then I'll take it in.

That will give me a chance to sound him about the last 50.

There won't be any delay so I don't intend to even look at "Candy" again 'till it comes out.

I'm glad you liked etc. the last chapter I sent — seems to me the book is awfully funny and that we were frightfully underpaid.

Love,

Viola

Chapter 15

A House O'Porn Extraordinaire

Girodias enjoyed playing the role of the grand impresario — not only of erotic literature, but of Paris nightlife as well. Exercising his penchant for vintage wines, fine dining, and cabaret, Girodias envisioned providing all these beneath the roof of his new publishing house. In the summer of 1958, with *Lolita* abuzz in the United States, Girodias abandoned his cramped quarters on rue de Nesle and found the building to make his entertainment dream come true. With two stories and a labyrinth of *grandes salles,* a refurbishable cavernous cellar, and a café at street level, Girodias christened the building, at number 7 rue Saint-Séverin, Chez Lolita. But not daring to tempt fate further with Mr. Nabokov, it was finally called La Grande Séverine. In a massive project that took years to complete, the building was transformed from a modest ground-level bistro into a full-fledged, talk-of-the-town nightclub. Mason was one of the first to see it in its infancy — when the project completely consumed Girodias. *Candy,* by this time, was finally finished.

Paris, May, 1958

My old,

The MS. arrived this morning whereupon I hurried to publisher with it thus bringing to a close *our* part of the job. Now, as Selznick so rightly put it, we can do nothing but cross our fingers and *hope.*

Whereupon Giddy took me on a jolly tour of his partially

> finished restaurant-bar-cave. He has socked, one after another, million upon million French franc into this splendid enterprise, and I have come to think of it as a rich tribute of his gratitude to little chaps like you and me and Harriet Daimler [the pen name of Iris Owens] since it is with funds cleverly gleaned from the sale of our novels — imperfect as they are — that he has staked this gracious dining club. I estimate it represents several hundred thousand books of smut.
>
> When I say that he has spared no expense; that the walls of the bar are graced with exquisite, individually-fired tile; that the stone pillars in the cave are authentic Roman ones, and fine enough to be displayed in our own American Metropolitan Museum; that every corner in each of the numerous rooms, antechambers, vestibules, *chiottes* contains some further delightful surprise, dazzling our view, and satisfying our inner sense-yearning for an alchemy of weights so that the very contour of being is seen harmonious.
>
> Then you will see how Candy will be transmuted to the steaming floor of a men's room; and see how this fanatical amateur of the plastic arts is unceasingly strapped for funds having just bid, who knows, 180,000 French francs [$360] on a Michelangelo salt-cellar at an auction, so that he is beset by plenty of niggling bill-collectors and has to stall them off as long he can. Or maybe his idea is to pay for Candy at the same oaken rhythm it was delivered. So I'll be sending you a "thick envelope" a bit later, or he himself, since I gallantly suggested he send you yours first since he was so beat. Perhaps it would be better if you wrote him yourself about this (7 rue Saint Séverin) as I think I'll be leaving soon for a brief visit to N.Y. — which is what is left of the original idea to go to the states to have the baby.

On May 18, Terry wrote back from Geneva with a note of mock concern about Mason's proposed trip to New York. "You won't rest until you get your big soulful hebe nuts off into some genuine fair-haired southern U.S. girl, so you may as well hurry up and get it over with, so you can settle down and start building toward some kind of future."

By the spring of 1958, Girodias's efforts to release his banned books via the French Administrative Tribunal paid off. *Lolita,* and dozens of other previously banned books could now be published. The reprieve was short-lived, however; with the election of de Gaulle in May, a conservative government returned to censorship, resulting in the banning yet again of many Olympia titles, including *Lolita*. The ban applied to the Olympia's original edition in English, so, in hopes of working around the authorities, Girodias had his brother Eric translate it into French.

With *Candy* completed, Terry and Mason asked their publisher for their final payment, knowing it would be some time before Girodias actually got around to settling up. Although Terry and Mason treated it as a simply another late payment, the final payment of 15 *mille* (about $30) would be all Girodias needed, from his perspective, to own the copyright to *Candy*.

In the summer of 1958, Mason and Couquite moved into Mason's parents' place in Connecticut, making forays into New York, where they stayed in the Central Park West apartment. Their baby, Juliette, would be born there that fall. Whether Mason's skill with numbers derived from his life of creative drug transactions, or some innate ability, it was a talent that was fast becoming an obsession and would occupy him for the next fifteen years. Though Terry had written asking Gid for the payment, no money had arrived. Couquite had managed to collect 10 mille before their departure.

Milford, Conn., July 23,'58

Hello there!

I've been a bit remiss, I know, in answering your kind letters, but I suppose you can understand the sort of bruhaha [that] attends a move of the sort I recently completed from the old world to the new, and what that does to an enormously elaborate mentality such as mine. . . .

Be that as it may, we are finally settled down in Connecticut, as you advised, and patiently waiting for our darling little hydrogen bomb to come forth in November. . . .

Business first, and then I'll give you all the oodles of news . . . When Couquite went in to collect my share he claimed he'd already given me my 25 and seemed to think that the ten he gave to Cooky was for you. She sent you five it seems. The result is that he owes us each 20 (unless he settled with you since). Well that's the sort of error in his accounts which he frequently makes, and I'm writing him in the same mail reminding him of the circumstances — that he didn't pay me when I delivered the MS, and that, since I didn't see him subsequently he couldn't have given me loot as he claims. I hope this will clear up the situation and that we'll all be able to go on with our mutually profitable affairs without you thinking that you've been diddled once again by a couple of big-city hebereenos.

Muriel

Girodias knew it would take some sorting out before Mason and Terry could corroborate who was paid what in which country when.

Rue St. Séverin, Paris, July 31st, 1958

Dear Terry Southern,

I am dreadfully sorry about this utter stupidity of mine.

1) Through a mistake of ours, the money has not yet been sent to Sunemasse. It is being sent today.

2) Mason was right: I had not payed the 25,000 [$50] to him. I must be affected by the heat, or old age, or something. I have sent my apologies to him — a difficult task in the circumstances. And I am conveying mine to you.

The money order will be of 20,000, as I understand Couquit has sent you 5 on this account.

This should therefore settle everything.

The book will only be out in September, due to a series of mishaps following the late delivery of the MS.

In all humility,

MG

In August, while Terry and Carol were traveling in Italy, British *Harper's Bazaar* published a feisty interview with Terry and J. P. Donleavy by Elaine Dundy (Tynan), entitled "Offbeat Americans and Why They Choose to Live Abroad." Donleavy praised the American publishing experience, saying, "The making and breaking of a writer in America is faster. And slower in Europe. And we all want to be made fast and broken slowly and gently. But when I saw the copy of the American edition of *The Ginger Man* I thought it most attractive and for the first time I really felt I'd got published." Terry blasted the American publishing establishment that continued to reject his novels. Terry would not be published in America for another two years, and he valued more than ever the smaller European publishers who were giving him a chance — Deutsch, and even Girodias.

> I think my book [*Flash and Filigree*] was first published in England rather than America because I think most American publishers' tastes are on the level of the comic-strip. They've become just ordinary businessmen. They don't have time to read; they're too busy hustling. Consequently they never develop any personal tastes. . . .
>
> They're the first real automatons trained quite simply to spot imitations of previous imitations. But then you take a situation like in England where there's a kind of *noblesse oblige* to be reasonably intelligent — well, then you may get a few people who, however outlandish otherwise, have highly developed individual tastes, and so there's a chance then that a manuscript will appeal *directly* to them, and moreover, a chance they'll have enough security and self-respect to respond properly when it does.

Despite Terry's view of U.S. publishers, one of them, Walter Minton, had just put out a book Terry liked quite a lot. In August 1958, Putnam published *Lolita* in the States — and sold 100,000 copies of the book in its first three weeks. *Lolita*'s checkered and controversial publishing history in France, its appearance in America, and its volatile mixture of humor, sex, and taboo, paved the way for *Candy*'s eventual appearance there. Terry and Mason probably didn't know about the terrible struggle that had gone on between Girodias and Nabokov, and how Minton intervened to settle it. Nabokov's temporary copyright was going to expire in 1960, and relations were so bad between Nabokov and Girodias that Nabokov wanted out of the relationship entirely. Girodias threatened to distribute and market his "own version" of the book in the States. As Minton recalls:

> He and Vera [Nabokov and his wife] were absolutely convinced that they had been swindled [by Girodias]. He said that he knew that at least three or four thousand copies of the Olympia *Lolita* had been sold in the United States whereas Girodias had only paid him royalties on a thousand or so. I said to him: "Don't ever open your mouth about that to anybody because if it ever became established [that thousands of unauthorized copies sold in the United States] your copyright wouldn't be worth *beans*."*

Girodias eventually settled with Nabokov and Minton for 5 percent of the book's American royalties. The book sold incredibly well for years, and the profits enabled Girodias to pay his lawyers, bribe French officials when necessary, and treat his authors (like Terry and Mason) to the occasional meal and open bar.

---

*Minton was referring to an obscure aspect of international publishing law at the time, which stated that a limit of 1,500 copies of a book could be legitimately imported for sale by an American publisher, beyond which the book fell into the public domain.

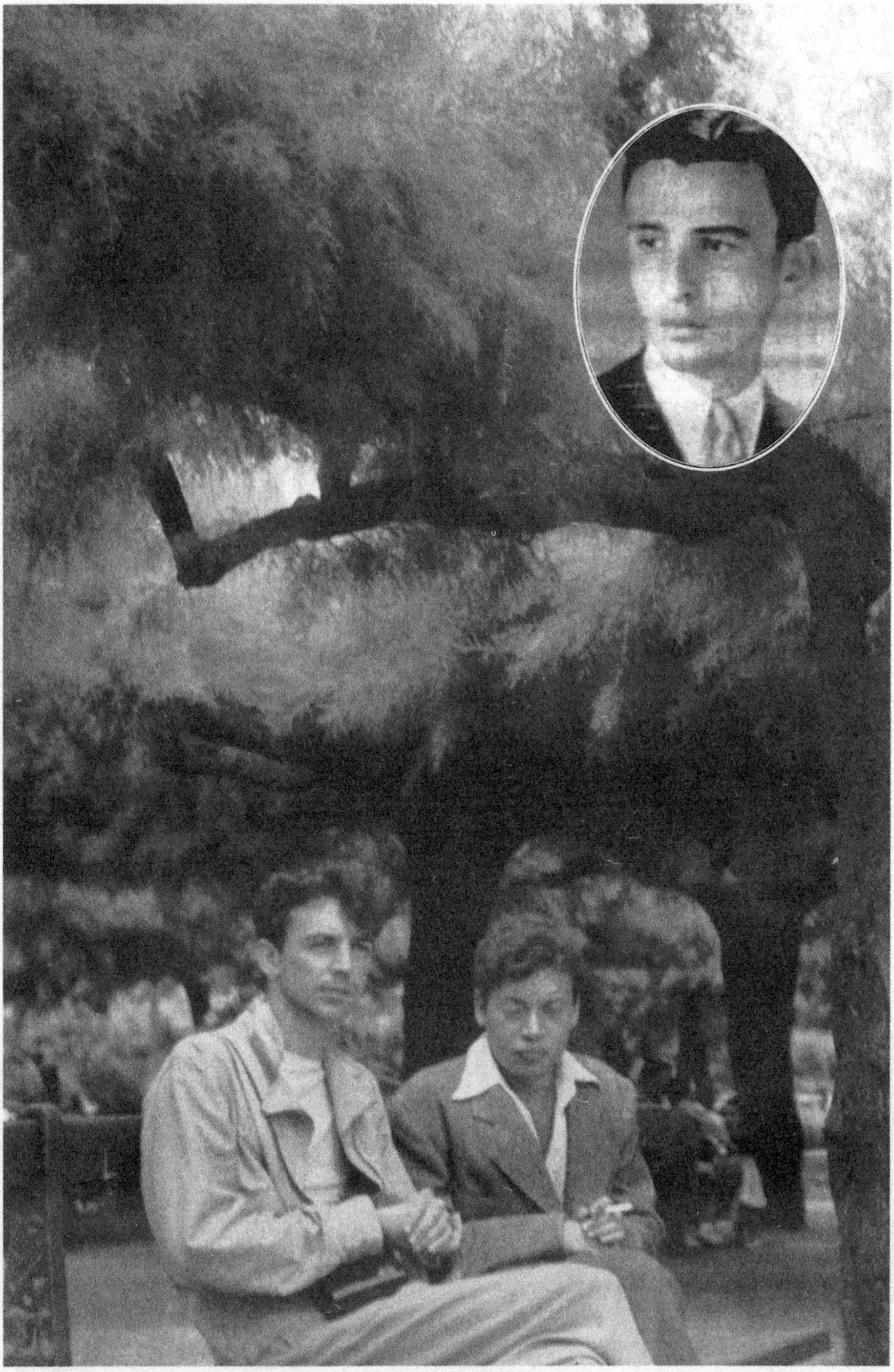

Under the Tree of Life: Terry Southern and Mason Hoffenberg in the Luxembourg Gardens soon after they met in the late 1940s. *(Courtesy Terry Southern Picture Collection) Inset:* Maurice Girodias at twenty. *(Courtesy Gilles Larrain)*

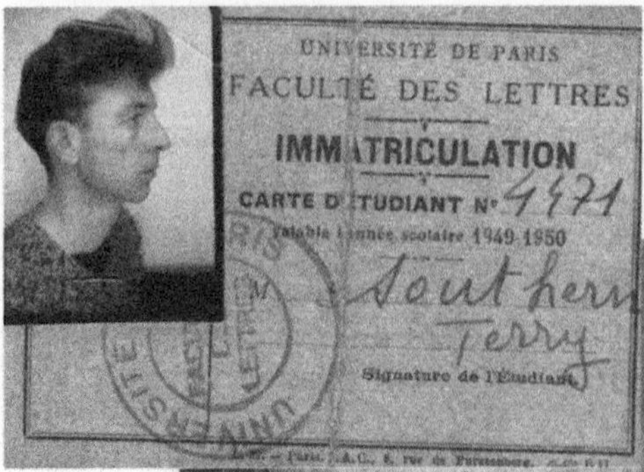

Left: Terry's Sorbonne identity card.
Below: Down and out on rue de la Harpe, Paris, c. 1948. *(Terry Southern Picture Collection)*

Left: Terry in Spain outside Gaudi's cathedral, c. 1953. *(Pud Gadiot/Terry Southern Picture Collection)*

Below: Terry's first wife, Pud Gadiot, c. 1952. *(Terry Southern Picture Collection)*

Above left: Mason on the family beach in Milford, Conn., 1956. *(Courtesy Couquite Hoffenberg)*

Above: A passport photo of Mason in 1954. *(Courtesy Couquite Hoffenberg)*

Left: Terry in his apartment with David Burnett, photographed by Terry's pal Aram Avakian. *(Courtesy Alexandra Avakian)*

Below: At home with the Hoffs: Couquite and Mason in Paris, 1956. *(Courtesy Couquite Hoffenberg)*

Below: Terry and Carol on vacation in Pisa, Italy, 1956. *(Courtesy Carol Southern)*

Above: Couquite Faure in her Bank Street apartment, New York, 1955. *Right:* Mason in Milford, Conn., in 1955. *(Courtesy Couquite Hoffenberg)*

Below: Carol and Terry with their intrepid 1938 Citroën, France, 1958. *(Aram Avakian/ Courtesy Alexandra Avakian)*

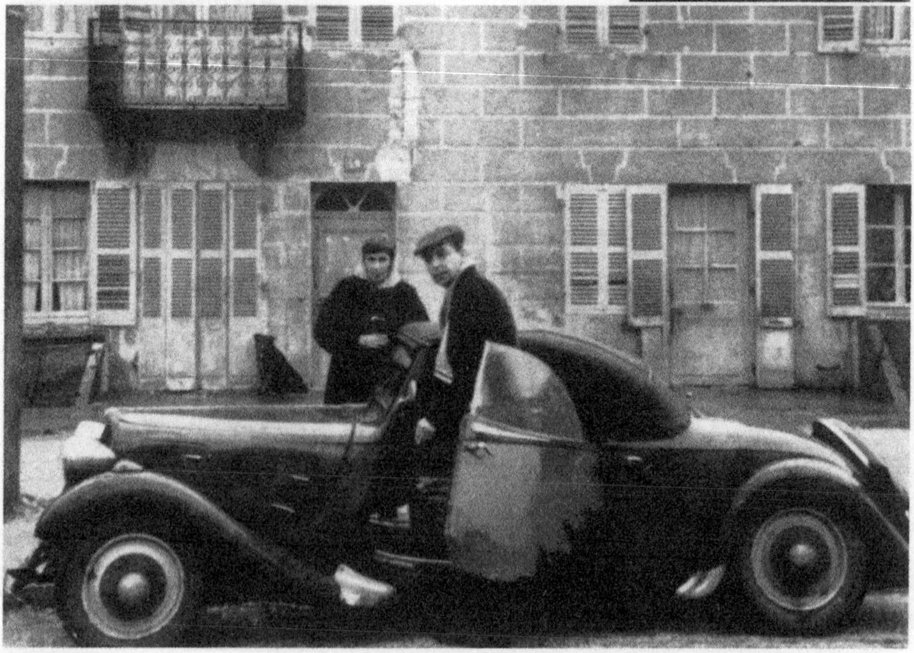

Above left: William Burroughs outside the San Remo, with poet Alan Ansen, who was W. H. Auden's secretary. *(Allen Ginsburg/Courtesy Allen Ginsberg Trust) Above right:* Gregory Corso outside the American Express office on the cover of his Olympia tome.

Left to right: George Plimpton, *The Paris Review's* designer, Billy Pene du Bois, *Merlin* publisher Jane Lougee, poet Christopher Logue, Paris, 1950s. *(Courtesy* The Paris Review*) Inset: The Paris Review* logo.

Top left: Terry at work on *Flash and Filigree* galleys in Geneva, 1957. *Top right:* Carol in Geneva, same year. *(Terry Southern Picture Collection)*

Left: Henry Green, Carol, "Puss," and Terry, outside the Green flat in Belgrave Square, London, 1957. *(Courtesy Carol Southern)*

Below: Mason and poet Marianne Moore, in Massachusetts, 1959. *(Courtesy Couquite Hoffenberg)*

Top: Tourettes sur Loup, where Terry and Mason finally got cracking on *Candy*, 1957.
Inset: Mason finds his *balcon*.
(Courtesy Couquite Hoffenberg)

Below: William Burroughs with friend Jack Kerouac on the cover of *Kulchur*, a literary journal.

Above, left to right: Terry and Mason play poker in Tourettes with black-listed Clifford Odets, whose *Sweet Smell of Success* came out in 1957.
(Courtesy Couquite Hoffenberg)

Below: Big Brother watching: Detail from an *Evergreen Review* cover, 1960.

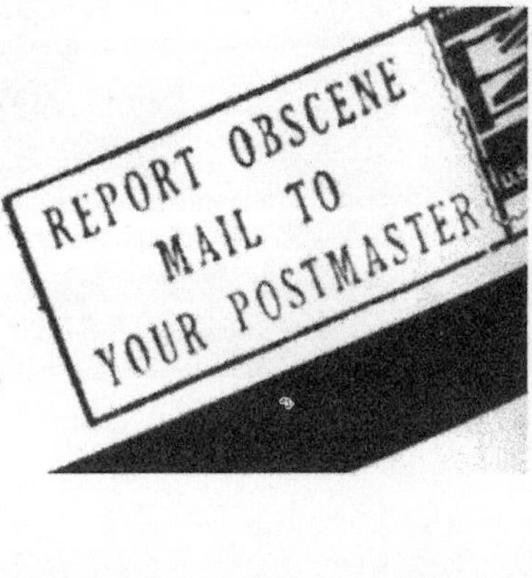

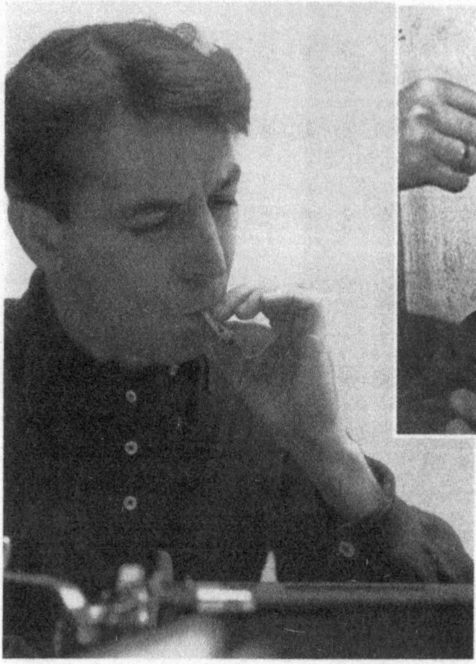

Above: Mason Hoffenberg in the zone. *(Courtesy Couquite Hoffenberg)*

Above: Terry before his Royal portable. *(Aram Avakian/Courtesy Alexandra Avakian)*

Below: Marilyn Meeske and Iris Owens, a.k.a. Henry Crannach and Harriet Daimler, prolific beauties. *(Courtesy Marilyn Meeske, Iris Owens)*

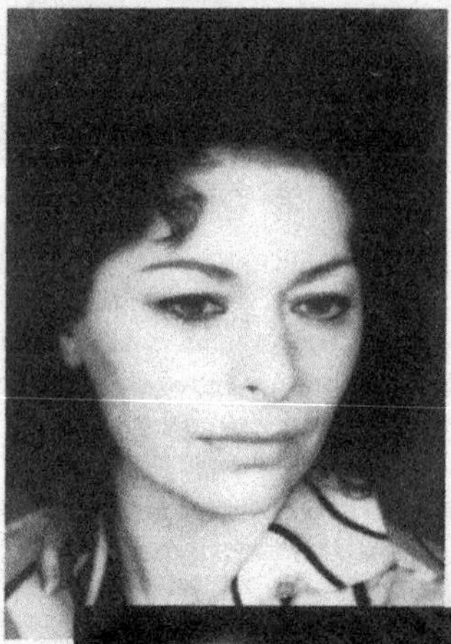

Below: Girodias at the Grande Séverine, c. 1962. *(Robert Doisneau/RAPHO).*

Chapter 16

Just Call Me Lollipop

In September of 1958, just as Terry and Carol were returning from Italy, Girodias wrote to Terry announcing *Candy*'s imminent release:

Paris, September 5th, 1958

Dear Terry Southern,

The book will be out within 2 weeks now.

What about sending review copies to a few well chosen columnists or reviewers? You've seen perhaps the noise they are making about *Lolita, The Ginger Man* and the strange Olympia Press. The book might attract someone's fancy, which might be useful. . . .

If you agree to my suggestion, I think I should send a short personal letter to the chosen journalists, presenting the book, and the anonymous author. Could you work out something?

Of Girodias's stable of DB authors, few used their actual names: Burroughs, Genet, and Corso were among those who did. Almost everyone else used a pseudonym, mostly because the books were, or could at anytime become illegal, possibly leading to deportation. While Terry (and Mason) eventually allowed their names to be associated with the book, Terry responded to Girodias in the summer of 1958 with some caution, saying he could not even send out "personal notes" to reviewers — as doing so would give away his identity.

Geneva, September, 1958

Dear Gid Girodias:

Thanks for your letter of the 5th and for returning the mandat with such considerate promptness. I do very much appreciate it.

As for your suggestion for proclaiming the authorship of *Candy*, I must ask you to put such thoughts from your mind for the time being. I assure you it would in no way help sales or reviews, for the simple reason that I am not as yet that well established. And, whereas I do think it a good idea to send copies to reviewers (without letter), I would for obvious reasons, wish to get the critical reaction *before* allowing it known that I was a party (don't forget, Hoffenberg is involved as well) to the authorship. Also, I have (ironically enough) a *children's book* [*The Donkey and the Darling,* written for the children at Carol's nursery school] under consideration by publishers just now, and any news linking me with a book "in questionable taste" would irreparably shatter my chances with that. And again, I am under contract at the moment with two (English and American) publishers [Andre Deutsch for *Flash and Filigree* and Random House who had purchased U.S. rights for same] and so might get into serious, ethical, if not actually legal, trouble with them. Finally though, and moreover, since I did not get to proof-read it, I should, in any case, want to see the book first — and I trust you will send me a copy, either free or otherwise — as soon as available. If it cannot be sent to Switz, you could send it to Annemasse (Switz though is preferable.) I do look forward to seeing it.

With best wishes,

Sincerely,

Terry S.

Girodias to Southern:

Rue St. Séverin, Paris, Sept 9, 1958

Dear Terry Southern:

I did not make myself clear: I *never* thought — or suggested — that your name should be disclosed.

I thought we might send review copies with a sort of half-serious blurb, and try to build — eventually — a sort of story about Maxwell Kenton.

That was just a suggestion, an idée en l'air. Don't fret, I won't betray!

Yours,

MG

The idea to do a bio for Maxwell Kenton was a brilliant stroke on Girodias's part. The cold war and nuclear issues were on Terry's mind (he had just written a play in which children at a nursery school not unlike the one where Carol worked had to dig their own fallout shelters on the school grounds) prompting him to make his nom de plume a scientist.

Geneva, 11 September 1958

Dear Maurice Girodias:

Thanks for your letter of the 9th.

'Maxwell Kenton' is the pen-name of an American nuclear-physicist, formerly prominent in atomic research and development, who, in February 1957, resigned his post, "because I found the work becoming more and more philosophically untenable," and has since devoted himself fully to creative-writing. "Instead of bringing brief horror into man's life," he has said, "I would like to think of bringing some measure of entertainment and happy diversion to it. There is certainly a dearth of it in our times."

The author has chosen to use a pen-name because, in his own words again, "I'm afraid my literary inclinations may prove in their present form, a bit too *romantic,* at least at this point, to the tastes of many of my old friends and colleagues."

The present novel, *Candy* — which, aside from technical treatises, is Mr. Kenton's first published work — was seen by several English and American publishers, among whom it received wide private admiration, but ultimate rejection due to its highly 'Rabelaisian' wit and flavor. It is undoubtedly a work of very real merit — strikingly individualistic and most (perhaps) engagingly humorous. It may be said that Mr. Kenton has brought to bear on his new vocation the same creative talent and originality which so distinguished him in the field he deserted. And surely here is an instance where Science's loss is Art's gain.

This might be a fair basis from which to work out the sort of thing you had in mind. Offhand I can think of three reviewers who should probably receive a copy, and are capable (by situation and temperament) of creating some interest in the book.

On no account mention my name though.

Best,

Terry S.

A postscript lists influential reviewers of the day: "John Davenport, Esq. c/o *The Observer,* Mr. Anthony West c/o *The New Yorker,* Mr. Edmund Wilson." At the end of September, Girodias sent Terry the galleys for *Candy.*

Rue St. Séverin, Paris, September 27th, 1958

Dear Terry Southern:

Here are the proofs of Candy. It's a funny book all right, especially the first half.

I am a bit preoccupied by the actual use of "Western Union" and "Quaker" denominations. Can't you alter the names? . . . which might owe us a libel suit. I am not joking. Such things have happened, and I must be extra-careful, because of my peculiar position, etc.

Please return the proofs as quickly as possible. You need not go through them entirely, I only sent them to you because of the Quakers, really.

All the best,

MG

A few improbable turns of phrase may also attract your attention. We have marked the places with a cross in the left margin.

Terry responded with characteristic attention to detail:

11 rue Cramer, Geneva, 1 October, 1958

Dear Maurice Girodias:

Thanks for sending the proofs, which I will put into the mail this afternoon. I made the changes you suggested ("Quakers" to read "Crackers" and "Western Union" to read "messenger") to good advantage, I believe. I also tried to improve those improbable turns of phrase marked with x, and a few besides that. Apparently there was some objection, on the part of you or your staff, to "Miraculous Mandarin Suite" by Bartok . . . which I could not perceive. Mason wrote that part and, while I don't know what he was getting at, it seems all right to me — though certainly I have no objection to your changing it. Do you mean it is 'improbable' that there would be such a suite? It ("Miraculous Mandarin") seems to me a fairly cryptic and engaging title, and more or less true to the spirit of the whole. At any rate, I wasn't able to think up a better one, though should you, do, and by all means, feel free, etc.

I'm going through a French *Candide* with the idea of getting one of those nice 'prefatory quotes' to use at the beginning — this would, I believe, lend a further literary substance and aesthetic justification to the work, and give the critics something to get their teeth into right away.*

You voiced no objection to the use of individual names (Huntz Hall, George Arliss, Edmond Lowe) in the Livia sequence at Halfway House — as opposed, I mean, to your objection to the use of "Quakers."† Did you overlook this? Or is it different?

I very much appreciate your thinking of me regarding the

*The Voltaire quote ultimately selected for the first edition was "*Candide, chassé du paradis terrestre, marcha longtemps sans savoir où, Candide, tout stupéfait, ne voyait pas encore bien comment il était un héros.*" (Candide, expelled from paradise, walked for a long time without knowing where he was going. Candide, in a stupefied state, did not yet see to what extent he was a hero.)

†Huntz Hall, prolific actor who played Horace Debussy "Sach" Jones in the *Bowery Boys* films; George Arliss, British stage and film actor, who retired in 1937; Edmond Lowe, American leading man of stage and film.

possibility of some work with your friends for Simca [an Italian poetry and arts magazine published in English], and I would be most happy to undertake this should it materialize. Do keep me posted.

All best,

Terry S.

Another prominent N.Y. critic (who prides himself on his unflinching appreciation of the off-beat and risque) occurred to me: Mr. Dwight MacDonald, c/o *The New Yorker.* He does a considerable amount of work for *Partisan Review,* which is not too unlikely an outlet for our purpose.

Candy was published in Paris in October 1958, as number 64 of the Traveller's Companion Series, with a print run of 5,000 copies. While the very funny and satirical look at sex in America immediately attracted the attention of the Beat and expat crowd, it also caught the eye of the Brigade Mondaine (the Paris vice squad), and the book was seized from booksellers all over Paris and hauled to the trash yards by police. Some dealers managed to hide the books and sell them in brown paper wrappers under the counter.

One of Girodias's main sources of revenue came through exporting and selling his books to the British market. *Candy*'s appearance as a *livre interdit* on the Customs Office list was a terrible obstacle for him. The Home Office in Britain was aware of many copies of *Candy* being smuggled into the country, despite the import-export ban on both shores. Girodias conceived a wily dodge in December, whereby he reissued the book using a different cover, initial pages, and wrapping so that it could pass through customs (and be sold to the bookshops) as an apparently different title altogether. *Candy* was thus reborn as *Lollipop.* Girodias had used this technique, in various permutations, before, and later recalled it with relish:

Whether the title changes were obvious or otherwise, the end result was much the same. The average French policeman, having no English and being as short on imagination as his professional colleagues everywhere else, was unable to equate a book entitled *Peals of the Rainbow* (1965) with one called *Seeds of the Rainbow* (1957) simply because it didn't appear on his list under the letter "S." It was an amusing game that was being played.

This "amusing game" was apparently not noticed by either Terry or Mason — perhaps because neither could afford to actually buy a copy of the book. Had they opened Girodias's secret printing which bore a "1959" copyright though it was printed at the end of 1958, they would have been horrified to see that everything about it was wrong, and absurdly so. The dedication seemed Hindu-zoological, and appeared in a ludicrously large font:

To Master Boon and Master Badj

The Voltaire quotation was now attributed to Rimbaud! But most distressing, Professor Mephesto's carefully orchestrated delivery of his pompous introductory speech had been entirely rewritten — apparently by Girodias himself — complete with self-conscious asides, allusions to invented scenes, and a maddening and unpunctuated attempt to have the professor repeatedly clear his throat. Regarding travel and how it "broadens one," Mephesto now said:

> "There is no finer way for exploring the depths of one's ahem," he fixed his gaze on the sweatered belly of a girl in the front row, "soul, you can call it . . . And ahem the soul is the seat," he smoothed his hands over his behind, "of the ahem ethical faculty."

No doubt Mason and Terry, with the "cootie pincer" attention they paid to every comma, would have gone through the roof had they seen it. But the deceit worked, and Girodias saved many thousands of copies from the rubbish heap.

In spite of the ban, and in part because of it, *Candy* and *Lollipop* quickly became sought after among Americans visiting Paris, and books began appearing in London and New York, in bookstores like Frances Steloff's Gotham Book Mart.

With its send-up of Americana, and its "capping *Lolita*" (as Terry apparently perversely said), *Candy* became a much sought-after bit of contraband for Americans traveling through Paris. The book was passed around and passages read aloud. "Give me your hump!" was said to be a rejoinder heard in bars throughout the Village.

In cold and controlled Geneva, Terry was beginning to feel cut off from his American roots, and the Southerns began planning their return to the States. Terry fantasized about country life and wanted to look for a "stone farmhouse." In the following letter, suggesting Terry move to New England, which Terry would do within the year, Mason once again brings up Girodias's recalcitrance in paying the authors what he owed them:

Milford, Dec 14, 1958

Dear Souterrain,

According to my calculations you have now come to the end of your supply of Vageline [contraceptive cream], and the last few globs are rapidly oozing out of your hourglass of gook so I am not entirely perplexed to hear you are once again pulling up stakes and coming home.

Our darling little two-week-old Juliette is shrieking steadily by my side as I write this.

I must confess, for Candy, that I have forgotten much about the book itself and the three years we spent our brains' labor on it. ONE thing I did manage to retain though was that he owed us 40 mille [$80] at the time I left, and even that this entailed a little comedy with you, Gid, Couquite et Dieu sais quoi. I wrote Gid a little letter to straighten out this mixup and to remind him that he owed me 20 and you 20. I then received a kindly note in return in which he agreed with my analysis of the situation and promised prompt rectification. SINCE then I have heard nothing and have come to suspect that this is more of your skunk-work. However, since you now ask in seeming innocence if there isn't something you can do while passing thru Paris, I say Yes! Goddamnit! You can pass by

Gid's and get my share of the loot (or fork it up yourself in case this is a new example of your Southwestern hospitality).

It's high time you found out a few things about your own country, Terry. I mean you've been over there toadying up to all those slants and wops, know your way around La Belle Belgique blindfolded, but you don't even know that there aren't any stone houses in Conn. (eastern Pa., yes) which is in the USA!

Might find a stark New England *frame* farmhouse with land at the price you mention. And southern Conn. has the advantage that should you get tired of "going back to the land," then you can go back to the sea which is the origin of all life. If I hear in answer that you're on the level about this thing, and that you've settled this irritating mixup with Gid, I'll get in touch with Mr. Elmendorf, a wily real-estate expert of Milford, who may know just the place for our artist kibbutz and poetry park. At any rate, he'll leave me with a realistic appraisal of the thing.

I can understand how you might have been carried away seeing the proofs of Candy, especially after a six-month interval, but to say it caps Lolita . . . well, excuse me, but that is downright San Francisco whistling in the dark. To say nothing of Doctor Zhivago which is No. 1 and which does cap Lolita. We're both too young (and you're too sneaky) to be in a class with men who have had long, rich careers, and who have the power to show.

Pensively

Suzanne

Part II

STEALING *CANDY*

"I don't know which is best — the freshness of rain, or the warmth of fire."

— *Candy*

Chapter 17

New Life, New England

As *Candy* disappeared into the black hole of banned books, Terry and Carol returned to the United States in the late spring of 1959 and took up temporary residence in the back room of *The Paris Review* offices. While Andre Deutsch was about to publish *The Magic Christian* in England, a chapter from it, "Grand Guy Grand," ran in *The Paris Review* and won the magazine's "humorous fiction prize," established by Gertrude Vanderbilt.

The publishing scene was still fraught with self-censorship and big-business conservatism. One publisher who gave Terry and all writers of the time hope was Barney Rosset. Rosset had founded Grove Press in New York in 1951 and began the *Evergreen Review* in 1957. The magazine, which featured poetry, plays, essays, short fiction, cartoons, photographs, and artwork, provided a window into what was happening in Europe and New York, and was dubbed by the Associated Press "the most adventurous collection of writing you can find on the stands today." Rosset ingeniously juxtaposed European writers, artists and philosophers — including Sartre, Camus, Beckett, Robbe-Grillet, Ionesco, Artaud, Gunter Grass, Octavio Paz, Heinrich Boll, Fernando Arrabal — with the Americans who were inspired by them and creating new expressions of their own. "Happening Scenes" were chronicled and contextualized; everything from pataphysics to "The German Scene" and *Hiroshima Mon Amour*. The *Evergreen Review* took the profound creative freedom and provocative, literary eroticism that had been flourishing in Paris a decade earlier and mixed it with the explosive underground scenes in America: the Beat and Black Mountain poetry movements, photography and the New York painting scenes. Rosset wanted to introduce to America to what he called the "Anglo-American sex radicals": Allen Ginsberg, Jack Kerouac, William Burroughs, Lawrence Ferlinghetti, Gary Snyder, Robert Creeley, Kenneth Koch, John Rechy, and Larry Rivers. It was a wonderfully incestuous ferment: McClure on Pollack, Stuart Davis captured on film, Frank O'Hara on Franz Kline, LeRoi Jones on Cuba. Rosset was fearless, and he wanted to help bring down all the walls of censorship in America — not only those around sex but politics and racism as well. In the years to come, Malcolm X, Frantz Fanon, and Che Guevara would each call for "Revolution!" within the pages of *Evergreen*.

Girodias wanted to copy Rosset's success with *Evergreen* and started planning a review of his own. In May, Terry received a handwritten note from him saying that there were "a number of new projects" he wanted to talk with Terry about. Avoiding the issue of the money he still owed, he ended the letter appealing to a subject he knew would engage Terry. "My night club is not yet open, but it will not take long now — 3 weeks I hope. Have you any idea how I could get hold of good new American records? Any information would oblige." Terry responded:

June 2nd, 1959

Dear Gid:

Thanks for your letter which I've only just received due to a faire suivre. It was certainly a pleasure to hear from you and to know that you're doing well. Perhaps by now your club is open and swinging; I know it shall be a great success. You asked about records; I would be glad to send you records from here, though I wonder if the customs expense would not make them as expensive in the end as in France. In any case I will send you the best price-catalogue here, and you can decide. . . . You can spoil the club if you have corny music, whereas if you have good music (Billie Holiday, Gerry Mulligan, Dave Brubeck, Modern Jazz Quartette, Ray Charles, etc.) you will build up a dependable clientele.

Candy is having a small success d'estime here in private circulation . . .

All best wishes,

Terry Southern

Girodias's club was appointed by his talented paramour, Michele Forgeois, who directed the Spanish craftsmen in refurbishing the interior, geared to highlight the many unique items Forgeois scavenged from Parisian demolition sites and flea markets. Seven rooms on two levels were each appointed with a perfect blend of opulence and taste. The Église Saint Séverin adjacent had a medieval burial ground, part of which the workers encountered when excavating the thirteenth-century cellars of the Grande Séverine. When it finally opened in 1959, Gregory Corso recalled being greeted by Girodias with a drink in one hand and a skull in the other. By 1960, the club was as much a curiosity as it was an exotic place to do business. As Thomas Quinn reported in the *New York Herald:*

> On the ground floor there is a "turn-of-the-century" bar with a 1900 tiled floor; a red room inspired by Chinese and Japanese examples; a blue room, Le Salon Cagliostro, so called because of the old Spanish tarot cards painted on its mirrors; a very green and refreshing winter garden with bird cages of the rococo school; while downstairs there are three rooms: a bar, a dining room and a central room with a dance floor.

Girodias used the club to pacify the growing number of authors, printers, lawyers, and publishers to whom he owed money. It was a revolving credit system — which had the staff often on strike due to lack of payment. His patrons, often angry with Girodias for similar reasons, would bring as many people as possible for free feasts. As Michele Forgeois rhetorically opined to interviewer John de St. Jorre in *Venus Bound,* "Maurice adored spending money even though he burned himself badly . . . Why? *Pour s'amuser.*" For the hell of it.

The rise of the Grande Séverine in 1960 would coincide with the success of Girodias's most celebrated titles; *Lolita, The Ginger Man, Candy,* and *Naked Lunch.* As the multidisciplined bad-boy impresario of the moment, *The Economist* dubbed him "the most celebrated avant-garde editor of his time." Girodias was like a child again, playing with what he called his "new toy."

Marilyn Meeske recalls that the club had a certain kitschy "wild and crazy guys" quality, and that Girodias couldn't really attain the serious press attention he desired. "He thought he would *get* to Paris on an international level — but no one would go there — they'd show up for the freebies — he couldn't get *Paris Match* or any of the important happening journalists to get interested in promoting him."

Girodias's nightclub became a great eclectic venue for avant-garde theatre and especially for jazz. According to St. Jorre:

> At its height, the Séverine employed sixty-five people, including a number of well-known singers and musicians. Jazz musicians Kenny Clarke and Chet Baker, Memphis Slim . . . Marpessa Dawn of *Black Orpheus* fame, Juliette Greco, the French singer, and Mae Mercer, another black American singer, all performed there. Mae Mercer, a large, powerfully built woman, had a tempestuous affair with Girodias that was marked by noisy rows and physical combat, with Girodias invariably on the receiving end.

When Gallimard finally published *Lolita* in the autumn of 1959, Nabokov, who was in Paris, refused to acknowledge Girodias's presence at the fête. Miriam Worms recalled, "Nabokov was contemptible. He couldn't accept that his best book was published by Olympia, which he regarded as a scandalous outfit." Eric Kahane, whose painstaking translation Gallimard used, remembers:

> We were talking. He was very nice . . . very complimentary. Then there was a commotion at the door and my brother entered. He

> came over to us and as he was getting near, Nabokov veered away like an old warship not "seeing" him. Gid was both upset and amused. . . . Nabokov . . . did not want to admit that he had been published by a professional pornographer when here he was at Gallimard being hailed as a king.

In Paris, Girodias had become friendly with an American publisher, Walter Zacharius of Lancer Books. Girodias, with his suite of identically bound, outrageously bold literary treasures, each one a cunning, artful, often mind-blowing provocation, made quite an impression on Zacharius. He later recalled:

> [Girodias] was a genius as a publisher . . . I'll never forget reading at the hotel that night — reading everything he gave me. I said, "I'd love to bring [Henry Miller] in [to the States]" — I said, "I don't have enough money — I'll go to jail." But Barney [Rosset], he used to be a wealthy fellow, and he brought him in and did very well with him. And I had *Candy* . . . I never forgot it. I saw humor in the book — the sex didn't really mean that much to me.

Girodias noted Zacharius's interest in *Candy* — and would later use that interest to good advantage. Another Supreme Court breakthrough occurred in 1959, boding well for *Candy*'s prospects in the States. Justice Julian Hoffman ruled that the U.S. Post Office's seizure of the first issue of *Big Table,* which featured material by Burroughs and Kerouac, was to be "freed" by the Post Office and absolved of its alleged "pornography" status.

As a theatrical impresario, Girodias was in a class by himself, putting to good use some of the more outrageous and visually oriented authors in his stable, such as staging an adaptation of Norman Rubington's *Fuzz Against Junk.* In a spectacular swan-dive, Girodias hosted a gala affair for the debut of Marquis de Sade's *Philosophy in the Boudoir.* Girodias encouraged his more outrageous friends to dress up, and he recalled, "A girlfriend and myself went dressed up in St Vincent de Paul nuns' habits, the ones with the winged hats, which we had rented. The place was packed, there were probably about 150 in the theatre." In attendance were Jean

Seberg and her husband the novelist-statesman Romain Gary, film director Roger Vadim, and actress Catherine Deneuve.

The Brigade Mondaine was also there, and without needing to see much of the performance, closed it down in a raid. Ironically, it was Zacharius who helped get Girodias out of jail:

> Lou [Ouillian, a friend] said, "We're coming down here tonight — they're putting on *Marquis de Sade*," and they invited the French press, and [Girodias] was going to interpret the play and tell them why it was great . . . right? And you know who he invited? De Gaulle's wife! De Gaulle's wife was the head censor, understand, in France . . . and so I'm sitting there, and I don't know, my French is imperfect — and Lou's interpreting for me and I'm saying "ohmigod," and during the intermission Lou said to me, "We're getting out of here, now!" I said, "Why?" He said, "Look around — the place is loaded with police. Let's get out of here before we get locked up!" So we left. We went back the next day to see him — the whole place was locked up. His publishing — everything was gone. So we visit him in jail. And he's screaming — he was a maniac . . . Lou and I put up some money and they finally let him out.

Girodias later recalled, "My friends from the vice squad were only too glad to use this as an excuse to have the club . . . closed down, which in turn caused it to go bankrupt and as a side effect forced the Olympia Press into bankruptcy as well."

In 1960 there were a great many changes for the Southerns. In February, *The Magic Christian* came out in the United States, published by Random House. Terry took jobs writing criticism (for *The Nation* and others) to bring in some money. They began looking for a country house — Carol's inheritance would cover the down payment — and finally found one in East Canaan, about three hours from New York City in the northwest corner of Connecticut. Blackberry River ran in front of the 1757 colonial, which came with fields, woods, an apple orchard and graveyard, and twenty-nine acres. With its mountain backdrop and sweeping views, Canaan was the quintessential fantasy farmhouse Terry and Carol had imagined. In his spare time, Terry fixed up the chicken house and prepared the fences for livestock — something he had learned growing up in Texas. Carol began digging a large vegetable garden so they could "eat off the land."

With a baby due in December, little money coming in, and recommendations he had gathered for this purpose over the last few years, Terry finally submitted his Guggenheim application with a proposal concerning *The Hipsters* — a novel he would never finish.

> *Statement of Plans*
>
> My plan would be to remain here, in this isolated farmhouse in Connecticut with wife and child, and complete . . . a novel, already several years in the writing. . . .
>
> Since undertaking this work — which in its nature has proved to be more demanding, deliberated, and lengthy than is usual — I have published three shorter novels and approximately 50 stories and essays. These have had a certain gratifying critical acceptance, but have not helped me to give an uninterrupted period to what I consider my principal work in hand — so that my energies are largely engaged now, as for some time past, by odd jobs of farm and construction labor.
>
> The basis for my application is the belief that with the aid of a grant I could devote myself more fully to completing the work, and, in so doing, perhaps make a worthwhile contribution to the field.

Terry's application for the Guggenheim and for the more conservative Saxton grant were both denied, but things looked promising, regardless. Lewis Allen, a theatrical producer in New York, liked Terry's play *Beyond the Shadows,* and offered to buy it and have Terry adapt it into a screenplay for $5,000 and points.

There was also a new book project afoot, begun with Richard Seaver and Alex Trocchi. *Beyond the Beat,* which would ultimately be published as *Writers in Revolt,* was to be an anthology of "the most controversial writing in the world today." Terry and Dick put the anthology together — Trocchi had absconded via Canada, one step ahead of the narcs. The book featured excerpts from *Howl* and *Our Lady of the Flowers,* as well as extended passages from Sartre, Sade, Burroughs, Hubert Selby Jr., Baudelaire, Herman Hesse, Artaud, Henry Miller, Samuel Beckett, Lawrence Durrell, Malaparte, Celine, among others. Terry's disdain for the state of American literary criticism rivaled the animosity he felt toward American publishers, as Terry revealed in a literary essay on William Gaddis:

> American critics — and this is true of no other contemporary culture — are themselves so far removed from the creative process, and from all imaginative thought, that their response to a work can never be on the basis of what the work is, but on what it seems to represent. It is psychologically untenable for such a person to admit the possibility of direct contact, or experience with a "work of art" or a "masterpiece" — other, of course, than those so certified and still smelling of the grave.

The *New York Times* was reciprocally disdainful of Terry (and his book's British acclaim) in their review of *The Magic Christian:*

> What all of this assorted dada leads to, besides some very funny samples of the author's vacuum-packed humor, is anybody's guess. "The Magic Christian" has been hailed in Britain, where any ugly American wearing a plastic pig mask and a diamond stickpin the size of a 5-cent piece is bound to be widely popular.

By the late summer of 1960, Mason, Couquite, and two-year old Juliette had returned to Paris. Mason's fantasy of living a country life had been realized by Terry, who wrote Mason from East Canaan with another Village update and an invitation to contribute to the almost-completed *Beyond the Beat.*

Blackberry River, 22 September 1960

My dear Hoff:

I was hoping to have heard from you by now, with your new address, what's shaking, etc. Also a piece of your heavy prose for our anthology, *Beyond the Beat;* we have selections from Celine, Malaparte, Ionesco, Beckett, Artaud, Canetti, Camus, Sartre, Hesse (Steppenwolf treatise, etc.), all big guns, so your heavy will *not* be wanting for good company; send at once as the project is earmarked for an early *succes du metier;* also any suggestions you may have as to inclusion of other classic heavies (we have part of *Naked Lunch,* beginning: "The President is a junkie, etc."); if you wish to participate in this phase of the project (i.e. bon conseil) your name will be included in the Advisory Committee, along with Richard Seaver and (if he can stop shooting and get cracking) Mel R. Sabe, *plus* receiving a fat stipend for your trouble! We are not using any poetry, so far at least, though it might be a good coup for you to have the only poem in the book; preferably a prose fragment (any length to 25 pages). . . .

Mel Sabre is in bad shape; all his veins crumpled and he is fixing in the neck; it is quite a sight to behold, him shooting with a mirror in one hand, craning his head about, eyes rolling wildly, trying for a hit, and hitting a nerve instead, screaming, leaping about on one foot and then the other, then spike dangling from his neck like a scorpion at last as he majestically sinks down on all fours, several rivulets of blood coursing across his bare bronzed chest, fresh tight-fitted jock-shorts bulging at crotch as though with deep sea catch inside them. . . .

Can you drop me a line as soon as pos.

Best,

Your Ted

As for advisory pay: $50 minimum; $25 for every text suggested which we do use.

Mason had a flair for high drama. Whereas Terry rarely wrote about his personal concerns or their relationship, Mason reveled in exploring these areas — often just to tease him. In this letter written from a new flat at 275 rue Charenton, he reproaches Terry for a rejection suffered the previous year when he was trying to kick.

Paris, Oct 20th, 1960

Dear Terry,

Are you surprised to know that I was tickled to hear from you? Tickled very deeply because even before your letter arrived I discovered one day that I'd revised my opinion of you and no longer held you in low, but in middle esteem. Let's not steep ourselves in old quarrels, revenge and bitter accusation. I'll just mention that I was so hurt when you refused hospitality of an apartment in Geneva when I was sick as a dog and needed the mountain air. "I won't ask you again," is what you may remember I said nobly, and to myself I quietly lowered you to low esteem. Thenceforth God knows we all have our faults, but yours became a malicious hobby of mine. It was trashbag this and vile fink that until, with the passing of three four years, I saw in a mellow glow the other day how I was blinded by my own loathsome paranoia like a scum to sting the eyesight. I could have told you at that moment that I understood, whatever your hideous motive, how you could stroll away whistling as they locked me in the reptile house. I know you'll make allowances for me knowing what a sourpuss character I have no means to prevent. Then there is the Future during which we must pledge a minimum of dignity for such an old palhood, else we diminish ourselves. . . .

I thought he was in prison but an unimpeachable source informed me that Haj [of the Café Soleil du Maroc] was busted just two weeks ago at the Belgian border in an abortive run to Brussels. Saida [his wife] was with him and was also bagged since the chit [hash] was pretending to be a clotted portion of underdrawers . . . Twice now, at night and far away, I've seen the venerable Sun scurry under brief lamplights wearing your old raincoat.

As Terry knew he would, Mason came up with a few ideas for the anthology, including a Papua New Guinean folktale. "Legend #32 is a gasser," Mason wrote, "where the women stick palm spikes on the hero's joint, then give him a cane to hobble home on, and he then lays for the ringleader of the women, sews her snatch together with vines, cuts *her* a walking stick, whereupon, 'She is confined to her house where she putrefies and dies.'" Mason continues, quoting the folktale:

> The word-for-word translation is especially nutty. . . .
>
> they emerge they hold him he stays
> they them thrust-into penis they thrust-in sago-palm spikes
> penis they it thrust — in they snap-off it
> they it thrust — in they snap-off it
> they it thrust — in they snap-off it
> they it thrust — in they snap-off it (repeat many times)
> swiftly swiftly finished they cut for him stick
>
> . . . I have another volume of the series, Pawnee Indian this one, not so peppery. . . . Worth a go, eh, you crafty old Navaho medicine-man?
>
> I am sorting through my beat old notes and beyond, to see if I can't find some heavily original, creative piece suitable for your mag as you so kindly requested. No doubt you and Troc are hilariously scheming to counter with your only rejection slip — "sorry Hoff, but this is a bit *too* seedy, even for B.T.B." Very well. I'm not going to whimper and whine. History has not yet had its say in the matter. What started as a vicious fascist prank may prove a horse of another man's poison, baby.
>
> As ever
>
> Ernst

Such matters as permissions were put on hold at the end of the year when I was born.

Chapter 18

Candy Goes to Italy, Mason Gets Nervous

In January 1961, Mason met with Girodias, who told him that he had received an offer for Italian rights for *Candy*. Girodias immediately sketched out terms for the Italian deal and used the opportunity to quickly construe a general contract covering all future editions.

Paris, 17th January, 1961

Dear Terry:

You will find enclosed copy of a letter I sent to Mason; he suggested that I submit it to you. It concerns *Candy* alias LOLLIPOP for which we have received an offer for the Italian translation rights.

It is quite possible that we will find other publishers who will want to buy translation rights and I therefore proposed to Mason that we make a general contract for that book. I have not written earlier because Mason has only just given me your present address.

If you agree to the terms outlined in my letter of January 6 to Mason, will you please send me a word and we will prepare a formal agreement. I would appreciate your answer as soon as possible as the Italian publisher would like to go ahead without delay.

Best wishes,

Yours,

Maurice

Enclosed with Girodias's letter was a memo outlining terms, which Mason had already signed — no doubt at Girodias's club after a sumptuous meal. Mason had also scrawled in heavy pencil at the top a note to Terry: "Will you please return [enclosed contracts] to us."

THE OLYMPIA PRESS 7, Rue Saint-Séverin,
Paris, 5e, le 6 janvier 1961

Monsieur Mason Hoffenberg
275 rue de Charenton
Paris 12e

Dear Mason,

I confirm the terms we have obtained from Longanesi :

- 8% on the selling price for the first 3,000 copies ;
- 10% on the following 5,000 copies and
- 12.5% above 8,000 copies.

The advance on royalties would be equivalent to half of the total amount due for the first printing.

They would pay 1.500 NF [$300] upon signature of the contract and the balance within 90 days (ninety) following publication of the book.

I also confirm my suggestion that we sign a formal contract concerning all English language and translation rights or any other subsidiary rights.

We would receive 1/3 (one third) of all reprint rights and 1/4 (one fourth) of all translation or subsidiary rights for our part and we would act as Agents as well as Publishers of the original editions.

Actually I have been carrying out the negotiations with Longanesi on this understanding.

Yours sincerely,

Maurice Girodias

Rather than signing, Terry seconded the idea of a separate "formalized contract," which would cover the original book and all subsequent editions. Around Christmastime, Girodias's club had burned in a fire, an event that Terry and many others found suspicious. Sylvie Forgeois, one of the club's managers, commented, "We wondered whether he considered the fire to be suitable punishment for whatever sins he attributed to himself. . . . Everybody thought Girodias had lit the match himself for the insurance. Only we knew that he wasn't properly insured."

Blackberry River, 24 January 1961

Dear Maurice:

Thanks for your letter of the 17th.

That is pleasing news about the Italian translation offer. I am not quite sure I understand the monetary (percentage-wise) arrangements — vis-a-vis Olympia Press and the authors — in the Longanesi negotiations (and I take it that these are substantially the same as those meant to obtain in the 'general contract' you propose), but since you seemed to be pressed for time in this matter, and since there was some delay in my receiving your letter, let us go ahead with the Italian contract, keeping it separate from the general agreement until such time as I am better acquainted with its terms and have conferred with Mason, etc.

I was sorry to hear about the fire at your club, though I suppose you picked up a pretty penny in assurance, eh?

Best wishes,

Yours,

Terry Southern

Mason began voicing his concerns about what he had signed, especially since he now understood that Girodias would be acting as their agent in making future deals — a potential conflict of interest. Moreover, he believed Girodias's percentage of the translation rights, 25 percent, too high. He wrote Terry about his suspicions:

Paris, January 30, 1961

I was on the point of writing you, by God, and today received your letter. You'll have to understand why I'm so remiss in these matters as was the case with the piece I fully intended to send you for your anthology (is it too late?). Put it down to my narcotical ups and downs. I am currently as clean as a hound's clit and more or less able to assume responsibility for my end of a fertile correspondence.

I am tickled pink at the idea of your having a baby boy. Deep down I knew that you would some day run out of vag jelly and that all hell would then ensue. This important event should supply you with the emotional maturity, respect for your fellow man, and oodles of anxiety needed to round out your personality.

When Gid told me about the Italian translation of "Candy" I got a similar reaction to yours, got cagey, thought what about having a veto on the translation which might not do justice to our work, and had the sound idea of writing you immediately so that you could have your agent give the terms the once over and advise. I then abandoned these worthy projects and plenty of others to enter a clinic for a couple of weeks and kick a brutal, Autumn habit contracted while doing research in French hip-talk in order to translate "The Connection"* (likewise abandoned). Right. I got out of clinic fortnight ago and am gradually becoming less corpselike. In my general apathy I took Gid's word (perfectly worthless) that he had gotten the best deal possible, and signed. What the hell, it's a windfall, I figured. I admit this was the kind of unjewishness which gained Henry Miller and V. Nabokov $300.00 apiece and $178,000.00 for Gid. Still, I can't believe "Candy" is in that jackpot class — if we had something like that, the shrewd thing would be to publish it ourselves over here. However show the contract to someone if you want, and if he says no go then you could still spike the deal by withholding your signature.

Soon after that you could expect to receive first payment which, if my understanding is correct, will be in the form of 47 kg's of dried lasagna. Should come in handy with a new little gentile around the house sucking everything in sight up his face and anus.

Here's something else: while chatting with Gid about the above I buzzed him about a new Maxwell Kenton book. He agreed with alacrity and mentioned the generous sum of $600.00. I pointed out "Candy's" Italian success and he smoothly rose to a thousand. I've

---

*Jack Gelber's play produced by the Living Theatre in New York.

> been thinking about it, not the book but the money. It's not enough to rupture our balls, but we could compensate somewhat by slenderness of length. What I had in mind was each doing 80 pages — say 4 20-page chapters. I could flip a coin for who does the leadoff chapter, send a carbon to other guy and so on. Might make it easier since it's stimulating to receive other guy's chapter and take off from there. What kind of book? Beats me. I can't see a sequel to "Candy" very well since the poor girl seems to have been so thoroughly worked over. I thought of a letter of yours I have with a hilarious bit about an exploding envelope of H. . . . Maybe we could cull a lot of bits like that out of letters, journals? Care to have a go? 80 pages = $500. I could use the loot and the work.
>
> Say hello to Mel if you see him.
>
> Giuseppi

A handwritten postscript was hastily added:

> PS. I've just been to see Gid and it turns out I was wrong in my analysis of what we're signing — you *are* agreeing to both deals if you sign. So don't. I'll write you tomorrow with details. Gid claims he needs to have legal status as our agent *before* he can sign with Longanesi. I imagine Longanesi assumes he already has some legal contract signed with us as publisher. One thing fishy is that Gid is asking us for 1/4 or 25% as agent instead of customary 10%.* Another is that he'd be effectively blocking us off in any deals that came up, we'd have to take his word for everything. I suspect he might have other possibilities besides Longanesi.
>
> I'd like very much to find out what our legal position as authors that signed *nothing* with a publisher. Can we deal directly with Longanesi? Cut out Gid? Or simply threaten to as a lever to make him straighten up if necessary. Can you find out about this or do you know an agent here, knowing the European scene, that I could go to and find out?

*While 10 percent was a customary agent fee in the United States, 25 percent was not unusual in Europe, particularly if the publisher was selling foreign rights without using a subagent.

In the following letter, Girodias draws a portentous line in the sand by reiterating that *Candy* was a work for hire. The implication (lost on the authors at the time) was that they would need to accept whatever terms he specified, for he was declaring himself the owner of the copyright as publisher. Had the authors accepted Girodias's point of view at this juncture, a fortune would have been made by all three men in the coming years from *Candy.* Instead, paranoia soon began to take over, especially for Mason. It would be a decade of haggling over percentage points before a settlement would be reached.

Rue St.-Séverin, Paris, 3rd February, 1961

Dear Terry:

Thank you for your letter of January 24. You are right in assuming that the Longanesi negotiations have been carried out by us on the premise that both Mason and you would agree to the general arrangement I suggested concerning this book. *Candy* having been commissioned by me, I think my offer is sound, fair and sensible and it goes without saying that I shall do my best to do something with the book (very profitable for you) if I have material advantage in so doing.

Could you, therefore, send me a word confirming your agreement to the division of proceeds in the case of English-language editions (two-thirds/one-third) and translation or other subsidiary rights (three-fourths/one-fourth). I shall work out a very simple contract between Mason and you on the one hand and Olympia on the other as soon as I receive your acceptance. But I could proceed with the Longanesi negotiations upon hearing from you and before we have this contract signed and sealed by the three of us.

I do not know whether you have heard from Mason recently. He was thinking of trying to talk you into writing another gallant little novel for me jointly with him. I would, of course, be delighted if this project were to materialize.

With all good wishes,

Yours,

Maurice

Realizing he was in out of his depth, and feeling the need to protect himself from Girodias, Mason found an experienced French agent, Helena Strassova, to interpret the situation. She discussed making a contract with Terry and Mason whereby she would represent *Lollipop* exclusively. Meanwhile, an agent named Cindy Degener at Curtis Brown's New York office began taking an interest in Terry and his work. Degener soon signed on with the Sterling Lord agency, which handled a lot of Curtis Brown's clients in the States — including Mason's friend, Jack Kerouac. Terry would follow Degener there, but not in time to have Lord vet either the memo Mason had signed or the upcoming contract from Girodias.

Mason wrote Terry from Paris on February 22, 1961:

Dear T,

. . . Yesterday I found [an agent] that seems quite adequate. I had a good long talk with her. She's had dealings with Gid, doesn't quite share my pessimistic paranoia about him. She looked at the contract which caused her to cackle with mirth and roll her White Russian eyes incredulously. She pointed out a few bits about it I hadn't picked up on, i.e. it doesn't even mention title of the book, can be interpreted as referring to anything you or I might ever write in the future; and it doesn't contain any expiration date or clause enabling us to renegotiate or break off if dissatisfied. In short it stinks.

I'm convinced we should use her and hope you'll agree. I'm enclosing necessary papers to this end. You keep copy with her signature, sign bottom of other copy and return to me. I sign it and bring it to her at which point she's authorized to represent us and draw up a proper contract with Gid. I imagine you'll have some questions about what we're signing with her and so I won't deliver our signed copy to her until they're ironed out.

Phyllis

Terry wrote to Girodias in mid-February, telling him he wanted to have his agent (whom he didn't identify) have a look at the situation, and to let him know that he and Mason believed that they should participate more in the profits — especially if *Candy* were published in the United States. Girodias's negative response — and reasons for it — expressed a position he would repeat often in the years to come, not only to Terry and Mason but to all his disgruntled authors:

7, Rue Saint-Séverin, Paris 5e, 24th February, 1961

Dear Terry:

I saw Mason yesterday and feel I must again try to clarify matters as there seems to be some misunderstanding between the three of us which I am anxious to clear.

You will certainly remember that *Candy* was a book written on commission. We agreed on a round sum which was paid to you in several installments before I received the manuscript (which, incidentally, was delivered a year after the agreed date). The book turned out to be of a quality definitely superior to what I expected but this, of course, did not afford larger sales than those we average with our other titles. In fact, it sold more slowly — precisely because it is written with a sense of humour which is entirely lacking in most of our customers. The first edition is not yet out of print although published two or three years ago. In short, although I am overjoyed to have had occasion to publish such a good book, it has not been a profitable venture so far. The fact that it was banned in France does not really affect our problems but it did cause some additional trouble and expense.

I have tried to explain to Mason that there are two attitudes possible with regard to the commercial potentialities of this book. It would be entirely legitimate for me to consider that the book having been commissioned for a definite sum, all rights belong to me. It would also be possible for Mason and you to argue that the book being the result of your joint efforts, all further publication rights belong to you. Actually, both attitudes would be morally and legally justified — although it would be quite difficult to get any court to designate the rightful owner of the publication rights. Indeed, we never made a proper contract providing for possible reprint and translation rights.*

. . . No literary agent in the world will be able to do as much as I can do to persuade various foreign publishers as well as English-language publishers to buy the rights from us: you must certainly know by now that literary agents are passive intermediaries between authors and publishers and I do not see the advantage you would gain from the intervention of an agent to whom you would have to pay a commission of 10% or more on your share of the profits.

In short, this is all a matter of trust and fair dealing. I am not asking more than a very reasonable share of the spoils. Nor do I see any reason in our past relations which would justify your distrust of our methods. I therefore ask you to reconsider the problem as a whole. I suggest that we draw up a contract between the two of you and Olympia which would stipulate [the] division of all proceeds. . . .

Yours,

Maurice

Back on the farm in Canaan, where Terry was juggling feeding the chickens and "the inf" (who had just turned one), Terry began exploring the kind of writing he had described in his Guggenheim grant application — one which used a first-person narration "as a *human* and *personal* narration, instead of a *literary* one." Exploring this impulse, Terry would soon be writing the scene with what Tom Wolfe dubbed "a new kind of journalism," one that would capture Terry's interest much more than mapping out the logistics of a book that apparently had no future.

---

*Girodias reiterated the terms he was proposing for a new contract in this letter: one-third for reprints, while Olympia would take one-fourth of all translated editions. Authors would divide a 12 percent royalty.

Chapter 19

Getting the Kaiser on Paper

In late February 1961, Terry returned to Mason the agent agreement they had both signed with Helena Strassova in France, believing that Mason would follow through with her, but he did not.

Paris, 25 February, 1961

Dear T.

. . . Here's what's been happening: when I went to see Gid the day after my chat with Strassova, armed with plenty of pertinent questions, he came on partly yukity yuk yuk, don't you trust ol uncle Gid, and partly (whenever I tried to pin him down to above questions) like Lee J. Cobb in "On The Waterfront. Whadya nuts or something?" he said in effect, and "Look, this is taking too long," and "Oy I have a stomach-ache — get the fuck out of here." He also mentioned that the paper he had sent us to sign was *not* the contract he had in mind (contradicting what he'd told me on my previous visit several weeks ago which had been what had caused me to warn you not to sign and gotten me started on suspecting all kinds of monky business), but merely a preliminary agreement enabling him to deal immediately with Longanesi. Also, when I asked about what was meant by "Agents as well as Publishers on original editions" (a phrase which Strassova had pointed out could be viewed as referring to *other* books since he neglects to mention any titles), he said this was an error of his secretary and should have read ". . . the original edition." (But, I wondered, in that case why mention it at all since he is, obviously, Publisher of the original edition, unless as "Agent" he wants to cop a further percentage or fluke the contracts that might come up?) I asked timidly for clarification on this point. "This is taking too long," he said, rising from his chair and rustling the papers on his desk energetically, "Get out, you crazy, impudent fuck!"

I emerged from this interview feeling confident that the meeting with Strassova was our best way of handling the thing and promptly mailed the papers to you.

Next, I slyly invited Gid's secretary to luncheon at my expense, having had a hot fantasy about throwing her one of my smoking, dock-walloping blasters, and when I shift into the final beanball cloverleaf she sobs out all the info on sales, sources, and shyster-clauses. Instead, she ate a very hearty luncheon and presented an impassioned defense of Gid which got me to wondering whether I hadn't been a bit carried away and gotten paranoic over what might have been essentially a difficulty in communications. . . . She advised me to write [Girodias] a nice letter, stating our position, have it countersigned by you. This was a cooler way to handle him, she said, than face to face when he had a tendency to blowtop at the slightest pretext like A. Hitler.

She also gave me pause on the case of N. Rubington ("Fuzz Against Junk"). Now I've been lushing it up with Rubington most every afternoon, and his story with Gid being remarkably similar to our own. . . . One of his complaints had been that Gid had slipped an ad for his frigging restaurant [the Grande Séverine had been rebuilt] into the back page of "Fuzz" starting out, "If you enjoyed this book you will enjoy a good dinner at la Grande Séverine etc." When Norm protested Gid said "Get out! This is taking too long. Oy!" Norm got a lawyer (who pointed out that it would take years to win the case since contract had been handled through Gid's Swiss agent for "tax purposes." . . . However, at mere notice from the lawyer that he was starting proceedings, Gid deflated and promised to pull out the ad. This is similar to his modification of tone since we've been balking and hinting of agents, because after all, this new letter of his (obviously written after his secretary recounted our luncheon conversation) is a good bit straighter then he's been coming on heretofore. It even contains a concession — 12% royalties on any new editions Olympia does of "Candy." . . . She [Girodias's secretary] had said vaguely at one point, "Now let's see, has Candy gone 2 or 3 editions?" (Gaït, of the Eng. Book Shop, says "Lollypop" is one of her best sellers among Gid's books, with orders coming in from the States etc.) *He* says in his letter that the first edition (5000 copies?) is not yet exhausted. Who knows? . . .

I'm not sure what to think now so let me know soon which course you favor and your reasons. Please write me businesslike like you do to Gid. I mean I found your last to be a bit light-hearted and kidding around, and as long as I'm becoming an obsessed maniac and forking out for Chinese luncheons (your share=2,700 francs [$5.40]) you could at least give me the benefit of your shrewd, hill-billy reasoning.

What happened to your anthology? Trok snort it all up? I find out a little more about contracts and I might publish it myself on condition it contain creative writing by me.

Hang on to Gid's newest letter. It might come handy in court and my copy's unsigned.

Emil

The due date for *Candy*'s first royalty statement (February 28th) came and went without a peep from Girodias. At the end of March, Mason sent a handwritten note to Terry about finalizing the agreement with Olympia.

Paris, March 27th, 1961

Dear Terry,

A slight delay in answering your last letter since we were preparing to leave for Easter Vacation in La Camargue which is where we now are, enjoying the beaches & horses and ever thinking of our dear pal Terry Southern, since this desolate swampland reminds us so often of his own home-state of Mississippi were it not that the stagnant canals don't contain no putrid corpses of negroes caught red-handed being uppity with gentle folks.

As for our business deal with Girodias: I used my judgement as you suggested, and told him that his last letter seemed to suggest that perhaps we could now come to a contractual agreement and that he should therefore, submit this contract, or a faithful synopsis of it, to us with the understanding that there might be a few final points to be haggled over.

Perhaps you have now received such a document and mine is in my letter-box at Paris — I left there a week ago. If this is the case, you will no doubt let me know aussitôt if there's anything you feel should be included or excluded. and I shall do the same, dear pal, the very goddamn same.

I expect to be back in Paris after 7 April, ready to get some good sober work done on our negotiations with Gid during the relaxed Spring season in Paris. As soon as a satisfactory termination is achieved in our dealings with Olympia I fully intend to fly to Blackberry River with my beloved loved ones for a well-earned New England & Autumn full of the winey sapo of vermillion maple leaves and pork sausage.

Shacknasty Jim

Mason was spending more time at Girodias's rebuilt club and quite enjoying himself. Girodias apparently sent Mason contracts which were never received. After updating Terry on happenings in Paris, he tells Terry to be on the lookout for contracts from Girodias as well.

Paris, Mayday 1812

Terry, I have known you now how long? Whole epochs have transpired since fate (or was it luck?) brought us together.

Is this any reason why you should just now, when things are finally breaking our way, neglect to answer a perfectly reasonable message, keep me waiting a month of Sundays? What would it be like if the U.S. Coast Guard took to responding in this leaden-ass manner?

Paris was really rocking with new faces, exploding police-stations, and big, rangy, Mach.12 headlines all month.* Mr Hadj, Mr. Zoom, and Violet Charly are no longer with us — Society's gain is our loss. . . . Gid gave a heroic party It was to celebrate Gregory's new book, "American Express." I understand not even Gre-

*During the Algerian war in Paris, as Meeske recalls, "You never knew when bombs were going to explode. I never gave it a thought . . . [but] Miriam Worms lost her eye."

gory has read it. While there, I met a man from Longanesi's "in Paris for a few days to sign contracts with Gid" . . .

Also, I have taken a great liking to Gid. We have been juicing it up and if you ever saw a royalty check to the tune of the whiskey he has sprung for it would do your heart good.

Furthermore, I'm not sure how much longer his press is fated to continue since he could crack up legally, or just nervously, at some constantly accelerating point in the near future.

For old time's sake then, if not for the above reasons, will you please stop beating your meat and reply whether you received two copies to sign and send to me of a contract of which a copy was sent to me to sign and send to you for your records which was stolen from my mailbox so that I have not as yet read it but am sure we should stop diddling round and unless there's something gravely the matter with it would you kindly stop beating your meat?

Ian

In early May, a note handwritten on Deux Magots stationery came from Mason, saying he had gone over the terms with Girodias (probably at the café) and they seemed okay. He also enclosed fresh copies of the contract for Terry to sign.

Paris, May 9, 1961
Date your letters like I do, you nut.

. . . As a general rule, I propose that we not joke about business affairs — at any rate not in a way to cause ambiguities. Humor is not that funny.

. . . I'm going to Gid's presently and will ask him about Frnc [an additional sum] as you suggested.

I finally read the contract and it seems all right to me. Besides, I no longer give a shit & feel we should get on with another Maxwell Kenton book. I hope to God I will write you soon with ideas for this matter.

Couquite is knocked up higher'n a kite and I would like to have an MS done when her time comes — Christmas, that is. If you see anything funny so far in this letter go right ahead and have a good chuckle, honey, but for purposes of lucid communication I swear to Christ that there are to my knowledge, no such jokes intended. . . .

Nothing that startling has happened here, and I can't say I mind as the least little histoire in my vicinity muddles my cool.

Mason

P.S. Gid says money should be there pretty soon
P.S. Initial first page of contract as I did

At the Deux Magots with Mason, no doubt over a bottle of wine, Girodias took up pen and added a note of his own to this most informal of cover letters for a contract. It simply said, "Love, MG."

At the tiny post office at the end of Lower Road, Terry received, countersigned, and immediately sent the contracts to Girodias with a handwritten note asking for money.

Blackberry River, May 15, 1961

Dear Gid:

Due to the urgency expressed in your *recommandé*, I am foregoing the usual formality attendant on such business affairs, and jotting this note at the post office itself, so as to return the contracts *by return of post* as you requested. I am sending both copies to you, since Mason's boite du lettre is quite obviously not the place to send anything of value or interest whatever, due to his involvement in extreme right-wing French politics. Can you please dispatch me as large an amount of money as possible, preferably by return of post. We are really getting on to another classic Kenton now and do require sustenance funds to see it through.

Is it true about the Olympia Press Magazine? [*Olympia Review*] Can you give more details?

Best wishes,

Terry S.

The contract Terry signed and returned had the one-third split for all editions in English, with Olympia taking one-quarter of all translations. The document began with the following point:

> 1) The Publishers being the owners of all publication rights pertaining to the Work by virtue of the outright royalty paid to the Authors when the Publishers commissioned the said work NOW FURTHER AGREE AS FOLLOWS:

Terms two through seven concerned joint approval of translations, the 12 percent royalty, as well as an "outright royalty" for the first edition, how payments were due (on June 30 and December 31 of each year), Girodias's option to purchase the next two books by "Maxwell Kenton," and how the agreement shall "automatically terminate" if Publisher fails to pay on time, or "if such default is not rectified by the Publishers within one month of receipt of the Authors' written notification."

And so the authors finally had a legal document parsing out the publication rights to their work. The question remained whether Girodias would pay any attention to it.

Chapter 20

The *Olympia Review*

As Terry and Mason were dealing with the contracts, Girodias was launching his new literary magazine, *Olympia Review.* Terry liked the idea of contributing to it, especially since Mason was serving as editor (Girodias first approached Allen Ginsberg for the editor post, but according to Mason he "went off to Tangiers irresponsibly"). Terry thought to contribute topical material — a cross between investigative reporting and personal observation. The title for a potential series was suggested by Mason: *The Spy's Corner.* Terry responds:

Blackberry River, June 7, 1961

Dear Mace:

That was a nice publicity-release about the mag you sent — the moment I read "obtain" in queer usage I knew you were in and I was out. I wonder if you aren't pushing your luck a little — the brushoff is a game two can play. Goodby and good luck (maybe you'll need it).

Fed Nash

Actually though I have worked with the Meeske before and know her to have a great head (try and get some of it, big boy, you may find a saucey comeuppance for your pains) and it looks as if you are setting up a billion dollar staff there in Paris, France (how about Jacques Stern for "Freak Shoot-Off Editor"? HAW HAW!)

I like the idea of Spy's Corner and feel I could make a go of it if money is real and forth obtains. How much outside material would I be expected to uncover for the balance? I can understand Gid's point of view in wanting where possible to pay off in BIG FROG COCK instead of money, but this simply cannot obtain in my own case due to strap.

Please consolidate my position there, without forgetting who is your real friend and true

Terry

Press for early Longassi settlement.

In a letter of early June, Mason gave Terry some guidelines for "Spy's Corner" submissions;

Paris, June 10th, 1961

Dear Tacky,

Got your letter today and showed it to G. Marilyn [Meeske] has now arrived and the three of us had a conference the other day about the magazine trying to decide what the fuck is happening. . . .

The magazine's to circulate mainly in the states, so can't be quite as juicy as some of the Olympia Books. Figure just a teentsy filthier than what is presently acceptable in Evgreen, Greasy Table [Big Table] etc. . . .

A. Truck [Trocchi] was in Paris briefly, mentioned that you'd "stolen" the anthology material . . . he was pretty steamed up in general, and seems to be in one of the most fucked up positions imaginable chemically, legally, domestically; but will no doubt land on his feet since he's a battling s.o.b.

See you soon

Big baboon

Yitzhak

The *Olympia Review* was to be a bold magazine challenging the conservative status quo in Paris, pushing the limits of "decency." In the second issue, Girodias would later define its (and his) mission:

> The purpose of Olympia Press has been, in the past ten years, to demonstrate that censorship has no valid reason to persist in a modern society. The purpose of this review is to push the demonstration even further, and suppress once and for all the old beliefs that certain things can be said, and others not; that art should coincide with morality; and that governments are qualified to play the role of spiritual mentors.

After a month in his new position, Mason wrote to Terry in the summer of 1961 describing problems at the *Olympia Review.* Mason wanted to use an introductory essay by Takis, the sculptor, on "behind the scene dirty work in the world of Art Galleries." Mason wrote:

> Think of it, a long poem in the first issue which immediately pegged the beatnick school for the worthless horseshit it is 90% of the time, a poem which would intimidate the readers and which they wouldn't be able to put down! Now you can stop thinking of it because Gid did put it down, and Takis' article too, for being criminally unsmutty.
>
> This experience depressed me and confused me.
>
> Along about there was the arrival of M. Meeske. Any illusions I may have had about how I would now have a buddy with whom to discuss the mag, engage a fruitful dialog etc., were rapidly dissipated. For me, she had a patronizing, insulting, maddening attitude — the head nurse's relationship with harmless Uncle Bob, oldest and battiest schizo in the hopeless ward; and for Gid, the bar none, most deadly nose of brazen brown I've observed in my life (which includes, as you know, 34 months in The Air Corps). Furthermore, I had adapted the infamous Sammy Glick as my hero and model, and had been shyly emulating him and feeling my way into

the role. . . . Well, my half Glick grew pale and wilted quite away in the scorching blasts of the true master which is Marilyn of the Bullshit Art.

Give you an idea: She, Gid and I are seated in his office having a mag Conference. Her behavior at such moments is so despicable I gag at the thought of it. One of her tricks (occurs when Gid and I are both speaking at once) is to raise her palm in my direction like a traffic cop. This is a rapid, seemingly involuntary gesture, and accompanied by a holy smile of trance and admiration in *his* direction. "Oh! Oh hark! Oh don't interfere the slightest teentsyweentsy bit with these glorious words which are causing mine eyes to sparkle with a tear of delight," is what she seems to be saying. Next, I propose an idea for the mag.:

> Mason: How about putting a piece of SEXUS in the first number? (Marilyn makes the face that invariably greets my suggestions. It says, "You know, you really should do something about this habit you have of saying anything that pops into your head." Gid says nothing.)
>
> Gid: (breaks the silence) — I just thought of a short piece that Miller wrote . . . I can't remember the name, but it would be perfect for the magazine.
>
> Marilyn: Has anybody here read *Max and the White Phagocytes?* It's *fabulous;* the greatest thing he ever wrote . . .
>
> Gid: Oh, now I remember the name of that story; it's called *Via Dieppe — New Haven*. It's excellent!
>
> Marilyn: (flipping) — Where he crosses the channel? BUT THAT'S EXACTLY WHAT I WAS TALKING ABOUT! THAT'S THE ONE I MEANT! IT'S FABULOUS! GID, YOU HAVE TO USE THAT ONE IN THE FIRST ISSUE. IT'S THE ONE I MEANT WHEN I SAID *MAX AND THE WHITE PHAGOCYTES!*
>
> Gid: (drily) If it was in *Max and the White Phagocytes,* then it's already been published in the States. We couldn't use it.
>
> Marilyn: Yes, well I didn't mean —
>
> Gid: We only want things that have never been published in the States.

Marilyn: Yes, of course. If it was in *Max And The White Phagocytes* we couldn't use it in the magazine.

Gid: That wasn't a bad idea of Mason's, to use something from *Sexus.* We should have something of Miller.

Marilyn: And it will be coming out just when everyone is talking about Miller, just after the trial for *The Tropic of Cancer.* (getting excited) My God! Think of that publicity! And not only that, but *Sexus* hasn't ever been published in the States. They've never seen it. Why, that's a wonderful idea! *What do you think of that* idea, Mason?

Thus the days passed, and the time approached when my salary for the first month was going to be due. "Have you heard from Terry?" Gid would ask occasionally. "Yes," I would say, "he wants to know what's happening with the money from Longanesi. I'm a bit curious about it myself. Should be coming in any day now," he said.

And the time arrived when my salary was due. Nothing happened. I waited a couple of days and then asked for my money. "I'm broke," he said. "What is this shit?" I screamed. "I'm walking around borrowing money to eat lunch with. I only have seventy-eight francs [thirty-nine cents] . . ."

He then gave me three mille [$6.00].

He sure is funny about loot. By hammering away at the problem, hounding him shamelessly, I have now (July 11) gotten most of my June salary. The Longanesi thing began to occupy my thoughts more and more, and I took to browsing in the filing cabinet when I was alone in the office to see if the answer mightn't be contained with all those papers and stuff. And by George, a couple of days ago I found it! A nice letter from Longanesi saying, "We have received *Lollypop* contract. Enclosed, our check for 150,000 [$300]." Or something to that effect. I haven't been able to find this letter again, but I have the distinct impression it was dated *March 15!* A question of months ago, at any rate. . . .

Lilian

Regarding work on the *Olympia Review,* Marilyn Meeske remembers things differently. After having been away from the office for a month or two, finding the old "River Styx" man posted there was a shock. She recalls, "I was surprised to find Mason — who really had never worked — in an office. We did not like Mason to be around finally."

In early July, Mason sent Terry a copy of the 1959 edition of *Candy,* which he had apparently never seen. This was the edition that Girodias had creatively altered to avoid the vice squad. Terry must not have examined it very closely, having been stopped cold by the dedication page: "To Master Boon and Master Badj." In his letter to Mason about it, Terry also could not resist the temptation to satirize the news of Ernest Hemingway's suicide, even though Hemingway was an inspiration to him.

Blackberry River, July, 1961

My dear Hoff:

Just a quick note to say danke for the copy of C. (who was the empty-head, I wonder, who changed the dedication from Hadj and Zoon to its present nonsensical and unfunny form? Let us by all means get this corrected for future reprints) and, too (danke) for your Mom Hoff's check, which saved us here at Black.

Am getting on with a solid Spy's Corner and hope to have that to you in an early post. . . .

An interesting sidelight on the recent death of Ernest Hem., straight from the horse's mouth (Miss Mary) though doubtless as yet too hot to handle in the Corner. Anyway Big E. observed a life long practice of performing his conjugal devoir trois fois par jour, rain or shine; that is to say: once at night, once in the morning (on waking), and once in the afternoon. Lately however he had been having trouble getting it up, and so had been giving Miss Mary head instead. On this particular morning he woke Mary out of a sound and peaceful sleep, as per usual (she always regarded him as a "big boob") to perform his devoir. When he had finished, or thought he had (though in fact he had only succeeded in annoying her) he was strutting about the room, a la Mel Sabre, spouting some jargon about "going out on the terrace and tossing up a few targets for the old 12-gauge". "Why don't you use that goddamn HEAD of yours for a target, you old fruit!?!" muttered Mary sleepily.

When she heard the shot, she waited a few minutes, then called out softly: "Still got the old eye, Ernie?" No reply, and she slid back into sleep with a sigh of almost immeasurable relief.

Right?

S.

Also enclosed some possible first issue cover material.

A few days later Terry wrote to empathize with Mason's life at the Olympia Press:

Blackberry River, July 20th, 1961

My Dear Hoff:

Thanks for yours of the 14th. (Without wishing to seem the perfect rat-prick or stickler for procedural detail, may I suggest that we open our letters with an acknowledgement of receipt, *by date,* of Coros' Let., done simply enough: 'Thanks for yours of (date)' as I have done above.)

Your conference skit was hilarious, albeit of negative import. I am surprised you did not bop her one — which is, of course, precisely what you must *not* do. Perhaps a Kenton book may be in order one day based on this character portrayal, titled: SOW. In any case I am confident your own position is secure; Gid, with his well-tempered perception and canny survival instinct, cannot fail in the end to recognize your superior qualities and invaluable hipness. . . .

He will ease away from [Marilyn], on one pretext or another, probably the very one (the valueless 'yessing' which now makes them appear allied) . . . Meanwhile you must keep your cool — *no showdowns, Hoff!* Meanwhile, too, however, it is of course a big drag about the long poem and good essay not being used if for the reasons he says. Does he then plan to use nothing to give the magazine some pretension, or purport thereof, to quality Lit.? Surely he is naive to imagine it can succeed otherwise — either commercially or free of interference from the authorities. It *must* have support from *some* responsible quarter; otherwise no coverage in Time mag! Even such magazines as Escapade, Nugget, Cavalier, etc. maintain a ration of about 1-4 (one no-smut to four smut) and those like Evergreen about 50/50. Even if the non-smut is regarded as mere filler, there is every reason to make it as good as possible, so as, as I say, to win some degree of support as a magazine of 'literary pretensions.'

When I 'stole' the anthology from Trok, at the peak of his criminal irresponsibility, Dick Seaver, of Grove press, came in as the third editor. We have become fairly good friends now, and I could show him the poem and essay that Gid refused if you would like; it might be a good object lesson to him if they were accepted by Evergreen.

I am sending the last copy of Evergreen. Note interesting writing by John Rechy — I have written him for material too. . . . It would be good, by the way, if you could send me some OPR [Olympia Press Review] stationery to use in soliciting mss.

Ed

Terry was a great supporter of the *Evergreen Review,* and felt it provided the political immediacy, eroticism, and Beat sensibility that *The Paris Review* and others were lacking. Rosset had published Terry's story "Put-Down" years earlier, in which the protagonists, disaffected Americans in Paris, high on hashish, are playing on the floor with broken balls of mercury — while cutting each other to existential ribbons. While *Evergreen* continued to be a source of inspiration, Terry would within a year find his own journalistic voice writing for a magazine that had been around for years, *Esquire.*

Chapter 21

sHit Habit (#6)

On the farm in Canaan, the Southerns had very little money. Still, they were living the life they had imagined — Terry was writing, mainly for *The Nation,* making occasional forays into New York; Carol was gardening and caring for two dogs, a cat, and baby. They raised their own chickens, two black angus, and a pig, and had an organic garden. By this time Terry had written up an interview story with Boris Grugurevich, who was perhaps the only American citizen to take part in the Bay of Pigs invasion. This was to be the first Spy's Corner piece for the *Olympia Review.* He wrote Mason about it, and offered a few suggestions for dealing with Girodias and the Longanesi affair.

Blackberry River, Conn., August 17th, 1961

My Dear Good:

. . . I am enclosing the Spy's Corner copy, though I must tell you frankly that if you are not going to be involved closely, I am not keen myself — I simply do not feel that familiar with Marilyn's and Gid's taste to undertake it with any confidence that we would be serving one another's purpose in the matter. The piece, as you see, is much longer than you stipulated and I am sorry for that, but it was inherent (such a length) because of the material and its treatment; the completion of this, which I have already done, is eight pages; after that I could keep it down, no doubt, to your 3–4 pages as per specification. Considering what you have said, and considering Marilyn's letter, I am not at all sure that this piece will meet mag requirements. If this proves to be so, even vaguely, do not push it, or rather not for my sake. Dick Seaver was here and saw the whole of it, and will take it for Evergreen if it is not suitable for Olymp.; so if there is any show of ambivalence, just say, well, I'll talk to T. about it, and let it go at that (they will soon forget in a monstrous fleshing out and absorbing each other in their gross passion — Marilyn's passion for Gid is *feigned;* Now she only digs young freaky cats who will let her eat their waste.)

Under the circumstances (of your own ambiguous engagement at the mag, and Evergreen on tap (for $225), and the fact that I am not keen to continue if your engagement *is*, in point of fact, ambiguous) I would have to insist, regarding this copy, *that any editorial changes, other than those which you yourself would approve, be submitted for my okay.* I know that sounds like a lot of pompous horseshit cunt cock crap, and it only occurs to me because I know that Marilyn, given an ounce of power, can behave as though she is suddenly omniscient. Moreover, this (copy) has a strong interest here, much stronger probably than is recognized in Europe, because of all the interest in the affair. It is, after all, the *first account* of the Cuban Fiasco *by one of the participants.*

King B. [Boris Grugurevich] was back, on 'leave,' and it was through him that I got much of the info.; now he is back in Guata., sucking young darks.

Regarding the use of an excerpt from Candy, *do* inform our *agent* [Strassova] of this; let *her* handle it, as, indeed, she *should* be handling the Longanesi affair. Why isn't she? That just occurred to me . . . and would have spared your elaborate mentality all that fucking around. What did you do, pay her in head and then get cross?

Speaking of pay, if the Spy copy doesn't go through, I can send you the 50 by return o'post, you grand thing! Later!

Gretchen

Mason wrote back that Terry's concern over Girodias and Meeske's editorial meddling was justified: "It's not just that they're unscrupulous," he wrote, "they're dumb sometimes, and both would instantly fall on their ass if the English language was something you needed in order to walk." Mason's life at Olympia was becoming evermore Kafkaesque for him, and he was afraid he was going to be fired.

Paris, August 23rd, 1961

Dear T.

. . . Gave me a bit of a start, your proposal to have "our agent" intervene. We don't have one. I thought you knew that. That letter you once signed to retain Strassova was just in case we decided to go through with the idea. When all that agent talk started was when G. sent us that nice long letter about how we had to "trust" one another and all that shit, and proposed the more or less legitimate contract which we eventually signed. Incidentally, I compared our contract with those for the other books involved in the Longanesi affair, which was a package deal, and that part's okay, it's identical, only one guy was smart enugh to stipulate that Longanesi should send him his loot directly and not have it go through G.

Which brings me to some cheerful news. Shortly before G. left I reminded him in a kindly way that I'd sent you your share and would it be all right if I finally started drawing this money. This he agreed to quite reasonably just as if it was the first time the matter had come up. I'm not sure why he suddenly shifted. Could be that Marilyn might have pointed out that I'd probably seen the Longanesi letter in the files which stated that payment had been made May 15. It could be also that he's got some little quirk about never giving money to anyone but if you find out the magic, hocus-pocus word — which is "comptable"* in this case — then his hands are tied and he has to give it to you. Because I went through this same bit with my salary, asking and whining, and having him give me three mille [$6.00] and a story, until one of the secretaries tipped me off that I could just go to the accountant and get huge gobs of loot. That's what I'm doing now anyhow with the Longanesi loot. I guess Gid just can't stand the sight of the loot escaping him *physically.* As long as he doesn't know about it it's all right, like a two-

*French for accountant

timed husband. I'll have my Mom send you a check for $62.50 therefore which, with the other 50, accounts for your half of our 3/4ths of the 150,000 francs [$300]. There'll be another payment within 90 days of publication which will represent the rest of whatever half the royalties on the first printing comes to. No doubt there will be a slight delay while this seeps through Girodias, but we can always write [Longanesi].

Mason signs off by steering Terry's Cuba piece away from Girodias, who apparently had been expecting something more "grotesque":

If Evergreen would pay $225 (without an "histoire") then you're right in not wanting to get involved in any kind of complications whatsoever with G. . . . No great harm done. It might be Miss Slut Slime herself, that you hear from in this connection, but the result will be the same.

That's it

Jessica

Terry continued to include Mason in his projects, asking him to help transform his "Beyond the Shadows" into a film or television script for Lew Allen. It was based on an outline Terry had written in Geneva, "The Ring," about an acting coach who, through Svengali-like control over one of his more intense students, produces a murderer. The acting assignment is to "be" a character for twenty-four hours, and the teacher, Manheim, encourages one student to be a vampire. In Terry's character descriptions, one is clearly based on Candy, the other, perhaps, on Girodias.

CANDY BARR — a pretty girl of 20–25 with a middle-class background. There is a unique freshness and trust in her manner, and a striking ingenuousness. Cheerful and optimistic without being vivacious, innocent without being prudish; she has a keen native intelligence and a natural sense of taste and propriety. It is this combination of directness and spontaneity with a wholesome innocence which sets her apart, make her sympathetic and genuinely humorous; unlike the characters portrayed by Judy Holliday and Marilyn Monroe, she is neither vulgar nor prudish.

MANHEIM — the director of the Actor's Workshop. He is middle-aged, European, with a very strong personality, at times almost hypnotic. His manner is flamboyant and eccentric; he is perhaps a genius, perhaps a charlatan; of the fact that he has great persuasive powers and a prophet-like talent for leadership there is no doubt.

By late August, Mason finally did send some suggestions for the script, but Terry was already well past the speculation stage and soon finished it without him. Mason wrote:

> The pressure you mention about the $$ script is a pity since those things take plenty of time to ripen in the head — you remember I daresay that Candy took 6 years to write and has got room for improvement. . . .
>
> What little I've been able to think of, in the sorry state I've been in with my frontbrain a shambles of clashing discordination from all the terrible things they pulled on us JEWS, is now coming up. . . .
>
> Gitou

By September, as Terry and Mason anticipated, Girodias rejected Terry's Boris/Cuba piece for the *Olympia Review.* In a letter of October 7, 1961, Mason tells of how he "spent three weeks at the seashore kicking a nervous little sHit Habit (#6) in record time, which I'd contracted while absentmindedly fixing . . ." He then gave Terry a lively update on the Paris scene, which included "sympathetic young beatnicks from many lands . . . guitars, pot, earrings; great spades from the village and the South . . . Limeys talking fluent hiptalk . . . suddenly, passing by, who I thought must have really died since I'd not seen him in so very long, not looking much older then in the old days, old Sun [Mr. Soun] did not recognize me, or pretended not to. Not one of the young beatnicks saluted their old grandpappy either."

Mason signs off expressing certain relief at leaving the *Review:*

Gid and I go down for a warm, personal drink; then, having cordially fired me, we have warm intimate handshake and best of the warm personal wishes for the future. God, what a prince! He pointed out how the hot gick of Marilyn's loathsome grunty had clotted his heart past any of the occasional thrills he might have received from the unpractised probings of my own uncertain brown-nose.

As Mason relates in the following letter, Girodias was distributing *Candy* to bookshops — suggesting that the ban was not being strictly enforced at the time. Despite their signed contract with Girodias, no money was forthcoming. Terry suggested to Mason that they approach the agent Sterling Lord. As Lord recalled, "Terry came to me asking if I could get him out of the Girodias contract and that's what we did — citing lack of payment." With Lord and his wife, Cindy Degener, who specialized in film, at his side, Terry's literary horizons were expanding on various fronts in the States. Mason's horizons, however, seemed to be contracting, and he became ever more desperate to work creatively with Terry again.

Fall, 1961

Dear T.

Return of p.[post] is how you continue to rate with me, Jim, even though you recklessly let entire seasons take their course before replying to my messages, thereby squandering the luck of the last of the Kentons.

How are things working out in Conn? Not too warm as toast, I take it. We too are prey to the sinister chill of Winter and depend, in our struggle against damp, on two highly unreliable and stinking mazout stoves put out by The Cro Magnon Warmth Company — "35,000 years of experience. Smoke Is Our Product!"

I frequently wonder if it wouldn't be nice to get an old farm in New England, with all these children I'm getting, and do some writing, grow a few steaks for my own use. It certainly would simplify our task if I were close enough to exchange chapters with you as I got to the end of my furrow.

Let's be realistic though and by all means lay keel on a new moneymaker story, even if it entails mailing carbons.

I agree there's no particular point in dealing with G. with his highly unethical way of operating and limited market. I think (speaking of ethics) that we should root swinishly in Candy for matter and ideas, producing, not so much a sequel as a different treatment. I'm not thinking so much of lifting the actual plot, or specific incidents, but the format and, particularly Candy's character and the general tone. Start her off with (Cherry?) joining the Peace Corps and getting sent to some unspeakable pig wallow of a country in arctic Asia. . . .

This wouldn't be Chap I necessarily which might be needed to establish C. in some family, and hometown romance situation (such as the town humpback). After that, the general rule would be to follow the "Candy" idea — around the world and through History with our bobby-socks sweetcrotch enduring various violations, brushing against the major movements and intellectual groups, and sustained by her tried and true philosophy i.e. "Well, it was my own fault, darn it." As I see it, there's quite a bit of material we didn't hit in "Candy" such as astronauts, Marxists, Castro, Olympic Games . . . there's the whole world baby, and, as I say, in a pinch we can always redo something from "Candy" mit a slight change like Quakers=Zen. The big danger is a certain monotony in the pattern: can't simply repeat the damn thing every chapter. Not that I think Candy did that, but that that's The problem.

For reasons contractual, we'd need another nom de plume since Max is tied up with Gid. . . . It would even give us the chance to think up a gogetter monicker serving as a sub-title and eye-catching sales inducement.

By the way, Gait [a bookstore owner in Paris] called to my attention that she no longer receives "Lollypops" but the original "Candy". Looks like he's scraping bottom and that the re-edition clause will soon be coming into play with plenty of sheckles any time we want to bring suit to get them.

New book will take years no doubt. All the more reason for starting pronto and leaving us a breather in our senescence in which to cash in on fame with Lit. chairs at Vasser and Smith. Old Man Pace resolves the Race.

Yolanda

Chapter 22

The Naked and the Sucked

Mason was envious of Terry's life of farming and writing. He downplayed his visits to the pastoral Dordogne region, writing, "When I think of 'country' I think of lovely New England, and not this chewed-out, under-wooded grime-strewn European Agricultural Community pock-marked with bomb craters and containing monotonous ranks of endives and peasant wine." But things were still very much a struggle for the Southerns in Canaan, and throughout the winter of 1961–62, they lived mainly on canned tomatoes and whatever Terry brought back from hunting, usually venison or rabbit. Mason's updates revealed his tenacity; he was actually getting blood from the stone Girodias:

Paris, February 6, 1962

Dear Terr,

Something seems to be up Longanesiwise. Few weeks ago, dropping in the office on other business, I noted the Longanesi edition of the Parker Tylor/Charles-Henri Ford book, "The Naked And Sucked" or whatever it's called, which was part of the four-title package deal containing "Candy" which Gid sold them. Which shows that they were merely buying up these properties to keep them from competition or to stash them towards some vague point of liberlized mores in the future. I was prompted to make some innocent query about the status of "Candy" — had it also been published? — and God and his secretaries shot their hands to their temples and moaned rhythmically as is their custom whenever it transpires that loot is to be paid *out.*

If you've had any separate info on this matter, or any communication with rue St. Séverine regarding it, for gawd sake fill me in and let's keep level. Because I assume we'll have to combine in some foxy con to get what's coming to us — he'll simply do nothing about it as long as he possibly can unless some pressure can be borne through legal threat or enticement of lit. properties of the future jeopardized by outraged authors.

You might, for a starter, mention in a letter to the office that a friend in Rome had his order for Candy accepted by bkstore and [that] soon delivery would take place. So far I've gotten as far as to have Gitou, No. 1 frog secretary, mumble something guiltily about having to "write a letter" to Milano for some un-named purpose before loot would be forthcoming. As you remember, our contract calls for a second payment upon publicatione. . . .

Yours,

Catherine

In early February of 1962, Berkley Publishers contacted Terry directly, seeking to reprint an excerpt from *Candy* in an anthology to be titled *Banned #2*. Terry did not consult Lord for this extremely small deal, clarifying some aspects as best he could:

Blackberry River; February 8th, 1962

Mr. Thomas A. Dardis
Berkley Publishing Corp.
101 Fifth Avenue; New York, 3, N.Y.

Dear Tom:

Enclosed is the agreement. You will note that I have deleted the word "author" in Para. #3. When you spoke of "public domain," I understood, of course, that you were referring to *your* position as a publisher *vis a vis Olympia*. However, as one of the authors of the work, I certainly do claim, on behalf of the authors, proprietary rights — even looking forward, in fact, to the improbable day when the book in its entirety may be published here. I could hardly be expected then to sign any sort of formal waiver of this proprietorship. With the enclosed agreement, however, and pursuant to its terms, you have been granted permission to use the piece. Surely that is sufficient. Right?

I would still prefer that the piece be presented as "an excerpt from the novel *Candy* (or *Lollipop*) by Maxwell Kenton" (with an asterick and the author's names, etc.) so as to bring attention to the novel itself. I should think this would be to your own advantage as well since you could then note that the work had been banned not merely in America but also in France (necessitating the title change). In other words, this is doubly hot stuff! . . .

Please let me know your feeling about these suggestions.

Sincerely,

Terry Southern

In March, Mason wrote to thank Terry for hooking him up with Sterling Lord. While deconstructing the Italian payments and studying the Girodias correspondence, he repeated his burning desire to break with Girodias.

Paris, March 14, 1962

. . . G. is such a squirmy man when it comes to payday and flooky contracts that I feel most strongly we should attempt to break the contract at the first opportunity, and even lull him into unsuspiciously trying to diddle us by being our usual imbecilic selves. "C" might be a tidy item in the States in the not too far ahead, as you were the first to point out, and I am dead certain G would lead us a merry chase and screw the fucking daylight as is his repeatedly proven nature.

Adieu,

Barry

Mason, at age forty, "balling it up" in Spain, continues to trade off one vice for another — as writing projects continue to elude him:

Paris, April 24th, 1962

Dear pal in the U.S.:

Just back from Spain where we hit on a town inhabited solely by friendly U.S., German and Brit millionaires, and where I became a new and better man.

After a while, dear wife and kids were obliged to return to Paris and I was able to devote myself devotedly to balling it up, falling madly in love with two gorgeous California high-school chicks and 72 year-old Brit poet-lady. Just swimming, laughing, fighting, and the love-juice just oozing and squirtin from my two orifices continually in bright jets of red and orange.

As a result of all this pleasure I am in the healthy pink of fine physical and moral ship — like I ran into a dozen shitfiends in Paris yesterday and had not the slightest friendly inclination. Couldn't care less. I got plenty of funny ideas also, and hope to be of some real support to you, baby, on our next meeting, in the frantic position you must be in.

Here's a little reminder of how "fair" this loathsome man was to us in the past. Do you remember when we were about to sign his contract and suggested that he cough up a lousy few hundred bucks retrospectively to bring his original "outright royalty" up to something like standard loot for what he admitted was a superior book? His answer was: ". . . the notion of sharing extra profits which Mason and you seem to favour is hardly logical."

Sweetballs

In April, Terry apparently wrote Mason that, anticipating an eventual settlement with Girodias, Sterling Lord was quietly showing the novel around and getting good but cautious reactions from U.S. publishers, some of whom were expressing concerns about racial "slurs" in the book. Mason responded:

Certainly good news was yr welcome announcement of thing finally breaking for C statewise with all the welcome bread this may imply. . . .

Not even having a copy of the contract I can't look myself but Oh BOY! It certainly would be nice if yr sharp Am. Agent could find something to break that contract now that we have State prospects. How about the fact that we didn't receive one goddamn statement so far on the book from G. in his capacity of our Lit. Agent? Because perhaps his plans to reprint now may queer, or tend to disgust Am. Publisher.

WORKWISE, if a deal goes through, I feel confident we can strengthen this book with some cool revision. "Dago greaser . . ." difficulty you mention doesn't strike me as a block of any proportions; offhand, it sounds like we could substitute sublingual exclamations (Vortch! Chark! Bumblitch!), or frog obscens in itals. (*Putain de merde! Ta bite, vite!* ZigueZIGUE!).

As I see it, and as you mention, the main change would be to jazz up the opening if possible. I have a hunch you did the first chap. while still locked in the mood of your previous novel, and that, after consid of what C. became eventually, you might get the key to this.

Leon

In the summer of 1962, to make up for lost time, Girodias decided to publish the premier two issues of the *Olympia Review* simultaneously. Terry was listed as a contributing editor of the second issue (which was banned in Paris), having helped secure an unpublished chapter of Henry Miller's *Sexus* and Mark Twain's *1601.* In issue number three, which came out in 1963, Girodias issued the following manifesto:

APOLOGY

We owe our readers many apologies: Olympia, we must admit, has had an erratic start. Following issue No 2 we had to interrupt publication . . . because a ban was pronounced against the magazine by the French government, only a few days after the first issue had been released.

The peculiar nature of this ban must be put in evidence. Our review, first of all, does not contain any material that could be classified as "pornographic" by the most demanding censorship experts. Furthermore, this review is printed in English; it has been examined

> by both the customs administration of the United Kingdom and that of the United States, and it has been admitted into these two countries — a circumstance which makes one wonder what excess of zeal can have inspired the French censors to ban Olympia on the French territory. . . .
>
> We believe that the richest source of individual experience and progress is sex — whose many cultivated variations are collectively known as "eroticism".
>
> It is our ambition to gradually evolve a new style of expression common to everything which will appear in the review — a style which will be the very style of freedom.

In his anti-censorship crusade, Girodias was as indefatigable as he was self-serving — and in this instance, he was also generous. True to his word, he instituted a $1,000 *Olympia* fiction contest prize and Jonathan Kozol was the first winner. But this did nothing to convince Mason that Girodias was not going to swindle them if *Candy* was ever published in the States. As his paranoia over Girodias's machinations intensified, Terry's interest in the whole *Candy* affair lessened.

On July 17, 1962, Girodias sent Terry and Mason the details (and terms) for the new edition of *Lollipop*. The print run would be 5,000, and the total royalty on sales, in accordance to their 1961 contract, would be 12 percent, or roughly $2,000. "It will probably take 2 or 3 years for this edition to sell out," he wrote. Royalties were due every six months, beginning in February. He ended the memo offering a $1,200 advance — of which half would be paid in four months. As Girodias had still not made good on previous monies he owed them, the memo was, from Mason's point of view, extremely suspect. Terry agreed to confront him.

Mason was especially suspicious of Girodias's statement to him that *Candy* would be reprinted in six weeks. Rather than going around to see him, Mason phoned, so Girodias wouldn't have the time to "stall and marshall his schemes . . ." and asked the publisher if, with *Candy* coming out again, it wasn't necessary, or customary, to consult with the authors first, especially since they were (according to Mason) considering "forthcoming" *Candy* volumes. With his intimate knowledge of how Girodias operated, Mason was sure Girodias's announcement of a *Candy* print run occurring "in six weeks" was a ruse designed to buy more time and another possible excuse for not paying them.

In early August, Sterling Lord wrote to Girodias introducing himself as the agent representing Terry Southern. His letter ended: "Terry has never received any statement or payments for the period ending June 30th, 1962, as promised in your contract. I wonder if you could please send that along to me." Girodias wrote back making an excuse why no such payment could be made.

The 1962 edition restored *Candy* to its original edition: gone were Girodias's odd phrasings from the first few pages. In deference to the ban, and perhaps in the hopes that it would give him squirming room with the police if caught — the back of the book had a tiny advisory: "Not to be sold in USA or UK."

With his exposure in *Esquire,* Terry's career was taking off. Mason's writing life was much less quantifiable and more fragmented, not only because he was a poet and there were fewer outlets for his work, but because he was not overly concerned about making a living. His father was a successful businessman (who distributed Buster Brown Shoes). Yet Mason needed an occupation — especially if he was going to support a drug habit. In the summer of '62, he took a job as a copy editor for Agence France Presse. This gig provided him with a repository of political, social, and simply weird information to add to what he had already stored away as a vociferous reader and student of esoteric literature and culture. Mason could spin incredible yarns with absolute credibility, and this new material had yet to see the printed page. But his grand, poetic impulses were relegated to the few and far between nights when he wasn't high or hanging out in cafés with friends. And writing while withdrawing, as he often did, was not the best technique.

No doubt Terry questioned Mason's decision to take a job; he felt Mason didn't actually *need* one, since his family supported him. Terry believed that the "writing for money" trap could dissipate or block even the greatest of talents. But Mason kept his job. He was married with children and had a stepdaughter, and he may have hoped that the job would somehow save him from falling completely into junkiedom.

As he began helping Terry break from Girodias, Sterling Lord began aggressively looking for a New York publisher for *Candy.* Peter Israel, a young, up-and-coming editor at Putnam, took an immediate interest in the book. Putnam publisher Walter Minton, his experiences with *Lolita* still fresh, decided to try to cut out Girodias by making one or both of the authors break with Girodias and do a deal with him. Whether or not Girodias knew of the American deal, he no doubt anticipated working such a possibility to his advantage.

Mason wrote to Terry wondering if they should pursue a Putnam deal (which he had apparently already mentioned as an *idée en l'air* to Girodias), or whether they should accept Girodias's latest agreement covering the new edition.

> Paris, September 24th, 1962
>
> I concluded . . . that Gid's reprinting proposal is not to be taken seriously, certainly not the delay of 6 weeks, and that the whole bit was some kind of reaction to the American offer you told me of, such as: he threatens to bring out his own edition if the publisher will not pay his price. A hype of some such kind. And agree with you that his offer of 450,000 [francs, $900] is designed to get us primed for the old diddle-aroony, mollified, numb with gratitude. . . . Therefore, I think we should consider the above loot as merely a lure and not something that could conceivably materialize by any feinting on our part. . . . we should reject his 450 in favor of the Am. Offer which would be more, n'est-ce pas, and might be jeopardized by *any* agreement with G. Or does that American deal seem to be petering out to you? Your latest letter seems a good deal less certain than the previous one. So that even G's phantasmic 450 seems more tangible and worth making commitments for?
>
> I'm confused when you indicate we could deal direct with Am. Pub. And G. could like it or lump it. If this be true it's boss news, and I urgently urge we take that course. But what about the "Lolita" episode where he successfully took on Nabakov & his Am

pubs and forced them to jig to his tune? That doesn't sound like he's so helpless in the States. . . .

I'm convinced the ideal thing would be for us to break off if we can find anything that shows he broke the contract . . . and be in a position to negotiate independently or attack him if he publishes C. without our okay.

I've still not gotten the status report I keep asking him for, on the Ital. and Olimp. Editions. After all, the contract calls for him to relinquish the rights if there isn't an Eng. Edition a year after exhaustion of the first; and it has been out of print for G. only knows how many months, but since we've no signed paper to this effect we couldn't do a thing even if a year did elapse.

Another angle — chances are the "Lollipops" actually do constitute a re-edition vis a vis the original "Candys" since it would seem he would print his usual first-printing quantity (?) in each case, and, this being the case, we never got anything on that 2nd printing and could maybe use that to cop out. Of course, he would say "prove it" and I'm not sure what we could do then. . . .

As always,

Katherine

P.S. I get the impression the O review is going badly $-wise. It's been banned in France as you may know and I picture "Uncle Gid" to be in a particularly voracious humor, and eager to make all us black folks foot the ball by conning, gauging, chiseling and gnawing away at any little sums coming in destined for the spooks. How is the revue doing in the states? Do you have the same picture? Even B. Burroughs, who usually claims to be content in his dealings with G., was bitching a bit yesterday about his loot being short and seldom.

In July 1962, Terry received a fateful assignment from *Esquire* to interview Stanley Kubrick. Terry had seen *Paths of Glory* and *The Killing* in Paris, and Kubrick had just finished what would become his breakthrough film, which was, coincidentally, *Lolita*. The decidedly removed approach Kubrick employed to portray sexual obsession was in stark contrast to Terry's literary playfulness with the subject. In the New York office Kubrick shared with his co-producer James Harris, Terry interviewed the director about the film.

> **INTERVIEWER:** Now, this is an *erotic* film — I mean, in the sense that sexual love is necessarily treated, and is sometimes in the foreground of a dramatic scene. Do you have any particular theories about the erotic?
> **KUBRICK:** Only that I think the erotic component of a story is best used as a sort of energizing force of a scene, a motivational factor, rather than being explicitly portrayed. . . . There's something so inappropriate about seeing it with an audience that it just becomes laughable.

Kubrick's artistic dilemma — that there may be something *too personal* about sex to effectively translate to the screen — so struck Terry that he instantly had the hero and plot of his next novel. *Blue Movie* would center around ahighly respected film director (not unlike Kubrick) who sets out to make a studio-backed "erotic" film ("with full vag-pen," as Terry would quip), thereby testing the limits of art and decency — his own, and the public's.

Their interview was a meeting of minds, and Terry wrote it up as a straightforward encounter with "this chess-playing poet" who demonstrated in his films and life a "kind of relentless honesty of principle and direction." *Esquire,* however, had been pressuring Terry to portray Kubrick as a "trouble-maker" and wanted him to follow up on stories concerning his fights with producers over *Spartacus* and with Marlon Brando over *One-Eyed Jacks.* A portion of this exchange:

> **INTERVIEWER:** Marlon Brando has been quoted as saying of you, "Stanley is unusually perceptive and delicately attuned to people. He has an adroit intellect and is a creative thinker, not a repeater, not a facts-gatherer." . . . If this was his opinion of you, why did you walk out on the filming of *One-Eyed Jacks?*
> **KUBRICK:** It's possible, of course, for two adroit, perceptive, delicately attuned people not to agree in any way, shape or form.

Ironically, both Kubrick and Brando would have profound influences on Terry and *Candy,* respectively. *Esquire* killed the interview as too high-brow.

* * *

Soon after their meeting, Kubrick read *The Magic Christian* and hired Terry to help him transform *Dr. Strangelove* from heavy-handed melodrama to "a Kafkaesque nightmare comedy." After his first transcontinental plane trip, Terry rented Kenneth Tynan's flat in London and began working with Kubrick from November 1962 through the conclusion of the filming in the spring of 1963.

During the flight to England he wrote to Carol:

> My True Darl:
>
> Taking this opportunity to write you on the plane itself. . . . We are two hours now from London and, I presume high above Atlantic ("33,000 ft" the announcer said). I sit next to the window, and outside a fantastic scene — the wing, gigantic, brown now, though actually aluminium and gleaming earlier, but now brown and shades of brown like a Mondrian symmetrically mottled, beneath it a floor of white fluff, and beyond, the horizon of blue, all extremely vivid, with two sharply parallel ribbons of thin clouds, very clean cut. Looking out there is no sense of motion whatsoever. A bright star hangs over the tip of the wing and stays exactly there — the tip of the wing does not rise or fall from it, nor move.

After Terry began working on *Strangelove,* the Southerns all moved into Kenneth Tynan's flat on Prince Albert Road. Kubrick would pick Terry up in a limo customized for writing, and Carol often took me to Hyde Park to feed the ducks and geese.

In a letter sent to Terry on the *Strangelove* set in Middlesex, England, Putnam's Peter Israel discussed the problem of *Candy*'s lack of valid copyright. The Manufacturing Clause of the Copyright Code in effect at the time specified that works written by foreigners abroad and published there were not protected by U.S. copyright unless the author(s) filed for an interim copyright — which Terry and Mason had failed to do. This situation would enable pirate publishers to flood the market with knock-offs. The copyright issue produced an entanglement that would plague the authors and the book for the next four years.

New York, NY, February 18, 1963

Mr. Terry Southern
c/o "Strangelove"
Shepperton Film Studios
Middlesex, England

Dear Terry:

I have every good intention of getting on with *Candy* along the lines we discussed when I saw you last, but the eminent Mr. Lord and I have hit a temporary snag, the problem being that I don't see how we can protect the book under copyright and am rather unwilling to sign an agreement under which Putnam pays a full royalty scale for a public domain book. I don't think the "unexpurgated" material will help. It would enable us to apply for a copyright, but it certainly wouldn't keep some unscrupulous fly-by-nighter from rushing the Olympia edition into paperback at the same time, leaving G. P. Putnam's current sons in the awkward position of being the only publisher of *Candy* in town who has to pay royalties to the authors. Sterling and I are working on a wrinkle or two, but I don't know at this particular moment where we stand. All I do know is that I have a desk drawer filled with copies [of the Olympia edition] ready to go out to the literati as soon as we get squared away. In the meantime, the more people I manage to expose to the book the more encouraged I feel about the prospects.

I see in the strike newspaper that STRANGELOVE is girding its loins to take on FAIL SAFE in the courts, but I don't believe anything I read in the *New York Standard* so would like to hear what is really going on.* It would be a pretty hefty duel at that.

*Though based on different material, *Fail Safe,* directed by Sidney Lumet, was so similar to *Dr. Strangelove* in plot and concept (but not execution) that Kubrick was able to win an injunction to delay the film's release, which had been scheduled for 1963. *Fail Safe* was released in 1964, some months after the release of *Dr. Strangelove.*

I'll let you know of future developments — i.e., how things stand, etc.

Best regards,

Peter Israel

Editor-in-Chief

Mason had gone to England in 1963 ostensibly to find drug treatment, but found instead the intoxicating scene of the Rolling Stones, their music, and the women around them. Mason hung out with one of the most dynamic couples at the time, Marianne Faithfull (who covered "As Tears Go By" in 1964) and Mick Jagger. He also met Anita Pallenberg, to whom he would remain close throughout his life. Terry also came to know this crowd, though not through the world of drugs but via the art scene happening around the Robert Fraser gallery in London. Fraser was the first to display the "modern" art of Warhol, Lichtenstein, and Jasper Johns.

In the summer of 1963, after the filming of *Dr. Strangelove,* Terry was back in Connecticut and on to new projects. Beginning in June, three consecutive issues of *Esquire* featured prominent pieces by Terry: the interview with Boris Grugurevich, which Terry entitled, "Recruiting for the Big Parade — How I Signed Up at $250 a Day for the Big Parade Through Havana, Bla Bla Bla, and Wound up Working for the CIA — a Hipster Mercenary's Account of the Bay of Pigs Invasion," followed by an ironic piece on Mickey Spillane, "I *Am* Mike Hammer," then, "You're Too Hip, Baby."

Chapter 23

Fuzz Against Junk

In Paris, it was business as usual for Girodias. Victoria Reiter, a young American, recalled her days at the Olympia offices in the early '60s:

> It was extremely staid — staffed mostly by down-to-earth women who took no shit from anyone, especially when Arabs would turn up expecting orgies. Most of the business with authors was done in Girodias's apartment or in cafés. The accounting was terrible, filled with as much fantasy as the novels themselves.

As for whether Girodias knew the extent of the problem of his accounts and his record-keeping, she said:

> Sometimes I thought he did; sometimes I thought he didn't. I never saw or made out a royalty statement during my entire time there. He never paid French social security payments and the authorities went after him for that, too. He ended up owing the government, he told me, 80 million francs [$60,000]. Being a secretary for Maurice was unlike being anyone else's secretary. He wrote incredibly long letters to lawyers, authors and publishers . . . rehearsing legal arguments for future court appearances.

Mason was equally calculating in trying to collect from Girodias. Since Putnam's had not offered any terms as yet (because of the copyright mess), from Mason's perspective there was *no* American deal, despite all of Peter Israel's assurances. Catching Girodias in breach of contract would help *Candy*'s cause overseas.

Paris, June 15th, 1963

Dear Partner,

Good Lordy, I certainly must excuse myself for owing you a letter 3/4 months, but as you know, I've been busy as a basket of butterflies with personal difficulties, and the host of beloved details that go with being a parent, an intellectual, an expatriate, and a Hebrew gentleman with frog ladies in his charge.

. . . I guilelessly passed by our wily publisher's last week and frankly asked him why we had not as yet received either statement or payment on the reprinted C. despite our contract which provides for bi-annual statements and payments to be made on June 30 and December 31 "and not later than two months after the end of each period. . . ."

When I called him on this little oversight, he shot me a charming, sheepish, forlorn little smile and hinted, with a gay twinkle in his eye, that he would take care of things as soon as the old pressure relented a bit — poor chap is in another of his financial squeezes as he explained it.

As you can quickly calculate again, this might be an opportunity to break the contract if we wished.

I feel however, that since we have no hot NY offers, we may as well try and get at least some loot from G. (he mumbled something about having sold 1,000 of the 4,000 reprinted which would mean 2000 NF [$400] for us)

I've had no word yet from the office although G's secretary said she'd send a statement in a few days when I paid my visit four days ago.

I suppose the next step is to send the letter called for in the contract giving him 30 days to settle up, however, I'll wait to hear from you on this in case there's anything you care to propose.

By the way, where was Sterling Lord when G. went past his deadline three and a half months ago? Or isn't he supposed to be keeping an eye on things?

I'm interested in seeing whether the statement (if we should ever get one) will mention how many copies of C. were reprinted. As I mentioned above, G. says it's 4,000, but knowing his jovial

> ways, I take that 4,000 figure, rapidly shred it to 4,000 confetti which I flush down the latrine.

Though Terry and Carol returned to Connecticut in June, Terry met only once with his old Paris buddy when Mason was in Milford — even though the Hoffenberg family home was only forty-five minutes away — nor did he revisit the Village scene. Terry had been changed not only by the experience of working with Kubrick but also by the honor of being published throughout that previous summer in *Esquire*. What was more, the London-based agency Gregson and Wigan was sending film work his way. Terry invited Mason to help him on the rewrite of *Wolsey Fricktt,* produced by Ronnie Kahn, while he began working on adapting *The Marriage Game* for Harry Saltzman (who later canceled the contract).

"That summer, he closed the door on his old friends who were junkies," Carol recalls. "The Village scene was finished for him. When he took the train into town, it was to see George Plimpton and that crowd."

In August 1963, Walter Minton began putting a deal together with Sterling Lord regarding publication of *Candy* in the United States. As Terry later rationalized it, "Girodias didn't pay us for a long, long time . . . so we felt free to go to another publisher." Walter Minton recalled:

> None of them had applied for a U.S. copyright, and so the book was in public domain. Since the book was out of copyright, Girodias had no rights in the United States. We signed a contract with normal royalties for the two authors, and an advance of . . . ten thousand dollars each. But we put a codicil in the contract saying that if anyone brought out a pirated edition of *Candy,* Putnam's would be relieved of the obligation to pay any further royalties to the authors.

At the time, Terry felt they should only pursue an American deal if he and Mason could first prove Girodias in breach of contract. Terry issued Mason a Power of Attorney, so that Mason's efforts would represent his own. Under instruction from Mason and Sterling Lord, Terry started the ball rolling by writing his coauthor a formal "letter of concern" about Girodias's overdue payments. Mason began exploring these issues in a series of letters:

79 Rue Daguerre, Paris, September, 1963

Dear Sterling and Terry (since I'm sending you each a copy)

I've received . . . Terry's power of attorney and his letter which I'm to enclose with my own as "notification" to Girodias — thanks for all of them.

I'm going to have to delay the affair for as long as it takes for you to answer this, however, in order to make the following point: if I send G. Terry's terse, legal-sounding letter (in which Sterling's name occurs) and a comparable letter of my own, won't we be tipping our hand — confirming any hunch or information he may have that a U.S. publisher is interested in our book and prompting him to hang on to the contract. (After all, the chance of a U.S. sale must have been one of his main motives in wanting the contract in the first place, and in giving me a "payment" when I stupidly asked for one last June — whereas he could just as well have fluffed me off as he usually does when asked for money he owes).

All he has to do in the present case is make another "payment" in the form of a check, for instance, which, presumably will show he's living up to his part of the contract even if we claim that it (the check) is not full payment and do not accept it. In that case we'll have accomplished nothing.

I think we have a slightly better chance if he receives a wordy, rather diffuse letter from me, not very angry in tone, containing a few false leads, and generally suggesting that I am trying to "play the lawyer" in my pitifully inadequate manner. This letter will, nevertheless, contain the "written notification" called for in clause #4 of the contract, which "automatically terminates" one month later if he hasn't "rectified defaults". It will also contain both Terry's, and my signature, and be sent registered mail (and wouldn't mention that Terry has given me power of attorney).

Such a letter might be more apt to perpetuate the image I'm sure he has of Terry and I at present (and quite justly) — a pair of idiot writers who dislike reading contracts since they don't understand them, and who have probably lost their copies in any event.

I've noticed, in the years I've been observing him, that G. will seize on any chance — including long shots — which would seem to allow him to renege on honest debts.

By the way . . . Gid may have sold out the "Candys" and is now unloading his old "Lollypops", or he may prefer to sell the "Lollypops" since he pays no royalty on them (and, in that case, there is nothing to prevent him from quietly reprinting "Lollypops" as required. . . . Perhaps I'm getting a bit paranoiac about the thing.) At any rate, an American trying to get a copy of "Candy" (and very few people are aware that "Lollypop" and "Candy" are the same) to bring home from Paris will depart empty-handed as far as I can see.

Yours,

Mason Hoffenberg

Mason's concerns about indiscriminate printings were not paranoiac. It is unknown how many printings of *Lollipop* rolled out of Girodias's S.I.P. printers in Montreuil over the years — suffice to say that between the 1958 debut of *Candy,* and the "official" 1959 and 1962 editions of *Lollipop,* Girodias had still not properly accounted for sales to the authors.

Back in Paris, Mason, from his new address in rue Daguerre in the 14th arrondissement, wrote a draft of the promised letter to Girodias, copying both Terry and Sterling.

September 7th, 1963

Dear Mr. Girodias:

When I saw Terry in Connecticut this summer, we finally had a chance to discuss our situation as "Candy's" co-authors. . . .

On this occasion, we would like to call to your attention that you have failed to give us a statement (or payment) for "Candy's" sales in the first half of 1963, and that, so far, you have paid us less than one third of the amount called for in the statement which you gave (five months late!) for the last half of 1962.

Needless to say, we would like payment in full for both these periods immediately.

We would also like to point out that the one statement which we received reported merely that fifteen hundred copies of the second edition of "Candy" had been sold, but made no mention of the publication date of that edition or of how many copies it consisted of. Would you kindly include that information on your next statement — which, frankly, we feel will be unacceptable otherwise.

Yours truly, Read and approved,

Mason Hoffenberg Terry Southern

Terry responded, warning Mason off sending such a formal letter:

Monday

My dear Hoff:

Thanks for your letter. Drugs and Jay-O have apparently clouded the issue in your great head. The letter I sent you and the Power of Att. were *not* meant for Gid's eyes, but simply to be retained as proof that your own request was in fact on behalf of us both. You must not, of course, mention these in your request to Gid. Sterling is writing you in detail about this, but briefly let me say that your letter to G. is the opposite of what we (I thought) had in mind — namely an informal (Dear Gid type) letter asking for full payment, but in such a way that it does not spook him (as we duck-hunters say) or otherwise hip him to what's shaking. Sterling said that he would draft such a letter and send it to you — he will make sure the legal parts vis a vis the contract are in there, so that all you need do is modify it to mesh with your *normal* relationship with G. (I mean if you use a letter-head and Dear Mr. Girodias approach he will surely know what's up.) The date should be on the letter and your address, but I don't think his — probably the only thing unusual about it would have to be that you sign your full name instead of just Mason, and that you send it registered.) However, as I say S. is writing you today about it.

Putnam won their case on Fanny Hill and sold 10,000 copies the day the ban was lifted, so the outlook for us is good at the moment.* Also Larry Rivers (very big here) said he thought he could do a book-jacket for it, which impressed [Peter] Israel. The Realist is running an announcement asking people to write the publisher expressing interest in the book being published (in Nov.) so things are going smoothly so far. . . .

Best,

Herb

Are you crack on the film scenario?

Mason then issued a breezier declaration:

79 Rue Daguerre; Paris; September 23, 1963

Dear Girodias:

It's autumn again, and as 1963 draws to a close Terry and I would like to remind you that the royalties due on "Candy", on June 1st, 1963, are overdue — and that you still owe more than half the royalties called for in the statement you sent for the previous period.

Yours truly,

Mason Hoffenberg

Mason was obsessed with the *Candy* imbroglio, his obsession further fueled by his tendency to paranoia. Hearing his fellow Olympians (like Norman Rubington, Gregory Corso, and William Burroughs) complain about specific aspects of their contracts, Mason was determined to beat Girodias at his own game. His frustra-

---

*Massachusetts appealed, and eventually banned *Fanny Hill* again. The famous case eventually moved up to the state's supreme court, where the "obscenity" judgment was finally overturned.

tion with Terry and Sterling's apparent disinterest increased as the stalemate with Girodias put the fate of the book further out of their reach.

On September 30, Mason composed a seven-page, single-spaced letter to Terry, which he begins by warning him, "We must never forget that we are up against a seasoned, unscrupulous COCKSHIT. . . . G is *Habitually* crooked (I mean you can depend upon it 100%; that contract is a masterpiece of attention to each little crooked detail.)" Mason's "Giant Brain" was working overtime on trying to catch "Uncle Gid" in a lie — which was like trying to catch water in a sieve. Mason was convinced he had uncovered "little riff[s] exemplifying his constant dillydocking," such as the consideration that five hundred books were to be deducted from the count as a contingency against those that may be "lost, damaged or seized." Mason wrote:

> OK, I can see where some of his mailed stuff might be seized, but I know from working there that he mails relatively few books and that 80% go through the French bookstores. But what is that "lost and damaged" crap? Does that mean that 45 copies fall off a shelf in the stockroom and land behind a radiator where they are "lost", or that the stock boy spills his lunch on ten copies getting them all gooey with soft boiled egg and woostershire?
>
> And note that this is an open-end category — "if we figure that we won't have more than . . ." because he might have really a bad run of luck and lose 2,000 copies through termites or God knows what.

Between Mason's job at Agence France-Press, his heroin withdrawal, and now the pressure of screenplay opportunities Terry was offering, he was a bundle of nerves. Writing to Terry, however, offered him a chance for self-observation — often to comic effect, as in his letter of September 30:

> I physically, and by accident encountered G in a public park near his office whither I had withdrawn with a beloved volume of verse. We both came on as if delighted to meet in this spontaneous

manner, and I did an A-1 imitation of myself as mirthful, scatter-brained, intimidated intellectual, gaily twitting him about his being remiss in payments with generous admixture of sheer admiration and appreciation of his storied deviltry.

I had to delay my registered letter to him after this meeting though (for about a week) since it seemed unnatural to smack him with this document the day after our hilarious encounter.

I asked him at this time about the point I made to you previously (that there are no copies of Candy in the stores, only Lollipop, and that absolutely no one is aware they're the same book so that the whole demand for Candy by hip Americans trying to cop a copy while in Paris goes unsatisfied). His answer was that Candy was never removed from the banned list and that he can only publish Lollipops therefore. This is probably true. In effect, it means that Candy has been unavailable to the public since the banning date (several years ago).

I am flipping with panic and chagrin at the way I've goofed on your request for script [*Beyond the Shadows*], and I'll be permanently fucked up if you tell me I'm definitively disqualified from this rare opportunity you were grand enough to turn me on. Good God, I hope it isn't true.

But when I got your letter that it had to be *a few weeks*, the same thing happened to me that happened in the army when I am one in a steadily advancing queue of hundreds of nude recruits . . . and suddenly it is my turn, in the cluster of smoothly functioning medics, to make an instant urine specimen in a jar. And when they notice that I have not immediately done this, like the 75 men preceding me, why do they think they are going to improve matters by all rushing up to me — "Hey! Hurry up PISS!" — making me drink water and already the 155 men behind me are starting to buzz angrily. "Hey up there! Lets PISS up there! He must be a fairy, that guy. Hey FAIRY! Hey lets get on the ball up there!" . . .

I might as well make a few reflections about collaborating, at this point. I take it for granted that your vanity as a writer is the same as mine (or anyone else's) and this vanity, which is a sine qua non for writers, takes the form of believing deep down in your heart that you're the greatest. Consequently, when two writers are collaborat-

> ing, since their vanities are identical it should be possible to cancel them out somehow and ignore them thereafter, or rather neutralize them as the potential troublemakers they are. Because this question of "who is the greatest" is surely the main wedge to cleave writing-teams asunder.
>
> Now, in the collaborating that you, dear Terry, and I have done with Candy and now, the script, it has always been a question of my working on material you've already done. This definitely gives me the beau role — sitting grandly with my blue pencil after you've done the hard art of actually pounding out all those pages. It stands to reason also, with more or less commercial writing of this sort, that a second, suddenly digging the material has a better chance of seeing the thing objectively and getting fresh ideas than the number one who is too embroiled, can't see the wood for the trees, etc. And so there arises the delicate situation of #2 writer conceivably sounding like he's *correcting* #1 because he's the greater writer. . . .
>
> Perfectly hopeless. No, what a pair of writers should have is complementary strong points and the conviction that all ideas and material derive from some neutral, middle area, and are to be thought of like elements in a science experiment.
>
> I think we've got something like this attitude (taking turns at the wheel while partner gets some needed sleep) and being able to contribute valid insights to each other's stuff without it being a cause for "offense."

Signing the letter as "Sophie," Mason concludes by providing an explanation for his "bad showing" on the *Shadows* script:

> I've reached a climactic point with h whereby I've been passing through the entire kicking-getting sick-feeling-a-bit-better-and-relapsing cycle on a weekly basis for the past couple of months. I've no idea where this is leading to, and often fear it may be the prelude to some inglorious debacle.

At the end of October, Mason wrote to Lord, saying he had reminded Girodias "that he still owed us more than half of the royalties called for in his statement for the previous period."

> I received no answer and the contract is therefore finished, I trust, although God knows what G. might say to prove this is not the case if he hears we signed with a U.S. publisher. . . . It would be best to simply go ahead with Putnam and let Girodias react when he finally hears about it. One other thing, does he (Girodias) still owe us back royalties even though the contract is no longer in effect?

Mason then brought up extremely cogent and important questions regarding the pending Putnam contract, especially concerning the termination of royalties in the event the book was pirated:

> I must say I don't quite understand why we have to lose *all* royalties if an unauthorized American edition of *Candy* comes out. Why wouldn't it be enough to waive royalties insofar as Putnam might fail to make up their costs? But what if, despite a pirate edition, Putnam still was able to show a profit. In such a case, it seems to me we should be entitled to something even if it were not the full 10%. Furthermore, what bearing would a pirate edition have on resale rights (clause c)? I can understand why their own edition might suffer from a pirate edition, but if someone wanted to buy reprinting rights from them, then it would be as if the pirate ed. didn't exist.
>
> It seems, according to these terms, as if the more chance the book has of selling well the more risk there is of Terry and I losing out on everything.
>
> Lastly, why do we get just a straight 10% royalty? Isn't it customary for the royalty to go up a few points after certain sales figures are attained?
>
> Maybe I'm prejudiced, but it seems to me that Candy has financial potentialities that are clearly superior to the average novels by not-so-well-known writers appearing on American publishing lists. It's one of the last of the "good" Olympia books, and has the distinctive quality (unlike Miller, Burroughs, Genet etc.) of being smutty in a wholesome, humorous and unobjectionable manner.
>
> Why then, should it not receive at least the same terms as the average novel?
>
> I certainly want to see the deal go through, and don't intend to be "uncooperative," but I would like to know how Putnam answers the questions I've been asking.

Left: Girodias at the top of his game, posing for photographer Doisneau in the garden of the Grande Séverine, 1964. *(Pierre Boulat/Cosmos/AURORA)*

Below left: Mason swam everywhere he went — in Spain, Connecticut, and in Tourettes, France. *(Courtesy Terry Southern Picture Collection)*

Below: Terry had great respect for the *Evergreen Review,* edited by Barney Rosset. *(Steve Schapiro)*

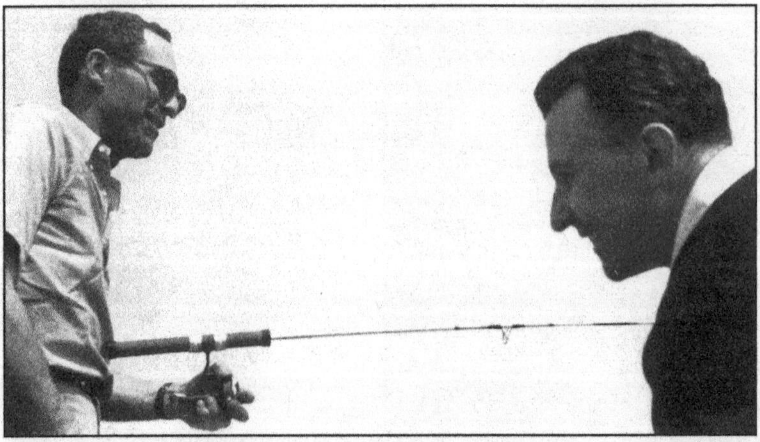

Above: Barney Rosset and Girodias fishing, East Hampton, 1960. *(Barney Rosset/Courtesy Suzan Cooper)*

Above: Bob Dylan trades in his cowboy boots for the British kind on Mason's terrace in rue Daguerre, 1963. Mason *(background)* with drink in hand. Couquite's cousin Hugues Aufray (seated), a guitarist, introduced them. (*Courtesy Hugues Aufray)*

Left: Bob Dylan and D. A. Pennebaker making *Dont Look Back* during Dylan's 1964 U.K. tour. (*Courtesy Pennebaker Associates)*

Right: James Patrick Donleavy, author of *The Ginger Man,* in London, 1958. When he first saw Girodias's edition of the book, he vowed revenge. *(Larry Burrows, © Larry Burrows Collection)*

Above: Girodias in the medieval cellar of his club, the Grande Séverine, 1964. *(Robert Doisneau/RAPHO)*

Below: The Spoiler: Walter Zacharius, 1965, and his unauthorized 75-cent edition — the first of *Candy*'s many "pirate" incarnations. *(Courtesy Walter Zacharius)*

CANDY
NOT ONE WORD CHANGED!
This is the ORIGINAL, UNCUT and UNEXPURGATED edition as first published and banned in Paris.

Above: The Victors: Barney Rosset and attorney Edward de Grazia remember their struggles against censorship. *Naked Lunch*'s win enabled *Candy* and many other books to stay in print — regardless of state and local actions. *(Mia Yun)*

Left: Putnam's paperback

Below: Terry with the *Candy* cover model at Elaine's, 1964. *(Steve Schapiro)*

Left: The 1750 house in Canaan in 1960, viewed from across Blackberry River. *(Terry Southern Picture Collection)*

Below: Terry with some hissing "honkers," Canaan, spring 1964. *(Steve Schapiro)*

ow: Zeline, Couquite, Juliette, Daniel, and son outside the Hoffenberg home, Milford, nn., 1963. *(Courtesy Couquite Hoffenberg)*

Below: Carol, Nile, and Terry, summer 1964, in Los Angeles. *(Steve Schapiro)*

Right: Jane Fonda and Terry at Elaine's, c. 1967. The image became the cover of his anthology, *Red Dirt Marijuana and Other Tastes.* *(Robert Dudas)*

Left: Gail Gerber, c. 1964. *(Camilla McGrath/Courtesy o*
Gail Gerber)

Below: Kindred spirits: Terry *(*
salutes Lenny Bruce, whom he
wanted to act in *The Loved On*
According to Paul Krassner,
Lenny had fallen through a
second story window after taki
DMT (while on acid for the fir
time). *(William Claxton)*

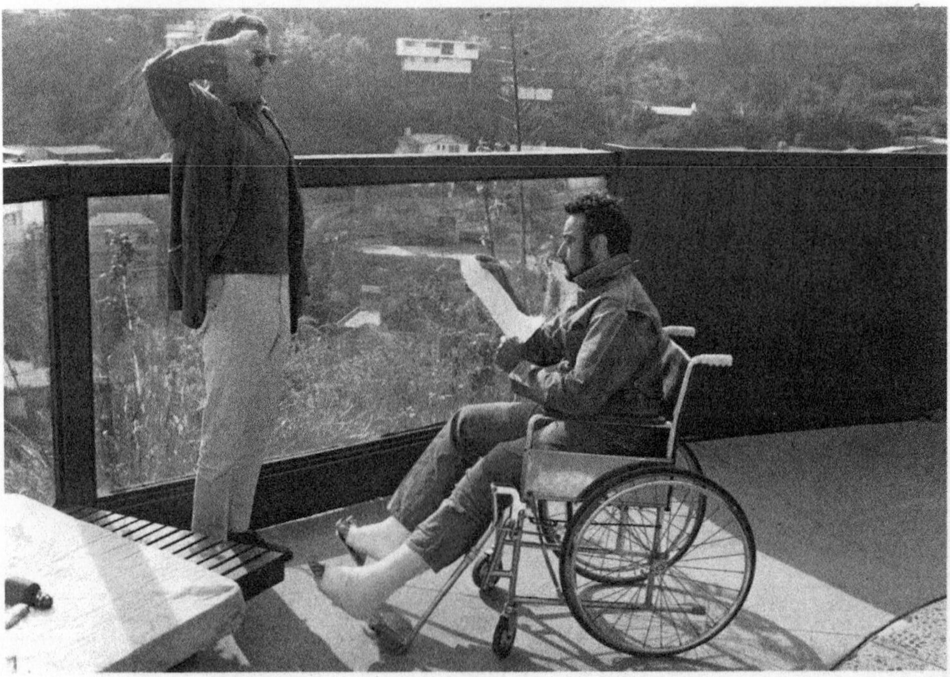

Right: Will he or won't he? Mason disappeared during the *Candy* promotion — just after the *Life* photographer got two headshots, summer 1964. *(Steve Schapiro)*

Above: Ewa Aulin and Marlon Brando, publicity still for *Candy,* and the cover image of an unauthorized edition of the book. *(1969 Selmur Pictures, Dear Film S.p.A)*

Above: On location in Rome with Sugar Ray Robinson, Ewa Aulin, and Richard Burton on the set of *Candy.* *(1969 Selmur Pictures, Dear Film S.p.A)*

Right: Director Christian Marquand and his seventeen-year-old bride, actress Tina Aumont, at their wedding, 1963. *(Courtesy Tina Aumont)*

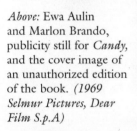

Above: Anita Pallenberg, a friend of Terry's and Mason's, was involved with the Rolling Stones, and starred as The Great Tyrant in *Barbarella.* *(© 1968 Paramount Pictures Corporation)*

Clockwise from above left: Girodias in his New York office, 1971. *(Gilles Larrain)* Terry out on the town, early 1990s. *(Nile Southern)* Mason, 1980s. *(Eric Michelson)*

Below: The first and the most recent editions.

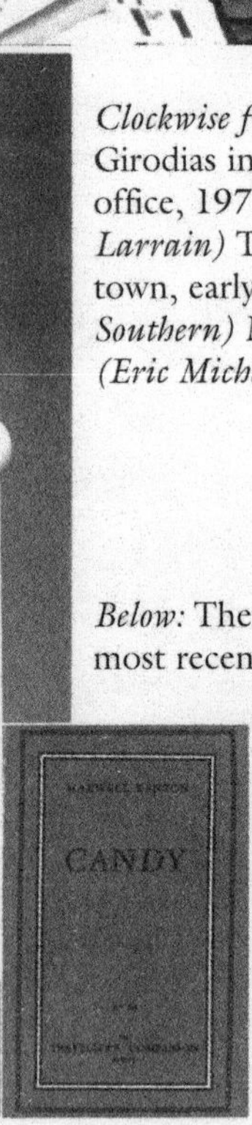

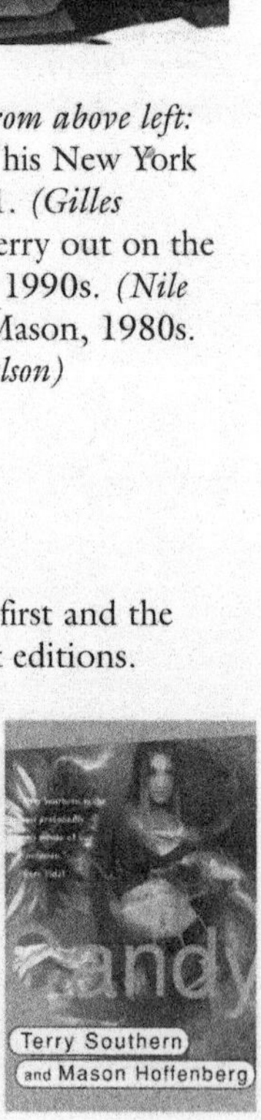

Once again, I'm sorry for the long delay in answering your last letter.

Sincerely yours

Mason Hoffenberg

Mason's points were well taken and Sterling agreed. But Sterling's negotiating power was compromised in that he was representing a book his authors didn't own. Perhaps this is why none of Mason's suggestions was written into the contract.

Chapter 24

What the Fuck Is Wrong with Your Eyes?

Terry's approach to writing was orderly, focused, and solution oriented, and he quickly mastered the mechanics of screenplay format. Mason, on the other hand, usually couldn't get past his own stream of consciousness. Mason wrote about his life-as-trapeze-act to great effect in his unpublished memoir. His hilarious look at the breakdown of his marriage reveals the satirical talent that drew Terry to Mason like a moth to the flame. In one sequence, he has just turned on, is due home, and realizes his eyes will give him away:

> I . . . suddenly remembered an idea that I'd had in the past and had never checked out. Which was a chemical optometrists used that dilated people's pupils to make them easier to examine — atropine. I had to go to three drugstores before finally being able to con somebody into selling me a bottle without prescription, and by then it was time to go home for dinner.
>
> All right. Driving through Paris rush hour traffic and at a red light I pour some on a wad of cotton and dab my eyes. Waited, keeping an eye on my eyes in the mirror. Now I'm more than half-way to the house and there's been no result. It occurred to me that perhaps it took a long time to work — I'd have to be late . . . tell her the car broke down . . . no, that I ran into Frank Lusardi and we had a drink . . . who is Frank Lusardi? I knew him in the army, you've heard about me speak about him. . . .
>
> I got frantic and poured a lot of atropine on the cotton and really doused my eyes.
>
> Now I'm just a block from the house and finally something

seems to be happening to my eyes. Pupils are definitely dilating. Excellent. I parked the car, take another peep in the mirror and they seem now to be getting a bit too big. They're not just going to stop when they get to normal. Well, tough titty, at least they're not pinned anymore. Definitely not. They're dilating to beat the band. Look like a couple of balloons blowing up. Better get home and hole up in a corner with the evening paper hiding my face. As I came in the apartment I noticed things were getting a bit blurred. Took one last look in the hall mirror before confronting the little woman and just have time to note, before the world becomes a vast blur, that my pupils are simply colossal. Not only that but that they're two different sizes of colossal. The right one is bigger than the left one. And the left one is so big you can't see any iris showing.

Beautiful. I enter the room and, for once, she puts down the knitting.

"Hi," I say, my voice terribly normal as I go crashing into a chair.

"WHAT THE FUCK IS WRONG WITH YOUR EYES?"

"My eyes? What do you mean, 'my eyes'?" I am stepping along with my finger tips tapping the wall over to where the couch should be. Things look like I'm standing under Niagara Falls. I get to the couch and immediately get engrossed in the piece of frosted glass which is the evening paper I'd had under my arm.

"YOUR EYES!"

"My eyes?" I say it once again. Things are as idiotic as possible. "What's wrong with my eyes?" And now I arise and look in the mirror behind the couch. I trust it's in its usual location and that I've got it lined up right and am not simply facing a bit of wall.

"Oh, you mean they're whaddycall it? The pupils are dilated? That's because I had a little amphetamine this afternoon. I had to. I was falling asleep —" There is a bit of turbulence in the general blur which is her leaving the room . . . accompanied by an explosion, a vase? an ashtray? Anyhow a distinct feeling of something smashing on the wall not too far from my head.

The other aspect of Mason's trapeze act was: keeping it together. During November of 1963, he took the initiative, making some corrections for *Candy*'s inevitable American edition. He also had last-minute trepidation about his name appearing on the book—because of the flak his mother would probably receive from her friends. He worried about Terry's parts, particularly Derek striking Candy with a wire coat hanger and the internal ejaculation scene with Guru Grindle:

> "Oh, please," said the adorable girl, actually alarmed, "not . . . not *inside* me . . . I . . . I . . ."
>
> "Don't be absurd," said Grindle, breathing heavily, "naturally, in willing the chemistry of the semen, I would eliminate the impregnating agent, spermatozoa, as a constituent — for it would be of no use to our purposes here you see."
>
> "Now then," he continued after a moment, "tell me if this does not almost exactly resemble philistine 'orgasm'?"

> 79 rue Daguerre, Paris, 14 Nov. 18, '63
>
> My Dear Chap, I got your wire of welcome action coming up at last on Candy. As for changes in the text, Peter Israel's point about the importance of presenting an "unexpurgated" version of the Paris edition is a strong one, and I think we can't make any substantial modifications therefore. I wistfully wish you could take the sting out of Derek's suckscene and Grindle's because of what it's going to do to my poor old Ma when her Canasta pals get an eyeful of that strong stuff. This is just what Israel was against though. Maybe we could blame it on Gid in the introduction — how he lashed us on to high smut content, the sickening degenerate.

Mason reiterates his strong feelings about the unfairness of the Putnam deal: "If a pirate U.S. edition appears, our royalties simply stop (and also our share of any book-club or reprint sales)."

> That might make sense if Putnam actually goes into the red on their edition because of the pirate edition, but if, despite pirate editions, Candy (Putnam's) still does well enough to make a profit does Israel mean we don't get our royalties therefrom?
>
> Fuck that detestable noise! . . . the minute they . . . begin making a profit then we should get our 10% for Christ all mighty!

For the U.S. edition of *Candy*, Mason suggests other possible dedications, such as "Dr. Freymann and Dr. Dent," who treated addicts. Mason, like Burroughs, had started seeing these doctors regularly in England for his drug addiction. He also suggests adding a new Voltaire quote:

> "Ce n'est plus le temps de plaisanter." ("It's time for us to get serious.")
>
> — Letter to D'Alembert
>
> I quit my job at AFP last week so as to devote full time to being sick and Olympia litigation. Later I hope will come creative energy and a chance to make up somehow for my hanging you up on the script.

Putnam was still allowing minor changes to the text, and Mason signs off offering some additional refinements:

> I found OSPHRESIOLAGNIA in a dictionary of psychiatric terms. It's a synonym of "osmolagnia" — "erotic pleasure derived from certain odors, usually body odors." (The patient in Livia's script is an osphresiolagniac.) . . .
>
> Trixie

Meanwhile, an anthology of *Esquire*'s best work was compiled by Rust Hills and the editors of the magazine, and two of Terry's stories were chosen for inclusion in the "Reporters Off-Center" section, including the Cuban piece. Wanting to give Boris more credit for what had become a popular story — Terry suggested a new title, "The Hipster Plans to Free Cuba; by Boris Grugurevich as Told to Terry Southern." The book would come out in the flurry of activity that was 1964.

Chapter 25

The *Candy* Wars

Despite the substantial income *Lolita* had been providing him through its American publication, Girodias was spending a great deal of money on his legal actions, as well as his expansion of the nightclub, bar, and theater of Saint-Séverin. Taking counsel from Sterling Lord, Sy Litvinoff, a friend of Terry's and his accountant and lawyer, and his partner Howard Singer sent a "cease and desist" letter to Girodias on November 25, 1963, terminating the 1961 contract for "failure to render timely reports and remit the amount of royalties due the authors." This showdown letter from Singer was Putnam's signal to quickly execute a *Candy* contract with the authors and officially commenced the *Candy* litigation — a roller-coaster ride that would continue for years.

Girodias promptly responded:

7 rue Saint Séverin, Paris 5, November 29, 1963

Dear Mr. Singer,

I acknowledge receipt of your letter of November 25 concerning "Candy" by Terry Southern.

I am frankly dismayed by its contents, and I am writing to Mr. Southern about it.

I will send to Mr. Southern a statement of royalties and corresponding payment as soon as possible. However, I cannot accept his decision to terminate our agreement and I would like to know more specifically on what grounds Mr. Southern rests his claim that he can do so.

Yours sincerely,

Maurice Girodias

7 rue Saint-Séverin, Paris, November 29, 1963

Dear Terry,

I have today received a letter dated November 25 from your lawyer, Mr. Howard Singer, informing me of your intention to cancel our agreement relative to "Candy".

I am certainly at fault for not having delivered statements and corresponding payments regularly. The reason is that I have been fighting against nearly unsurmountable difficulties in the past two or three years to keep my business on its feet. My publishing activities have been practically paralyzed by the innumerable bans, fines, and other niceties showered upon me. You know that Candy itself was banned, and was only reprinted under a different title at great risk to myself — to myself only.

I should certainly have explained all this to you before — but I was quite certain that you were being kept informed of my situation by Mason, and frankly I did not see much point in sending whining, apologetic letters to you such as this one, as long as I was unable to pay what I owed you.

May I also remind you that Candy was written on commission; that you and Mason were to receive an outright royalty for the manuscript; that I gave you advances on that royalty but that the manuscript was finally delivered more than two years after the agreed date. You must realize that the book was bought by me for a definite sum and that, in accordance to our original verbal agreement, I had no obligation to pay you anything in addition to the first payment, in the event we would print another edition. As the book finally proved to be an article of a much higher quality than what I had expected to receive, I considered that it was only fair to propose to Mason and yourself to turn our initial arrangement into a conventional contract, after the first edition had been sold out. But, once again, nothing forced me to do that.

You will certainly understand, in those circumstances, how surprised I was to receive your lawyer's letter without any advance warning from you. It is both unfair and unfriendly, and quite apart from the practical complications this is going to cause between us, I must say that I was deeply surprised by your attitude in the matter. By God, I think I have been patient and friendly enough when you needed my help. Now that I am in a jam worse than anything you have ever known, I think you could try to be a little more generous — whatever my past and present faults may be.

Naturally, I will answer Mr. Singer's letter, but I would be sincerely relieved if you should step down from that legal pedestal of yours, and I can promise that I will do my inhuman best to get some money to you as soon as I can.

Yours,

Maurice

cc: Mr. Howard Singer

Although Terry had been a boxing champion in the army, he disliked and actively avoided confrontation. After all of Mason's hysterics and accusations and the fact that legal proceedings had begun, Terry was still uncomfortable about breaking with Girodias and Girodias's letter gave him pause. Mason, on the other hand, was adamant about pursuing legal action, summing up in one of many vitriolic letters that Girodias was "entitled to have the fucking shit kicked out of him." Mason carefully detailed Girodias's deviousness and lapses. In a letter to Terry in December 1963, Mason estimates that the first edition printings had brought about $35,000 to Olympia. The second edition, "my bookstore informant tells me," was out of print, and whereas Girodias said it would "probably take two to three years" to sell out, it took around 14 months, "and Gid made 18 thou (5,000 copies at 1,800 francs each = 9 million francs [$18,000].)"* Mason seemed to be the only one paying attention to these details and continues to explore them in his letter to Terry of December 12:

---

*Mason is using old francs here. Further, in calculating Girodias's "profit," he is using the publisher's list price rather than the bookstore discount price. Even taking all this into consideration, it is clear that Girodias is pocketing most of the spoils.

Our 12% royalties came to 1 million 80 thousand francs ($2,160). According to the contract we should have received two statements . . . not later than Aug 31st and each one of these should have called for roughly half of the total $2,160. *Actually,* we received one statement, in *June,* declaring that our royalties came to about $500 at that time . . . of which we received $200 *after* I went into his office and made a scene.

I'm going through this brief review because you ask me if I'm sure we are right "morally," in our action.

Now, bearing in mind these two figures — Gid = $18,000 Maxwell = $200 — hear this: ". . . I must say that I was deeply surprised by your attitude in the matter. By God, I think I have been patient and friendly enough when you needed my help . . ."

In reviewing his Girodias correspondence, Mason became particularly irked by the last line of a Maurice letter from 1961: "Neither you nor Mason will have any reason to complain."

Isn't that swell? Oddly enough, I find I *do* have reason to "complain." I "complain" that he hasn't given me my thousand bucks of the C. money and that now he's going to try to cut into my share of the Putnam royalties where I have a chance to recoup some of this. That's tough shit that he's had "nearly unsurmountable difficulties in the past two or three years". I, for my part, have got child Daniel, child Juliette, child Zeline, wife Couquite, and habit Edna to worry about, and I'd just as soon that my $1,000 went to their support and not helping him surmount his difficulties.

Maybe you think I'm pissed off because of my fiasco as editor of the Olymp Review. It's true, I am. That episode is going to leave an ugly taste in my nose for the rest of the deal. I'm also pissed off at getting robbed of the C. loot, however — and other things, like conditions for the contract — that if he hadn't wanted to sign we would then be free to sell C. in the States and there was nothing he could have done about it with his "verbal agreement". As it is, he got his contract rights to sell the book or take his cut if we did, and when it came to our royalties he reverted to the previous arrangement by simply not paying them. You bet I'm pissed off; I'm positively flipped on the subject and, as you can see, can go on ranting for pages about it.

I am "deeply surprised" myself that you could take that bullshit letter [Girodias's "apology letter," 29 November 1963] seriously. Terry, it's nothing but lies.

While Mason pushed Terry's concerns about breaking the contract with Girodias aside, Putnam was moving full steam ahead. To hype up and substantiate *Candy*'s "banned in France" status for marketing purposes, Mason began looking for a sample of the formal banning notice he had seen stamped in copies of *The Story of O.* Mason was also homing in on the perfect Voltaire quote.

79 Rue Daguerre, Dec 12, 1963

Dear T, you gave me a hearty laugh with your assassination wave* and I got right down to creative work to write a fittingly funny reply. This work was going along fairly smoothly and I'd just about completed the third draft when your latest letter arrived reminding me I was getting the old time/quality ratio distorted again, so I'm rushing off this low-quality job with its high fact-content to get caught up on crass material matters. (This much is certain.) . . .

The first point being the new Voltaire quote, I feel it is better to use a real citation and thus enhance C's high lit. tone. I finally found one which resembles what was used in the Olymp ed, is easy to understand for yanks with low French-content, and which gets things off to a nice moral and philosph start:

"Elle ne savait pas combien elle était vertueuse dans le crime qu'elle se reprochait."†

(Quite apt for C. don't you think? Her "It's my own fault, darn it," tagline being nicely summed up.)

---

*In Terry's "Impolite Interview" in *The Realist*, he launches into a routine about a wave of assassinations prompted by the killing of JFK.

† "She did not know how innocent she was of the crime for which she reproached herself.

"Ainsi, a chaque action honnête et généreuse qu'elle faisait, son déshonneur en etait le prix" [Thus, for each honest and generous act, dishonor was the price] is another which I think not as good as the first since the paradox is not as pithily expressed and it is a little harder for Americans. Both of these are from *L'Ingénu* which is about the same length as *Candide* and was published the same year — 1767. The hero — the "ingenu" — is a Huron Indian who comes to France out of intellectual curiosity about European civilization and encounters some vice and corruption like they never heard of back in the tribe. The "elle" in the quotes is his pure, young French chick who is forced to frig a government minister in order to free her boyfriend after he has been thrown into the Bastille for naively defending Hugenots to a Jesuit spy. It's not as good as *Candide* — too much pious philosophy at the expense of the narrative.

The expression you asked about is: "Il n'y a pas à tortiller du cul pour chier droit," (You don't have to twist your ass to shit straight). . . . [P]utting this in a prominent place in the book seems to be accenting the obscenity angle needlessly, and sacrifices our valid right to associate ourselves with scholarly traditions of the Satire. Even disregarding the question of possible censorship problems, I still think — for correct merchandising, let's say — that C. should be presented as high-class stuff. . . .

Sol

Terry responded that he favored using the "elle ne savait pas" quote and forwarded same to Peter Israel, who responded:

G.P. Putnam's Sons, NYC, 20 December 1963

Dear Terry:

I like the new quote and we can incorporate it in galleys (for the book is already being set). . . .

On the question of pricing, our minds seem to work the same way. We have decided to put a $5.00 price on the book, which is $1.00 higher than what we might normally do. It will have a stained top and colored end papers and a handsome binding. This is not quite what I would call "an expensive deluxe-type edition" but I think it is where we should be with what is really a short book, and it is a higher price and better "package" than we would be using for the run-of-the-mill novel of the same length.

Best,

Peter Israel

Editor-in-Chief

By the way, I am much in need of some biographical material on you and Mason. Could the two of you drum me up self-profiles and get them in before long?

Terry then submitted his and Mason's biographies for use on the dust jacket:

Mason Hoffenberg is an American poet who has lived in Paris for the past ten years, where his work has appeared under a variety of pseudonyms. Until recently, he was the literary editor of *Olympia Review* and a writer for *Agence Press Francaise.*

Terry Southern's stories and articles have been widely published and anthologized, both in the United States and abroad. He is the author of the novels *Flash and Filigree* and *The Magic Christian;* co-editor (with Alexander Trocchi and Richard Seaver) of *Writers in Revolt;* and co-author (with Stanley Kubrick) of the screenplay for the film, *Dr. Strangelove.*

As the publication date drew near, Mason reread their Girodias contract and panicked — pointing out some stomach-turning clauses to which they had agreed:

79 Rue Daguerre, Paris, Dec. 22, 63

FIRE! FIRE!

Let's go everybody. FIRE! FIRE! FIRE! Take out your [1961] contract and read clause #1 . . . You got it? . . . "Publishers own all rights by virtue of *outright royalty*" . . . See it? . . . just what you warned we shouldn't say, no? . . . only we signed it.

Now look what comes next, how clause #1 is isolated from the rest by that "NOW FURTHER AGREES AS FOLLOWS" . . . because later, when clause #4 states the contract terminates 30 days after he fails to make payments following our notification, the wording is, "The *present* agreement shall automatically terminate . . ."

Get it? In other words, it doesn't refer to clause #1 which is given a special, unviolable status the way the thing is set up at present — *that* agreement, which is his interpretation of the original verbal accord, is not covered by either of our two escape routes in clauses #4 and 5, both of which refer to the "present" agreement.

That's the way I suddenly saw it at any rate while glancing at the contract in connection with the letter you asked me to write Singer. It would mean that G. continues to have his hooks in, no matter how he goofed on our royalties — and he must have been fully aware of it all the time he was not paying them. I hope that answers your question about "morality."

Could this be one of those things that you and Sterl and Israel are all aware of, and know the answer to, and only I am in the dark? I'm rather afraid it's the other way around — that I'm the first one to have dug it, unless Gid has already come on about it.

I particularly don't like the effect it will probably have on Putnam's. How come they haven't dug it already, for that matter? Doesn't it mean that G. can hang them up if they don't get his ok? I mean, even if we had a friendly judge that saw what a swindle G. was attempting and was of the opinion that the contract itself was invalid, I'm still afraid that Putnam's might not want trouble and would find the most expedient thing was to pressure us into giving G his 33% (out of our royalties, of course).

. . . The trouble is he's got our signatures on that damn ownership of all publication rights clause which sounds like it entitles him to *some* kind of consideration. Of course I've no idea on how strong a point we might have in that he simply doesn't have the right to own our damn book like that. . . .

We should look to our defense because I will never agree to have that scumbag wriggle into the deal. He's gotten enough out of that book for his $700.

Raoul

Ignoring the above considerations, Singer followed up the contract termination letter as the year drew to a close with a threat to sue if payment was not made.

Mason kicked off the new year with a letter covering a bullet-pointed host of loose ends, from the blurbs they were still waiting for, to the true identities of Hadj and Zoon and their suitability for the dedication:

79 Rue Daguerre, Paris, January 6th, 1964

Just drop you a line, dear T., as I post off the cons to Sterl, since there seem to be a number of trivial issues to settle.

- I felt your Bio was stunning, pinching the tenuous stuff of my Bio into tangible, bite-size matter for the public. Please change "poet" to "writer" though, you vicious cockcracker.
- You haven't mentioned if "L'Histoire d'O", or a just as groovy Customs Seizure Announcement have arrived. I went to awful trouble turning up this hard-to-get number, and it seems least you could acknowledge the inconvenience you thoroughly put me through. Also, I have culled through your hundreds of letters, skimming off the top gassers, but hesitate to send them on to an alert and libidinous, circlejerking Customs lady. "Looks like Hoff's trying to slip through more hot matter to T in detached pages disguised as ex-correspondence," she thinks, hefting the turgid bundle, and begins a peephole at which your irreplaceable, purple pulsing ZUMBA bursts forth spitting viciously after its unaccustomed confinement. Well, it's your zumba. Let me know if you want to try your luck.

- The P[utnam] contract seems to leave British rights open. That right? Don't you or Sterl have any limey leads? I could go to London if reality demanded. Why not give 'em both barrels. I wrote Sterl to tell Longanesi he's our sole representative now, and to ask for accounts if any.
- C is still banned here. If it comes out in NY, that will be a bit of switch and might make a telling publicity point.
- I've written Burroughs [for a blurb]. If [James] Jones has goofed [by not sending] let me know and I'll toddle over to that harp hypocrit and drub him soundly with my flexible arms.
- Is the preface going to be a problem? Strikes me there's material in your letters that could well serve here. Let me know if you need anything for this item.
- Deep in your heart, you know that "Hadj" applies to any gook that makes Mecca. Our friend's name was Sherif with last name like Abdelkader or something. . . . On the other hand, he was generally known as "Mr Hadj" all right, and that is best perhaps. I've gone to plenty of inconvenience on Zoom [ascertaining his real name] till I finally found a signed document. This signature consisted of three of your dink characters, and required some brushing-up of my previous work with this inscrutible medium. I am now satisfied that these three characters should be romanized Sun Wu Kung, but suppose it is best to leave the dedication as originally, perhaps, if that's what makes you happy, Mom. "Take care of your thoughts is the best!" Zoon had written on this document.

I feel somewhat easier about the clause in the G contract I wrote my last fire-fire letter on. I mean, the implication seems to be that all rights revert to him in case he defaults — a patent absurdity, goddamn it to hell.

I still feel he will pull something — probably this clause — though, since he's so much at home on legal street and can't stand getting coldcocked on this hot deal no doubt.

I heard from Litvinoff and Singer how they're in hot pursuit of our royalties. Actually, I'd thought, tactically, of holding up a bit here and using this issue for leverage to maybe bar him from trying to queer the P deal. Give it to him later, when he's let it slip by. Or intimating something along these lines. But I guess Lit and Sing know their business, and it's probably good to start waving the bat at him in any case. I dig their style. . . .

I hear conflicting tales about G. — that he's flatass broke with the dish washers chipping in to keep the Grande Séverine going; and that it's doing very well.

Take your pick. Either way, have to keep our guard up with this type person.

God bless you in advance,

Sherm

The Putnam contract was finally completed and signed in late January of 1964. The document (with various annotations initialled by Terry, Mason, and Minton), was for the U.S. territory only and was not favorable to the authors in many ways, as Mason had been pointing out, and as Girodias had no doubt predicted. For one thing, the contract was predicated on Terry and Mason guaranteeing they owned the copyright — something everyone knew they could not actually do.

The contract provided only a $1,000 advance and 10 percent royalties. In a complicated rider, Terry and Mason were completely liable for any award judgments against the publisher, i.e., for pornography or, presumably, a bad copyright. If a pirated edition came out, the publisher would be released from its obligation to pay royalties. One thing Mason did achieve was the deletion of the word *scandalous* as a liability. This was fortunate, especially considering that Putnam made *scandalous* the book's primary selling point.

With *Candy* coming out in a matter of months, Mason's concerns about the fairness of the contract faded into the giddy denouement of his near decade-long relationship with the publisher. As for Terry, he was proud of the book and was eager to see it reach a wider audience. The day Mason signed the Putnam contract is a day Girodias later recalled:

I had this fantastic nightclub, and [Mason] would stand on the sidewalk across the street for hours and hours and hours looking at the people coming in and out. You know, watching the place, and hating me for the fact that I was displaying all those things which he felt he had contributed to. That was before Putnam but after the publication of *Candy* in Paris. One day, he came walking into the nightclub. There was a bar at the entrance where I was usually sitting getting drunk. And he sat down next to me very quietly. I said, "Hello, Mason." And he said, "Do you have a pen?" So I gave him my pen, and I turned around to the woman I was talking to, and when I turned back to talk to Mason, he had gone. I asked the bartender, "Where's that fellow with my pen?" And he said, "He just walked out." Well, this is just what I imagine, but at that point he signed a contract with Walter Minton. And I think he needed my pen to sign that contract.

Chapter 26

Something Worth Blasting

The year 1964 was Terry's year. It began with the premiere of *Dr. Strangelove* on January 12, in New York City. A whole new world had opened for him — the world of cinema. Meanwhile, the much anticipated *Candy* was to make its U.S. debut in the spring. After the film's premiere, Mason wrote to Terry about an introduction to *Candy* — now lost, or perhaps never completed — which he was writing.

79 Rue Daguerre, Paris, January 23rd, 1964

Dearest Darling

I can see you're hopping mad at this delay as well you may, but in two-three days, not more, I'm posting you a draft of intro — more of a curtain raiser, but something I feel will do nicely in case we don't have a really good conventional preface of some kind which I, at any rate, find a lot more difficult.

Also sending pics of me to Putnam's and big bonus statement from Big Bill [Burroughs], who just came to Paris and hadn't gotten my Tangiers letter — also in two/three days tops. He's reading C now and getting his lean South Texas nuts off accordingly.

My intro will be needing a good going over by your sharp donkey cock for style and amplification — if you think it makes it — and I'll really have it off in 2/3 days. Could perhaps save some time if you'd tip me off — as I asked in my last — as to whether I should spend valuable afternoons editing your letters, looking for a 2nd copy of out-of-print "L'Histoire d'O", and other exciting projects you have hipped me to but queries about which you ignore. . . .

Big Bill came here to pick up 5 thou sent by Grove via Olymp which Git had of course spent on his restaurant and black paramour. Even Bill has finally soured a bit on G. at this blow, and he (Bill) used to be the only one I know who said he had no cause to beef.

Hold tight

Raff

As Putnam began its marketing campaign in New York, the Parisian authorities were preparing for Girodias's public ruin. General de Gaulle's conservative government was controlling media throughout France in an effort to ensure that nothing could embarrass the regime. While the Radio and Television Federation became a mouthpiece for Gaullist views, newspapers and magazines found themselves scrambling to conform to fear-and-favor pressures. Laws changed with the wind and were crippling to those who did not conform. Girodias, a continual source of scandal for over a decade, was particularly targeted; his numerous banned books could not be displayed in or outside any bookstore, no publicity could be given to them, and all future manuscripts were to be submitted to the Ministry of the Interior for review prior to publication. Christian Bourgeois, director of the prestigious Julliard publishing house, commented in *Newsweek,* "It's a scandal that illiterate policemen can interfere in my business." Cited for numerous violations, Girodias was sentenced for "outraging good morals" to a year in prison, a twenty-year ban from publishing, which he avoided, and a $20,000 fine, which he no doubt escaped paying.

In a letter of early March, 1964, Girodias blamed falling behind on payments to the authors on "the enormous difficulties I've had to deal with in the past two years," culminating in a jail sentence "not suspended this time." He goes on to imply that his legal troubles could be linked to *Candy:* "I took much greater risks in publishing *Candy* than a conventional publisher would have," and further, that "no legal necessity obliged me to sign a contract with you." Girodias pleaded with Terry to see the error of his betrayal, while also laying out his endgame strategy:

If our last contract is legally declared null and void by a French court, then our former agreement will be reinstated which means that I would be able to consider myself as the only rightful owner of the publication and licensing rights of a book which I bought for an outright sum. This may sound absurd to you but I can assure you that it is not; and, furthermore, the situation of *Candy,* from whichever angle you may wish to consider it (copyright for instance), is much too delicate to make a feud between us profitable. It would be rather interesting to have this case judged in a French court, *Candy* being banned in France and, therefore, illegal.

My proposal is as follows: I suggest that the validity of our contract be confirmed by both sides; I would reduce my share of the US publication rights (only) to 25% of the income and my share would be retained by you and Mason against the royalties I owe you, until our accounts are balanced. There are minor clauses I should like to have incorporated in that arrangement but the main thing, for the time being, is to know if you accept my offer or not.

Frankly, I would be relieved if you were to do so because, although you have good cause to be dissatisfied with my present financial dilemma, I still think that I have always acted in a loyal and friendly manner towards both Mason and you in all our previous dealings and I feel that this entitles me to being treated in a more understanding manner now that I am in a mess which defies description.

I know that Mason is furious at what he judges to be a total lack of concern on my part for other people's difficulties and problems. If I were that kind of person I would certainly be rich and safe from trouble. In the present case, you may be certain that it was not to frustrate or antagonize you both that I failed to pay what I owe you on time.

I hope to hear from you soon and am sending a copy of this letter to Mason.

Best,

Girodias

Terry apparently did not respond to Girodias's logic and pleading, preferring, no doubt, to write whimsical letters to others.

Seymour Krim, who had published an early story of Terry's in 1960 ("The Face in the Arena"), was publishing an advance excerpt from *Candy* for the men's magazine *Nugget.* With his typical humor, Terry wrote the editor regarding certain cuts and changes that had been requested.

March 29, 1964

RE: Publication of Excerpts from *Candy* in Nugget Magazine.

Dear Seymour:

I am very sorry to have to say so, but in my view the selections you propose to publish contain omissions so extensive, and alterations so radical, as to seriously misrepresent the actual and distinctive character of the novel itself.

Therefore I must ask for your full assurance that you will present these excerpts as such (i.e. as "excerpts") and not as a "condensed" or "abridged" version of the whole novel; and secondly, that you preface them (in type-face no smaller than that used in the text) with the following note (or similar note, acceptable to Mr. Litvinoff) in regard to their editing:

"Note: The authors wish to point out that, in accordance with prevailing magazine-publication standards, and in conformity to existing public-statutes concerning "obscenity," the following excerpts from *Candy* have undergone considerable editing of their form in the Putnam edition."

Now, Seymour (I mean, really!) I can understand your position in regard to wanting to avoid the use of the more dramatic of the so-called four-letter-words; and, out of my friendly feelings for you, and with a nightmare grimace of hilarity frozen across my heartbreak, I cheerfully went along with *all* of those deletions. Other deletions however — such as "damp" (proof #1A132), "jellybox" (proof#1A139) — are just too highly (and senselessly) crippling in terms of style and tone, and have got to be restored, or corrected, as indicated on the proofs enclosed.

I certainly cannot go along with such changes as Aunt Livia's "hot greaser cock" to "hot greaser stuff" (proof #1A157). The word "stuff" has vague and amorphous connotations, whereas it is well known that Livia required organ of stout and smart definition, and it does, I must say, reflect editorial shoddiness of a very shocking order indeed. I'm not insisting on the word "cock", but you have turned it into *chili* or something ("hot grease *stuff*"!) "Hot greaser joint" is acceptable, as is "bit", "wood", "rod", "dip-stick", "shaft", "staff", and "jelly-roll" (or "jumbo", *or* the very contemporary "zoomba"!). So here's a nice optional layout for you, Sy, (with a little Rorshack-test thrown in, eh? Hee-hee.). Anyway just make sure you don't use "stuff" (mah people don talk dat way).

Well, I guess that's thirty for now. You'll be hearing from my powerful solicitor who is charged to oversee these instructions.

Best,

Terry Southern

Paul Krassner, who had been publishing Terry throughout the early '60s in *The Realist,* prepared his "Impolite Interview" with Terry to coincide with the release of *Candy.* Terry's move away from the "quality Lit" arena, toward a kind of cultural and social activism, led to some interesting questions. Aware of his ambivalence about "mindflow," and Kerouac's writing in particular (which Terry finds "cloyingly sentimental"), Krassner quizzed Terry on the Beat scene:

Q: Do you think that the "beat movement" accomplished anything constructive?
A: Yes indeed — and something far greater than anyone seems to realize. No one, insofar as I know, has recognized that the Beat Generation is the source or origin of the great wave of Civil Rights action.

White participation is, of course, the thing that gave the Civil Rights movement its real center of momentum, in terms of *scope,* vastness of scope — Martin Luther King stressed this time and again, the necessity of not alienating the whites who were part of it — and this participation can be traced directly to the spirit first engendered by books like *On the Road* . . . that kind of personal, impulsive, do-something-crazy-and-impossible spirit — setting out for California with only three gallons of gas, or walking through Georgia armed with nothing but a beard and a guitar.

Krassner picked up on the hyperbolic accolades that Terry's contemporaries were so eager to shower upon him after *Strangelove*, but here, in a rare display of politesse, Terry gives credit, and defines what it is all about for him personally:

Q: Nelson Algren says that *The Magic Christian*, *Candy*, and *Dr. Strangelove* are each aspects of the same novel. How would you say they're related?
A: They might well be part of the *same*, but they are not all mine, because the basic conception of treating the bomb as "absurd" was Kubrick's. I think what you'll find they all have in common is that they blast smugness — and where you find smugness, there is sure to be something worth blasting.

"Smugness" probably sounds like an oversimplification of *Strangelove*, but I think that's what it finally comes down to . . . smugness over a foolproof system which may not be.

Chapter 27

A Suitable Vehicle for Prosecution

> What are the benefits of censorship? First of all, the preservation of government authority! The citizen reads what he is told to read by the State or by its newspapers. Then you have sexual frustration organized on a national scale: there has yet to be found a better method for keeping the masses in step, the working classes as well as the others. The consolidation of prejudice, and the destruction of authentic culture, of invention, and free will. The spirit of independence is cut down to its lowest common denominator. The State needs censorship to maintain itself alive.
>
> — Michel Bogous to Jack Kahane, *The Frog Prince*

In 1964, Walter Minton was confident that a decade of Supreme Court decisions concerning obscenity—culminating with the popularity of his own *Lolita*—had signaled the inevitable: censorship in America was finally losing its grip. This boded well not only for a society shedding its McCarthy skin, enjoying *Playboy,* and about to embrace the Pill, but for the artists, writers, and publishers who for generations had endured the wrath of censorship's visible and invisible expression in bannings, prison sentences, canceled contracts, fines, smear campaigns, injunctions, boycotts, shreddings, and the stigma of being labeled "pornographer."

Candy's instant popularity in the United States in 1964 represented the ultimate shrugging off and irrelevance of U.S. censorship laws, which had been abusively enforced across the nation since 1922 when they were used to outlaw the Shakespeare & Company edition of *Ulysses,* published by Sylvia Beach.

The rules facing Minton, Barney Rosset, and every other publisher in the United States, were hardly less amorphous and subjective in the mid-'60s than they had been in 1934. That was the year Bennett Cerf, publisher of Random House, challenged the illegality of *Ulysses* and won a judgment wherein the high court approved the "literary merit" of the book, and pithily defined "decency" as a work that "would not arouse the average person."

Every issue of *The Paris Review,* which was primarily a magazine of poetry, was sure to contain something that would offend some average person somewhere, and George Plimpton and the *Review* staff were very aware of the power of the port police. George had had a censorship issue with Terry in the early '50s over the phrase "don't get your shit hot." The line, excerpted from Terry's novel *Flash and Filigree,* had been transmuted by the *Review* to "don't get your crap hot" out of fear the magazine would be impounded. When the issue came out, the line had been further changed to "don't get hot." Terry was incensed, and George issued an apology in the magazine.

The issue of censorship arose again between George and Terry in 1958 over the word *cunty* in the "Writers at Work" series. In Terry's interview with Henry Green, the following exchange took place:

> **TS:** When you being to write something, do you begin with a certain *character* in mind, or rather with a certain *situation* in mind?
> **MR. GREEN:** Situation every time. . . . I got the idea of *Loving* from a manservant in the Fire Service during the war. He was serving with me in the ranks and told me he had once asked the elderly butler who was over him what the old boy most liked in the world. The reply was: "Lying in bed on a summer morning, with the window open, listening to the church bells, eating buttered toast with cunty fingers." I saw the book in a flash.

The censorship climate was slightly more relaxed because of a 1957 Supreme Court decision, enough so that George was not so concerned about the use of the word *cunty*. However, he was still aware of possible library bannings and distributor problems. Here is George's letter to Terry:

541 East 72nd Street February 11th, 1958

Dear Terry,

Well, of course I called a Crash Meeting to discuss the four-letter derivative spelled out in your last letter. It took me some time to get to the point, or rather to screw up my courage to pronounce the word in question, and eventually had to resort to chalking it up on a blackboard, tastefully inserting asterisks for at least two of the letters. Consternation was immediate. Jean Stein didn't know what the word meant: Humes explained it to her, but he was rather too complicated about it for her, and my impression was that she inferred the word had something to do with navel fluff. No matter. Her vote is a small one. Tom Guinzburg said he finally understood why the Viking warehouses were full to overflowing with copies of *Loving*, that any book that comes to one in a flash generated by a c**nty finger was bound to end up in the bins, and as for Peter Matthiessen, who, as you know, has been an anal man from way back, he suggested 'crap*y' or even, and he gulped, 'shi**y'. William Pene du Bois suggested — a urinary tract worshipper — 'pissy'. Bob Silvers recommended 'hincty', and Jean Stein pressed as a substitute "wolly' (I think she got 'cu**ty' somehow mixed up with 'cottoney' — thus my 'navel fluff supposition), and among us, a majority fortunately, favored a non-asterisked c**nty, and thus it will appear in the magazine, provided, of course, that's what the good manufacturer wishes to have in there himself. I do think, frankly, that the Viking Press will bring up the question again when Volume Two of the Art of Fiction appears; they are concerned with High School readers, whose reading, regretfully, is controlled by librarians and school boards who are down on odors of any sort, much less those of the orifice to which you refer. . . .

As ever,

George

The interview was published with "cunty fingers" intact.

* * *

It is no accident that 1964 was the year America finally cast off its bookish sexual shackles. Years of litigation had led up to that point — spearheaded by Barney Rosset, the tireless publisher of Grove Press and *Evergreen Review*, and his dynamic team of editors and attorneys. Team Rosset included over a dozen First Amendment experts at the American Civil Liberties Union fighting in district and state superior courts across the country, as well as the brilliant lawyers Edward de Grazia and Charles Rembar. Their eloquent and compelling arguments for the cultural significance of erotic literature and the value of a society free enough to enjoy it were honed over nearly a decade of arguing literary obscenity cases before higher courts. Grove's team demonstrated the "artistic merits" and "redeeming social value" of authors and artists including Henry Miller, Lenny Bruce, Claude LeLouche, Allen Ginsberg, Hubert Selby Jr., and now Terry Southern and Mason Hoffenberg. To appreciate the importance of Grove's efforts, one need only remember the climate of fear among publishers concerning anything potentially "offensive" to anyone. A banned book could be financially ruinous, and the "decency" laws were vaguely defined and frequently abused.

A watershed event in the loosening of the censorship laws was Chief Justice Brennan's 1957 Supreme Court decision stating that the First Amendment protects works even if they might appeal to prurient interests and affront community standards. Brennan's decision arose from the case of Samuel Roth, an author and publisher, known to authorities to have sold copies of James Joyce's *Ulysses* and other books since the early '30s. In 1955, Roth was arrested and convicted for sending through the mails "obscene materials," erotic cover illustrations by Aubrey Beardsley.

Chief Justice Brennan, who would be involved for two more decades with making obscenity decisions, upheld Roth's conviction, but for the first time attempted to define obscenity, stating that a work that was "utterly without redeeming social importance" was *not* protected by the First Amendment, but that *literature* was. He also determined that the test for obscenity was "whether to the average person, applying contemporary community standards, the dominant theme of the material taken as a whole appeals to prurient interest."

By 1960 Grove was making history testing the Supreme Court's sketchy definitions, challenging in 1959 the U.S. postal ban on its unexpurgated edition of D. H. Lawrence's *Lady Chatterley's Lover.* Grove's attorney Charles Rembar argued not only that *Chatterley* had literary merit, but that the work elicited a "normal sexual interest" as opposed to a sick, morbid, or prurient one. Grove fought for over a year for *Lady Chatterley*'s freedom, and when it finally came turned its attention to Henry Miller.

Terry wrote about the significance of the long-overdue appearance of the *Tropics* in his *Nation* review of November, 1961:

> What is rare . . . and quite possibly unique, is for a culture to have at its bosom an artist whose major work has not merely gone unpublished in his own country, but has actually been outlawed there; work, that is to say, hailed throughout the rest of the world as of the very first importance, and more widely read, according to the University of California Librarian, Lawrence Powell, than any American living other than Upton Sinclair, or any dead, other than Mark Twain and Jack London. Yet it is only within the past year, through the sustaining wisdom and courage of Mr. Rosset's Grove Press, that *Tropic of Cancer* and *Tropic of Capricorn* have at last appeared on the open market. . . .

Shortly after its publication, Grove's edition of *Tropic of Cancer* was banned from sale across the country. By the winter of 1964, fifteen lawyers from the ACLU had become involved in the *Tropic* fight, defending obscenity charges in as many as sixty different suits nationwide. As it was outlawed in state after state, the book was finally, decisively liberated from the "obscene" standing by a victory in the Florida Supreme Court. In his ruling, Chief Justice Brennan further defined what could *not* be branded as obscenity and denied constitutional protection: "Material dealing with sex in a manner that advocates ideas, or that has literary or scientific or artistic value or any other form of social importance."

The decision had far-reaching implications, and even made life temporarily more livable for persecuted comedian Lenny Bruce. On the day of the decision, the Illinois supreme court overturned the 1962 conviction that stemmed from his arrest at the Gate of Horn in Chicago for a nightclub act deemed obscene. Grove's victory opened doors and jail cells for artists, writers, and performers across the United States—but the fight was far from over.

The Kennedy era signaled a vibrant, healthy attitude toward sexuality. In a Democratic White House, the Kennedys invited such writers as Jack Gelber, author of the so-called subversive play *The Connection,* to literary functions. But after JFK's assassination, the FBI began routing out "obscenity" with renewed vigor. "Pornographers," especially those who were prominent, Democratic, East Coast writers, like Terry Southern, were targeted, and their works often branded obscene—often through a coordinated effort of anonymous "complaints," police raids, newspaper articles, and legal actions designed to go to higher courts. While the U.S. Supreme Court was occasionally making painful, stammering decisions on whether or not certain works were "obscene," there was a continual nationwide effort—spearheaded by the FBI, aided by police, and implemented by district attorneys—to rustle up and bring through the courts suitable "vehicles" for prosecution.

In March of 1965, the FBI reported that the U.S. district attorney "*at Department instruction,*" was preparing to present *Candy* as an obscene work to a federal grand jury in Houston. They further advised that the book be read by the U.S. Attorney General himself:

> In view of the alleged extensive printing of the book "Candy" and the fact that complaints have been received in two different geographical areas of the country concerning same, a copy of this book is enclosed for your review, and it is requested that this Bureau be advised as to its suitability as a vehicle for prosecutive action under the interstate Transportation of Obscene Matter Statutes.

The case was closed on April 20, 1965, "in view of the Department's ruling that 'Candy' was not a suitable vehicle for prosecution, no further investigation is being conducted." *Candy* was off the hook.

By the spring of 1966, the "Brennan Doctrine," which protected works like *Candy,* of "redeeming social value," was put to the test with *Fanny Hill,* a.k.a. *Memoirs of a Lady of Pleasure.* The book, originally written in 1749, was the first ever to become the subject of an obscenity trial, in 1821 — and now it was back again. Both the Massachusetts and New Jersey attorney generals demanded it be shuttered away forevermore as an "obscene" work. Representing Barney Rosset, Charles Rembar convinced the Supreme Court justices that this classic book concerning a young girl's sexual awakening and descent into prostitution "had literary merit, historical significance and psychological value." In a victory for literary expression, Rembar further convinced the court that there could be no such thing as "well-written pornography."

If any book provided a test for that "no such thing as well-written pornography" argument, it was *Naked Lunch,* which, by 1966, was still the subject of a three-year old lawsuit. Rosset had published *Naked Lunch* in 1959 and had warehoused the books until 1963, when he decided to try his luck and distribute the book — resulting in the arrests of booksellers nationwide, including one in Boston where the case moved up to state superior court. In the history of censorship, not surprisingly, works of fiction (and poems such as *Howl*) that used expressive, innovative language to exorcise social and political taboos invited prosecution as a matter of course — not because of "prurience," but because these works often questioned the status quo. *Naked Lunch* incited much more ire and outrage than *Candy,* because of Burroughs's panavision treatment of homo (and poly) sexuality, drug life, and the intersection of sex and drugs with government corruption, corporate decadence, advertising, and greed. As Terry wrote of *Naked Lunch*:

> It is a devastating ridicule of all that is false, primitive, and vicious in current American life: the abuses of power, hero worship, aimless violence, materialistic obsession, intolerance, and every form of

> hypocrisy. . . . No one writing in English, with the exception of Henry Miller, has done as much towards freeing the writer (and tomorrow the reader) of the superstitions surrounding the use of certain words and certain attitudes.

In the Boston trial of *Naked Lunch,* attorney Edward de Grazia had Allen Ginsberg and Norman Mailer testify on behalf of the book's "social importance." Grove Press was the defendant. At issue was no longer whether Burroughs, Grove, or the bookseller had engaged in any criminal act, but whether Grove had the right to publish the book without censure. The testimony was provocative and passionate. At one point de Grazia quoted a letter from Burroughs:

> What we are dealing with here is a barrier of what can only be termed medieval superstition and fear, precisely the same barrier that held up the natural sciences for some hundreds of years with dogma rather than examination and research. In short, the same objective methods that have been applied to natural science should now be applied to sexual phenomena with a view to understand and control these manifestations. A doctor is not criticized for describing the manifestations and symptoms of an illness, even though the symptoms may be disgusting.
>
> I feel that a writer has the right to the same freedom. In fact, I think that the time has come for the line between literature and science, a purely arbitrary line, to be erased.

But the real star of the show was Allen Ginsberg. De Grazia had given Ginsberg access to the empty courtroom chambers at night to practice his oratory, and they rehearsed arguments together in Ginsberg's funky hotel room. As de Grazia recalls in a recently published article about the *Naked Lunch* trial:

> In those days . . . with his great shaggy beard, balding pate, and mane of long stringy hair, Allen looked like the Lord of the Beatniks. When he took the witness stand, however, Allen tried to make a good impression on the judge by wearing a white shirt, a figured tie, and a jacket for what I like to think was the first time ever.

> The presiding Boston Irish-Catholic Judge Eugene A. Hudson peered down at the New York Jewish-Buddhist poet and said "straighten your collar!" He seemed to regard Allen as a schoolboy who had come up to the front of the room to recite his lessons. The poet responded by straightening his collar, peering up at the judge, and saying "Yes, sir."
>
> And then, responding to my questions — among those that he and I had developed together . . . He talked virtually without interruption for nearly an hour about the structure of Burroughs' novel and about the social and political importance of its images and ideas. . . .

Judge Hudson, however, was not persuaded, and ruled *Naked Lunch* to be obscene. Grove et al. had lost the battle, but the brilliant testimony and compelling arguments which had been amassed over time in the case, won the war, for on July 7th, 1966, the Massachusetts Supreme Court reversed Hudson's decision.

Naked Lunch was thus the last work of fiction to be censored by the U.S. Post Office and Customs officials. The world finally was safe for erotic works of the imagination to see the light of day.

As De Grazia said recently, "The Nixon administration tried and failed [under Warren Berger] to blunt the radical, revolutionary, libertarian gains for art and literature of the Brennan doctrine" but "our *revolution*, in terms of sexual expression, particularly in works of the imagination, remains quite secure." In film and photography, however, artists are still vulnerable to prosecution — particularly if children are involved. De Grazia was called in to help with the pre-production of *Lolita*'s 1986 remake — because the film's producers were prepared to cut the most important scenes in self-censorship.

"Alarming today," says de Grazia, whose focus is now on civil rights, "is the term *terrorism* in the hands of this [Bush/Ashcroft] administration . . . Protests, antiwar speech, criticism of the government — these are all endangered again." Indeed, unprecedented rollbacks have occurred such that "terrorist" and "terrorism" are in many ways more chilling yet undefined labels than "pornographer" and "pornography" ever were.

Chapter 28

Candy Does America

While Terry had been waiting for this moment — when America would discover his writing talents — Mason was embarrassed and alarmed by the attention. Whether this was because he had little else in his oeuvre to fall back on or because Terry's hand was so evident in the book, there were plenty of reasons for Mason to feel awkward. Mason's literary background was impossible to quantify, and the press focused on Terry's "undiscovered" backlog of European-published works, his unsung novels, the phenomenon of *Dr. Strangelove,* and the scandal that everyone seemed to know *Candy* would be. Many of Terry's friends and admirers in the "quality Lit" world leapt at the chance to endorse him as the serious writer of brilliance and dedication they considered him to be.

As the spotlight kept missing Mason, he began a downward spiral into oblivion. Rattled by his inconclusive dealings with Girodias in Paris, with the prospect of a lot of money from G. P. Putnam's coming in — but still unclear if the authors would receive any of it — and with his jealousy of Terry intensifying every day, drugs became a central way out. Erratic behavior and paranoia ruled his day, and during the next few months of critical negotiations between Putnam and Girodias, Mason would occasionally appear — only to say "no," and create more confusion. The chemicals were taking their toll. As he wrote in his journal around this time:

> My arms are without legs. Now what are they going to do with the pants for a shirt my mouth gave them for Christmas?

My shoulders used to like my teeth, and my hands would sleep with my eyebrows.

And then my brain had this heart-attack. . . .

Now everything refuses to work anymore, and they've gotten to hate one another and play dirty tricks on each other. . . .

My left foot isn't going to walk anymore; it wants to lie around in blue jeans and be an intellectual like my brain.

Mason stopped writing to Terry shortly after he sent the following handwritten note from Spain:

Spain, April 9th, 1964

Dear Dad:

I've been down here living it up with a groovy group of anglo-Jewish expatriates, but am soon returning to big town, U.S.A. I think, where we can get on with the job.

I saw a spectacular American chick fall flat on her face in a puddle of mud in one of those narrow streets down here.

Also seen it rain in Spain.

In Paris I saw Gid. He's got his fangs out and must be beaten to a pulp pronto. Tell our attorneys to attack at once. (I'll pay my share gladly out of royalties.)

I'll write in more detail on return to France.

Kindest personal regards,

Brett

In late April, *Newsweek* ran an article about Girodias's censorship woes in France and prison sentence. Girodias responded to the magazine shortly after:

7 rue St. Séverin, Paris, May 4th, 1964

Your article "Creeping Censorship" (INTERNATIONAL, April 20) is substantially correct, except on one point.

The reason I received such a brutal sentence, including one

year's imprisonment, was not the publication some ten years ago of "Our Lady of the Flowers," but of six other books, also quite old. The judge took a particular dislike to one of them, Harriet Daimler's dainty novel "The Woman Thing," which he insisted was sheer pornography. My pig-headed refusal to accept that definition sealed my fate. . . .

Censorship, be it Russian, Portuguese, or French, is everywhere the same. And you were quite right to put moral and political censorship in the same bag in your article, as they always have the same purpose.

Maurice Girodias, publisher

In New York, Peter Israel knew *Candy* would provoke a national dialogue debating the book's "decency." Fearing a national backlash to ban the book might take hold, he hoped to build a public consensus against a pornographic reading of it. With the authors' help, he solicited these quotes for *Candy*'s jacket:

"As among other things, it is a satire on pornography, it might be mistaken for pornography; but to discuss *Candy* as a pornographic book would be as crass and unfounded as to catalogue *Gulliver's Travels* as a 'travel book.' The inspiration of *Candy,* as is implicit in its title, is Voltaire's *Candide* — a book which also outraged people at the time, but I don't think any sane person today would maintain that it should not have been published."

— FRANCIS WYNDHAM, Literary Editor, *The Queen*

"Morally bracing . . . in its satirical foray against sickbed sex, both scientific and literary . . . Candy is a girl who has been freed of all unreasonable puritanical restraints yet who dwells in a limbo where up-to-date females are expected to give sexual pleasure without, however, experiencing pleasure themselves. . . . This is the stuff of heartbreak."

WILLIAM STYRON, *New York Review of Books*

"Although Byron did it at times in *Don Juan,* sex and humor are extremely hard to combine. Candy does it, however, by sharpening the humor to satire — and what a rogue's gallery of high (brow) fashion we meet! Mephesto, Krankeit, Grindle! Yes, lots of satirical novels are coming out now, but they are almost never funny. Congratulations—*Candy* is the funniest book I've read in a poon's age!"

— DWIGHT MACDONALD

"A work of genuine literary merit; I like its satire, its grotesqueries and its inventiveness."

— ROBERT B. SILVERS, Editor-in-Chief, *New York Review of Books*

"*Candy* has all the salty, irreverent wit and penetrating humor one has come to expect from Terry Southern—and from Mason Hoffenberg. It should be a good shot in the arm to the American reading public."

— JAMES JONES

By early May, the advance reviews were coming out for this most anticipated book. *Newsweek* dubbed *Candy* "the first genuinely comic pornographic novel" and enthusiastically summarized the book's hip, Beat, and banned Parisian origins. Putnam's full-page ads proclaimed:

> Stand aside, Franny and Zooey; the age of Hadj and Zoon is upon us. The new era promises to be . . . a lot more fun. The most marvelous . . . denouement in modern letters — the climax of a Greek tragedy rewritten by Nathaniel West and S. J. Perelman."

Candy was released by Putnam in hardcover on May 12, 1964. Putnam placed an ad in *Publishers Weekly* introducing the nation's booksellers to a gift-wrapped surprise — Candy Christian:

> Meet Candy
>
> THE LOVED AND LOVABLE COED FROM RACINE, WISCONSIN
>
> FIRST PRINTING: SOLD OUT; SECOND PRINTING: IN STORES; THIRD PRINTING: ON ORDER.
>
> Can a little girl from a small town in the Midwest find love and understanding in this troubled world? Meet Candy, the beautiful, big-

hearted heroine of the wildest, funniest romp since *One Hundred Dollar Misunderstanding.* *

The culture wars were on — the *New York Times* and *Chicago Tribune* refused to advertise the book. Many reviewers ignored *Candy*'s literary aspects, focusing on the cultural phenomenon and controversy. "Want to Read *Candy*? Don't Go to the Library" was the headline of a typical article reflecting the kind of censorship that was alive and well in America;

> Unavailable in all [Northern Illinois] libraries are "Candy," a satire on pornography; Harold Robbins' profanity-filled "The Carpetbaggers," and Henry Miller's controversial "Tropic of Cancer." . . . One library has reported guarding the community reading habits so tightly that certain psychology and anthropology volumes are not placed on the open shelves, but held "only for serious researchers."

But librarians resisted the "literature vs. pornography" debate and ordered *Candy*, following the American Library Association's Library Bill of Rights, which stated:

> Censorship of books, urged or practiced by volunteer arbiters of morals or political opinion or by organizations that would establish a coercive attempt of Americanism, must be challenged by libraries in maintenance of their responsibility to provide public information and enlightenment through the printed word.

Alfred Chester, writing in the *New York Herald Tribune,* put it bluntly, stating that *Candy*'s publication, "is an event of sociological rather than literary importance." Chester explored the contradictions in censorship firsthand:

> Official United States, or Texas, policy on literature is completely incomprehensible. When I came in from Mexico last year, two

*Robert Gover's 1961 satirical novel.

Brownsville inspectors flipped through my treasured Olympia books and returned them to my suitcase, but they wanted to seize Stendhal's *De l'Amour* and Sartre's *La Nausée,* both in French. I was kept waiting for two hours while the books were cleared by some masterbrain in the Customs building. America would do well to establish special ports of entry for people carrying books, wearing beards or other dress not considered standard uniforms of respectability.

Candy was arousing outrage and ire, especially in the Bible Belt and the Midwest. Many letters to the editor were written by self-proclaimed "Christians" outraged by Candy's actions, not to mention her sacrilegious surname. Terry was astonished by one of them in particular:

SMUT IN THE LIBRARY
Editor, Daily News:

Well, now that the forces of decency have finally asserted themselves in the case of the movie, "Lorna", I feel it's my Christian duty to alert the citizenry to the same type of degenerate smut that exists in our public library: not in Greenwich Village or other places of sin and iniquity, but right here in good old Lebanon, PA.

Well, here we are fortunate enough to have a newspaper which fights on the side of good and righteousness. The book to which I refer is "Candy," by Terry Southern. Now, I haven't personally read this book, but a friend told me that it is the worst sort of smut he has ever put his eyes upon, and is an abomination to every God-fearing individual. Innocent children, into whose hands this book might possibly fall, would be done great harm by reading it. They are always the ones who are hurt, our young people. To imagine that it is allowed in our public library is difficult to understand. The atheists, fellow travelers, communists, and communist dupes who write this sort of thing should not be allowed a place in our community.

Christians, unite in this great season we are now enjoying and purge these atheistic elements from our midst.

The Holy Warrior

After Lenny Bruce weighed in, calling *Candy* Terry's "second coming" after *The Magic Christian, Publishers Weekly,* usually temperate in its editorializing, surprised many in the publishing world when it bottom-lined *Candy* in its March 23 forecast as "sick sex."

> "Candy," originally known as "Lollipop," is a hot potato originally published by Olympia Press in Paris. In a dubiously humorous style and with very bad taste, the authors put their pretty, addle-brained, college-student heroine, Candy Christian, through a fantastic and aerobatic series of sexual adventures.

"Sick humor," was a calculated term that the media had used to vilify and quarantine Bruce, and *PW*'s hostile allusion was not lost upon people like Nelson Algren. Algren wrote the first national review for *Candy* in *Life* magazine. In its May 8 issue, Algren warns of the impending culture wars *Candy* was bringing to a head:

> UN-AMERICAN IDEA: SEX CAN BE FUNNY
>
> Sex in America, after this event, is not going to be the same. Horrified warnings are already being issued by defenders of public morals. The usually bland *Publishers Weekly* has waved off the nation's booksellers by branding *Candy* as "sick sex, pulp writing." That kind of criticism is both childish and inaccurate, but the fact remains that this is definitely not a book to give your mother — or your nephew. . . .
>
> The awkward truth he presents is that sex is not sick, but innocent. And worse news yet to reviewers — Southern is an absolutely first-rate writer. So now the whole bicycling throng of literary begrudgers, too obsequious to oppose yet too chintzy to praise, too canny to hate and too careful to love, will have to pedal like mad to fit Southern in to some acceptable preconception.
>
> "He's like Nathaniel West!" is sure to be one guess. "No! — he's Lenny Bruce!" another will insist. . . . "Not at all! He's a combination of Orwell, Burroughs, Joe Heller, and Evelyn Waugh!" *The Magic Christian, Candy,* and *Dr. Strangelove* are the work of a major satirist. Furthermore, each are aspects of the same novel. In short, Southern is holding up a triple-angled mirror to America in

which, given a rudimentary sense of humor, we are enabled to see ourselves as we really are.

As sex and satire simultaneously broke into the American consciousness with *Candy* and *Dr. Strangelove,* so too did Terry Southern. The press began to package him as a self-made man who had arrived to save America from its stuffy Puritanism and Eisenhower hangover. In the din of this kind of press, Terry did not rise to thwart these assertions quickly enough (if at all) for many of his former collaborators — particularly Kubrick — who began taking ads out in major newspapers to set the authorship record straight regarding *Dr. Strangelove.* With every new article proclaiming Terry as deus ex machina, Mason's anxiety about his old buddy grew greater.

William Styron, a friend of Terry's since the Paris days, wrote the review for the *New York Review of Books.* The piece appeared with a large illustration from *Alice in Wonderland. Candy* represented a chance for reviewers to reexamine America's puritanical and hypocritical attitudes toward women's sexuality and the spate of self-help books on sexual fulfillment. Styron seized the opportunity to skewer the kind of sexual "training manual" popularized by Dr. Albert Ellis in his *Sex and the Single Man, Sex Without Guilt,* and *The American Sexual Tragedy.* Styron wrote that Ellis

> pits the bachelor trainee ("you") against a hypothetical foe known as "your girlfriend." Most of the tactics in seduction are elementary, and the physiological terrain described by Dr. Ellis is old and trampled ground. The book's real distinction lies in its style; and since the style, among sexologists as among poets and novelists, is the measure of the man, let Dr. Ellis speak for himself: "Coitus itself can in some instances be unusually exciting and arousing. If your girlfriend is not too excitable at a certain time, but is willing to engage in intercourse, she may become aroused through doing so, and may wind up by becoming intensely involved sexually, even though she was relatively passive when you first started to copulate."
>
> It is this kind of mechanical howtoism, with its clubfooted prose and its desolating veterinary odor, that constitute the really

> prurient writing of our time. It is pornographic and disgusting, and it is one of the major targets of *Candy* in its satirical foray against sickbed sex, both scientific and literary.

The May 18 issue of *The Nation* featured a cover story by Nelson Algren, "Donkey Man by Twilight." In this major profile, which also explored Terry's short fiction and new journalism, Algren said of *Candy:*

> [S]ex in this country has been sick for so long, has been a wasting affliction instead of a joyous fulfillment for so long, that by restoring the comedy of it, Southern has done something we should be grateful for. . . .
>
> Candy is simply a honey-haired girl-child with a marvelous aptitude for wriggling out of her panties in noble causes. When the cause happens to be a humpback, what could be more noble than to give oneself to his hump? . . .
>
> Candy is a girl who can't say No to men who need her, and from Greenwich Village to Tibet, they all do.
>
> Like Alice ducking down the rabbit-hole, Candy never pauses to wonder how she's going to get out again. Like Alice, she fits herself into any circumstance and then wishes "it would stop happening." Her search for the father through a setting as changeful as Alice's is really a journey through the country of America's sexual myths. Before it is concluded, I'm afraid, Henry Miller will be startled to find *Tropic of Cancer* in the same league as *The Good Earth.* After *Candy,* sex in America is never going to be quite the same.

Walter Minton and Terry appeared on a TV show together to publicize *Candy.* Though Mason was in New York and apparently eager to do promotion, Putnam apparently decided not to use him. His chagrin emerged in an interview conducted for *Playboy* much later:

> Dig a thing like this: I finally came to the States during the big promotion and I met this public-relations guy from Putnam's who was handling the book. We talked and he said public-relations shit like 'Beautiful, baby. You can really go,' and he got me onto a TV show for that night. Then he took Terry out to lunch separately and suddenly

everything went on like I had leprosy. I never got onto the TV show or any other one. And I never found out what Terry told that guy at lunch — or if he said anything at all. For some reason, I was just cut out of the whole scene.

Two days after the book's release, Minton, who had only recently met Terry for the first time, provided him with an update on the book's publication. Ironically, the *Candy* contract was not yet executed between them—having been delayed on Mason's end in Paris.

G. P. Putnam's Sons, New York, NY, May 14, 1964

Dear Terry:

It was a very hectic day — and I'm sorry that we didn't have an opportunity to talk a little more. But it was very good to at least meet you.

It's a bit early to spot definite trends, but I thought you might like to know how *Candy* is starting off in her American debut.

As Peter told you, we shipped books so that they would not arrive in stores much before the first of May — this being a purposeful act in this instance. Last week, May 4-8, we had 280 reorders. This week we had quite a flurry on Monday, 406, and on publication date, May 12, there were 458. I think this, in good part, had to do with the LIFE review, since the orders came from all over the country, although about 60% of them were from New York, where we had the heaviest advance subscription — which is normal in any case, but especially predictable in the case of *Candy.*

On May 13 we had 90 re-orders; this morning there are 3,500. So *Candy* is finding an audience. We have a good gauge of best-sellerdom in THE SPY WHO CAME IN FROM THE COLD which continues ensconced at the top of the best-seller list. *Candy*'s reorder pattern is such that I think we'll hit the list fairly quickly, although at what level I can't yet predict. I'll be in touch with you again.

It was good to see you, even briefly.

Best regards,

Walter J. Minton

Minton was correct in his analysis. By May 25, Putnam had exhausted its second printing before it ran, with over 5,000 reorders from booksellers. To add fuel to the fire, Putnam began shipping insert cards of Nelson Algren's *Life* review inside every copy shipped to bookstore owners. Meanwhile, novelist Jane Howard began an in-depth story on Terry, with *Life* photographer Steve Shapiro to provide a visual essay on Terry, including his family life in Canaan.

On June 8, Sterling Lord submitted the Putnam edition of the novel to the U.S. copyright office — knowing full well that the basis for the claim was contentious. Two weeks later, *Newsweek* ran a piece profiling Terry and *Candy,* which portrayed Terry as the "idea-man" behind *Strangelove* and *Candy,* proclaiming, "Terry Southern has assaulted mankind for its perverse misuse of the two most dynamic forces in the modern world, sexual energy and nuclear power." Mason's worst fears were materializing: Terry was getting all the credit. *Newsweek*'s profile by staff writer Mel Gussow firmly established Terry's arrival. Ironically, the media was finally discovering Terry the novelist as he was leaving literature for film — literally boarding a plane for Los Angeles. Gussow wrote:

> Terry Southern is a new kind of best-selling novelist — a comic pornographer with a profound moral sense. . . . His prose has a weirdly old-fashioned grace, like antique gold filigree, in which his radical new ideas glow like blood-red stones. . . .
>
> "Attacking smugness is the novelist's and moviemaker's most important function," Southern said just before taking off from New York for the Coast. In an interview with NEWSWEEK, he reports that the campaign seemed to be going well. Publishers are already clamoring to see his latest work in progress, "Blue Movie," a novel about "a very strong Bergman-Fellini-type movie director" who is concerned, like Southern himself, with "testing the limits" of the esthetic acceptability of erotic art.

Riding the media wave like a seasoned cowboy, Terry's pronouncements articulated his mandate to shake things up, and, as

Ginsberg would later put it, "change the curve of culture." The "quality Lit" world was now in the rearview mirror, and Terry even had a parting shot for its current luminary, Norman Mailer:

> "I think this is a golden age for creative work of any kind," the long-haired, unpressed, unbuttoned, chain-smoking Southern said. "The people who go all out will make it. We've only scratched the surface of our Freudian heritage. We are undertaking an exploration of the mind and we're making some interesting discoveries. We have discovered the value of not being prejudiced. The assumption has always been that there have been limits. But we now know that there are no limits." . . .
>
> Ironically, Southern now has a 29-acre farm in the Berkshires, complete with cows, chickens, and sheep. But he has no intention of going square. Until the last lingering taboos are destroyed, he says, "the effect of art should be iconoclastic. But the motivation should be impulsive, natural. Unfortunately, not all our writers should trust their impulses. Some of them, like Norman Mailer, have lousy impulses."

Candy was selling even faster than *The Spy Who Came In from the Cold* — or any other bestseller the company had ever had. According to Putnam sales records for June 15, 10,000 copies were sold in the book's first two days on the market, and 14,000 copies were sold during that first week. New York's two best bookstores, Bookards and Brentano's, reported *Candy* to be their number one bestseller.

Putnam's second wave of advertising appeared in the *New York Times,* announcing, in a font that could be read across the length of a subway car:

> "Sex in America, after this event,
> is not going to be the same." — LIFE MAGAZINE
>
> In just a few short weeks America has made an unprecedented bestseller out of this unique comedy. Why? Because *Candy* is a refreshing breeze in America's house of hearts, a comic chop at all our false

totems, and a veritable earthquake in the underground literature of our time.

With Terry now being identified in *Candy*'s advertising as "co-author of *Dr. Strangelove*" and talk of *Candy*-the-movie bubbling about, Mason's fears about being left behind on any film deal were so great that he hired his father's New York attorney, Gideon Cashman, to draft a sharing agreement. In it he and Terry would forever share all proceeds 50-50, including any screenplay fees, even if Mason himself didn't do any writing.

Chapter 29

Going Hollywood

Terry's fairy-tale initiation into the film industry — working with Kubrick in Europe — fueled his newfound dedication to the medium. And the press frenzy surrounding *Candy* — plus *Strangelove's* critical success and Academy Award–nominated screenplay — sold the film industry on Terry. MGM's studio chief (and a friend of Kubrick's) John Calley recruited Terry to work on an all-star movie that needed screenplay help and a black comic touch, *The Loved One*. Its director, Tony Richardson, was fresh off the mega-success of *Tom Jones,* which had won several Academy Awards that year. Calley flew Terry out for a month of initial meetings, and Terry and Tony hit it off immediately. *Candy* had risen from ninth to seventh place among America's bestselling novels. While Terry was all too aware of the horror stories concerning the dismantling of writers in Los Angeles (including Faulkner, whom he had met through Jean Stein in the '50s), the time and sensibility seemed especially right for Terry.

Shortly after working on *The Loved One,* in a radio interview with Casper Citron broadcast in July 1965 on New York's WOR, Jack Gelber and novelist Elaine Dundy talked about *Candy* and the state of the novel. Terry, arriving late with a drink audibly tinkling, was dark, brooding, and cynical—a cross between an über-hip Lenny Bruce and his old nonplussed self.

> **GELBER:** New ground, Terry . . . new ground . . . that's a theme that keeps going on in your work, or your talks with me . . . What kind of new ground do you think *Candy* breaks?

SOUTHERN: There are no books that treat the erotic as *romantically*, as *explicitly* as *Candy* does.
CITRON: And you think this is why the public is going wild?
SOUTHERN: I don't know what the *public* is doing, but I mean, this is something *I'm* interested in . . . the novel . . . has to move *ahead*, because, you get something like Bergman and Fellini . . . *man*, the novel has *got* to move ahead! . . . What I'm saying is very simple. The most *powerful* empathetic sensory perceptions are sight and sound. Right? . . . *Sight and sound* engages you more than —
GELBER: The act of reading.
SOUTHERN: Right.
GELBER: I'm not sure I like your hierarchy. There is no doubt in my mind that physiologically speaking, sight, sound, smell, touch are much more *active* sensory perceptions than *reading* about something . . . but that has nothing to do with *meaning*! I mean, after all, people don't *write* things just to get a *visceral* reaction — they obviously *mean* something. If you mean something, you don't necessarily have to go out and use the most immediate sensory apparatus such as the movies.
SOUTHERN: You'd better.

Terry's overnight celebrity ushered in all kinds of opportunities, and some still knocked from the East Coast. Bennett Cerf, editor in chief at Random House, offered him $35,000 for his next novel, sight unseen. Terry led him on, despite his promise of *Blue Movie* to Peter Israel of Putnam, with whom he had already discussed publication. It was ironic that the publishing world, which had so long ignored him, was now offering him one hundred times the amount Girodias had given him and Mason only six years ago. Such incongruities reinforced the cynicism with which Terry viewed the whole "writing game," and he didn't think much about burning the tenuous bridges these merchants, agents, and co-writers were standing on.

In August 1964, Terry was profiled in *Playboy* magazine. In the full-page, glossy photograph, Terry sits cross-legged in a white room, dressed in a well-cut black suit. Looking penetratingly into the camera, clean-shaven and sharp, an alluring *Candy* nymphette in the soft-focus background, he cast an arresting, provocative image. Terry's name was in bold caps, and underneath it the words CANDY MAN. The *Playboy* piece declared, "There is an unbridled wildness to his prose — as wild as the pilot's exultant cry in *Dr. Strangelove* as he straddles the plummeting H-bomb."

While Kubrick actively tried to counteract the misconceptions about him being fostered in the press, Mason was simply bewildered by being ignored. In Spain, he retreated further into drugs. As he would later reflect, "It was my fault. I was lying in Paris, suffering because my family was breaking up. It's like you win the lottery and your life falls apart. I lost my kids, I had a big dope habit. I just didn't give a shit. And that's not the right way to handle it when you suddenly have a gold mine."

Apparently Mason's bravura concerning his authorship was not offered to the press, but rather to publisher Walter Minton, who recently recalled how "Mason swore to me many times he alone wrote *Candy* and Terry only added a few paragraphs."

In the August 21 issue, *Life* ran a photo essay and profile of Terry. One of the pictures featured him clean-cut and driving in a white convertible, wearing shades, a giant billboard above him promoting *The Loved One*'s upcoming release. The photographs of Terry were breathtaking, from holding forth at Elaine's restaurant in New York to Hollywood's Sunset Strip, from the farm in East Canaan to Leo Castelli's SoHo gallery. Jane Howard, a staff writer for *Life,* gave Terry a megaphone to the world such as he had never had before:

> "The important thing in writing," he says, "is the capacity to astonish. Not shock — shock is a worn-out word — but astonish. The world has no grounds for complacency. The *Titanic* couldn't sink, but it did. Where you find smugness you find something worth blasting. I want to blast it."
>
> And so, blast away he does — currently from the bastion of a rented Beverly Hills mansion which has an electric gate and a swimming pool visited once a week by a gardener who fishes out the five

or six leaves that might have fallen into the water. His helper is Nile Southern, now three-and-a-half.

"When I first met him, his teeth were clenched," says Carol. "I was a little afraid of him." . . .

The very thought of collaboration makes some writers' hair stand on end. Not Southern's. "It's the purest form of writing there is," he says. "It's like writing a letter to your best friend. There needn't be hard feelings."

In his more optimistic private moments, Southern may possibly admit to himself that he *is* breaking through the barriers and finally achieving some results. At any rate, says his wife, "Terry's teeth aren't clenched anymore."

Meanwhile, Minton continued his summer ad campaign:

Have you read Candy, the novel
that's fast becoming as famous as LOLITA?

This comic classic is unique in its Un-American look at the American scene. . . . Among other facets of American life that may never be the same: THE CAMPUS, ZEN, UTOPIA, PSYCHIATRY, PEACENIKS, PREVERTS . . . Read *Candy* and see why! National Best Seller; 65,000 copies in print

The ads appeared in New York and Chicago, and Terry wrote to Minton, objecting to what he considered a pandering comparison to Nabokov's book. Minton wrote back a four-page handwritten letter from the Hotel Flora, in Rome, taking Terry to task for accepting the Random House offer when they were in discussions on *Blue Movie*. He wondered if fame was getting to Terry:

[Late August] 1964

Dear Terry

Your letter, forwarded from New York, was waiting for me in Rome.

I suspect that ad could have been improved by expanding the "etcetera". But it was put through in a great rush because time was very much a factor. And it accomplished more than any single ad I've ever seen. It got a message across to reader and bookseller in New York and Chicago. It resurrected a very valuable *Life* story [Algren's review] that had been passed over several weeks and was on the edge of limbo, and together with the *Life* piece it sold enough books to boost Candy (at least for one week so far) into the #1 spot in June's bestseller list.

Mr. Nabokov agrees, vehemently, if on different grounds, about the comparison of Candy to Lolita. I do not because no comparison was made — we merely asked a reader if he'd read a book that was becoming as well-known, as talked about, as controversial as Lolita. And, with the spectre of censorship still there (I hear there are new rumblings in Chicago) as well-received, as (to use a word I hate) "literary".

And, what can't be forgotten for a moment, a quarter of a million copies of the hardcover edition were purchased, followed a year and a half to two and a half years later by over three million paperback copies. Of course some of them were helped by what I felt to be a poor movie [*Lolita*] that left people saying "you should have read the book" — which hasn't happened with *Candy* — but it still means the word *Lolita* has passed into the vernacular and I just don't believe there are enough intellectuals in America to account for such a sale — and it does the book (Candy) good to stand in the same sentence.

But that is not too important for it is in the past, as our publishing relations seem to be. I regret your position and while I obviously accept it, I cannot either understand or appreciate it. As I wrote before, Sterling Lord insists he acted on your specific instruction and was willing to do whatever had to be done to alter the situation at your request. Indeed, to the day of my departure for Europe on the 19th he still said no contract had formally been signed despite the fact I've dealt with it as a "fait accompli". And Bennett Cerf even reconfirmed on the telephone his feeling about Candy and implied he'd release you from your agreement if you wished — for he knew of our counter-offer — and he was still concerned with Blue Movie's future if you followed the outline.

You speak also of your regard for Peter [Israel] — yet I've never seen an editor calmly given such a kick in the teeth.

You don't really like Bennett's position on Candy yet you deal with him on Blue Movie.

You repeat your confidence Sterling kept us fully informed whereas Peter and I have told you he did not—and most of the New York publishing community knows he did not.

The conclusion of that Life piece seems regrettably correct. You have always had the ability to spot phonies and phoniness — as your books testify and as I'm sure your own life shows evidence. And phonies have always bothered you — your teeth were indeed clenched.

Well if your wife said so, they must indeed be unclenched. But I, for one, think the perceptiveness may have been dulled as well. And I hope they are eventually clenched again. Time will tell and we'll still be in business.

Sincerely,

Walter Minton

Peter Israel dropped Mason a line to keep him in the loop. He had apparently discussed a new project with him, perhaps a follow-up to *Candy*.

Putnam's and Sons, September 2, 1964

Dear Mason:

Candy got up to No. 1 on *Time* Magazine's list last week! It dropped to No. 2 this week. We continue to be No. 5 in the New York Times and are No. 4 in *Publisher's Weekly* this week. Sales are not as exciting as they were during one stretch but we continue to be selling the book strongly and I expect this will go on for some time now. We will have a new round of advertising across the country this month.

Needless to say, I am excited to be involved with a new venture with you and I am counting upon it being a good one for all concerned. I hope all is well with you and your family. Let me hear from you if you have time.

Regards,

Peter Israel

Editor-in-Chief

During the shooting of *The Loved One,* Terry met an actress named Gail Gerber, who had appeared in the Elvis Presley movie *Harum Scarum* and who was cast in (but ultimately cut from) *The Loved One*. The twenty-six-year-old member of Les Grands Ballets Canadiens had moved to Hollywood seeking fame and fortune. Terry, who only a year ago was unknown, scrambling to make ends meet, found it impossible to resist a whole new world of temptations, which, in addition to Gail, included fast cars, interesting people, drugs, and international film production. Terry began seeing Gail and in September, Carol and I — then nearly four — returned to Canaan alone. Terry checked into the Chateau Marmont to begin doctoring scripts for MGM executive John Calley. A new kind of existentialism was about to begin for Terry: here and now in the fast lane — with booze, dexies, and Acapulco Gold leading the way.

On October 2, nearly five months after publication, Peter Israel wrote to Mason expressing his horror that Mason's attorney in France had still not yet gone over the *Candy* contract sent a month earlier. He signs off positively: "*Candy* goes on. No.1 again in this week's *Time* and we have slipped to No. 4 in the *New York Times.* Sales have passed 100,000."

Ironically, the first state to launch a pornography suit against the book was that of Candy Christian's fictional birthplace: Wisconsin. In September, a bookshop in Milwaukee was cited for distributing an "obscene" book identified as *Candy.* If the state attorney general successfully enjoined against sales there, it would set a precedent nationwide and could affect booksellers' willingness to carry the title. Putnam's vice president and treasurer wrote to initiate the required legal response from the authors. Mason complained to Israel about being held responsible for violating such subjective standards as decency. Israel wrote to Mason, explaining that "this is an action being brought against the book itself (not against any individual) on an obscenity charge.

Couquite was increasingly upset by Mason's drug problems.

He would kick, only to begin using again, and they separated. Mason saw the children frequently. One day, about to pick up six-year-old Juliette and two-year-old Daniel, Mason asked her for their coats, saying he was taking them to the Luxembourg Gardens as he often did. In fact, he took them to Italy and later to New York. Couquite later recalled:

> When I heard they had been kidnapped and were in New York, I jumped on a plane and flew over there. I took my aunt, a fierce lady, with me and we found the children with Mason's mother. My aunt said she would sit in the parlor of Mason's mother's house until the children were handed back to me. I had to get lawyers involved.

Frustrated by the weak contract he was being asked to sign with Putnam, and paranoid about the Wisconsin suit and the others that were expected to follow, Mason raised issues concerning *Candy* with his new attorney in France, Howard Koerner. Mason had been objecting to fine but significant points, such as the authors' liability for any "obscenity." Israel reported that Putnam had modified the liability from "scandalous" to "obscene," but that "author and publisher must jointly assume the risk":

> As in the case of Candy, we further agreed to share the cost equally with the author in the event that any charges were brought against the book on that count. If you will check with your friends who have contracts with book publishers, I think you will learn that this is in itself an unusual concession, for just about every publishing contract I have ever seen holds the author fully responsible in such areas.

Candy fever was spreading into other countries, and with it, the mistaken impression that Terry was its sole author. In England, the January issue of *Ace* magazine, a men's tabloid, featured a cover story, "Terry Southern—The Man Who Made Candy Quicker Than Liquor." This kind of press escalated the tension between Terry and both Mason and Kubrick.

With the publication of *Candy,* and the release of the motion picture "Dr. Strangelove," for which he wrote the screenplay, the man has rocketed to fame and success as suddenly and unexpectedly as any other "overnight success" who had to struggle for years before finally being recognized.

Concerning his own naughty novel [*Candy]* Southern waxes . . . practical. "Hopefully we'll be banned in all the right places," he says, but he doesn't actually think it will be banned anywhere. "America's come a long way since the fifties — and elderly ladies like my books."

However, it's hard to keep Southern serious for long. Of the most memorable episode in *Candy,* the sexual encounter with the hunchback, Southern had a snappy reply when asked how he'd treat the scene when it's made into a movie.

"Simple," said Southern. "I'd have him keep his shirt on."

Despite his wild novels, Terry Southern is a happily married family man. He chuckles a lot. He drinks daiquiris. He's easily pleased.

But watch him carefully. Terry's made out of strong cloth. And he's the hottest and fastest-moving item on the American literary scene today.

He's shoved *Candy* right down the throats of "The Establishment," and made them like it.

Chapter 30

Enter the Pirates

Back in New York in the new year of 1965, Walter Minton was preparing to issue the paperback edition of *Candy* with Dell Distributing Company, but delayed because the hardcover was selling so well. The unprecedented success for what many across the country were calling pornography, quickly led to speculators examining the book's copyright. Pirate publishers on both coasts began typesetting their own editions. Word soon got out that Walter Zacharius of Lancer, the New York publisher, had printed up 500,000 copies of the book and was ready to "drop them on the street." Dell, not wanting to partner with Putnam on such shaky ground, would not offer its usual advance payment on the printing and only agreed to distribute the book for a much higher than usual percentage.

"The cruel irony," Terry told John de St. Jorre, "was that the book was not copyrighted, and so Girodias went to Walter Zacharius and did a deal. It was a pretty rotten thing to do." Walter Minton later commented:

> I never heard that Girodias had anything to do with getting Zacharius to do the book. . . . But if he talked to Zacharius about it, that's all he needed to do. I doubt very much if Zacharius paid Girodias anything. I never heard of Walter Zacharius paying anybody anything unless you put a gun to his head, and you'd probably have to shoot him halfway to prove that the gun was loaded.

Walter Zacharius himself said:

> Girodias told me the story of how it was written. "Who's got the copyright?" I asked, and he said nobody had the copyright and that I could do it. He gave me all the correspondence he had on it—between Terry and Mason and himself. The attorney said, "You can't pay anybody, or you'll end up in a lawsuit."
>
> So, I put it out, and the next thing I know: Girodias challenged me to a duel! I got a call from my office saying Maurice Girodias was there, and that he was demanding to *duel* me. I said, "Let's have a drink of cognac at the Stork, I'll pay you." And I paid him in a way so that I wouldn't get in trouble. . . . I always felt bad because the authors never got anything.

Putnam denied the authors any royalties because of the appearance of the Lancer edition and the Chicago Greenleaf edition, which soon followed. Mason's worst nightmare had come true: not only would he and Terry be denied royalties because of the pirated editions (and there would be more), the knockoffs didn't even carry their names (only Maxwell Kenton's) and, priced twenty cents cheaper than Putnam's paperback, the "anonymous" editions would sell better.

Lancer boldly advertised in the *New York Times* and *Booksellers,* claiming to have the true, definitive edition by the original author (!), Maxwell Kenton. "No one knew which book was the 'real' book," Zacharius said, "Minton didn't even know. I knew more about the book than he did — because Girodias gave me all the paperwork . . . the copyright Minton put on the book wasn't worth beans! Minton put a phony copyright in the book. . . . We almost put it out as '*Lollipop.*' "

Lancer's plain white cover had a generic warning across the top:

> NOT ONE WORD CHANGED!
> This is the ORIGINAL, UNCUT and UNEXPURGATED
> edition as first published and banned in Paris.

As Zacharius recalls, "I didn't like the cover. We had a young lady in the office who had nice lips — used a lot of lipstick — and I said, 'Kiss this for good luck.' So I put those lips on the cover and said to her, 'Your lips are going to be on a million copies.' She was the daughter of our own wholesaler in Ohio."

As other unauthorized editions began to appear, Girodias, with Machiavellian aplomb, lamented to his lawyer Leon Friedman about the pirates—not telling him about his secret deal with Zacharius, steering the prosecution toward Greenleaf instead:

> Lancer are a bunch of odious boors . . . and they have behaved in a way so low and treacherous with me . . . that they deserve a lesson, and should be made to pay punitive damages . . . But Greenleaf! . . . they are the most cold-blooded, malevolent trio I have ever met. If Lancer deserves some punishment, the Greenleaf people must take a beating such that they will at least stop stealing my property.

Minton wanted to begin legal action against the pirates before launching his own paperback with Dell. The paperback wars were now under way. But Terry, not wanting to alienate Girodias further, and bitter about not being paid, refused to sign any action without having the Girodias settlement in place. Minton held up the paperback run. As he recalled, "A lot of legal people at Putnam were angry at Terry. Because of the uncertainty, we didn't print any copies of the softcover until the last minute. Lancer was very organized — they had already talked to a bunch of distribution outlets — so Lancer had a big head start, and we lost a lot of sales." Minton then realized he needed only approval from Mason (who still had Terry's power of attorney) and cut a side agreement with him in exchange for $10,000 cash — which Mason demanded on the spot. Mason also agreed to help Putnam and sue the U.S. Copyright Office for the book's copyright. "I don't know why Terry didn't do it," Minton said, "I guessed he was pissed about the fact that we stopped paying him royalties."

As the Putnam paperback edition flooded America, Lancer,

Brandon House, and the other unauthorized editions of *Candy* sold hand over fist during the 1964 Christmas holiday season. Meanwhile, in Paris, Girodias's financial misfortunes had taken their toll. Olympia Press went into bankruptcy on December 14. Once again, Girodias would try to rise from the ashes, and *Candy* would either help resurrect him or be the final salting of his wounds.

Walter Minton recalled the race to get the paperbacks into the stores and onto the stands: "Dell did a remarkable job in getting the book out in a week. . . . Lancer got out first, but we caught them up on the West Coast. In the end, we sold between two and two and a half million copies and Lancer sold about a million."

Minton may have "caught them up" on the West Coast, but his distributor was surprised to find many more publishers printing *Candy* than just Lancer and Greenleaf. At least seven pirates from the West Coast published editions of *Candy* between 1965 and 1969:

1965: AMPOC PUBLISHING, Burbank, CA
1965: SUNDOWN PUBLISHING COMPANY, El Cajon, CA
1965: DANIEL PUBLISHING COMPANY, Riverside, CA
1965, 1969: BRANDON HOUSE, North Hollywood, CA
1967: EUROPA BOOKS/AMPOC, Los Angeles, CA
1968: PARTHENA, Venice, CA
ALL STAR BOOKS*

With no authors to pay and Putnam's nationwide advertising in full effect, printing *Candy* was like printing money. All of the pirates were careful to use the Girodias edition word-for-word, since its incarnation in France had the cloudy copyright. Perversely flaunting their piracy while bolstering their legal stance, each pirated edition proudly declared:

*No publisher's information of any kind appeared in this edition, which was grotesquely marketed as child pornography.

This edition follows the text of the original Olympia Press edition, published in Paris in 1958. It is complete and unabridged.

They also used the Maxwell Kenton pseudonym, and the original dedication: "To Mister Hadj and Mister Zoon."

The California pirates, especially industrious, printed numerous alluring editions, often changing cover designs slightly from printing to printing to confuse authorities as to which "edition" of theirs was current.

The pirated editions probably averaged print runs of 50,000 each. However, in an FBI interview, an anonymous West Coast pirate admitted to printing a million and a half copies. Girodias called the pirates "porno-gangsters" and claimed that "more than 15 million copies were sold in some 30 to 50 unauthorized editions, of which not one cent was paid to either myself or the authors."

While many used the jacket quotes (from Wyndam Lewis, etc.) Putnam had secured, Greenleaf in New York had the audacity to use verbatim Putnam's marketing slogan, "The world's most talked about book." Other marketing copy, though no doubt upsetting to Terry and Mason, was playfully tongue in cheek:

> Good Grief Daddy . . . All I was trying to do was find someone who truly NEEDED me, you know — who wanted my understanding and comfort to . . . well, SHARE the beautiful and thrilling privilege of giving fully. Silly old Daddy! How could YOU comprehend? But, oh, Daddy, when Uncle Jack looked at me THAT WAY, and when he beseeched me to give him all my TRUE WARMTH on the hospital floor . . . his need was so great, so so — ACHING — of course, I GAVE to him, just the way Professor Mephesto, that truly GREAT man, taught me to.

Terry's fame, on one level, was beginning to work against him. The frenzy over *Candy*, and in particular the obscenity suits, had made him the focus of an FBI probe. "Obscenity," which had been charged against his friend Lenny Bruce, was being prosecuted to the full extent of the law, and though highly subjective in its determination had become a national threat seemingly as dangerous to society as drugs and communism. In February 1965, the FBI began surveillance on Terry and the commercial phenomenon of his "dirty book." They sent an agent from New Haven to watch the Canaan house — even though during this period Terry was with Gail, either in Los Angeles or abroad. Carol remembers a black car frequently parked across the house by the river but thought nothing of it at the time since fishermen sometimes parked there.

Although its investigation predated the notorious COINTEL program, which infiltrated and sabotaged popular figures and movements in the United States (such as the Black Panthers and the peace movement), documents released through the Freedom of Information Act make it clear that the FBI was poised to help instigate a COINTEL-type smear campaign against Terry as a "pornographer" if such a course of action was deemed advisable, or ordered from above, and that the FBI was offering protection from prosecution to the pirate booksellers and over seven hundred distributors in exchange for their information and cooperation. As the FBI focused on Terry, an anonymous tipster in Los Angeles made a most interesting claim about Terry's supposed pornographic film collection, prompting the agent to report enthusiastically, "This is not the ordinary type of pornographic film but is high quality, the best made, including some for KING FAROUK." The agent goes on to state, "With reference to the pornographic library of films . . . it is not known to this office whether it is a local violation in Connecticut to display films to 'guests' and it is therefore left to the discretion of the Bureau as to whether such information should be made available, strictly on a confidential basis, to a local law enforcement agency covering SOUTHERN'S place of residence."

Perhaps this rumor can be traced to the Plimpton/Becker collection, which had a loose association with the Sadre Aga Khan (who funded the *Paris Review*) or, more likely, to the myths surrounding the famous Kubrick viewings of stag films on the set of *Strangelove*. In any event, Terry would have been pleased to have actually had such a collection.

In late March 1965, the FBI "reviewed" the book internally and concluded it was "not a suitable vehicle for prosecution":

> "Candy," for all its sexual descriptions and foul language, is primarily a satirical parody of the pornographic books which currently flood our newsstands. Whatever erotic impact or prurient appeal it has is thoroughly diluted by the utter absurdity and improbability of the situations described.

In 1965, while Terry was in California finishing his latest rewrite job, *The Cincinnati Kid,* Girodias arrived in New York to make a fresh start. With his company defunct, and legal cases such as J. P. Donleavy's *The Ginger Man* still simmering, Girodias was anxious to take what he could of his catalogue and begin anew. From a base in New York, he could also deal more directly with the *Candy* issue. He chose Barney Rosset as the ideal partner with whom to continue pushing the limits of publishing. Rosset and Girodias were flip-sides of the same coin — both fighting censorship, often for the same authors and causes. Rosset had already published and gone to court to defend *Lady Chatterley's Lover* and had won a very costly court battle over *The Tropic of Cancer,* first published by Girodias in Paris.

Just as the contracts between the two publishers were drawn up and ready to be signed by Girodias's lawyer, Leon Friedman, the deal suddenly fell apart. "It was a good contract," Friedman noted, "and Maurice would have made good money out of it." Why did the deal fall apart? The answer is typical Girodias. As Dick Seaver, then Grove's editor-in-chief, recalls:

> One day I received a phone call from another publisher, saying, "I've had a visit from your friend Maurice Girodias. He wants to make a deal with us for a joint venture with his Olympia Press. I heard he had made a deal with you guys." I had actually thought the Olympia-Grove deal was already signed, so I marched into Barney's office and asked him point-blank if it had. "I signed it," Barney said, "I'm waiting for Maurice to countersign." At which point I told Barney about the phone call I had just received. "He's shopping our deal around," I said. Barney shook his head. "Goddamn Maurice," he said, "He'll never learn, will he?"

Leon Friedman summed up his client best: "Maurice's attitude was, 'if the other guy wants to sign a contract, it can't be a good deal.'"

Girodias ended up dismissing Rosset, calling him "Sadistic Superman." Rosset responded by publishing in the September issue of *Evergreen Review* a bitter and scandalously detailed account by Vladimir Nabokov of Girodias's dubious behavior over the previous ten years regarding *Lolita*. Nabokov wrote:

> From the very start I was confronted with the peculiar aura surrounding his business transactions with me, an aura of negligence, evasiveness, procrastination, and falsity. . . . What always made me regret our association were not [as Girodias had often claimed], "dreams of impending fortune," not my "hating" him "for having stolen a portion of Nabokov's property" but the obligation to endure the elusiveness . . . the duplicity, and the utter irresponsibility of the man.

Reinventing himself yet again, Girodias set up an office in an apartment in Gramercy Park and began living at the Chelsea Hotel. Some of the Girodias international network came to help run the New York office, such as Gerry Williams, an American who had run an Olympia affiliate in Holland. Williams had also been an editor and translator in France. Financing came from a stranger Girodias had met on a plane. Williams recalled an odd assortment of characters who appeared at Olympia USA as Girodias put together the American money and distribution network. Williams also recalled for John de St. Jorre a group of men "in camel-hair coats, gold cuff links and Florsheim shoes coming into the office and putting their feet up on the desk as if they owned the place — which they probably did."

In New York, Cindy Degener was chomping at the bit to get the movie sale going, but there was nothing she could do. As she forwarded Samuel Pisar's mounting legal bill to Terry (which Mason shared) for the litigation going on in France, she tried to remain optimistic:

If we had a settlement with Olympia's successor, I really think the possibilities of a good motion picture sale on "CANDY" are substantial. If I had the copyright situation in France straightened out today, I could make a big sale to the Skouras family with one phone call.

Part III:

UNREELING *CANDY*

SCREW: Did you get any ideas, or background, for your book [*Blue Movie*] from the making of *Candy*?
TERRY SOUTHERN: No — I'm not aware there were any ideas at work on the filming of *Candy*.

Chapter 31

"Good Grief, Me a Movie?"

As the *Candy* men's prospects for receiving any book royalties from their literary confection became increasingly remote, each began to set his sights on a film deal. In April of 1964, a film producer friend of Terry's, Frank Perry, saw *Candy*'s number-one spot on the bestseller list as an opportune moment to set up a movie deal. He began constructing an agreement with United Artists in which they would option the property regardless of the status of the rights. Attorney Robert Montgomery ironed out the terms between all parties, which was signed May 6. If the authors could settle the copyright issue with Girodias, and the movie could actually be made, UA would pay a total of $130,000 to acquire the rights. However, the option money ($60,000, of which the authors would see very little because of the legal costs) was to be returned to Frank Perry and his production company in June 1966 if the rights to *Candy* could not be delivered. The race was on to secure the copyright before the option expired.

Meanwhile, Girodias was working up his own scheme to entice some high-powered French friends to get cracking on the film — telling them the copyright wasn't a problem — secretly hoping he would win the inevitable lawsuit that would play out in France. Mason was fearful of any film developments — sure that he'd be cut out of both the creative and financial aspects — just as he had been cut out of the limelight.

Mason's fears were not without justification. In June of 1964, in the form of a joint venture, Frank Perry contracted Terry to deliver a *Candy* screenplay within three months, for $15,000. Mason was now literally out of the picture, since the two men — Perry and Terry — would, according to their contract, make "all decisions relating to . . . the Motion Picture and rights therein." Terry was defined as an equal producer with Perry — sharing all proceeds. The price for the purchase of the screenplay was to be equal to Perry's directing fee. Sterling Lord was to take 10 percent of any income.

Meanwhile in Paris, Mason renewed his acquaintance with Bob Dylan, a character who had greatly impressed him when they first met two years earlier. At the time, Dylan was on his first tour of England, and had hooked up in Paris with a French guitarist who was Couquite's cousin. As Mason later told *Playboy*, "The first time Dylan did a London concert, he wanted to see Paris. . . . Naturally they came over to my house, because I was an American who smoked dope. And I didn't know who Dylan was. That was about the last time he could still meet people normally. . . . I actually thought he was a hillbilly."

Mason had stayed in touch with Dylan, and now traveled with him during his 1965 European tour. As *Dont Look Back* filmmaker D. A. Pennebaker recalls:

> Mason was quite manic and funny. . . . He rode around in the car with us for a few days. . . . He had met Dylan in Paris — and he was around during Dylan's '65 tour. There was talk of making *Candy* on the cheap — and having us [Pennebaker and Leacock] do it — Dylan was interested. At one point someone told me, "You know, if they decide the book is pornography, you could go to jail!" That's the first time I realized these things were actually dangerous.

By the summer of 1965, Cindy Degener was navigating the good ship *Candy* through the rough seas of litigation on a daily basis. The legal fees at home and abroad were mounting, and she was desperate to see the case rushed through the French courts and to beat Girodias for the copyright on his own turf. The celebrated French trial lawyer Samuel Pisar, whose firm, Kaplan, Livingston,

Goodwin & Berkowitz had offices in New York, Beverly Hills, and Paris, launched the lawsuit for the authors against Girodias in France, using the renowned French trial attorney Pierre Bréchignac. Meanwhile, United Artists' option was set to expire, and it was doubtful that Terry and Mason would be able to return their share of the option money if it did. Degener announced in a memo to all concerned: "We now have only until June 1966 before [United Artists] forecloses and takes the book away from Terry and Mason." Meanwhile, she was getting offers from film financiers. "The Skouras family is extremely serious about making some kind of a deal with me." But *Candy* was still far from saleable. The best Degener could hope to achieve was a guarantee of protection to anyone who bought the property from any lawsuit coming from Terry, Mason, and (the biggest challenge) Girodias.

Vying for Terry's time among many producers wanting his services, Frank Perry put Terry up at the Beverly Hills Hotel to start adapting *Candy*. A place to work, dexamyl, booze, and a television (usually with the sound off) were all he required to get cracking. Gail Gerber recalls the scene:

> He was writing the script and typing and laughing and he had a new bottle of B&B [scotch] there and I'm ordering food, doing whatever, reading and fooling around . . . and I see the bottle and it was a third empty. I thought, "Wow, that's interesting." The next time I look at the bottle, it was half empty. . . . I thought, "It must be evaporating". . . . Then I realized that it was going down — yet he was not drunk — he was cold stone sober. Typing and writing. Terry had an enormous metabolism for alcohol.

Terry's 139-page script for *Candy* was written quickly and required ingenuity in its treatment of the grotesque. In the hunchback scene, for instance (a scene that everyone, including UA, was hesitant about, as it involved deformity, near-rape, and sadomachochism), Terry used an interior monologue voice-over technique — something he usually objected to:

INT. BATHROOM

Candy enters, pauses before the mirror while picking up a towel.

CANDY (V.O.)

Gosh, a real hunchback!

Then, in her mind (a la Walter Mitty) occurs an imaginary exchange.

YOUNG MASCULINE VOICE

Hey, look at that humpback!

(proudly)

Wouldn't see anything like that back in Racine, would you?

CANDY (V.O)

(blasé)

Come on, I'll . . . introduce you. . . .

To break the ice with the demented Hunchback, Candy brings down a book of Blake.

She has to stretch up to get it, giving a provocative delineation to her figure. PAN DOWN. CU, the Humpback observing her.

CANDY (V.O)

(as stretching motion lifts her short blouse above waist of her jeans)

Good grief, I just hope he doesn't think that I'm . . .

(sighs)

Oh well, it's my fault, darn it!

HUMPBACK (V.O)

Girl want ruba-dub!

She gets down the print, brings it over, somewhat flushed.

CANDY

(sitting down beside him, extending print)

Isn't this just too much?

(points)

You see, just here, where the —

HUMPBACK

(ignoring this, grasps her)

I want ruba-dub you!

CANDY

(upset)

Oh please, don't say that . . .

Terry wrote three screenplay drafts of *Candy* over the next two years for Frank Perry. As Perry's option ran out, and the film remained unfinanced, the value of Terry's *Candy* script became dubious.

In the fall of 1965, both *The Loved One* and *The Cincinnati Kid* were released simultaneously. *Dr. Strangelove* had been nominated for an Academy Award for Best Screenplay, making Terry one of the hottest, best-paid screenwriters around. But Terry's natural impulse to stretch a project's envelope earned him, as James Earl Jones later quipped, a reputation as "a bad boy" as well. *The Loved One*'s advertising campaign was "Something to Offend Everyone."

The Chateau Marmont on Sunset Boulevard became Terry's new home in Los Angeles. He finished the *Candy* screenplay there as well as others. Ironically, his script would ultimately be rejected by the film's producers.

George Plimpton wrote Terry in Hollywood, hoping that despite the big money he was reportedly earning he wouldn't forget their old ways, which apparently included the occasional screening of stag films:

> What with the Big Lettuce (the rumor is you're pulling in 7 thou a week) you should come on in for the weekend. . . . I trust you're keeping an eye out for Philms Bleu. [Bill] Becker & I have elected you an associate librarian of the famed "Blue Collection" — and will hurry on Small Lettuce to you if warranted, so that said delicacies can be purchased and hurried East for showing to S. Kubrick at odd hours.

In early October, while Degener, Lord, Cashman et al. were launching their assault to gain control of the copyright, Girodias, with the cool demeanor of a seasoned gambler, offered Cindy, Terry, Mason, and all the American lawyers his shrewd, sobering, and defiant overview of their "regrettable conflict." Writing that he would be "only be too glad to envisage the possibility of . . . a settlement," he set forth in a one and a half page letter the problems and offered solutions (shrewdly omitting any mention of Olympia's recent bankruptcy). His key points were:

> *Litigation in France* — could take "between three and five years"; complicated to prosecute from either standpoint, as the book is banned and sold illegally.
> *Film Rights* — no film company will sign a contract with litigation going on. "A dead loss."
> *Copyright Situation* — neither Putnam nor authors can claim ownership of the copyright — but Olympia has a "very good chance of obtaining" same, since "the copyright notice in the original edition was correctly worded in our name; and the fact that we commissioned the book to be written for a set sum."
> *Putnam Contract* — authors forced to accept hard terms; agreement "could no doubt be renegotiated."

Afraid of further complicating the Putnam deal and the developing movie deal, the Lord team delayed negotiating with Girodias—waiting to see Pisar's results in the French courts. Mason signed up with Pisar as well, so that in France there was a unified front. Meanwhile, in October, *Candy* was still holding strong as one of the top ten bestselling books — where it had been since the spring of the previous year.

By the end of 1965, Putnam had printed twenty editions of *Candy*: thirteen in hardcover and seven in paperback. The sheer volume of sales nationwide was overwhelming, and at the Frankfurt Book Fair in mid-October, an outraged and threatening Girodias found Minton, who agreed that a deal could be worked out, but only if Olympia settled its differences with the authors first. In a last-ditch effort to screw Minton before "settling" with him, Girodias wrote to the U.S. Copyright Office in Washington, D.C., requesting that Olympia Press be granted a copyright for his original edition of *Candy*.

In November, Girodias met with Putnam's lawyers in New York. Girodias knew that Terry was no longer acting in concert with Mason, but that Mason still had Terry's power of attorney, so, like Walter Minton, he first proposed the settlement to Mason in a letter, urging him to forget about their "stupid, suicidal feud."

As John de St. Jorre points out in *Venus Bound*, it was now a waiting game:

> *Southern and Hoffenberg*: were waiting for a favorable verdict to their Paris litigation, for Girodias to self-destruct in his bankruptcy, and for a lucrative film deal. And for Putnam's blocked monies due them, including revenue from the booming paperback sales.
>
> *Walter Minton*: was waiting for a chance to derail the pirate publishers who were an embarrassment to all.
>
> *The Pirates*: were waiting for the statute of limitations to expire on their printings so they could avoid prosecution, and for their cases to be thrown out of court in the confusion.
>
> *The Film Producers*: were waiting for everything to be cleared up so they could capitalize on Candy's great success.
>
> *Girodias*: was waiting for the Library of Congress to grant him U.S. copyright, for the Paris litigation to cease, and for his financial troubles to let up. Girodias was now bankrupt — Olympia was up for auction.

In December, Girodias received word from the U.S. Copyright Office. *Candy,* he was informed, was already the subject of two copyright court cases: *Putnam's v. Lancer* (Walter Zacharius), and the suit Putnam forced Mason to launch against the Copyright Office itself — and thus the body would not make a decision on Girodias's inquiry. However, it did advise him that if he could prove he had an employer/employee relationship with the writers, then Girodias as publisher could be considered the author. If it were a "commissioned work," however, the authors could eventually claim ownership — through eventual reversion. It was a fine distinction and one whose definition rested with the employer. Girodias claimed they were employees, and immediately turned to Leon Friedman to contest legally not only the book's ownership but its appearance in America.

Near the end of 1965, after *Candy* had finally fallen off the bestseller list, Girodias wrote to Cindy Degener proposing a solution. Despite all the personal and professional animosity among all the players, Girodias's assessment is reasoned and calm:

> 7 rue St. Séverin, Paris, December 6th, 1965
>
> Dear Miss Degener:
>
> I suppose that you have heard from Mr. Pisar that the first hearing of the "Candy" case in Paris has been postponed until March of next year. . . .
>
> We are thus wasting our chance to dispose of the film rights; we give the pirate publishers a clear field to exploit the book without any interference; and we leave unsolved the situation between the authors and their American publisher.
>
> May I add that I talked to Mr. Minton and to Mr. Rembar [a copyright specialist], and that I know that a money-producing compromise is quite possible — with *my* participation. That could lead easily to a compromise concerning film rights, and to a joint action against the pirate publishers.
>
> But naturally all this depends entirely on your advice to the authors. When I saw you, you seemed to think that it was your duty towards your authors to try to let Mr. Pisar win a case in France

against us. Since then time has been flowing. More time will pass, and finally it will not be worth anyone's efforts to reach a compromise. As a film property, "Candy" is losing value constantly, and all our common chances of making money out of that Olympia-Press-originated bestseller are fast disintegrating . . . And for what purpose? Just in order to punish me? Or what, I wonder! . . .

I do hope that you will see where your authors' interests really are.

With best regards,

Yours sincerely,

Maurice Girodias

Chapter 32

Half of Paris for the Rights

During the book's nine-month reign on the bestseller list, and the Lord team's hope that United Artists would hang in long enough for the rights to clear, Girodias had his own strategy for getting *Candy* made as a film. In February 1966 he wrote to Leon Friedman that Christian Marquand, a pal of Marlon Brando's, wanted to help facilitate a settlement with all the parties so that a film deal could be done — with Brando starring and Marquand directing. Marquand, who began his cinema career as a child in Cocteau's *La Belle et la Bête,* was a powerful force with a pedigree in French cinema; not only was he married to the sexpot ingénue Tina Aument, and appeared with Brigitte Bardot in *And God Created Woman,* but his sister, actress Nadine Trintignant, was a favorite of Godard's. Nadine's husband, Jean-Louis Trintignant, was a French star who had worked with such luminaries as Claude Chabrol, Abel Gance, Claude Lelouch, Jeanne Moreau, Costa Gavras, Anouk Aimée, and Jean-Paul Belmondo.

Girodias reciprocated Marquand's enthusiasm by assigning him one hundred percent of Girodias's share of *Candy*'s film rights. Naturally, he did not inform anyone in America of this transaction, preferring to stir the pot himself. Marquand and Brando would now become the nexus of energy around which the film's development took shape, and although Girodias was not involved in the film's production, he became a silent, quickly disappearing partner.

Never one to miss an opportunity for intrigue and then to boast about it, Girodias flaunted to Leon his intention to pocket money on any film option through a side deal whereby he'd net twice what Terry and Mason were to receive for the rights.

> Litvinoff does not know the details of my negotiation with (or through) Marquand: the official sum I am supposed to have agreed to is $5,000. Nobody is to know the real figure (the remaining $30,000 . . . to be paid in Switzerland, tax-free). It is essential that the secret be restricted to you, Marquand and me. Naturally, the idea was to show Mason and Terry how willing I was to reach a general compromise, by accepting a ridiculously low figure for my share of the film rights. Naturally, I am well aware of the possibility that Marquand may have secretly offered more to Mason and Terry than the $10,000 or $15,000 they are supposed to get. . . . Everyone is lying to everyone else, but isn't that better if it is done sincerely?

Leon wrote back to Girodias that Litvinoff had already said he did not care if Christian Marquand gave Girodias "half of Paris" for his share of the rights, so long as the authors got what they considered a fair deal. Friedman advised, "You must have no illusions about pretending you are only getting $5,000 from Marquand. . . . Everyone here knows there is more coming and I doubt whether you can get any negotiating value from the fact that on paper you are getting only $5,000."

Early in 1966, New York District Judge Edward C. McLean found two competing suits before him related to *Candy*: Putnam sought to enjoin Lancer against publishing and selling their 75-cent paperback edition of the Olympia version of the novel, and Lancer sought a declaratory judgment showing that its book did not infringe on Putnam's rights.

The judge denied both motions, but ultimately ruled in Lancer's favor. He declared that Putnam's "revised version" of the novel, which the authors had registered for copyright on June 8, 1964, did not apply to the Paris original, and that since Lancer's edition adhered to the Paris edition, there appeared to be "no basis for charges of copyright infringement."

"Plaintiffs never applied for registration of copyright on the French edition," the judge said, "hence they never obtained one.

Since they do not have one, it would seem that they may not sue for infringement of something which they do not have." As Walter Zacharius of Lancer recalled:

> I remember being on a witness stand. 'How many books did you distribute at 95 cents?' came the question. "Over a million," I said.
>
> Minton jumped up and down in the courtroom — I thought he was going to fly through the ceiling! He couldn't believe it — he still had the hardback out [for $5] and we had it out in paper everywhere, for less than a buck!

As the lawyers formulated their responses and the intellectual property specialists were hired both in France and in the U.S., the amount of speculation, coupled with arcane international copyright law, provided the attorneys a field day for speculative (and costly) analysis. An excerpt of a letter from Samuel Pisar to Sy Litvinoff is a typically mind-numbing example:

> Even if Girodias were right, then the copyright will still be deemed to have reverted to the authors if the French court affirms the alleged breach of contract as of the date of breach or of the author's notice of termination. . . .
>
> We leave it to you to decide whether an agreement based on Olympia's continued ownership of the copyright would help you establish U.S. copyright to the first French edition.

Direct when he wanted to be, Girodias took the bull by the horns and called Minton on the phone. In a February letter to Friedman he described the conversation he had with the publisher while he was in New York:

> Minton's position is quite simple, in a way, healthy. If no copyright can be established on the book, then he has no reason to pay royalties to the authors. But he would be willing to settle the roughly $68,000 he has offered to pay them if the authors and myself acting jointly were able to give him a regular copyright . . . which he would use to win a victory against Lancer and the other pirate publishers.

Armed with this information, Leon Friedman immediately began what would be a year-long negotiation with all the principals involved: Walter Minton, Sy Litvinoff, Gideon Cashman (Mason's lawyer), Terry and Mason's agent Sterling Lord, and Terry's indefatigable ally in Lord's office, agent Cindy Degener. Much of Leon Friedman's efforts were spent tempering Girodias's expectations. He wrote:

> I would be lax in my duty to you, Maurice, if I did not give you my honest appraisal of how the situation stands after talking to the various parties and analyzing the law and your assets in this matter. You do have some bargaining position, but as of now it is certainly not worth more than $100,000.

March 4, 1966, was the date of the French hearing of the authors' suit against Olympia for breach of contract. If Terry and Mason proved bad faith on Girodias's part, the authors could gain authorship control over their work and copyright protection. Pierre Bréchignac, the powerful French attorney who spearheaded Samuel Pisar's efforts on the ground in France, advised that Terry's allowing New York's Berkley Press to publish an extract was detrimental to their case. But Bréchignac also thought that as far as England was concerned, Terry and Mason were required by the 1961 contract with Girodias to *jointly approve* any foreign editions, thus that fact "should be enough to prevent any publisher in England to publish a new [i.e., unauthorized] issue of *Candy*."

Girodias, however, was gleefully leading British publishers along, showing Mason and Terry he could do whatever he wanted and leave them behind. He had sold U.K. rights to Tandem, then told them the copyright could not be guaranteed. Tandem then assigned their contract to Jeenspress. Typically, he hadn't told Friedman about his efforts to sell the British rights, until they went awry:

> We now have a superlative imbroglio to disentangle. . . . I have sold the rights to Tandem, or rather a substitute company acting for them [Jeenspress], with a £5,000 advance which has been received

> by me. . . . But the secret about the Tandem deal was not kept very carefully by them, and I myself deliberately told Mason Hoffenberg a few weeks ago that I had sold the British rights for a good deal of money, without saying how much or to whom. My motives in doing that were to show how absurd the feud between us was, etc. But that piece of news did create something of a commotion. . . . Yesterday in London . . . the Tandem man . . . seemed a little nervous.

The problem was that it wasn't just a publisher he had swindled — it was a part of London's underworld.

Girodias predicted that the French litigation would take years for him to win, as Terry and Mason's lawyers were "totally ignorant of French law." Knowing that a film could not be made without a settlement, and with £5,000 from the British Tandem deal in hand with which he could begin settling with his creditors in France, Girodias seemed to enjoy pulling the strings:

> Let them fume and rave about the British situation. Time is on our side: they want the film to materialize, they want to avoid tying down the British edition with a number of local lawsuits as they have done in America, and they are increasingly aware of the fact that I am no longer bankrupt, that my position is being fast consolidated. . . . Let's be foxy.

In his response of February 14, 1966, Leon Friedman indicated alarm at his client's bravura:

> I am not as sanguine as you are about the effect of the British imbroglio. This will prove to Terry that you are dealing behind his back. . . . if we cannot settle with Terry and Mason in the near future and they enjoin Tandem's publication of the book, you must repay that £5,000. I realize that Tandem is obligated to publish an edition within six months . . . or they will forfeit the £5,000. You have a horse race here to see whether Terry will enjoin Tandem before April 22nd or whether you can get past that date and keep the money. Bedlam was never as hectic as this. . . . Time may be on your side with Terry and Mason . . . at some point [Walter Minton] is going to decide to proceed on his own and not pay you anything at

all — including the $30,000 which is now in the bank on the soft cover sales. If we can settle with Minton, this would put great pressure on Terry and Mason also. . . .

Maurice, I wish I could get a million out of this but $100,000 is not a bad figure. I don't mean to sound pessimistic but your optimism in this situation strikes me as unrealistic. . . . There is always the possibility you will end up with nothing . . . if we go on too long without settling.

It was a battle of nerves and self-righteousness. Loose ends abounded: not only was there no settlement with Girodias, and legal cases pending on both continents, but the authors' contract with Putnam had not even been signed. In terms of the royalties, the brass ring was long gone — but there was still the movie sale and the possibility of cashing in on some of the pirate's booty. As Putnam's royalty payments silently stacked up somewhere in escrow, the authors drifted further apart into the din of the swinging '60s, where nothing seemed to matter all that much — not yet.

Chapter 33

Bedlam Was Never So Hectic

By springtime 1966 the chess game became ever more complex and tension-filled. The Copyright Office was expected to rule on who owned *Candy* in the United States, while a copyright decision from the French court was also imminent. Girodias was overplaying his hand, believing that *any* complication only worked in his favor, as he'd have to be dealt with. The $60,000 option payment from United Artists would have to be returned if a solution to the copyright problem did not materialize within the next few months — when the option was due to expire.

Suddenly there was a breakthrough: in May, the French court ruled that Southern and Hoffenberg had the right to break their 1961 contract with Olympia Press because they had not been paid what they were owed, nor were they paid on time, and that Girodias had to pay the royalties he owed them. Cindy Degener was thrilled, as she wrote to her Italian co-agent at the time:

> We won hands down . . . with a decision . . . by no less than the President of the Third Tribunal. The Victory is absolutely stunning in terms of what it involves in the actual written judgement. We own everything now, and there is no question of any kind.

Before Girodias launched a counter-attack, he had his own good tidings: the Copyright Office in the U.S. ruled that Olympia owned the U.S. copyright to *Candy*. It was a stalemate.

With Girodias's power of attorney, Leon Friedman continued negotiations between all parties in earnest, and told Girodias that with Putnam's good copyright news, he hoped to leverage some money out of Walter Minton right away. Girodias called Terry to tell him a settlement was on the horizon with Minton, and that they must meet to resolve things immediately, as he was about to return to Paris. They met and made a deal, which Girodias then asked Friedman to begin shaping into a final settlement between all parties.

From the One Fifth Avenue Hotel in late June, Girodias wrote to Mason at the Sorbonne Hotel on Cromwell Road in London. In a move resembling checkmate, he sent a four-page letter trying Mason's hand: showing there were no moves left, how his "Queen," Terry, had been captured, and the deal was a fait accompli. Mason, of course, was either too skeptical, too angry, or too stoned to accept a word of it. Girodias reminded Mason that he received a copyright certificate from Washington. He states that it is "ever more important for us to reach a settlement, and to try to recover jointly whatever can still be recovered," which he estimated to be "between $400,000 and $600,000." He goes on to say:

> I met Terry last week and he said he wanted to settle everything immediately. He offered to let me have one third of everything. I considered the offer, discussed it with my attorney, and told Terry that I accepted it. Our lawyers resumed talks, but Litvinoff argued that Terry's offer must be disregarded, and that I had to content myself with 25%; or Terry would start suing me in England. I sent a note to Terry to say that in those circumstances he could forget about the settlement. And I want to repeat here that I mean this absolutely. I am sick of hearing that Sterling Lord, his wife [Cindy Degener] and Litvinoff keep repeating to everyone that I am a crook, a thief, a *sale type* [dirty rotten scoundrel] and all that. They are (and you are) responsible (with Terry of course), for the loss of one million dollars we could have shared equally between us. I feel very badly about that, and I remind Terry that ten years ago Donleavy played a similar trick on me and that now, after ten years of litigation in London, he will have to pay for it. . . . I may have had my responsibilities in the faults committed: but they are like nothing at all as compared to the accumulation of errors, mistakes and follies committed on your side. . . .

> So, I think that at this point, you have to take your own responsibilities, as we will either settle by next Wednesday, or never.

Girodias then laid out a ten-point plan to Mason, in which he would follow Terry's three-way split, stating that he would share with the authors (and eventually with Putnam) "the benefit of my copyright, and we sue jointly the pirates," specifying that Putnam was to finance the litigation against the pirates. "I am asking for one third of the money we will get from Putnam," he wrote, "Sy offers one fourth, which I will never accept."

In conclusion, Girodias urged Mason to "make [his] own decisions" and either cable Cashman or take a plane to New York to sign his settlement.

Girodias was performing a balancing act as no one else could. Dodging Tandem and Jeenspress around the back streets of London, he was still trying to sell the rights to other British publishers, including New English Library and Mayflower Books. When these companies caught wind not only of Girodias's dallying with Tandem but also the copyright problem in general, they refused to negotiate until the authors had reached an agreement in the United States. In response to a publisher's question about *Candy*'s copyright standing, Girodias casually replied, "Our ownership derives from a contract with the authors; our New York attorney can supply all the necessary information in that respect." Meanwhile, Jeenspress made it clear they needed to have their money back by August 20. Ever the gambler, Girodias managed to get them to agree to give up the U.K. rights and call it square, *if* he made the deadline — which he didn't know how he could.

After months of negotiations spearheaded by Leon Friedman, which included formalizing a solution to the British Tandem/ Jeenspress mess, Girodias's draft settlement (based on his meeting with Terry and as presented to Mason) was agreed to by the Lord-Degener side, but now Girodias himself was not satisfied. He harped on how unfair it was for him, the original publisher, to be forced into Putnam's terms concerning the authors' royalties, which he also claimed were too low. Girodias's motives often vacillated from the practical to the moral — and no one ever knew which one he would leverage at which time for what purpose. After Friedman thought all was settled in early August, Girodias pleaded with him at the end of a letter: "Really, Leon, is there any way for me to walk out of that agreement without doing anything illegal? I expected something pretty disappointing, but what I got is something like complete lunacy . . . can we get out of it?"

Leon ignored Girodias's protestations, trying to focus on the money and the settlement. He informed Girodias that Minton was "acting in a peculiar fashion . . . and does not want to start talking to us until all the parties, including you, have executed the agreement."

With this in mind, and with Girodias about to leave Paris for a week's holiday in Ibiza, Friedman signed the document for Girodias on July 29. Cindy Degener broke the wonderful news to Terry care of John Calley at MGM, where Terry was working as a ghostwriter on a film called *Don't Make Waves.*

New York, NY, August 2, 1966

Dearest Terry:

It almost makes me cry to say I enclose herewith three copies of the now completed agreement with Girodias and Mason. You will notice that Leon Friedman has the power of attorney for Maurice (which power of attorney both Sy and I have seen with our own eyes) and he has already executed these copies of the agreement. Please return them to me in the enclosed self-addressed, stamped enveloped signed by you.

Please do this as rapidly as possible, because I think we can at last begin to recoup some money from this incredible experience. Sy has seen these and okayed them. . . .

My love to you Terry. I could never have gone through this for anyone but you.

As ever,

Claire S. Degener

Believing they had everything settled between them, the next hurdle to overcome would be the ever-cautious and calculating Minton. As Degener reported in early August:

> The real money will probably come from Minton, but we are being very careful and cool in that area, and I think through that approach we will do better than fooling around with Minton. I suspect that he does not yet believe that this agreement will be signed, so he is still being coy.

On August 22, Girodias, writing from Paris, surprised everyone with a total refutation of the agreement Leon had signed for him, announcing he would "irrevocably refuse [to] execute it . . . as explained in my unanswered letter August 4th." Friedman was infuriated, and sent an ultimatum back to his client immediately:

> I received your cable today and was absolutely floored. I never received any letter dated August 4th relating to your thoughts about the *Candy* contract. All I received was a copy of a letter dated August 8th to Michael Rubinstein in which you acknowledge that you have "at last completed our settlement with the authors of *Candy*." (I think it strange that of all the letters you have sent me over the past months, this is the only one never received.) . . .
>
> I must tell you that unless you sign the agreement as I sent it to you, I can no longer represent you in any matters whatsoever. I feel my professional integrity is at stake here. You represented to me and to other parties that I had full authority to negotiate and execute the settlement agreement. I cannot allow myself to be used in the way you have done, Maurice, any further. I put hundreds of hours into the settlement and I think did far better than anyone could have done. It is only because the other side trusted me that I was able to get what concessions I did. . . .
>
> I am sorry that everything had to end this way, but you must understand my sense of frustration. I believe I have helped straighten out a number of your affairs very advantageously and that my skills could be very useful to you in the future, but I cannot let the rug be pulled from under me the way you have done.

Girodias later explained his actions to Cindy Degener (and eventually to Friedman), by letter:

> I am convinced that Leon . . . signed a contract which he thought was in my interest. Unfortunately one essential issue was completely ignored in the said contract, concerning the practical conditions in which the Jeenspress agreement could be abrogated. As a result of a first payment of £600 not having been made by August 20th, our agreement with Jeenspress to recover the British rights could not be executed; and I was personally placed in a very difficult situation, with many repercussions.

Friedman finally received Girodias's missing August 4 letter, marked *Affranchissement Insuffisant* (Insufficient Postage), and wrote to Girodias regarding the situation;

> My guess is that since you had no return address, they sent it on to me by ship rather than air so it arrived in three weeks rather than two days. . . . But no matter. Too much has happened in the interim. I cannot help but feel that you simply changed your mind about the settlement, decided you wished to continue your vendetta with the authors and therefore deliberately misread the contract and looked for an excuse to repudiate it. . . .
>
> I would have had no problem if you had simply said 'no deal' when you were in New York. But when you tell me to go ahead and complete everything . . . and then you change your mind again, I cannot go on anymore. . . . I realize your emotional reaction to the way the authors betrayed you. But that cannot guide your actions forever. I believe now you just want to deprive them of any return from *Candy* no matter what it costs you. I am not going to be a party to that kind of revenge. I don't know what they are planning to do now. They have the option of enforcing the contract which is most certainly legally binding on you . . . I have no choice but to acknowledge I had the authority you represented I had and I will sign affidavits if necessary. . . .
>
> I still consider you a friend, Maurice, but I feel your method of doing business is foreign to me. I can be as aggressive as necessary

> when the occasion demands . . . but I demand some kind of honor from those I work with.

With typically unapologetic verve, Maurice wrote back to Friedman, "What an exceptional muddle! . . . My August 4 letter travelling the slow way. . . . It would be comical if so many other uncomical things were not involved."

Girodias then wrote a breezy memo to Terry and Mason, stating that the settlement was null and void. Terry's lawyer, Sy Litvinoff, responded with a brisk retort to Paris:

> I am sure that your long and distinguished career in publishing has familiarized you with the meaning of . . . a Power of Attorney. I enclose herein a copy for your perusal, should you have forgotten the document you signed. . . . If it is your great desire to spend more time in the French Courts, you have certainly chosen the direct path. We at this end will hold you to your Contract, and will, of necessity, have some more lawsuits to bring against you.

Refusing to acknowledge that Leon's efforts on his behalf were binding, Girodias wrote to Friedman with his "last and final offer," which he said would expire in a week if not signed. Girodias's seven points were similar to his previous ten, and to show he was really serious, he added that the agreement before them was "definitely binding for myself and my company, its successors or assigns." Friedman incorporated Girodias's "last" terms into a final agreement. Girodias's problems in London were becoming complex and dangerous for him. Tandem's backers didn't play games, and retained a professional muscle man, who threatened to break his legs if he didn't return the advance. Mason's situation, though not physically dangerous, was little better. His former buddy Terry was writing the screenplay for *Candy* alone and probably producing the film; his nemesis Girodias was calling the shots; the American publisher was cutting out the authors until further notice. Like Lenny Bruce, who was so obsessed with his own persecution that it became part of his "routine," Mason became a caricature of the "wronged writer": disasters burning behind him, always on the verge of getting it together, his suitcase of unseen wonders forever in tow, the monkey still on his back. From a journal entry dated 1966, written at the Chelsea Hotel, where he was living:

> I told myself I'd see what I could do starting at 9pm. Thursday night Corso, Emmet . . . a girl I didn't know named Loretta or Minetta or Vendetta, resembling an anemic Norwegian midshipman, and poor Edie Sedgewick made the awesome acid trip from which I am only (Sat. evening) now finally finished. Causing, after hilarity all night, the, I think, most frightening worst depression all that following Friday when I silently promised God I'd stop mainlining if only my right wrist would ever unstiffen and not be puffed and like a bloated sponge. . . .
>
> I decided I'd start work on a story based on the sex/money switch, while fresh, and perhaps later work an hour on sorting the suitcase crammed with papers (relating to the war with Couquite, my U.S. income tax, correspondance on the "Candy" affair, etc.), which I brought in a taxi to this Chelsea Hotel more long than two months past. And one day midway through January, Anita visiting me in the second of the three rooms I've had here, I accomplished a first sorting session with this pile. But by eleven pm I still had not a word down and thus am writing simply a faithful account of my present state (the lowest in my life) in order to do *something* as if writing, no matter how tenuous attachment.

Mason's other way of dealing with turbulence was to shoot up — then get clean. As Marianne Faithfull recalled of her friend:

> I got very depressed over something . . . I was crying and he said, "Let's get together and walk around." That's nice, I thought. I was crying and trying to talk. I think it must have been about a romance. He said, "I've got some junk at home and I think if you start on that it will make you feel better." That was his solution to everything. . . . But that was his way of helping.

Chapter 34

Tangled Up in Gid

Sy Litvinoff had strong ties to England, and as he stepped up his involvement in resolving *Candy,* found that the U.K. situation for Girodias was far worse than anyone imagined. Leon Friedman recalls being in the Hamptons and receiving a frantic phone call from Girodias:

> He was desperate and contrite. He said if he didn't get the British rights, he'd be in serious trouble — not just money trouble. I called Cindy and said we've got to redo the deal. Maurice is in physical danger. He must have the British rights and can have less elsewhere.

Degener, who had been in London looking for the film financing, agreed.

It seemed that Girodias had one of the most notorious gangsters in London breathing down his neck, someone who specialized in straightening out problems in the pornography publishing racket, and who could deliver old debts — within hours. This tough guy came from one of the seven richest families in England, but after many notorious incidents, the other sons took over the family business and eventually forced him out. Walter Zacharius, who knew him, recalls, "If you want to talk about a pirate, this guy was the real thing. . . . He was involved with a bunch of rough characters. . . . I was with him when Scotland Yard picked him up for killing somebody."

Like the Resistance fighter he had been, Girodias managed to keep his head — even from the gangster, whom he apparently appeased by promising to help him put out a pirate edition of *Candy* in England. While Girodias had been sorted out for the moment, it seemed that things for *Candy* would never be, especially in England. Michael Rubinstein, Girodias's British attorney, wrote: "The *Candy* affair generates the most extraordinary confusions! . . . The situation appears to have reached maximum confusion, and it certainly presents major dangers for my client."

He also explained that Tandem was keeping the British rights until Girodias paid them (or Jeenspress) back, which Friedman made sure would be part of the settlement.

Girodias cabled Terry on November 16:

> PLEASE CONSIDER MY APPROVAL CANDY CONTRACT OCTOBER 1966 COMPLETE AND FINAL NOTWITHSTANDING HAND WRITTEN QUALIFICATION STOP PLEASE APPROVE CHANGES ALREADY APPROVED BY ME AS PER YOUR AGENT'S INSTRUCTIONS AND TRY PERSUADE MASON COUNTERSIGN IMMEDIATELY OTHERWISE ANOTHER STERILE ENDLESS CONFLICT UNAVOIDABLE THANKS. MAURICE GIRODIAS

Though Girodias tried to settle with Terry alone, Friedman wanted to get both authors' signatures to wrap things up. At the end of November, Friedman tracked down Mason in Los Angeles, where he found him in a West Hollywood hotel. Friedman reported back to Girodias:

> Mason was, as usual, fairly incoherent when I talked to him. . . . It turns out that his real concern was not with Walter Minton at all. He wants to be guaranteed that if Terry is signed to do a screenplay on *Candy* he will also participate. In other words, he wants to be treated the same way that Terry is down the line with respect to the movie.

In late November, Girodias cabled back to Lord a single directive from Paris, threatening litigation. "IF NO SATISFACTORY DEVELOPMENTS MUST IMMEDIATELY START ACTION." Degener concurred, and wrote to Litvinoff, Terry, and Samuel Pisar:

> Mason must sign. We are nowhere without his signature in movie sales and litigation, and Maurice's "new approach" must be discouraged. . . . Please let's the three of us talk. Does anyone know where Mason is?

Despite all the mutual animosities and competing interests among the parties, Friedman had created a workable settlement. Just when everything seemed set, now it was Mason who refused to sign, since he was insisting on keeping the $10,000 Minton had given him as an advance against future royalties. This put the agreement into yet another tailspin, which Friedman was determined to smooth over.

In early December, Walter Minton emerged—having been unusually quiet throughout the turmoil. He wrote to Girodias, pushing for a *Candy* settlement which rivaled the calculating complexities of even Girodias. He also revealed how and why he had given Mason the problematic $10,000.

> You must understand I am in a difficult position. . . . When we began action against the pirates we had to have the signature of one of the authors on the complaint — that's under our strange copyright regulations. Southern would not do it. Mason did — on the condition that we came to an agreement with him about royalties on the paper edition. . . .
>
> So we have a perfectly valid contract with Mason that has nothing to do with the copyright situation or anything else. It is why . . . it was necessary that Mason saw more in the agreement with you and Terry than he would lose by settling for one-third of a 25% share rather than the one-half that he had by agreement. I postponed making the accounting to him that was due — on the grounds that there was a possible settlement with you and Terry in the air. But when he showed up in New York and demanded money, there was nothing I could do. Except pay him. . . .
>
> God knows I'd like to see this matter settled. And believe me, my position is that the money is there and it makes absolutely no difference to us whether it goes to Mason, to Mason and Terry, or to Mason, Terry and you — aside from the fact that I would like to see you get some reward for your efforts. Is that clear?

Around this time Friedman reported to Girodias on the stalemate with Mason:

> We are coming to the end of the road with Mason. . . . Cindy is so disgusted that she has given me virtual carte blanche to arrange a deal with Mason. Gideon Cashman is so disgusted with Mason that he is thinking of dropping out altogether. Mason is coming to see him [tomorrow]. He will again tell him that he must sign at this point or forever give up any possibility of getting money from *Candy*. . . .
>
> Mason may just be playing some elaborate game to get everyone's attention at this point. . . . [His] travels around the country and his refusal to talk sense make it impossible to move any quicker than we have been. I will cable you as soon as anything significant happens.

By the end of 1966, Terry was living the high life of a highly paid international screenwriter, with such projects as *Barbarella* and *Casino Royale* in the works. At the height of Mason's stalemate, Terry wrote to him to set the record straight, and urged him to stop holding out for "another $10,000" and sign the deal before it was too late:

> East 55th Street, NY; Winter, 1966
>
> Dear Mason:
>
> I think I understand your attitude and feelings about Candy and related matters. I don't believe, however, that you understand mine. Since I have found it somehow impossible to communicate them to you in conversation, I want to try to set them down, as follows:
>
> (1) The reason our royalties were withheld, and the reason there has been no movie deal to date, was the appearance of the pirated editions. Girodias instigated the pirated editions because we cut him out of the Putnam deal. You will remember that it was your idea and at your insistence that we *did* cut him out. Admittedly I was

at fault to go along with this, but I was not in favor of it. So that in my mind, the whole fiasco is basically your responsibility.

(2) We had a very firm contract with Putnam in *one respect*, i.e. that they could not issue a paperback edition before *one full year* of the hard-cover distribution. You sold out (for [$]10,000) this one piece of negotiating leverage we had with them by signing the waiver allowing them to publish it in advance of the contractual period.

(3) After all this time and a great deal of work by a lot of people to negotiate a settlement with Gid, which would clear the title for a movie sale and get us our royalties from both Putnam and the pirates, your obstreperousness in not signing is incomprehensible — except as some absurd form of blackmail.

(4) If you accept another 10 (or 11) from Putnam, you will have received 20 (or 21) to my zero. The only money I've received directly or indirectly from *Candy* was the screenplay money — of which you got half.

Mason had been telling the attorneys, and others, that Terry owed his screenwriting career to *Candy*'s success.

(5) In fact, the only money I have made from writing has been through screenplay work, and had nothing whatever to do with *Candy,* but stemmed directly from my work on *Dr. Strangelove.* Kubrick hired me to work on *Dr. Strangelove* because of *The Magic Christian. Candy* had not then been published in America, and Kubrick had not read it. *Dr. Strangelove*, in addition to being a great commercial success, was voted "Best Screenplay of 1964" by the Writers Guild of America, very nearly won the Academy Award in that category — and led to my getting more work scriptwise.

(6) Finally, but without I assure you, wishing in any way to underestimate the value of your contribution to the work in question, I feel I must remind you that of the total 224pps. (Putnam edition) you wrote 64 and one half pages (i.e. pps. 64 — 121 and 1/2 and pps. 123 — 130) which constitutes little more than one third of the whole, and which, you may recall, I rewrote entirely.

In view of all this you can surely understand how I find it difficult to agree that you should realize more from the project than I. Right?

T.

As a last resort to try to get Mason to sign, Girodias tried enlisting the help of Hoffenberg's family and convinced Couquite to call Mason's mother. Girodias apprised Friedman, "Just had a call from Mason's wife, who says she had a call from him yesterday. She feels that Mason is going to keep going just in order to show how important and desirable he is. That we already knew. The only way to convince Mason is to show that we don't need him. . . . This is not a situation where logic will prevail, but only childish bluff."

Mason finally appeared in New York and Friedman advised Girodias to stay away for fear of spooking Mason, and cabled Girodias as follows:

> MASON IN NEW YORK HIDING WITH CASHMAN AND SOUTHERN STOP INTERVENTION ON YOUR PART UNDESIRABLE UNTIL SITUATION CLEARS.

Understanding that Terry could sign alone, Girodias tried again getting him to sign, hoping that Mason would feel pressured to do the same, or be left behind. He then cabled a beaten-down Mason in New York:

> OLYMPIA HAS IRREVOCABLY ASSIGNED CANDY COPYRIGHT TO SOUTHERN STOP YOUR CHANCE COLLECT SHARE DEPENDS ON YOUR WILLINGNESS SETTLE . . . PLEASE UNDERSTAND YOU WILL BE EXCLUDED VERY SUBSTANTIAL MONEY UNLESS SETTLEMENT IMMEDIATELY EXECUTED . . . HOPE YOU UNDERSTAND YOUR RESPONSIBILITIES.

Friedman then wrote to Girodias in Paris saying that he had arranged a round-table conference "which everyone will attend and straighten the whole matter out once and for all." He reported that "Mason is back in town and everyone is treating him as if he had the plague. He is still determined to get equal screenplay credit with Terry Southern for any movie made of 'Candy.' . . . Terry will not even countersign the changes until we have settled with Mason one way or the other."

The meeting was held on December 15, 1966, in Gideon Cashman's Park Avenue office, attended by all the principals: Cashman and his client Mason; Friedman, representing Girodias once again; and Cindy Degener, representing the authors and the movie deal. The main objectives were to settle with Girodias, for the authors to be paid by Minton, the movie deal sealed and the screenplay authors settled, and to start suits against the pirate publishers. Southern and Hoffenberg sat in stony (if not stoned) silence, no doubt both wearing shades as the final terms were explained and agreed upon in Cashman's spacious but cluttered office. The contract would now go back once again for a final drafting by the attorneys, then to be signed by all before Christmas, only ten days away.

Friedman then called Girodias to report that the final agreement was imminent. Girodias wrote back, believing his luck had finally changed for the better:

> What next! . . . Leon, again thank you for everything. Without you that gory business would never have been resolved. Let's hope that things will take a turn for the better and that we will all be millionaires soon. That would be a nice change, wouldn't it?

But Mason, as if on cue, told his lawyer that he would not sign, and suddenly disappeared again into the holiday rush. As promised, Friedman approached Terry to see if he would sign independently of Mason. Friedman then sent the agreement to Girodias's lawyer in England, while conferring to him via telegram:

> SOUTHERN AGREEABLE TO ACTING JOINTLY WITH YOU ON BASIS OF LATEST REVISED AGREEMENT WITH HOFFENBERG SHARE SPLIT EQUALLY AND HELD IN ESCROW.

In another last-ditch effort to get Mason to sign, Girodias proposed bribing him. There was such desperation to get Mason's signature, that even Friedman himself was not above offhandedly suggesting a little intrigue, as he does within this letter to Girodias;

> The last contact I had with Mason was to give him a flat ultimatum that he must sign the contract by December 30. He said he was not

> going to, and I said Terry and I would go it alone. There is no other way to deal with that man. He may wake up in about two weeks and decide to sign; but cajoling him was finally self-defeating: he thought it just showed weakness, and was trying to hold out for more money. . . .
>
> Terry is so angry at Mason that he is very anxious to sign a deal with us and proceed to exploit *Candy* between the two of us. I am preparing some papers along those lines, and I am sure I can get Terry to sign them very shortly.
>
> To try to bribe Mason at this point would jeapordize a continuing relation with Terry. For that reason, I would not like to approach him. However, there is no reason why you could not do so on your own (without my knowledge, of course). If it ever came to the surface, I could probably smooth over any difficulties with Terry. . . .
>
> Terry is now very much with us and may be very co-operative on the English deal. . . . Approaching Mason may destroy Terry's good will. I would strongly recommend that you act in a conspiratorial tone with Mason, telling him to tell no one else about it. You should destroy this letter immediately after reading it.

With Terry now on their side, Friedman's letter and telegram fanned the flames of Girodias's grandiose fantasies, and he wrote back to the attorney suggesting yet *another* agreement, which would not only redefine all the Putnam terms but would cut Mason out of profit-sharing all together:

> Now that Mason is out of it for all practical purposes, we have regained our freedom to get decent royalties from him [Minton], not peanuts (the $100,000 he offers is half of what he should pay on 150,000 hard cover and a million and a half paperback copies). . . . What do you say?

Friedman urged Girodias to focus on closing the deal, not reopen its terms. Now that the *Candy* wars' end was in sight, Girodias was determined that it should end well for him in France. He longed to rise triumphantly before his detractors with his ultimate prize, the American bestseller *Candy,* on its way to Hollywood moviedom —

and still banned by the provincial French authorities. Thinking to kill two birds with one stone, and aiming to get back at Hoffenberg for all his obstreperousness, Girodias suggested a last ruse to Friedman, that they take advantage of an arcane French authorship law that could potentially strip Mason of *all* his rights.

While it seems likely that Girodias could have continued scheming indefinitely until a resolution occurred, with the cold of winter setting in, Mason finally relented and visited his attorney, who wrote to Cindy Degener;

January 11, 1967

BY HAND
Dear Cindy:

After many a swallow, comes the spring. Similarly, after many a delay, comes Mason Hoffenberg.

Yesterday, Mason was in my office and signed the documents which I am enclosing herewith. . . .

May I express to you my continuing awe and respect for the perseverance which you have demonstrated in connection with this matter. It reflects credit on you personally and on your organization.

Best regards.

Cordially,

Gideon Cashman

The final settlement detailed the following terms:

- All income to be divided: 40% for Mason, 40% for Terry, 20% for Girodias.
- Hoffenberg to keep the $11,000 from side deal with Minton, considered an advance against future royalties.
- Olympia granted U.K. rights, to pay authors 5% on hardbacks. Authors to receive £2,500 advance on sale of U.K. rights.
- All previous monies received by Olympia for sales of *Candy*

to be retained; monies received by writers for the film sale and U.S. rights to be retained, no accounting required.

- Copyright to be in authors' names, all rights to *Candy*, except in Britain, to be held by authors.
- Authors and Olympia to act together against the pirate publishers and share legal expenses and recovered monies. Any other party (i.e., Putnam) joining would share in monies and legal fees, the amount to be negotiated.
- Authors to account for previous film deals, and money left from repayments to be divided between authors and Olympia.
- Legal action in France to be terminated.

As agreed, Walter Minton paid the $64,000 in royalties he had in escrow for the hardback and paperback sales of *Candy*, but after legal and other fees and expenses were deducted, and with legal fees to wind up the movie deal, and with lawsuits pending to go after the unauthorized editions, the only ones who made any money on *Candy* besides Putnam were the pirates. "The pirates killed us," reflected Minton. Friedman later recalled:

> Putnam and the authors made a big mistake cutting out Girodias in the first place. Maurice was right when he said they hurt themselves in order to hurt him. If we had done at the beginning what we did at the end, we would all have made an enormous amount of money.

With his control over the U.K. legitimized by the authors, Girodias quickly cleaned things up in England. All his efforts and grief paid off there: he settled with the London toughs by making good on his debt (and encouraged Gold to do a small pirated edition while he looked the other way). He also sealed a deal with New English Library for £50,000 in exchange for the rights to a wide range of Olympia titles, including *Candy*.

Cindy Degener wrote to Litvinoff saying that in addition to Leon Friedman obtaining a litigator copyright specialist, Don Eagle, for the suits against the pirates, he was also going to arrange a story in *Publishers Weekly* "which he hopes will shake up some of the pirates."

Finally, the *Candy* men were working toward a common goal. However, the case against the elusive, dangerous, and in many cases politically connected pirates was a long battle that required the attorneys to reconstruct the entire saga concerning the contested chain of title at home and abroad.

Chapter 35

With the Spring Comes Mason and Brando

As the dust cleared, United Artists was bailing out. Besides the harrowing and embarrassing copyright conundrum, Terry's script seemed too outrageous and erotic to make in the States. But like his quiet maneuvering with Lancer, Girodias's stealthy encouragement of Christian Marquand tipped the scales and changed everyone's reality. Unbeknownst to him, Girodias had an ally in Cindy Degener. In February 1967, unaware of Girodias's behind-the-scenes involvement with Christian Marquand, and unaware that he had actually *sold* Marquand his interest in the rights, she wrote a memo to the "Candy Committee," which included Terry, Mason, Litvinoff, Cashman, and Friedman:

> For the next few days I will be at the Connaught in London. I want you to know that in spite of all the columns in the less toney papers, we have not sold *Candy* to the movies. We are awaiting the success or failure of [Christian] Marquand in signing Taylor and Burton. . . . All the brain work and expenses for attempting to retain Taylor, Burton, Starr, and Sellers is being paid for by Brando on behalf of his friend Marquand.

Exercising damage control through spin, Degener circulated a press release to the studios, New York tabloids, and film and literary trade publications announcing that the rights were finally theirs.

> FOR IMMEDIATE RELEASE:
> Ever since the novel *Candy* established itself as an international best-seller, there has been much surprise that it has not been made into a movie. Now a motion picture can be made.
>
> Because of its unusual nature—a copyright case in French courts involving two American citizens and a French publisher—the case has attracted widespread interest in France and in publishing circles throughout the world.

Degener focused on the legal victory in France, announcing definitively that Terry and Mason had "recovered from Maurice Girodias and Olympia Press all rights in their own work," and that "the decision was based upon Olympia's failure to pay royalties due." She wanted the press to focus on the legal fight — and its "resolution."

Degener's press release put a spotlight on *Candy* in the Hollywood trade papers, New York City dailies, as well as in Paul Nathan's "Rights and Permissions" column in *Publishers Weekly.* Nathan used the opportunity to provide an update on Terry, quoting him as saying:

> "Within the last couple of weeks [the case] was decided in our favor, in a French court. He [Girodias] was going to appeal, so we made a settlement: he gets a substantial percent — I think it's 25 — of whatever we receive from a film. It's a parallel case to 'Lolita,' where he did the same thing.
>
> "Earlier, United Artists had taken an option on 'Candy.' . . . Now it's available again."
>
> Not only is it available, but a certain amount of advance legwork has been undertaken by the French actor Christian Marquand, who, I gather, would like to be in it. A crony of Marlon Brando, Marquand has obtained a commitment from Brando — and also from Richard Burton and Peter Sellers, according to Southern — for "cameo" appearances in the film, if and when.
>
> Southern himself isn't sure this would result in the best picture. "I think maybe it should go the underground route and achieve its success like the book," he said. "I'd like them to try to make it an interesting, low-budget movie. But United Artists has already paid me

for two drafts of a script, and there's about $100,000 invested in it. That makes it hard to go and do something cheap."

At the moment Southern is occupied with preparations for a co-production by his own film company, Maldoror, Inc., and Colossal Pictures Ltd. [Litvinoff's company]. . . . The joint project is Anthony Burgess' "A Clockwork Orange."* Published here by Norton, the novel, as adapted by Southern, will be shot on Colossal's home ground, London — probably with young David Hemmings of "Blow-Up," as star.

Two weeks later, Girodias used the same venue in *Publishers Weekly* to launch his counterattack, ending his piece with an ominous warning against the publishing industry at large: "It is a sad fact that many of my [finds] have been printed by various publishers in the United States . . . (sometimes with the authors' misinformed complicity . . .). In order to cover up their actions, some publishers have been busy discrediting me professionally — and I have not always had the opportunity of replying. . . . My firm has decided to bring a series of lawsuits against every publisher in the United States, 'respectable' or not, who has [used] what I have every legal and moral right to consider as Olympia's property."

Girodias's inflammatory comments in the *PW* piece came as no surprise to the Lord team, but the word of mouth now coming back from Hollywood that Christian Marquand controlled the rights — was a shock. To make matters worse, Marquand was not only saying he would *be* in *Candy,* he was insisting on *directing* — and his ability to rein in a favor from Brando would allow him to do this. Marquand, well connected politically in Paris, had recently cajoled Premier Georges Pompidou into sending a letter to the governor of French Polynesia to help Brando purchase over 1,000 acres of *Teti'aroa* from the Tahitian Territorial Assembly.

Marquand sent Terry a telegram, hoping his enthusiasm

---

*Terry held the option to the novel at the time and co-wrote a screenplay based on it with photographer Michael Cooper. This screenplay was not ultimately used for the film version, which was directed by Stanley Kubrick and realeased in 1971.

would somehow help cut through all the problems. Marquand's feigned hipsterism in this telegram offers hints of the kind of self-absorbed, drug-fueled chaos that would soon arise with Marquand at the helm:

> MR TERRY SOUTHERN MALDOROR INC
> 65 E55 ST NEWYORK
> REMEMBER YOU VADIM BURROUGHS AND ME STOP NOW YOU ARE VADIM BURROUGHS IS MICK JAGGER MICK COOPER IS YOU AND I AM STILL MYSELF STOP ATTENTION
> LOVE CHRISTIAN

As the UA deal fell apart, an Italian-American producer named Robert Haggiag, who had a distribution deal with ABC television, stepped up. As Haggiag recalls:

> I liked the book. I was told that United Artists was giving up the project, and at the same time, had a proposition from an actor, Christian Marquand, who told me that he was very friendly with Brando, and that if he directed the picture, Brando would be involved.

Haggiag would pay for half the film's production costs if Brando indeed signed on. ABC television was getting into movie production for the first time, and *Candy* would be the vehicle by which the new studio would test its mettle in the film business. As Sy Litvinoff recalls:

> Ultimately what persuaded ABC was Christian Marquand. I mean, along comes this guy who says he can deliver Brando and all these stars. Christian knew everybody — he was a not only an actor but a celebrity in Europe. His [Trintignant] family and marriage gave him total credibility — like Vadim.

But Cindy Degener was outraged by Marquand potentially interfering with the rights aspect of the deal, and wrote to Allen Susman, an attorney whose name had been associated with Brando.

May 19, 1967

Mr. Allen Susman
Rosenfeld, Meyer & Susman
444 United California Bank Building
Beverly Hills, Calif. 90210

Dear Mr. Susman:

I do not know where to address a letter to Christian Marquand and Peter Zoref. Therefore, I am taking the liberty of writing you and hoping that you will pass along this letter to Christian and Mr. Zoref.

It comes to me from all sides that Christian and Mr. Zoref are categorically stating that they own the rights to *Candy* for motion picture production. Of course, this is not true. During the next week, I will write letters to all of the major movie companies restating what I have told them on the phone and in frequent other discussions; that is, the rights to *Candy* are available and that due to the settlement as among Mr. Southern, Mr. Hoffenberg, and Mr. Girodias, we now have world-wide copyright protection.

Thank you for any clarification you can bring to this situation by helping straighten out Christian as to the fact that he does not own the rights.

Cordially,

Claire S. Degener

Degener then wrote to Mason's attorney, Gideon Cashman in New York:

> I think that we are near a movie deal. There are two parties of substance really interested. I continue to ask $200,000 for the novel and the three screenplays. . . . I think I may actually get $200,000 or very near it.
>
> Please do not let Mason let himself down by not getting these papers to me.

On September 17, Cindy Degener was now in the process of tidying up the UA deal. In a letter to a United Artists executive, she wrote: "I am in a state of shock that I have gotten this far. If all goes well and any of the reports I receive are accurate, you will receive the rest of the money due you in early December." She wrote that "the entire experience has been horrendous," and because UA did not try to seize the rights or bail out sooner, she wrote, "I am most appreciative to you."

The same day, Cindy issued a check to Mason, c/o Gideon Cashman, for $7,200, indicating more money should be coming soon. The check was also designed to get Mason's attention on signing the settlement.

By the fall of 1967, Terry's finances had imploded, and he was becoming more and more erratic in his personal and professional life. Two years of lucrative film work had netted him over $600,000, but, believing there was always another big deal coming, he had failed to set aside money for the IRS, which was now breathing down his neck. The money was long gone — spent on caviar for all at the Russian Tea Room, betting in Italian casinos, and enjoying the high-life. His novel *Blue Movie* was overdue to New American Library, and Cindy Degener worried that the strain would prompt Terry to take quick screenwriting jobs instead of finishing the novel. In fact, that is what eventually happened; once *Blue Movie* was completed in 1969, Terry would not escape from the cycle of fruitless speculative script development. Seeking to steer him clear of this temptation, Degener wrote to him care of Litvinoff, who had an office Terry used on East 55th Street.

September 18, 1967

> Terry Dear:
>
> I have tried to phone but cannot reach you. I have just spoken with Dave Gotterer [Terry's new accountant] to let him know that the Internal Revenue Service put a lien on your income Friday afternoon. I enclose a thermofax of the documents the Internal Revenue left with Karen. . . . I was terribly sorry to hear that you could not

make the meeting with him last week, and now I gather that you have cancelled the meeting today at 4:00 p.m.

I am very sorry about the obvious difficulty you are in, and do want to remind you that upon delivery of 10,000 words of "BLUE MOVIE" to NAL you will receive $9,000, and upon delivery of an additional 20,000 words . . . you will receive another $9,000. . . .

I do hope that the situation does not make you feel desperate, and I hope that you will try and finish the novel, rather than take odd movie jobs. . . . I realize you are overdrawn at the bank, and this may be putting a terrible pressure on you, but on the other hand, if the novel gets done by November 1st, you have $54,000 coming to you, which is in addition to the $18,000 I have mentioned above.

The "CANDY" news looks increasingly good — so good that ABC Films is paying for Gideon Cashman to fly to Spain in order to obtain the signature of Mason Hoffenberg. Mason is the only real stumbling block left, and it is quite serious, but we will pray for the best.

Cordially,

Claire S. Degener

As Terry was fielding a variety of offers for speculative script work — from re-writing *Barbarella* for Dino DeLaurentis in Rome, to helping Peter Fonda get his as-yet-untitled *Easy Rider* off the ground — his romance with Gail intensified. Terry and Gail moved into a townhouse on 36th Street, where they lived for a couple of years before moving permanently into the house in Canaan. Gail, who had given up her acting and dancing career, began to teach ballet to help supplement Terry's dwindling income. During this tumultuous period, Terry made a half-dozen attempts to return to Carol, but as more and more time passed, his romantic ideal of house and family receded.

Neither of the marriages of the *Candy* authors survived the '60s. Mason's heroin habit, which Couquite found increasingly hard to bear, led to their separation in 1965, just as *Candy* was enjoying its greatest success. Mason had left his family in France, came back to the States and settled in Stone Ridge, near Woodstock, New York, shuttling to the U.K. for alternative drug treatments.

Terry, like Mason, left his marriage and was separated for long periods from his young son. However, unlike Mason, Terry never seemed to dwell on his personal life — no matter how complicated or painful to others (and himself) it became. Whereas Terry was not one for self-reflection, Mason desperately wanted to save himself, and knew what was at stake, as he wrote in his journal of a "standing sleep" dream — which eerily featured Terry:

> A dream briskly switches on. Terry is talking. He wears just pyjama tops and Couquite, therefore, at once, exists, and can see his dangling cock is not small and shriveled. Thinking of how much I want Daniel back—he's five, and needs me, his father, as much as I want him at my side—I realize it's a thing, finally, that I would unhesitatingly pray for to God (. . . "Please God"). Just then, Terry says, "Haven't you got an ashtray in this place?" and I, glancing and seeing none in the room am about to go to get the one in the bathroom feeling it's what I need — held offered before me in both hands, or placed on the floor with me, somehow, kneeling in it — in order to pray to God. . . .
>
> And now, in truth it's seen how he cannot get along alone. More and more it's apparent that he is the fumbling, cowardly, indecisive mediocrity his wife depicted — or is it that by the very nature of his loss (exactly as in the conventionally described mother "crazed with grief" by loss of her children) he has begun to rot like someone in an oubliette.

In mid-October, while writing to Samuel Pisar in Paris concerning legal fees and payment, Cindy apprised him of the movie situation:

> I am hopeful that within a matter of two to three weeks the *Candy* movie contract will, in fact, be signed with Selmur Productions [Robert Haggiag]. Lee Steiner, lawyer for Selmur, is increasingly certain of production.

> I am sure you are following all this in Paris, as Selmur is employing Christian Marquand.
>
> Mr. Cashman is flying to either Paris or Spain to hopefully obtain the signature of Mason. I am a bit concerned about Mason's signature, but I am hopeful that Mr. Cashman can achieve it.

Cashman recounted to John de St. Jorre his attempts to find Mason in Paris:

> The [ABC] producers asked me to go to Paris to persuade Mason to sign the contract. I arrived on a night flight and to my surprise was met by Mason himself in a Citroën 2CV. He took me to my hotel and told me to meet him at the Coupole at midnight. I went along, but he wasn't there. I waited until about two A.M., but he didn't show up.
>
> The next day he telephoned me to apologize and set up another meeting. Same time, same place — midnight at La Coupole. Same result. Mason didn't turn up. He called again the next day and set up the same arrangement once again: midnight at La Coupole. Well, when he didn't show this time I tracked down his fleabag hotel at one-thirty in the morning, found his room, and knocked on the door. I heard a groan, opened the door, and there was my client facedown and spread-eagled on the bed. He muttered that he would meet me at a nearby pizza place at four A.M. I went there, and he turned up in surprisingly good shape. We discussed the movie contract, and, as dawn was breaking over Paris, he signed it and I caught the next plane back to New York.

On December 7, 1967, Selmur issued a check for $150,000 and exercised their option to make *Candy*. The film was finally under way and would be released a year later. Shooting soon began at Haggiag's Dear Studio in Rome. Terry had hoped that Jane Fonda would take the role, but he had long since soured on the whole production, especially when UA backed off his script. As Haggiag says, "They thought it couldn't be done. It was too extreme."

As Terry recalled in 1968, "Regarding *Candy* as a film, I had nothing to do with it—having withdrawn when they insisted on taking out the hunchback." He later elaborated:

> When Christian Marquand, a friend, begged for a short option, I persuaded Mason that he should have it. Marquand, through Brando, signed up Richard Burton and got financing. I had already written a script, and they said it needed some rewrites. But then Marquand went and got a Swedish girl, Ewa Aulin, to be Candy. I couldn't believe it, the girl had *got* to be American. But he insisted. He said: 'I want to give the film a universal quality.' She couldn't speak any English and had to be looped and dubbed in.
>
> At that point I withdrew. Both Mason and I got some money from the film. They changed the script and . . . Richard Burton was a kind of Dylan Thomas poet who had a wind machine sweeping up his scarf. Brando was some kind of holy man. Charles Aznavour played a Richard III figure who was supposed to represent the hunchback. No, he didn't sing. It was nothing like the book, but, due to its all-star cast, it did make money.

As for Ewa Aulin, Miss Teenage Sweden of that year, Haggiag recalls:

> She had made a picture in London for a small Italian producer, and this producer showed it to me. We had brought many girls to Rome and were testing them, but we couldn't find anyone satisfactory. One of them, a good one, was American, but she had a bad nose, so we wanted to operate on the nose. She was operated on [but not cast] — and because she was so good — we used her as dialogue coach. She's the one who taught English to the girl.
>
> We were very close to beginning the picture and we didn't have the right girl. I felt she [Aulin] had something.

Aulin was only eighteen. To be suddenly thrown into the lead role of a movie of one of America's most successful books, and then surrounded by top celebrities, many of them accustomed to casual drugging and sex — the pressure on her to "perform" was extreme.

Haggiag made sure the film made money. Part of his deal with Cinerama was that the distributor agree to "a minimum guarantee of three million dollars." Haggiag recalls, "It was a very good deal with Brando, $20,000 a week, and a nominal percentage of the gross — I think 2 or 3 percent. I thought, even if we don't succeed, I won't lose much money. We found Buck Henry — who was interested, so I said, 'Let's start writing for Brando, and if it goes well, then we will extend it.' "

Marquand had said at one point, "We're going to throw the book away — and dig in." With Brando involved, other top actors quickly came onboard: Richard Burton, Walter Matthau, Ringo Starr, James Coburn. Regardless of the quality of the production or the integrity of those involved, Girodias had ultimately prevailed in the race for the movie. It was his production that persevered, and his under-the-table payment that enabled him to walk away feeling, again, like the lone fighter of the French Resistance — always playing both sides, always ending up with enough money in his pocket to know he had won.

In Peter Manso's biography, *Brando,* James Coburn recalled the initial days of shooting:

> We were all kind of gathered around the idea of doing a sixties movie. Our attitude was "Let's see if we can do it." Nudity was beginning to come in, fucking on-screen, and it was all much freer. Also, everybody would have a say, and we knew we'd be inventing as we went along, with Buck Henry there all the time altering whatever came out. It was supposed to be a total collaborative effort. . . . [When] I came in . . . Christian Marquand met me at the airport and said, "There's been a little problem."

Coburn soon learned that Ewa Aulin had suffered some sort of breakdown during her scenes with Marlon Brando. "She was this young, naive thing," Coburn said. "She had this wonderful ass, man, and Marlon just couldn't resist. She would look at him in his fright wig and just get hysterical. He was so funny and ingratiating to begin with — only now he wanted to fuck her, so that was icing on the cake."

Aulin was sent to a coastal hotel and given shots to keep her asleep until she recuperated. Soon, rumors reached Hollywood that the decadent production had kept Aulin high just for the fun of it. "It was overwhelming," Coburn said. "She just went over the edge."

This rumor of the star being doped up strangely mirrored the action in *Blue Movie,* where the studio head unexpectedly visits the set in Lichtenstein, and is subdued and kept under heavy sedation as the filming goes on.

As the movie *Candy* began its production in Rome, attorneys were hard at work in the U.K. trying to determine how the book *Candy* might legally be published there in the wake of Britain's successful litigations banning "indecent" literary works.

In early 1968, Cindy Degener updated Terry and Mason on the current prospects. Hubert Selby Jr.'s *Last Exit to Brooklyn* was still banned in Britain, and there was a great deal of cautiousness on the part of publishers who feared another "American porno" would be held up to scrutiny and meet the same disastrous fate. If published, Degener wrote, the publisher, New English Library "has excellent advertising and promotion facilities. Tied in with the movie, the book ought to do awfully well."

Lord/Degener hired Richard Du Cann, a famous English barrister, to report on the prospects. As he pointed out, "The book is one which is bound to attract the attention by the authorities. Those who read allegedly obscene material for the various prosecuting bodies have certain rule-of-thumb standards of judgment which if infringed will provoke proceedings." To prevent same, Du Cann provided a blueprint for a "pornectomy,"* to which N.E.L., much to the dismay of critics and readers alike, adhered. The book appeared in the autumn of 1968 and quickly became a London bestseller, but the press was so vicious regarding N.E.L.'s cowardice that pressure began mounting to save face: the *Times Literary Supplement* had this to say:

> What the publisher and his advisers have done to *Candy* might be called bowdlerization: but that would be unfair to Bowdler. That censor was trying in difficult times to popularize his author, claiming correctly that Shakespeare would still be excellent, even with all the bawdy cut. *Candy* is a very different matter. It depends on the bawdy from beginning to end: the cutting has removed the point. It is a joke without a punchline, not worth reading in its present shape.

---

* See Appendix B

It wasn't until April, 1970, that N.E.L. followed up with an unexpurgated version. In a preface, the publisher recalled its change of heart: "We were aware that powerful literary figures, who were promoting an increasing literary and legal tolerance, were ready to defend the merits of the book." With a highbrow intro by an eminent scholar, *Candy* was published, and with that, England seemed to hobble past its censorship woes — a far cry from the passionate speeches and concerted legal efforts with which Rosset Superman and his band of literary lions had helped destroy censorship stateside.

As the filming got under way, and money was being spent liberally in Rome, Girodias was closing shop for good in Paris. He wrote from New York to Holly Hutchins, who, in addition to being a part-time bookkeeper, was the last bastion of the Olympia Press overseas, at his relocated and downscaled offices at 6 rue Séguier. "Can you find yourself another job?" he wrote. "Unless you have a better idea, like opening a tearoom in rue Séguier with your own money, or a laundromat, or a fortune teller's office."

Holly wrote back: "It's been a great experience, I would not have had it otherwise for anything! And who knows perhaps someday 6 rue Séguier could be a *librarie-bar ou quelquechose* and with me under the counter (in a plain brown wrapper of course) . . . Many thanks for everything and all best wishes for a Happy New Year, and *merde* as we say over here!" Girodias said good-bye: "I . . . feel . . . very bad about the whole thing . . . my whole Paris establishment has now become a ruinous burden which I have to liquidate."

This was the end of the Olympia Press and its incestuous inspiration, father Jack Kahane's Obelisk. For Girodias, it was a sad defeat and truly the end of an era in publishing. No doubt the French Ministry of Culture (and the Paris courts) breathed a collective sigh of relief, having endured two generations of continual browbeating, innovation, and challenge.

Chapter 36

Scrawlings on a Cave Wall

As the Olympian house from which *Candy* rose fell to ruins, *Candy* the motion picture emerged as a most expensive production ($3 million), with an all-star cast. Capitalizing on the movie-marketing frenzy and a new generation of readers, and despite the copyright rulings in France in their favor, a number of new pirate editions of the book came out during the film's release, appropriating a movie-still of Brando and Ewa Aulin on the cover. Putnam's official movie tie-in edition also came out, with this copy on its back cover:

> Good Grief! *Candy* a movie?
>
> To the millions who read Candy's outrageous adventures in this famous bestseller, the fact that *Candy* is now a movie will be startling. *Life* magazine called *Candy* "unfilmable." But the "unfilmable" is now a star-studded motion picture starring Richard Burton, Marlon Brando, Ringo Starr, James Coburn, Walter Matthau, John Huston . . .

The cast also included John Astin (who later starred as the mustached father in *The Addams Family*), Anita Pallenberg, prizefighter Sugar Ray Robinson, and Judith Malina and Julian Beck of the Living Theater.

The "universal quality" Marquand sought was translated to screen quite literally, with Candy depicted in the opening scene as a protoplasmic celestial energy field — courtesy of *2001* special effects artist Douglas Trumbull. With a spaced-out euro-pop soundtrack (by the same composer who did *Barbarella*) the "universal energy" touches down on the parched surface of the earth, then gathers into the shape of . . . Candy Christian. The notion that this "celestial being" comes to earth to quench and heal, subverts the very "human" — and delightfully degraded — point of the book.

The ending of the film is even more "trippy," with contrived scenes of youth protest culture at a "be-in," as the entire cast assembles in an open field where a mass acid trip is in progress. Various circles of peaceniks sit contemplatively; Daddy Christian is smoking pot maniacally; Hare Krishnas are doing their thing; and Candy, as she has throughout the film, just walks impassively through all. James Coburn, playing Dr. Krankeit, injects old men and himself with a youth serum that has instant transformative effects — courtesy of a simple curtain people walk behind. At one point, this "no walls" environmental theater features Christian Marquand himself, with a Bolex movie camera, his jacket bedecked with burning sparklers, turning his camera toward a giant funhouse mirror in the field, that reflects the bloated *Candy* movie crew itself — cameras turning, money spinning, as if to say that they were having the last laugh (on the audience).

Candy, the classically told send-up of romance and pornography, had become a careless indulgence of '60s narcissism, painful for its authors to watch.

With a running time of close to, and in some foreign releases over two hours, the film was panned worldwide, generating some vicious commentary. *Time* compared Buck Henry's script to "scrawlings on a cave wall." Here is a sampling of the film's reviews:

> For sheer ignominious ineptitude, *Candy* takes the cake. . . . What this shabby European production is really about is money: a whole bunch of actors getting rich in Rome, an American television network footing the bill in hopes of cashing in on some sexy stuff they can't put on the air.
>
> — *Newsweek*

> Frenzied, formless and almost entirely witless adaptation of the enchanting Southern-Hoffenberg pornographic parable. No longer does Candy blithely chirrup "Good Grief!" at each new sexual calamity, while welcoming the opportunity to give herself to alleviate sex-suffering humanity. Instead, she defends her modesty with some vigour — her falls from grace being obscured by bowdlerization as well as censor cuts — thus robbing the book of its point as well as its charm.
>
> — *British Film Institute*

> An incomprehensible mess. *Candy* keeps getting worse than seems possible. The movie doesn't look directed: One has visions of the editor holding his head — his brains slipping through his fingers.
>
> — Pauline Kael, *The New Yorker*

Despite its negative publicity, the film made money. "It was like a coffee table book of its times," producer Haggiag recently said. Indeed, it was one of the few films which (like *The Magic Christian,* released a year later) seemed to capture some of the irreverent, out-of-the-box, anarchic spirit of the '60s. Made in Europe, and rated "R" before such classifications were strictly enforced, *Candy,* and the "PG" *Magic Christian,* became "must-see" films for preteens too young to be taking part in the psychedelic '60s.

In December 1968, after premiering in Los Angeles and New York, *Candy* went into wide release. Radio spots featured the voice of Marlon Brando and the other stars, with hucksterish announcers chiming, "The sweetest little movie this side of *psychopathia sexualis*" — a reference to Lenny Bruce's hip, hallucinatory spoken-word riff. As Bruce had died vilified by the popular media only two years earlier, the reference to Terry's old friend must have irked him even more.

Additional radio spots featured Orson Welles intoning, "Is Candy *faithful*?" to which a breathless female replies, "Only to the *book*!"

Terry attended a screening of *Candy* and by his own account walked out. He apparently never saw the film in its entirety. Soon after, he wrote Mason — with whom he had not been in touch for two years:

163 East 36th St. NYC; 26 December 1968

My dear Hoff:

Would like to know your feelings about a certain Mister Frog version of our *Can*. In my view, it was a Dumbell and Tom Fool from the opening frame.

En tous cas, the real point is that, good or bad, it bears precious little resem to the true *Can* — a view which would seem substantiated by the reviews in both Time and Newsweek mag this week, the former going so far as to say the picture "is based on the novel in the same way a flea might be based on an elephant." Such not withstanding the distrib continues to use the ad : "Is Candy Faithful? Only To The Book!" I think it is important that we make serious representation to them to drop that slogan; not only is it embarrassing, but it could dramatically curtail sales of the new edition — from which we stand to make a pretty, *if* 'word of mouth' doesn't become mere 'bad mouth'; in other words, it seems fairly important that the book be identified as little as possible with the movie.

Do you agree? And if so, will you join me in action — the plan being to threaten them with TV, etc. interviews blasting the pic, unless they drop that particular ad. And to go through with it if they refuse.

Please let me know, *and* give me your grand guy news.

Best,

Gretchen

Mason responded in early January 1969.

Dear Terry,

Returned to Paris from yuletide in the little-known "Ardeche" section of France where I stayed with in-laws and dear kike kids of my own, you can easily imagine my extreme displeasure and what a rude return to the crass it was for me abruptly to have a letter from the likes of such a sneaking fair weather s o b as yours truly.

I heartily agree in any case that something ought to be done about that " . . . faithful only to the book" nonsense, and will get in touch with you in a few days after returning to the U.S. But where? At Litvinoff's. Can you leave word there for them to give me your phone? Or else try calling me either at the Chelsea Hotel, or in Woodstock, NY a partir de Jan. 15.

Clair

Mason was about to move to the rural upstate New York community known as Woodstock, where his old friend Bob Dylan now lived.

Like Terry and Mason, Girodias cultivated extreme people, sometimes to his own detriment. In 1967 Girodias met Valerie Solanas, a fellow resident of the Chelsea Hotel, who had written an anti-male play, *Up Your Ass,* and a tract called *S.C.U.M Manifesto* named for her group, the Society for Cutting Up Men. Impressed with her "strident aggressivity," Girodias offered her $2,000 in installments for her autobiography, which she accepted. Things quickly deteriorated when she couldn't finish her book, was thrown out of the Chelsea, and became homeless. Calling him a "thief and vulture," and demanding money, Solanas came looking for Girodias in the summer of 1968, but luckily he was in Canada at the time. Instead, Solanas shot Andy Warhol (in whose film *I, A Man* she had appeared) at his studio in Union Square — firing bullets into his chest, spleen, and liver. Shortly after the shooting, Solanas appeared at Barney Rosset's office with an ice pick, steps ahead of the police who arrested her. It was a new kind of uniquely American threat Girodias had brushed up against: celebrity stalkers on the edge of quality Lit city.

The following year, Olympia was evicted from number 6 rue Séguier by the building's owner, M. Lamy. True to form, Girodias relished any fight, even the most trivial: "Lamy has now made the irreparable mistake of suing me to collect the key money I had undertaken to pay him. . . . He has given me the weapon I needed to exercise my REVENGE — which will be swift, terrible and absolutely ruthless. . . . As to Mr. Lamy's goose, it is being cooked with most tender care and attention."

In a last-ditch effort to save his New York operation, Girodias teamed up with a wealthy girlie magazine publisher. He was able to continue his various lawsuits, including one against a publisher of *The Story of O*. "I am now *winning* all my lawsuits. I am going very soon to win against Donleavy. Isn't that a scream!"

Girodias continued launching *Candy* suits against pirate publishers he happened across, such as Unique Publishing in Canada, which had been pirating the book since 1965. However, Girodias had so many competing agendas worldwide he often found himself in bed with his own enemies, which surely fit in with his morally ambiguous view of the world. In discussing strategy with his Toronto solicitor, he wrote, "I would like the action to be initiated in the authors' name in the first place, since Mr. Geller [owner of Cross Canada News] is still our distributor and I would like to avoid appearing as the originator of that action. I am sure that can be easily arranged."

In one of his last communications regarding *Candy,* Girodias wrote from the Gramercy Park Hotel to Cindy Degener concerning his action against the Toronto pirates. He also took the opportunity to summarize his feelings of betrayal by Terry and Mason—and copied them both on the letter.

February 4th, 1969

Dear Cindy,

My personal feeling is that the reason why Putnam payed Mason directly was to involve him in a situation such that he could not question Putman's accounting. Said accounting does not make much sense. One year ago Bill Callahan, then vice president of Dell, told me that the actual sales were over 2 million copies at that point. No doubt that it is time to ask for an examination of Putnam's books. I would appreciate having your thoughts on the subject. May I use this opportunity to make a personal remark. My conflict with Terry and Mason over *Candy* has been painful enough and I have no desire to revive it. Let me only say that I have a clear conscience about what happened, and that I consider that we would never had been in any trouble, and we would have avoided piracy, had not Terry and Mason allowed the contract with Minton in the first place. However, now that everything is said and done, and that we have effected at least our legal collaboration by signing a new contract, I would be most grateful if you could use your influence with Terry and Mason to refrain them from discrediting me publicly as they have done too often in the past, and which they continue to do even today.

. . . It has become fashionable to betray me, and then to pile false accusations on me to justify those acts of betrayal. I certainly have not deserved to be treated in that manner, and if you could help me in restoring some measure of sanity in that area, I would be greatly obliged to you.

Many thanks.

Best regards,

Maurice Girodias

In 1970, the payment from Putnam was finally accounted for and distributed to the *Candy* men—but after the legal fees and expenses, there was not much left to allocate. The judgments against the pirates did not yield much money, either, and took a long time to settle. By 1972, Putnam's case against Lancer had been thrown out of court. Even though Girodias had made a deal with Zacharius about the unauthorized edition in 1965, he had no qualms about suing him for piracy. And he eventually won. Consequently, $9,000, after attorney fees was divided among the *Candy* men — bitter and paltry spoils of a dissatisfying war.

Part IV

BIRDS OF A FEATHER, FALLING

At that precise moment, she thought of New York City, and decided to go there . . . someplace where she knew no one, and where no one knew her . . . where she could lose the old Candy in the nameless city streets, she thought, where she could finally . . . be *herself*.

— *Candy*

Chapter 37

Weird Scenes Inside the Big Pink

The '70s were disastrous for all the *Candy* men.

First, Girodias. By 1970, the Olympia Press was bankrupt again. In the unpublished third volume of his memoirs, Girodias wrote that he had been keeping the company alive for the sole purpose of continuing his legal battle with J.P. Donleavy. The disagreement over Donleavy's right to sell the book in England without him had escalated over the years into a full-on war, with many court appearances attended by both men and their teams of attorneys. Again, it was a question of the copyright — and who had it — which led to years of litigation. But the significant difference here was that *The Ginger Man* was not a work for hire. As Donleavy, who lived in Ireland, told John de St. Jorre:

> Girodias would never admit clearly that I was the owner of *The Ginger Man* and that he was a licensee of it. He had it in his head, as he did with the pornographic books, that he owned it, that it was his. It never occurred to him that I was the owner . . . having written it — that it existed — before he came on the scene.

Donleavy said he had a verbal agreement with Girodias that they would split royalties in France and America, but that England would be 100 percent his. When Girodias stubbornly reneged, Donleavy, who passionately believed this book was his crowning achievement, and that its critical acclaim was the key to his literary ascendancy, fought over the rights with his very life. The book was published in England and became a great hit there, and later in

America, where it was finally published in its unexpurgated form in 1965. Girodias's suits for the French and English rights had prompted Donleavy to hire the best French and British attorneys he could find.

The fight continued throughout the '60s and prevented any film from being made. By 1968, the expense and bad blood had reached its zenith. As Girodias writes in his unpublished autobiography:

> Since I was unable to keep [Olympia] out of bankruptcy, which I was doing only in order to continue the litigation against Donleavy on both the French and the British fronts, I would keep fighting through the receiver (who profited copiously by it), feeding more and more money to the lawyers in Paris and London; all this from my command post in New York, and through a Swiss holding company.

In 1969, a French court ruled in Girodias's favor, which Donleavy appealed, and the case then moved up to a higher court. Girodias envisioned getting Donleavy for good:

> I could then force Donleavy to pay me one half of all the subsidiary sales he had made unilaterally over the past 14 or 15 years, plus interest, plus eventual punitive damages: hundreds of thousands of dollars. Half of his castle, half of his seventy-five heifers and the other cattle, tractors, limousines, the lot.

But Olympia Press was in receivership, and Girodias needed to have a live company to win the case. In his inimitable way of thinking, it all seemed possible:

> I bribed the receiver some more to organize a public sale of the assets of the bankrupt company, [for me] to be the buyer of the company, and to do it in such a secretive manner that at this public auction at the Tribunal de Commerce, I should be the only one [there] . . . nobody else would know about it.

However, Donleavy discovered the impending sale through one of his Paris lawyers, and in a moment of crafty spontaneity, Donleavy's wife, Mary, suggested she go to Paris to try to buy the company. Mary and Donleavy's secretary, dressed to the nines, left with $15,000 cash and hired a French bankruptcy specialist to do the actual bidding. Girodias had only brought $8,000 with him and was summarily trounced. He recalls an interview:

> I looked at the group of three people who were bidding. The man was obviously a Paris lawyer, and the two women were obviously crazy American ladies. I couldn't understand who would do this, you see. Who would benefit? I thought it was a silly rich American girl who wanted to have the name of the company and then make me an offer to run it.

Girodias did not immediately discover the ruse. He wrote to the mysterious new owner "Mary Wilson" at the New York address she had given to the auctioneer. "I understand you have bought my old Paris firm. Would you be interested in publishing my memoirs?" When Girodias learned it was his old nemesis, he was furious. Donleavy was euphoric and especially relished Girodias's frustration in not knowing who had done him in. Donleavy recalled, "I heard that he suspected Mason Hoffenberg . . . of being behind it. Girodias wrote to him, 'Dear Mason, why have you done this terrible thing to me? What have I ever done to you?' "

Thus the Donleavys had their revenge in spades. The Paris Olympia Press was utterly defeated — not by the courts or tax collectors — but by one of its own authors.

Donleavy was not the only author who had intensely hostile feelings toward Girodias. John Stevenson, a.k.a. Marcus van Heller, who had written a dozen books for Girodias between 1955 and 1961, told John de St. Jorre:

> At one point Alex [Trocchi] and I found our books being pirated because they were appearing under the Ophelia imprint. We took them along to Girodias and said, "God, Maurice, look what's happening!" "Oh, the bastards," he said, "these pirates!" But it was his own imprint. He had simply reprinted our stuff under the Ophelia name and didn't want to give us the money.

Christopher Logue, an amazing talent who wrote witty books of limericks, bawdy ballads, and tales, often wherein adopting the persona of Count Palmiro Vicarion, was not amused by Girodias's professional dealings:

> I regarded him as a bully and this to me was unforgivable, this thing of attacking the weak — when he thought you were weak — and retreating from the strong. . . . I always regarded him with a certain degree of contempt for this reason. He treated his authors as kind of serfs and he forgot that a man who signs his name to his own work is somebody who believes in this work. They were not people to be trifled with.

During the last days of his Paris operation, Girodias tried to circumvent the Paris authorities by floating a new company in Copenhagen, which would publish a new imprint: The Odyssey Library. Of the thirteen books published, six were collections of finely drawn satirical collages in the tradition of Max Ernst, created by the surrealist illustrator and writer Norman Rubington, a.k.a. Akbar Del Piombo. The books were published in English and also appeared under the New York imprint. The Odyssey Library didn't get far, however. According to Patrick Kearney, who edited *The Paris Olympia Press: An Annotated Bibliography*: "His reputation preceded him and despite the fact that censorship had effectively been abolished in Denmark, the French police put pressure on their Danish counterparts, or in some other way influenced them, and the venture collapsed."

Nor were the '70s kind to Terry. The highly creative and philosophically charged world of cinema that Kubrick had ushered him into in 1962 had become a far less inviting place, particularly since Terry's last film, *End of the Road,* which he wrote and co-produced for his old friend Aram Avakian, was rated "X" and therefore practically unreleasable. If it had been made today, it could have been released "unrated," but at the time, an "X" rating — which *Midnight Cowboy* had received but later got rescinded — was the kiss of death. Terry was undaunted by the untouchable label that seemed now to be following him. In fact, he liked the sly in-your-face marketing slogan for the paperback version of *Blue Movie,* "Rate This One 'X'!" The book itself could not have been more of a slap in the face to the Hollywood that fed him — its climax featured the head of the same studio that had been duped into making an "X" film having sex with the corpse of the dead contract star. The studio's most valuable asset had committed suicide (after having sex on film with many African tribesmen) by eating her lead-based makeup and electrocuting herself in the bathtub while wrapped in anti-cellulite plastic. Terry thought he was telling a good yarn — à la Nathanael West—but others thought he had gone too far.

Blue Movie was published by Quadrangle in the fall of 1970. With school tuition due, and the IRS closing in on the Canaan house for unpaid back taxes, Terry needed the book to do well. But the *New York Times* had given *Blue Movie* a pithy 600-word review, in which David Dempsey (a relatively obscure novelist) not only panned it but made fun of the '60s argot Terry used:

> I found this a tasteless, kinky book, one that should be published in Liechtenstein. Dig? That way we could order it by mail and get the postage stamps . . . surely, this is one of the longest peep shows ever made, and the dullest. It is pornography without Portnoy.

To buttress his pornography charge, Dempsey stated that the book "has no redeeming social value," and ignored whatever positive impact on sex and social mores *Candy* (and Terry) had previously inspired. "I think a good case can be made for it as an anti-aphrodisiac. It should set back the cause of sex for some time to come."

Though Terry held no grudges or ill will toward the industry and the press that now shunned him and those with whom he had once worked and played, a slow unraveling had begun.

By 1970, the big salaries from the film studios, issued throughout '66 and '67, were long gone, the only thing left being debt and a "monstro tax burden." Despite Terry's producing and writing work on *Easy Rider,* Terry did not share in the profits. Films of his own novels, *Candy* and *The Magic Christian,* had been "botched," as he put it. The IRS seized all of his and Carol's liquid assets as well as Carol's inheritance. Terry and Gail moved back into the Canaan house (Carol had moved to New York), but now there was an IRS lien on the property and seizure was imminent unless the sizable amount owed, including interest and penalties, was paid.

On the West Coast, things were not much better. There was the impression in "pre-synergy" Hollywood that Terry, operating on the East Coast, was working with "fringe" people like William Burroughs, Larry Rivers, Mick Jagger, Michael Parks (*Then Came Bronson),* and even Hopper and Fonda on potentially pornographic, druggie, racial, or otherwise unreleaseable projects. This despite Terry advertising that the films he worked on made money — providing actual numbers to those who would potentially hire him. Increasingly isolated from Hollywood, Terry took rewrite jobs from practically anyone who stumbled down the long driveway in Canaan, so long as they had an idea and a little money up front. These were usually not bona fide, Guild-approved deals, but Terry welcomed these people and their projects with as much enthusiasm as he did jobs originating from ICM, CAA, or William Morris — all of which he had worked for at one time or another, depending on the producer. Terry's desperation for money, in conjunction with his lack of political savvy or perhaps his indifference to making a distinction between "real deals" and speculative ones, made him a dangerous collaborator. He refused to play by anyone's rules, and he had no rules of his own. His "no limits," take-it-further philosophy began to work against him.

Most damaging to his career, perhaps, was Terry's perverse insistence that Hollywood was ready to make an "A-list" pornographic film, vis-à-vis his own novel, *Blue Movie,* believing it could be done in such a way that an "X" rating could be avoided. While people like John Calley, Mike Nichols, Julie Andrews (of all people), Ringo Starr, and even Stanley Kubrick indicated they would shepherd the film, it soon became clear that Terry had been banging his "stars and sex" drum on industry deaf ears for too many years (he had first conceived the idea in 1962). No one in Hollywood really dared go near the film — regardless of how *funny* it could be.

By 1970, Mason and Couquite had been separated for five years. His dislocation from Europe complete, Mason had gone to Woodstock at the behest of Bob Dylan, whom he'd met in Paris. As Mason told *Playboy,* "We had a ball. . . . He was beautiful. And he said if I ever got back to the States, to stay with him in Woodstock. Which I did when my family broke up."

After his famous 1966 motorcycle accident, Dylan had decided to live a more reclusive family life. He moved into a large stone house in Bearsville, near Woodstock, which had a "guardhouse" occupied by Dylan's manager and lawyer Albert Grossman and his wife, Sally. D. A. Pennebaker recalls visiting the compound a number of times to show him cuts of the second Dylan film, *Eat the Document* (rarely seen). "Grossman," he said, "lived at the gate house—and if you were smart you stopped there — and didn't go on. There was a sign out front that read something like: 'IF YOU DID NOT TELEPHONE YOU ARE NOT INVITED.'" Pennebaker recalled, "That place was the undoing of many," referring to those old friends who got turned away.

Woodstock was a free-spirited, politically progressive community with a pool of eclectic talent. Mason formed tight bonds with many in Dylan's Woodstock crowd, and lived with Paul Stookey of Peter, Paul and Mary, for a while. Soon he was hanging out regularly with Levon Helm and Richard Manuel of The Band.

The "Big Pink" house was the famous rehearsal and recording space that led to such legendary albums as The Band's *Music from Big Pink,* and their collaboration with Dylan, *The Basement Tapes.* Mason's mother had rented the "Little Pink" house for him down the street.

"What's up? What's goin' on? You mind if I get laid?" was the standard greeting Mason issued to anyone he encountered, day or night — much to the amusement of local teens.

Life in the Little Pink was bedlam, as Couquite, who visited with the children for summer vacations, recalls:

> We had many visits from Dylan and The Band. It was messy. This was 1969, the year of the Woodstock Festival. Mason and the Band had to get there by army helicopter, as the roads were blocked by thousands of cars. One night, Richard Manuel overdosed in the bathroom. I heard him fall with this loud "bang." I was furious, and broke the bathroom door with a beautiful guitar of his — rendered totally useless after my brutality. Of course he had passed out and we had to rush him to the hospital. Mason would regularly set fire to different couches with his lit cigarette butts, the Little Pink would be full of smoke and neighbors would call up the fire department. Somebody stole the family jewels I had stupidly brought with me, thinking this would be a normal household.

Eventually, with his mother's help, Mason bought a small house in the nearby town of Stone Ridge. Soon after, he met Marianne Palmer, a twenty-year-old local, and they began living together. Their son David was born in 1970.

Mason joined the methadone program in Poughkeepsie, and drove there every other day to get his drugs. He found a new interest in raising a vegetable garden.

Off junk, Mason had turned to booze. While Terry quietly drank in the evenings and tried his hand at raising organic livestock, Mason's carousing was often out of control. His driver's license was revoked after he pinned a police officer against a fallen tree with his car — luckily, the officer was not injured — and later crashed into a barber shop — both times while drunk. Mason later told *Playboy:*

> I woke up as I was going through the window, and I said to myself, "Oh, shit. This didn't happen." It was three o'clock in the morning, so I made a U-turn around the barber chairs, pulled out and started

> driving again. They nailed me within two minutes: there were like a hundred witnesses. And one of the cops asked me, "Have you been drinking?" So I said, "I swear, officer, the only place I ever drive is to the bar." It seemed like an excuse at the time.

Mason's problems were compounded by the deaths of two people for which he was indirectly responsible. One of the victims, former *New Story* editor/publisher David Burnett, had been a close friend of both Terry and Mason's throughout the '50s and was a major influence on their sharp, outlaw sensibility. As Mason recalled:

> I'm wandering around with two bottles of methadone in a basket and some clean underwear, and suddenly I'm face to face with Burnett, who's one of the few people from the past I have nothing against. So we went into this bar [Malcolm's], talked for a while, and I left. But I forgot my basket. So he very naturally went through it. He and another guy drank the methadone, and they both died.

Though Mason's days were ever more complicated, he at times saw his life as a blissful trap. The dissolution of his marriage, his stormy relationship with Marianne (a.k.a. "Hedwig"), his poverty, and lack of purpose often led to bursts of writing, allowing him to escape the sense of futility that dominated his existence. In this excerpt from Mason's memoir, written during the summer of 1970, he describes the labyrinthian disaster that his life had become:

> Now, secretly, the important revelation that I am happy! But the world must never know. This occurred to me last night in bed that now, having clearly achieved the conditions of maximum destitution and difficulty I've sought and approached all my life, starting from the too secure and comfortable days on Riverside Drive . . . till the present miserable conditions . . . spending days on guard duty of a pear tree 2 years old against possible tent caterpillars, and similar dramatic pastimes, while meanwhile, I've only got $350 left and Daniel, Hedwig, the baby and doggy to care for it got me very mor-

bidly afraid, numb with perplexed thinking how, after all, as recently as a year or so ago . . . I had the pleasure of my French wife's company for the summer with the children. . . . Which, like all the costly behavior in the lonely six years since our separation, was designed to achieve reconciliation whereas now, when for the first time I no longer send the alimony she at last has accorded me Daniel for a *year* instead of a speeding, unreal summer vacation. And Hedwig . . . who the same day that I once received a check for 3 thousand . . . demented sobbing in terror on the couch after I belted her after she struck at me while I held the baby she was so furious that I refused to take off immediately with the money for a mad journey anywhere. . . . I'm good God allmighty poor at last. My mother realizes it and gives me 100 a month, my French wife also and accepts that I no longer give her 200, my lovely Swedish maid likewise and turns over her 80 from public assistance for an unwed mother with fatherless babe.

Mason was recruited by Levon Helm, with whom he had become friendly, to "rescue" Richard Manuel and keep him off heroin. Mason became a kind of guardian to Manuel, answering the phone to keep druggies and groupies away, and playing the mother hen. It was exactly the kind of chaotic backdrop for a self-imposed spiritual discipline that challenged Mason all his life — but this time it involved taking care of someone more dysfunctional than himself. Instructing Manuel how to outfox his demons gave Mason the "teacher" archetype he would practice throughout the '70s and '80s. Manuel's wife had left him, and the house (which Mason now lived in with him) had been taken over by a young dog named "Hashish," notorious for chewing the furniture and defecating everywhere. As Mason later told *Playboy:*

> He can't do anything. He's drinking like I never saw anybody drink. And now I'm drinking a lot. . . . We just sit around watching *The Dating Game,* slurping down the juice.

*

Girodias spent 1972 creating *President Kissinger,* a mélange of current events, science fiction, and pornography. It was, as Girodias put it, "very original in form." Girodias marketed the book as "political science fiction," probably in an attempt to protect himself from libel or worse. Nonetheless, his distributor Kable News found it scandalous and refused to release it. Girodias, his staff, and friends began personally distributing the book to eclectic bookstores and *President Kissinger* developed a small cult following. Girodias later wrote, "The book was hardly printed when I was invited by the U.S. Immigration Department to leave the country within forty-eight hours — on orders from the State Department."

Firming up a romance to avoid deportation, Girodias immediately married Lilla Cabot Lyon, a self-reliant diplomat's daughter who was studying medicine in Boston. But the authorities were on his tail and he was the victim of a bizarre sting operation. Lured from his office by a beautiful woman who claimed to have the "connections" he needed to solve his various legal problems, he wound up in a cab with her going to New Jersey. At some point during the quasi-seduction and bogus legal talk, the New Jersey police appeared, searched Girodias and found marijuana, which he contended she had planted on him. It was later discovered that she was a Scientologist.

As Girodias later summed up, "I was neatly framed by a beautiful lady who slipped drugs into my pocket and caused me to be arrested, and this in turn led to the destruction of my American publishing enterprise and to years of litigation."

Girodias was convinced that he had been set up by the Church of Scientology as payback for the book he had published earlier that year, an investigative exposé called *Inside Scientology: How I Joined Scientology and Became Superhuman.* Scientologists were notoriously sensitive to criticism, and Girodias suspected that they may have been behind the notice sent out to 5,000 booksellers on Olympia Press stationery saying that his company was out of business, which at the time was untrue. Girodias also recalled that many of his files had disappeared after one of his assistants quit and suspected that information in them was used by someone to tip off the State Department regarding his immigration status.

Leon Friedman secured the letter in question through the Freedom of Information Act, and found it had been addressed to Kissinger at the State Department and warned him about the upcoming publication of *President Kissinger*, pointedly noting that Girodias was under investigation for tax evasion and visa issues. The letter also described Girodias as "an un-American activist who should be stopped" before he slandered the government further. It was signed: "A PATRIOT."

Olympia USA never recovered from its Kissinger/Scientology debacle. Its downfall in 1975 marked the end of a courageous and scrappy publishing career for one of the industry's most entrepreneurial and indefatigable characters. A bout with cancer, and his continuing legal problems, which now had migrated from his business to his alien residency, reduced the "Frog Prince" to a penniless interloper, invisible to an industry and, indeed, a culture that was once aflame over his books. He wrote to a friend around this time:

> I am paying a heavy karma for all I did to the race of writers. . . . I have lost most everything I had brought here with me; not just the authors, but faith in myself, the belief in the game itself, and the ability to cope with so much atrocious vulgarity. If I make a comeback, it must be an educated one, as I cannot afford another failure.

Girodias became severely depressed after moving with Lilla to Boston, where she was completing her medical internship and residency. The marriage became strained as Girodias's mood swings took their toll. Though they separated on more than one occasion, they continued living together in New York and Paris for the next decade.

Chapter 38

Mason Licks Terry

In late October 1973, Terry was staying at artist Larry Rivers's loft on East 13th Street when an old friend called to tell him *Playboy* had come out with a piece called "Mason Hoffenberg Gets in a Few Licks." It included long hostile passages about Terry. Having just seen Mason a couple of months earlier, Terry was astonished. Sam Merrill, the freelance journalist who conducted the interview with Mason, was unknown to Terry or any of his friends, nor did it seem that Merrill had corroborated any of Mason's defamatory statements against Terry.

Merrill describes Mason as "a subterranean-holyman-ex-junkie . . . [and] perhaps the most famous unknown author in America." He had arranged to meet Mason — seemingly homeless, and living on borrowed dimes — at a local bar in Woodstock. Most of the interview took place there while Mason theatrically nursed a line of eight martinis set up on the table before them. Mason portrayed his old Paris pal as his apprentice, saying Terry was unable to score, or come up with any original writing. "I'm the guy who turned him onto everything in Paris: I taught him hip talk and smoking grass."

Perhaps most cutting were Mason's attacks on Terry's originality. He accused Terry of stealing ideas from mutual friends and "ripping off" people for their stories, citing David Burnett and Boris Grugurevich as examples.

> Terry's a redneck, like Levon Helm of The Band, except Levon is much greater than Terry. Levon is much more original. . . . Terry's

> a good re-writer, and he writes some funny shit himself, but he always grabs top billing. Boris became the only non-Cuban to get in on the Bay of Pigs thing, and Terry taped an interview with him in New York. The article came out in *Esquire* and it was very big for Terry — this great cat telling about a wild, historic fiasco — except Boris's name was mentioned only once in the piece. Boris didn't take that too well.

About *Candy*, Mason says, "It was a disaster. . . . Everything went wrong with my life after *Candy* came out." "Everything went right for Terry Southern," Merrill interjected, "he was ejaculated to fame and screenplays." Mason tried to recall specifics of his issues with Terry on *Candy*, but instead simply said, "I probably should have punched him in the mouth after *Candy* was published in the States . . . I think he screwed me. Terry always said I was his best friend. But I always knew what most of my best friends were thinking. Terry had this thing about secrecy. I should have figured he'd hurt me."

Mason's characterization of Terry as a kind of naive "trainee" who had doors "slammed" in his face by Camus and Françoise Sagan was offensive enough, but his charge that Terry "couldn't get laid" in Paris — and the inference that Mason *did* — and that the comment appeared in *Playboy* seemed to be the ultimate insult. Terry wrote a letter to the editor immediately:

> Blackberry River, October 27, 1973
>
> Editor
> PLAYBOY
> 919 North Michigan Ave.
> Chicago, Illinois
>
> Dear Sir:
>
> Regarding "Mason Hoffenberg Gets In a Few Licks," I think it only fair you realize that the identity crisis of "Mason Hoffenberg" (if, indeed that *is* his name) and his fantasyville existence, were at full cry

and whack-off, before he encountered yrs tly, or for that matter, most of the other people he refers to. In fact, the one thing that rings true in the article is what is implicit in the title-phrase "*gets in a few licks*" — the 'few licks' being the jerk-off and self-delusion he's been into for the past 30 years. And all the rest is, to put it at its most generous, sheer bullshit — especially the part about Hoff getting laid in Paris; he most certainly did *not* get laid in Paris.

Terry Southern

More than pride was involved. Terry and Gail Gerber considered the interview damaging to Terry's professional standing and feared it would further minimize his chances to work in the film business. Hoffenberg's insinuation that Terry had few original ideas hit a raw nerve, since Terry's most celebrated work was collaborative (including *Easy Rider, Dr. Strangelove, Barbarella, The Cincinnati Kid,* as well as *Candy).* Although his voice always came through, even in melodrama — and connoisseurs of his work can easily identify his lines — his true contributions were open to question and often downplayed. Uncharacteristically, Terry decided to sue and initiated suits against not only Mason but *Playboy* and Merrill as well.

It is a sad irony that in the *Playboy* interview Mason said Terry stole an idea for *Flash and Filigree* from their mutual friend David Burnett, when David had *died* due to Mason's own carelessness: "A lot of the funny shit Terry wrote was just the ideas of David Burnett. Like, we'd be sitting around smoking hashish in a café or something, and David would come up with an idea for a quiz show called *What's My Disease?* Now that's in one of Terry's books." In the deposition that Terry filed in advancing a case against Mason and *Playboy,* he stated: "The implication that my writing was not original and that I just wrote the ideas of others . . . is not true." Those on *Playboy*'s side questioned Terry regarding the contested "routine" Mason had cited:

> **QUESTION:** State the date and place you first heard or read the phrase "What's My Disease?" and . . . how did it come to your attention.

> **ANSWER:** I was at the Café Flore in St. Germain-des-Prés in Paris — early in 1952, January or February, with Mel Sabre, and someone at the next table was talking about a new TV quiz show they had seen in NYC called "What's My Line?" The idea of a satiric take-off on this occurred to me then and there — in the form of a quiz show called "What's My Disease?" and I mentioned it to Mel Sabre at the time and then wrote a story about it. The story did resolve itself as a *story* on its own. I later incorporated the story into a novel, *Flash and Filigree.*

The case was "dismissed with prejudice" by a New York judge in 1975. In lieu of a cash settlement, Mason, Merrill, and *Playboy* no doubt agreed never to say or publish such things about Terry again.

Terry was not the only recipient of Mason's barbs. Mason also managed to put down his old friends James Baldwin and D. A. Pennebaker, whose film *Dont Look Back* he described as "a commercial" contrived by Dylan's label Columbia Records. Even Dylan himself, who had taken him in, comes off poorly, as Mason describes him as a freaked-out head case: "It's like something out of *Candy,* except multiplied by a factor of about a thousand. Everybody wants to fuck him. . . . Millions of girls were going berserk to get to him and he was doing things like hiding in the closet whenever the door opened."

But the article does most damage to Mason himself. A bizarre and depressing portrait of him emerges, though one sadly familiar to those who knew him at the time.

> "I am absolutely broke now, penniless. But I'm living like a king. People buy me drinks and food," Mason says, before breaking into a coughing fit. Mason . . . was doubled over on the couch, gasping, trying of all things, to get a cigarette into his mouth.

In the mid-'70s, Mason, clean after his methadone treatments, moved back to Los Angeles, where he met and soon began living a kosher life in a Jewish neighborhood with Eliza Brown-John. The daughter of a famous graphic artist (best known for his work on the James Bond title design and ad campaigns and a friend of Terry and

Mason's in Paris), twenty-five-year-old Eliza soon became pregnant. She wanted an abortion, but Mason, who was now heavily into Orthodox Judaism, objected, and the two split up. Eliza moved to Australia.

After the breakup with Eliza, Mason moved in with his next-door neighbor, Stuart Cornfeld, a film student at USC who was working for Mel Brooks. Stuart recalled Mason as a very special mentor:

> The guy was absolutely the *premier amusant* in a room. He put everyone to shame. . . . He never name-dropped, yet he knew *everybody*. He was hysterically funny, and had that same twisted, massive contextual shift kind of comedy which Terry had. He could pick up a dead party in an instant. I remember him doing so, by saying at one point: "I have an idea for a party game: boys on one side, girls on another. Everyone gets naked. The first guy to fuck a girl gets to kiss her."

Cornfeld talked about his other mentor, too:

> Mason and Mel [Brooks] were both fifty-six. I was in my twenties. It was crazy for me, because during the day I worked with this older, Jewish, outrageously funny guy from New York, and then I'd go home to this older, Jewish, outrageously funny guy from New York. Mason and Mel were both threatened by each other — and when they were together, or when Mel called on the phone, they just talked about the weather — not making a crack. Mel Brooks in a room is funny — but Mason was right up there with him.

Like Gregory Corso, with whom he had become close at the Chelsea, Mason was living proof of the worldly Beat life to those who had missed it. To many young people who met him, Mason made living life an art in itself. "Mason had the sense of humor that was like firing an assassin's bullet with the tongue," recalls former roommate Eric Michelson, a photographer who met Mason in 1979. "He could slaughter the person next to him — but it was hilarious — because he talked like a nasally *dick,* missing some of his teeth . . . He was a total gift."

Cornfeld, Mason, and their trusty sidekick "Minky" were voyeuristic groovers of this lively neighborhood where old Jewish met hardcore gay. The anarchic cultural mix was such that just cruising around provided the trio with numerous opportunities for goofing, observation and Mason's unique brand of put-on. As Cornfeld recalls:

> We were West Hollywood "freaks" in our young twenties. We were like his bad habit — he'd be doing religious stuff during the day, then go hang with the bums and a quart of whiskey at night. He'd go with us to clubs.

Speaking of their time in New York, Michelson recalled, "It was like being in a movie. The wit . . . he would interpret the most mundane things — it was like walking around with Man Ray or Duchamp — he was more like an old troll than a human. But unlike the paternal figure of Man Ray wanting people to follow him, Mason was a bitter failure . . . which made it fascinating. He was bitter beyond belief."

"Mason's mom kept giving him money. He never paid the rent — we did," recalls Cornfeld. "He went on assistance, and got $50 to $100 a week. At one point I got him a job working for my father, who was an accountant. All he had to do was file these new tax code pages into a large book — but it was disastrous. It's funny, because Mason was so *sharp.*"

Mason by this time was back on drugs, but discreet about using. So much so that his own apartment mates didn't know about it. "We never knew Mason was a junkie," says Cornfeld, "until one day Mason blurted out, 'Why do you think I haven't been writing all these years?' We were kids," says Michelson. "Mason would send us out to score when he was sick."

The hardest thing for Mason to withstand was each morning's temptation to mainline. As he wrote in his journal:

> I noticed quickly that for once, and first thing in the morning (of a new week) I had cigarettes, matches, coffee, sugar and milk, no

> overnight companions yakking — none of the inconsequential but irritating hangups which ordinarily furnish the substance of my jam. This backed up the miracle of getting a clean hit in the morning with a fix so large its size alone comprised a gamble of all day turned into a shuddering shambles. Where do I get such courage? It's as if I'd pledged a maiden's prayer to snap into a saint if only for this last once the Lord grant me a quick flash from smack in the first hole of the morning.

Cornfeld still recalls Mason's encyclopedic knowledge of esoteric subjects. Mason believed in the mystical Jewish ritual of swimming on your birthday. One cold November, Mason accompanied Cornfeld to the beach to help him consummate the act in the Pacific Ocean.

> He would *teach* us things. . . . He gave us exercises to do. Before going to a party, he'd say, "Write down ten things you think will happen at this party. And when we come home, write what *really* happened and you'll prove to yourself what a mindless idiot you are." One day he drew the Japanese character for adultery — which he explained was a painting of a woman three times. "Who are the three women?" he quizzed us. I said, "OK, the first is the wife, the second is the lover . . . " I was stumped on the third, and Mason says, "It's the woman she tells about it." An unreal flow of bizarre and interesting information came from Mason. When he got into the Talmudic math, his eyes lit up and he said "Now, some of *these* people are *really* smart."

By 1975, Terry's professional writing life — in both film and literature — had essentially dried up and his reputation was at its lowest level. He had fallen into the cycle of speculative script work that Degener had predicted, taking his attention away from serious writing or high-level script assignments. Arlene Donovan, an agent at ICM, was now handling both Terry's film and his writing work. Years earlier, with Carol's help, Terry got together pages for an autobiographical novel, *Youngblood*, begun as *The Hipsters* in Geneva, and the proposal was sold to an old admirer of Terry's, Sam Lawrence, an executive of Delacorte/Dell. Just before the holidays, Lawrence wrote to Terry, tersely inquiring why they hadn't received anything from him since he had received an advance payment from them two years earlier:

December 16, 1975

Dear Terry:

Dell paid you $20,000 advance in June 1973 with the understanding that you would deliver a manuscript by April 1973. Additional payments of $60,000 were scheduled to be paid at various stages of delivery. We've not seen a word.

Unless we now have concrete evidence that there is a novel-in-progress, you will soon receive a tough legal letter from the Dell general counsel. I would hate to see this situation develop. I believe in you as a writer and I want to publish your work. I am now being put in a difficult position. Please treat this as a very serious matter. . . .

With best wishes.

Regards as ever,

Sam

Despite this threat, Terry was unable to deliver, nor was he able to repay the advance. Terry and Gail's phone in Canaan was often disconnected, and the only way to reach Terry was by driving up to the Berkshires to see him—as many (such as Rip Torn and Geraldine Page, William Claxton and a score of budding unknown filmmakers) continued to do.

In the face of mounting problems, as Terry became an occasional drunk, Mason was becoming something else entirely. Hoffenberg's socializing with those half his age and his recreational use of pot and heroin seemed to have an opposite effect. "He was amazingly charming, sly, and funny. He loved women, and he knew how to get laid," recalls Cornfeld; "He was a great *mentor.* His condescension was constant and unnerving. He'd say, 'You're a *moron,* but since you appear to be paying the rent, I'll listen to you.' "

In the late '70s, Mason returned to New York and was reunited with his daughter Juliette, who was teaching and studying at NYU. He lived with his mother until she died in 1978. "Mason *was* New York City," recalls Michelson, who was dating Juliette Hoffenberg during this period. He recalled their father-daughter relationship:

> She and Mason lived like poor hermits in his mother's apartment on Central Park West. Mason was funny about his daughter. I was talking to him once about Juliette's sexuality, and Mason became really agitated. He was very protective of her. He said, "I am going to get a large can of crushed tomatoes to smash in your head."

But there was another side to the drug life that was alienating and loathsome, an illness side Mason often wrote about in his journals, as in this excerpt about a visit to old friends:

> Late that night in the guest room I, of course, am taken sick with withdrawal symptoms. As usual, I have stupidly underestimated their severity. Now it really is going to be embarrassing because, as the sickness sets in, I realize that it's not going to be over in a night; it's going to be a question of weeks before I'm even in shape to leave the guest room on legs that tremble. . . .
>
> I am beginning a first day of being sick . . . [I sense] a very cold pin pushed up through the under side of my skull, which will puncture my scalp right in the middle of the top of my head.

Despite Terry's grand gentlemanliness, which was in full effect whenever he was socializing, his isolated life in the country, lack of meaningful work, and increasing use of alcohol and Dexamyl led him into a steady state of undiagnosed depression.

In the early '80s Terry's friend Michael O'Donoghue, an inspiring producer of *Saturday Night Live* and former editor of

National Lampoon, asked Terry to work for the show. Terry stayed a year, writing some memorably funny bits, but found the situation extremely stressful and difficult. He also discovered that, as so often happened, his humor was out of step with what could be broadcast. Terry found protection from the cutthroat atmosphere of competition and one-upmanship in Nelson Lyon, a burly, bald, imposing filmmaker, and former Warhol Factory member who was also a writer on the show. "People were pitching these ideas and they were just funny sketch ideas and had a certain snap—there's a routine for sketch comedy, a formula. Then it was Terry's turn and everybody was waiting for the great Terry Southern." As Lyon recounts, Terry diffused the panic of the competition and weekly deadlines by getting heavily into cocaine and playing practical jokes: "His office was like a whole fucking den, bottles, a cocaine grinder. . . . He would put weird clippings on my desk so the production assistants would see them. He had this little voodoo doll that he had taped to the top of the desk. This girl was supposed to give blow jobs and it was a blow job device."

Hal Wilner, the show's music producer, who became a friend, said, "I think NBC was just a weird kind of atmosphere for Terry. Michael [O'Donoghue] left midway through the season, so Terry didn't have his guy up there. . . . He got involved in this *Dr. Strangelove* sketch. You could just tell Terry wasn't happy with this and he made the most horrifying remark to me, 'I feel like the professor at the end of *The Blue Angel.*'"

The *Saturday Night Live* job was the last occasion he had to spend much time in New York other than weekly forays to his jobs at Columbia and NYU, where he was teaching screen writing. Back in the country, the TV was constantly on in the living room while he worked, and in his bedroom while he slept — which he did, more often than not, with numerous pillows piled on top of his head, drowning his quiet desperation in a continuous chattering drone. Terry never stopped writing, though, and CSPAN, his favorite channel, fueled many incisive political critiques published in various venues such as *The Nation,* the *Lakeville Journal,* and *In*

These Times. When not critiquing his students' screenplays with Post-it notes, he was writing outrageous letters to friends.

In the '80s, Mason took Michelson out to the Rolling Stones' refuge on Montauk Point (where Terry had often gone with Peter Beard during the band's heyday years earlier). Michelson recalled bizarre outings:

> We went out with Anita [Pallenberg] to this amazing place on Long Island — it was right out of *Performance.* There was no furniture there — just a white piano, and a pinball machine hooked up to Marshall amps — so that one's score blared out like the end of the world. They lived like white trash, heating up soup cans directly on the stove, no plates or pots or anything. There was an old guy there — it was Keith Richard's father. Anita was beyond junked up. She was also quite fat and grotesque, sitting there watching MTV and instigating these outrageous *screaming* fits. Now, I'm a surreal photographer, but nothing compared with these people. They were like the mole people — they were not connected to reality. But their reality, which was Mason's reality, was so much more interesting.

Mason introduced Michelson and Cornfeld to the extremes of living. Despite these often tempting perversities, they recognized their limits — and were perhaps inspired by them to become the successes they are. Michelson is a highly sought-after photographer. Film producer Cornfeld (*The Fly, The Elephant Man)* made films with Steven Soderbergh and Amy Heckerling (a former student of Terry's) and formed a production company with the actor Ben Stiller.

"Mason got very good at being sick," recalls Cornfeld, "he'd work a habit until it became financially prohibitive, and then he'd kick. He wasn't the type to boost. It caught up with him in the end. He had cancer, and the doctors took him off the methadone. Mason was comical even about his own death. 'I thought I was going to *die,*' he said, 'I felt the expanding sense of death growing within me . . . I was prepared for it. Turned out it was just a *fart!*' "

In 1984, Mason was given two years to live, having been

diagnosed with lung cancer. "Cancer schmancer! As long as I have my health!" he would say. Mason joked and philosophized until the very end. Anita Pallenberg recalls Mason joking that coughing was the only exercise he got.

Because of the pain, Michelson said, "Toward the end, he wasn't able to lie down. He was like something out of a vampire film. He'd take a long scarf and hang it from the ceiling and he'd run it through his armpit to pull his lung away from his body — and he'd just *hang* there, exhausted — that's the only way he could sleep."

As Mason lay dying, many people visited him, including his lifelong friend Anton Rosenberg. Also visiting him were Mei Wah, a Chinese expat who knew him in Mallorca, and illustrator Patti Dryden, who got to know him in New York. Eric Michelson came by with some photographs: "I could immediately tell by his expression it was the wrong thing to do — to say, 'Hey what's up?' and pretend like things were normal. 'Look,' he said, 'I'm dying . . . what the fuck do I care about pictures.'" Mason's existentialism, combined with his Jewish kvetching, never let anyone off the hook — not even on his deathbed.

Mason died of lung cancer in New York in 1986 at the age of sixty-four and was buried in the Hoffenberg plot outside New York City. "The only cure for cancer is death," Mason once said, "same with dope and sex."

Chapter 39

The Refreshing Ambiguity of the Déjà Vu

Girodias, his publishing operations closed down, turned to writing his memoirs in his last years. Crown published the first installment, *The Frog Prince,* in the late 1970s (*J'arrive* was the title in French). He wrote a second volume (still unpublished in the United States) in the 1980s. He spent the last decade of his life in Paris, moving from apartment to apartment and haunt to haunt, always in search of the restaurant, bar, or club that had the pulse of the times. In 1990, Éditions de la Différence published his collected memoirs. Well reviewed, the hubbub sparked life and verve into his soul again, prompting him to write to Lilla, "In the space of 3-4 weeks, my story has become so fashionable in this country that I could sell my toenails for a million each." *Le Monde* called him a "kamikaze publisher."

On July 3,1990, during the promotion of his book, shortly after appearing on Radio J, an eclectic Jewish radio program, Girodias died from a sudden heart attack. On his tombstone in Père Lachaise cemetery in Paris is engraved the title of his collected memoirs, *Une journée sur la terre* (*A Day on Earth*).

Patrick Kearney, Girodias's bibliographer and friend, commented:

> There are too many stories about Maurice's unorthodox business practices for it not have be at least partly true. Having said that, as a publisher, he was probably one of the most adventurous and perceptive of the twentieth century. His record of spotting great books is testament to that.

Echoing the sentiment, Barney Rosset once said:

> If Maurice was a pornographer, it was a very special kind. . . . People like Terry Southern, Norman Rubington, and Marilyn Meeske (a real Maurice Girodias person) were closest to Maurice's kind of taste. I could always spot a Girodias book — it would have an intellectualized sexual content and political style. *Candy* was the quintessential Girodias book.

In 1992, shortly after the Gulf war, Jean Stein, Terry's longtime friend and publisher of *Grand Street,* asked him to contribute something to the magazine. Terry wrote a brief *Candy* installment and credited the piece as co-written with Mason Hoffenberg, though Mason, of course, had been dead for years.

Terry used to tease Mason (and Girodias as well) about his "extreme right-wing politics," and a certain anti-Arab prejudice he displayed at times. Mason, who had been to Jerusalem, once joked, "If this Arab thing ever settles down, Israel will probably turn into a big Miami." Terry never lost sight of his progressive agenda, and as a friend of Edward Said's and a constant critic (through letters to the *New York Times* and *Village Voice)* of the Israeli occupation, the issue of American imperialism and "gunboat diplomacy" was often on Terry's mind. During the Gulf war, Terry contributed to *The Nation* criticizing the "cakewalk" and "turkey-shoot" aspects of the military action, as well as the United States's oil-related motivation for dominating the region.

The new *Candy* segment portrayed a satirical vision of Saudi Arabia, with Candy Christian and her baseball team part of the surreal American occupation there, but it is unclear who is being occupied, Saudi Arabia or the baseball team. The Hunchback makes an appearance as the bat boy. Early into the piece, Terry vicariously exercises Mason's interest in the occult:

> The bats had fallen in such a way that two of them were lying across a third, while the fourth lay apart nearby. The large man kicked the fourth bat farther away, then addressed the audience:

"The remaining sticks are in harmonious and mystical arrangement — and thus may be interpreted in accordance with the world-renowned *Book of Changes.*"

He spoke with the toneless inflection of a man half-drugged, an impression given further credence by his general mien of repose, especially his partially closed eyes, which seemed to grow more heavy-lidded as he continued:

"In order to assure that an absolute reading may obtain, various and personal information concerning those present is required. I shall now pass among you, handing out a simple questionnaire — which you are asked to complete, and to return to me, along with a certain amount of money or monies as per the designation on the back of the card. Payment may be made in Traveller's Checks or in the currency of any existing government. Refreshments will be served during the intermission which follows, and after that you shall see the fabled . . . *Candy Christian!* Miss Christian will be performing her authentic U.S. of A. mile-high bumps and grind!"

The image of Candy as a dubious "oasis" of Americana in Arabia is bookended by a figure (and symbol) very different from Candy, one who seems to be a new kind of global capitalism hipster: "a lithesome oriental woman, of indeterminate age, half reclining across the velour interior, her black *crêpe de Chine* clinging sensually to her slender curves, slowly raised herself and peered ahead."

Inside the car, the woman opened a bag, fished out several notes of currency and cast them in a haughty manner through the window, as the car surged up and away from the huts like a plane peeling off from its squadron. Then, out of a golden jewel-encrusted vial, she gingerly tapped a small mound of white crystalline powder onto the back of one thin delicate hand; and in a graceful birdlike swoop, she drew it into her nostrils, her breasts softly pert beneath the *crepe de Chine,* nipples pouting coyly, as she momentarily closed her eyes; but suddenly she opened them, and a frown clouded her lovely face.

"Wait a minute!" she snapped. "'Candy Christian' — that sounds like . . . an *American* name!" The driver gave a bemused grunt, then shrugged heavily. "But what on earth," she demanded, her dark eyes flashing in consternation, "would a nice young American girl be doing here . . . *in the middle of the Gobi Desert*?!?"

Upon a nighttime visit to Canaan during Terry's last years, visitors would often encounter a veritable festival of lights — nineteenth-century lanterns, North African oil lamps, and various candles in ornate colored glass fixtures, all burning and glowing around the chairs on the breezeway under the towering two hundred-year-old oak and locust trees. Terry was always jovial, never one to complain. His priorities were cold beer and fresh bones for his dogs.

He had acquired, over the years, a distinctive, and somehow reassuring manner of speech — one which combined the existential *ennui* with the undying put-on. George Plimpton once described his old compatriot as follows:

> In appearance he is rumpled, soft-spoken, courtly and rather owlish. The distinguishing feature is his speech. Texas-born, he has developed a curious mock English complete with little harrumphs ("What? *What?*") delivered in fits and starts, with words often abbreviated in hipster style ("fab" for fabulous) and marked with qualifying endearments such as "Tip Top Tony" for Tony . . . very unique and not unlike how Goofy would sound if he were born an earl.

Inside the house, among the crackling fires and antique oil lamps that blazed in the winter, with a yellow legal pad and no. 1 pencil, Terry was often seated on the couch. Work of some kind (a script polish, essay, letter to a friend or an editor) was always under way, but rarely paying much, if at all. Despite moments of clarity which were often unnerving — his eyes might lock with yours over his drugstore granny glasses — a despondency was detectable under his jovial "hrrumphs" and humorous remarks. Tuesday would roll around and it was time to lug a dozen heavily annotated student screenplays to the car and head for New York. Gail, who would normally be found teaching ballet or gardening, would take the day to drive him to his classes at Columbia University and back.

Financially, Terry never fully recovered from the IRS "wipe-out" that came down on him in the early '70s, and though he eventually settled with the IRS, he and Gail always managed to fall behind. In 1986, Terry and singer songwriter Harry Nilsson formed an entertainment venture called Hawkeye. Terry was VP in charge of literary development, but, ironically, didn't have a fax machine or secretary to follow up on business. He still ran down to the pharmacy to collect faxes, often picking up the occasional dexedrine refill with his *New York Times*. One project Hawkeye managed to finish was an audiobook of Terry reading *Candy*. Soon after, the company, which had paid a handsome salary for a year or so and leased Terry a new car, imploded when Nilsson's CPA business partner embezzled the company's money, was indicted, and sent to prison.

By the fall of 1995, Terry was teaching two screenwriting classes back to back so that he wouldn't have to stay overnight in New York. His longtime friend Jack Gelber, teaching at Brooklyn College, exclaimed, on hearing his schedule, "That's nuts. Back to back is a killer." It was. In late October, Terry collapsed on the steps of Columbia on his way to class. Students called 911 and he was rushed to nearby St. Luke's Roosevelt, where he died four days later of a heart attack. In the hospital, the attending physician asked if he had ever worked in a coal mine, because it seemed he had black lung disease. The autopsy didn't offer any further explanation, but perhaps one could say simply that Terry's "iron in the soul" and his notoriously black humor had become physically manifest. His ashes were spread about the Canaan pond.

Afterword

Shortly after Terry's death, while in the Canaan house, I received a call from Marc Toberoff, an entertainment lawyer specializing in intellectual property copyright, in Los Angeles. Marc informed me that under the GATT Treaty, 1996, a special provision allowed retroactive copyright registration for works published in European countries in English. Heretofore, these works were not covered by the manufacturing clause of the U.S. copyright code.

When I returned to Boulder, I printed the appropriate forms off the Internet, and, after signing them, forwarded them to Juliette Hoffenberg, executrix of the Hoffenberg Estate, via Sterling Lord. And so, in 1999, *Candy* received its first legitimate U.S. copyright.

In 2001, the film *Candy* came out on DVD. It was brilliantly marketed as a limited edition, in bright pink packaging resembling a tin of expensive chocolates. Another version was packaged as an exact replica of a 1960s circular birth-control pill dispenser. With kitschy coasters of all the stars and on-set gossip about the film, the limited edition sold out within a few months. A new print of the film was re-released theatrically in 2003 in France, Portugal, and Japan.

But perhaps the most astonishing thing to happen in the baroque history of *Candy* occurred in the early 1990s. The Book-of-the-Month Club offered *Candy* as a selection and produced a handsome edition for their mass readership. Sterling Lord was elated. The book that a mere thirty-five years earlier had to be smuggled into the country and was deemed "unpublishable" was now endorsed by the largest, most popular book club in America. Good grief— *Candy* had gone mainstream!

APPENDIX A

Selected Interviews with Terry Southern

Concerning *Candy* and "Pornography"

From an unpublished interview with Albert Goldman, 1973:

ALBERT GOLDMAN: Why do you sometimes sign your letters with girls' names?
TS: Because they're chatty. And obscene. The chattiness gives it a girlish thing, and then signing "Cynthia" or "Paula" after a lot of obscenity makes a curious juxtaposition. . . . Letter writing, I think, is the best of all writing, because it's the purest. It's like writing to yourself, but you've got an excuse to do it because this person will dig it. And you can transmit information in a strange way, you can sort of mix it, so they wonder, "Well, is this true?" You say something outlandish, and then you throw in, "John and Mary just ran away to Hawaii," and so it's hahaha, but in fact it's true.

There's always, and I don't know why, but I have a kind of feeling of necessity about writing things that are beyond that moment of acceptance, that are too offensive or something. They read it and say, "Hahaha very funny. No, we can't print that." I mean *The Realist* has turned down stuff of mine. I've got one there now that they turned down a couple of years ago. It's supposed to be Frank O'Hara, so it's "Fun at Frank's and Other Places," and it's very weird — it's not obscene, but it violates a lot of taboos.

That's the whole history of writing, really, trying to emancipate images, and languages. It's not just a question of four-letter words — you can get away with that — but of attitude. In great books, like Celine, and Miller, they affect attitudes, weird attitudes. Like Miller, dancing with a girl, and moving her up against a doorknob. He isn't really like that, of course, I mean he doesn't *do* that — he simply felt compelled to have a first person narrator who could say, "Yeah, got that doorknob up her cunt," because he felt you've got to be able to print it, even though it's disgusting.

He's really quite finicky . . . I mean he's not Greg Corso.

ALBERT GOLDMAN: Maybe he was, thirty years ago.

TS: No, I don't think so. The beauty of it is, he *created* a first person narrator, and made it very believable. What Salinger did, taking a thirteen-year-old, pre-sex kid and making him believable as a first-person narrator, is relatively easy, but when you've got a Lucky Jim age person, or Henry Miller, then it begins to get a bit dicey, because you got this sexual thing to deal with. The whole thing is frankness, candor, directness, and when men start being candid, and frank, and direct about sex, how far are you going to take it? Well, Miller tried to take it as far as he could, but it wasn't self-expression — he had an obsessive interest in the whole development of literature, the idea of being able to go farther than D. H. Lawrence.

In *Candy,* one of the strongest things was to try to do something that hadn't been done, to go a little farther, but on a different level, to try to make it funny rather than disgusting. It's like a painter looking at a canvas, and he sees there's something missing in a certain area, and so he tries to put it in. In an abstract painting it's just color, or form, but it can get to be very specific when you start narrowing it down, like in a particular novel, or treatment of a theme. No one's ever written a novel about the relationship between a girl and her father, for example. I mean, from the girl's point of view. Someone like Susan Sontag should devote herself to that, try to put herself into an imaginary situation of a girl making it with her father, or being attracted to her father, say like Jane Fonda and Henry Fonda. There'd be some weird competition with the wife — different wives — and so on, and, you know, it could be very feasible and believable.

ALBERT GOLDMAN: What about pornography on the screen, which is in one way the theme of your novel, *Blue Movie,* would that be a next step?

TS: Of the things that thrive unjustifiably, very salient among them are the clandestine — things that are taboo thrive, almost by definition. These dirty movies are so bad, and so expensive, because they're taboo. If you allowed those things to be played freely, it

> would be much easier to make better ones than exist now, because the bad ones just simply couldn't survive. And then, when they got better, they wouldn't be called *pornographic* — they'd just either be good or bad. And then you might say "Well, this is stimulating," or "this is erotic," but there's no law against eroticism. I mean, it's stock in trade for all filmmakers.

Mike Perkins, of Al Goldstein's *Screw*, interviewed Terry in the October 26, 1970 issue:

> SCREW: Have you read any of the new pornographers, say, Sam Abrams, Angelo D'Archangelo, or David Meltzer?
> SOUTHERN: No, but I must say, I'm suspicious of that word *pornography*. I would think that eroticism would be the better word.
> SCREW: I like the word eroticism too, but I use pornography just to anger the snobs. I'd like to violate "respectability" — which is a dirty word to me.
> SOUTHERN: Pornography, to me, is simply eroticism which has failed to make it, and so it just falls into the semantic garbage can of being called pornography, or obscenity. I mean they're *negative* words, whereas eroticism and eros . . . well, you know, *love*, that's like a good word. A strong, positive word.
> SCREW: What's the most erotic book you've ever read?
> SOUTHERN: Well, I think probably some things *I've* written: probably passages in *Candy*. I was really writing those certain things with the idea of trying to turn *myself* on, you know, which could, of course, include other people. I mean there's something very erotic about imagining how a *girl* feels sexually . . . that sort of immaculateness being violated or something. . . . The mind of a girl, you think, is *different*. I mean it's probably a myth, of course, but we do tend to believe it.

APPENDIX B

Anatomy of a Pornectomy

Letter from Cindy Degener:

February 6, 1968

Dear Terry and Mason:

Re: *Candy*
New English Library
Publication for England

I am both happy, and at the same time, concerned by my meeting last week with Christopher Shaw, now director of NEL. I had given up all hope of publication for *Candy* in England since the defeat in the English courts last November as regards Hubert Selby's book, LAST EXIT TO BROOKLYN. To my delight, and in spite of the Selby defeat, NEL wishes to publish *Candy* as fast as possible; specifically to coincide with the release of the movie *Candy* which NEL has learned will be released in London in September of 1968. Of course, tremendous speed is needed if the book is to be published and be in the bookstores by September of 1968.

On the other hand, there is a negative aspect to this happy news. In view of the Selby defeat, NEL cannot take the risk of publication without some cuts in the original manuscript.

I enclose herewith *Advice* (as the English call it) from a famous barrister, Richard du Cann. Attached to his *Advice* are the *Candy* deletions which du Cann feels are absolutely essential in order to avoid the same seizure and financial losses which LAST EXIT TO BROOKLYN encountered.

The decision to permit or not permit cuts must be made by

both of you. Mr. Shaw is very concerned and anxious to obtain your consent to these cuts so that NEL may publish. . . .

My usual reaction to a cut version of any book is to say "no." However, there are special circumstances which make me particularly anxious to get *Candy* published, in England, as fast as possible, even if it must be in a cut version.

For many months now the West Coast pirates here in the United States have been shipping their editions to England. This increasingly cuts into the potentiality of sale for your own edition on which you earn royalties. Although many jobbers in England are carrying the pirated editions from the U.S., the two biggest offenders are Del Books (no relation to our Dell) in Bradford, England, and the big London jobber, Rodney Books. I am concerned about the traffic in pirated *Candy*'s and think you should be. Until our present case here in the United States against Putnam is won, we are powerless against the pirates. Our only course of action is to get an authorized *Candy* published.

I suggest you both agree to the cuts, but that in so doing, we tell NEL that instead of the 5% which you now have, we would want 7% royalty from both hardcover and softcover sales. NEL can either obtain the additional 2% royalty from Girodias or itself.

On the Conservative Projection, you would earn approximately $95,729.85 at 7% and on the More Probable Projection, you would earn $149, 311.35 at 7%.*

The book will certainly be published by September of 1968 and this money would begin to reach you in early 1969 and would give you a handsome income for 1969.

Please let me hear from you as soon as possible.

Cordially,

Claire S. Degener

Letter from Richard Du Cann, Regarding U.K. Publication:

---

*Girodias controlled the U.K. rights (as per the final settlement) such that the authors never saw any income from N.E.L.

15th February, 1968

Ref: *Candy*

My meeting with Counsel yesterday yielded the following:

It would be extremely inadvisable, in Counsel's opinion, to reduce the number of deletions and amendments originally recommended. Counsel was emphatic on this point. He stressed that, although in many cases neither the narrative situation nor the vocabulary employed was objectionable in itself, it was the cumulative effect which would draw unwelcome attention to the book and render it more vulnerable to prosecution under English law. In the present climate, it would be foolish to dangle and bait at all in front of vigilantes. In short, he stood by his Opinion of 29 January.

He was prepared to concede, however, that it is not necessary to perform a straight pornectomy in every case — i.e., many of his suggested deletions could be reinstated in a revised form. After examining each condemned passage, he decided that the following could stay in provided that the objectionable words and the explicitness were removed:

Pages: 44, 45, 52, 53, 59, 60, 64, 66, 76, 126, 130, 143, 144, 145, 160, 161, 162, 215 and 216.

In some cases he has already indicated that amendments would be acceptable, so I have not listed these. In other cases — such as pp. 52/3 — rewriting would probably be a waste of effort as the cuts are minimal and specific. In some of the foregoing passages, too, there are no objectionable words *per se* but the scene described could be found to be objectionable by someone prepared to be outraged (who is, ultimately, the person for whom we are making these changes).

Finally, Counsel felt that both the book and its chance of avoiding prosecution would be greatly improved if in each instance above the authors attempted to sharpen the humour while blunting the sex.

DC [initials]

Re: CANDY

Further Advice

I return herewith the American edition of 'Candy' [Putnam hardcover] and my earlier advice dated 2nd May 1967. I attach below the amendments which in my view will be necessary to make to any version of the book if it is to be published in this country without facing certain prosecution. I must make it clear that publication as the book stands at this moment would invite prosecution. I need hardly remind the publishers that "Last Exit to Brooklyn" despite the most favourable circumstances of the trial was condemned by the jury at the Old Bailey and that as a result the climate is by no means propitious for launching a work which designedly deals with explicit sexual matters.

I should explain the basis on which I have made the suggested deletions and amendments. The book is one which is bound to attract attention by the authorities. Those who read allegedly obscene material for the various prosecuting bodies have certain rule-of-thumb standards of judgement which if infringed will provoke proceedings. Some of these are difficult to align with the test which the courts have to apply, that is whether the work read as a whole would deprave and corrupt those into whose hands it is likely to fall. The so-called four-letter words are a very good example. The repeated use of these would almost certainly lead to prosecution although it is very difficult to see in logic why the use of one such word on one occasion is less likely to deprave or corrupt than its use on more than one, on how repeated use would deprave and corrupt at all. Such arguments as these I fear carry very little weight. I have therefore sought to reduce the language and the incidents described in the book in such a way that no ["excuse" typed then X'd out] justification can be given to an official reader to advise proceedings against it. I cannot begin to justify some of the individual deletions I recommend on the grounds that the particular words or passages would in fact deprave or corrupt but only on the grounds that the number of such words or incidents in such an explicitly sexual theme would together be sufficient to lead to action being taken by the prosecuting authorities.

I should add that the American test of obscenity allows the dissemination of all written material unless it appeals to the prurient *and* is utterly without redeeming social value it is now increasingly clear that in England these tests have no validity. If a work can be judged to be obscene then it is only if the literary or other merits of the book outweigh "in the public good" the obscenity that it is safe. This in effect shifts the onus onto the publishers. Since even more now in the post-Last Exit period the boundaries in this field are going to be difficult to determine with exactitude and safety, the publishers will be on much safer ground presenting a work which is a satire with a sexual connotation than one which is sexual with a sexual connotation.

Richard Du Cann

Enclosure with Du Cann correspondence:
Candy: Amendments

Page 24	lines 26 to 31. Delete entirety.
Page 27	line 26 "flailing . . . onto page 2 line one . . . frenzy" delete.
Page 44	lines 18–24 delete "breast sucking"
	line 25 "stroking . . . sacrifice" delete
	line 31 "as he . . . giving fully" (on top of succeeding page. delete.
Pge 45	line 19 to page 46 line 1 " . . . as well" delete
Pge 52	lines 26 to 27 delete
Page 53	line 8 "Yes . . . hot" delete
	line 18 "organ. later" delete
	lines 27–8 "why . . . sopping" delete
Page 54	lines 6–7 "I'm . . . want" delete
Page 58	lines 15–16 "I kept sucking him off" delete or amend
Page 59	lines 6–10 "I wanted . . . stick" delete
Page 60	line 7 "COME" amend to 'come to you' without capitals
Page 64	lines 3–5 delete in entirety
	lines 10–16 delete in entirety
	lines 19–20 "but . . . out"
Page 66	lines 6–7 "as he . . . his ecstasy"
Page 76	lines 12–13 "You know . . . explained"

Page 92	line 12 "jack . . . mean" delete line 15 "jack-off" amend to 'liberate'
Page 93	line 2 "exactly like an erection" delete
Page 95	last line delete up to the word "evidence" line 2 on page 96.
Page 96	lines 7–8 "and . . . V" delete lines 17–19 delete in entirety lines 26–27 "take . . . and" delete
Page 97	lines 1–3 "the . . . decision" delete lines 6–7 "and . . . there" delete lines 13–14 "before . . . hand" delete lines 8–12 "if . . . examinations" delete line 22 "genitals" delete
Page 99	line 4 "wrench off" substitute 'get rid of'
Page 122	line 29 "JACK" delete lines 30–31 delete in entirety
Page 123	lines 1–2 "mand . . . and" delete
Page 126	lines 1–2 "lifted . . . member" amend to "undressed completely." lines 9–10 "and . . . her" delete lines 17–18 "His . . . sight" delete line 31 "member" delete
Page 130	lines 8–13 "Meeow . . . succession" delete lines 17–19 "One . . . up" delete lines 22–28 "Wu . . . amphitheatre" delete
Page 135	lines 13–15 "The . . . up" delete
Page 137	line 11 "You . . . lady" delete lines 12–13 "Fuck . . . dub" delete
Page 139	lines 25–27 "eating . . . squad" delete
Page 142	lines 23–30 "I want . . . mushroom" delete
Page 143	lines 29–30 "to . . . month" delete
Page 144	lines 3–5 "And . . . tummy" delete lines 11–31 "holding . . . tongue" delete
Page 145	lines 5–6 "with . . . honeypot" delete line 14 "I need . . . to page 149 line 24 . . . night" delete

Page 154 line 23 "somehow . . . to page155 line 13 . . . and" delete

Page 155 lines 10–12 "I'D . . . to-night" delete
line 27 "I want piss" delete

Page 160 line 20 "quickly . . . to page 161 . . . clutching" delete

Page 161 line 16 "to keep sucking and yet" delete

Page 162 lines 5–5 "snatching . . . labes" delete
lines 30–31 delete in entirety

Page 168 lines 2–3 "and he . . . inside" amend to 'forced his attentions on her'

Page 180 lines 10–12 "just as . . . you" delete
lines 25–26 "but . . . testis" delete

Page 201 line 4–4 "inadvertently . . . moment" delete

Page 203 lines 18–20 "as . . . own" delete

Page 205 line 20 to the end of page 209 must either be rewritten or amended or deleted, it cannot stand with this specific detail.

Page 215 in the letter lines 2–4 "I had . . . minestroning" delete
line 6 "not . . . mile-a-minute" delete

Page 216 lines 3–4 "he . . . and" delete
line 9–13 "I put . . . JEW" delete
line 18 "she ain't shit" amend
last line of the letter "and don't take any wooden organ" delete
First line of the text again requires a consequential amendment to omit "menstruating"

Page 217 line 1 "jacked off" delete
lines 27–30 "It was . . . somehow" delete

Pp. 222–4 These will have to be rewritten without the sexual connection.

Acknowledgments

Many thanks to the Seavers, Dick and Jeannette, to Greg Comer whose editorial advice and guidance were invaluable, and Arcade Publishing in general for their patience and support. To the Hoffenberg Estate; Daniel, Juliette, Zeline, Couquite, David and Kerry. Lilla Lyon and the Maurice Girodias Estate and the Olympia Press, George Plimpton, Leon Friedman, the Terry Southern Literary Trust, literary agents Susan Schulman and Sterling Lord, and the Fales Library at NYU. Carol Southern, for her spot-on editorial input, and Erin Clermont for her copyediting. Thanks also to Girodias biographer John de St. Jorre, bibliographer Patrick Kearney, Sam Merrill, Lee Hill, Walter Zacharius, Walter Minton, Cindy Degener, Leon Friedman, Gideon Cashman, Peter Israel, Mare Meeske, Alston Anderson, James Grauerholz, Edward de Grazia and Yeshiva University, Barney Rosset, Tom Lisanti, Michael McClure, Lee Server, James Marquand, Roger Mexico, Albert Goldman, and Jim Yoakum. Photographers: Steve Schapiro, William Claxton, Allen Ginsberg Trust, Aram Avakian courtesy of Alexandra Avakian, Jean Mohr, Pud Gadiot, the Southern and Hoffenberg Picture Collections, and Suzan Cooper. Al Goldstein and *Screw,* Eric Michaelson, Stuart Cornfeld, Han-Peter Litscher, D. A. Pennebaker, Michele Clarke and *The Paris Review.* Ken Fricklas for Web-hosting *terrysouthern.com,* Webmaster Damon Gitelman, Rob Smoke transcriptions, KGNU Boulder Community Radio, the Dahn Center, Neil Parker and Timeless Graphics, Mike Golden and Instant Classics, Jim Sikora, Lynn Munroe, Bo Altherr and Anchor Bay Video, Free Speech TV. Also to DJ Cheb i Sabbah for the tunes: 1 Giant Leap, Natascha Atlas, Tariq Ali. The Greek contingent: Yiannis kai Venettia, Panos kai Noni, my wife, Theodosia, and my daughters, Nefeli-Marie and Chloe-Caroline Southern.

Grateful acknowledgment is made to the following for permission to reprint unpublished and previously published materials:

The Terry Southern Estate and The Terry Southern Literary Trust: Letters and other writings by Terry Southern. Reprinted by permission of Nile Southern and Joe LoGiudice cotrustees, and by special arrangement with Susan Schulman, a Literary Agency.

The Mason Hoffenberg Estate, Daniel and Juliette Hoffenberg: Letters and excerpts from Mason Hoffenberg's journals. Reprinted by special arrangement with Sterling Lord Literistic, Inc.

The Maurice Girodias Estate, Lilla Lyon, Juliette Kahane and Valerie

Mandacé: Letters and other writings by Maurice Girodias. Reprinted by permission.

Nelson Algren: Excerpt from a letter to Terry Southern. Reprinted by permission of Donadio & Olson, Inc., copyright by Nelson Algren.

Black Spring Press (U.K.): Excerpts from *The Paris Olympia Press, An Annotated Bibliography with Introductory Essays by Maurice Girodias & Patrick J. Kearney* (Black Spring Press: London, 1987). Reprinted by permission.

Fales Library, the Elmer Holmes Bobst Library, New York University: Excerpts from letters from the archive of Sterling Lord. Reproduced by permission.

Grand Street, Jean Stein, ed.: Excerpts from Terry Southern's "Flashing on Gid" (Vol. 10, #1, 1991) and "The Refreshing Ambiguity of the Déjà Vu." (Vol. 11, #3, 1992). Reprinted by permission.

Grove/Atlantic, Inc.: Excerpts from *Candy* © 1958, 1959, 1962, 1964 by Terry Southern and Mason Hoffenberg. Reprinted by permission.

HarperCollins, Inc.: Excerpts from *A Grand Guy: The Art and Life of Terry Southern,* by Lee Hill, © 2000 by Lee Hill. Reprinted by permission.

Instant Classics; The Culture Quick Mart, www.instantclassics.com, Mike Golden, ed.: "The Next Man to Go: An Interview with 'Accursed Publisher' Maurice Girodias" by Mike Golden, ©1999 by Mike Golden. Reproduced by permission.

The Nation: Excerpt from "Donkey Man by Twilight" by Nelson Algren. Reprinted by permission from the May 18, 1964, issue of *The Nation.*

The Paris Review: Excerpts from "The Art of Fiction: Henry Green," (Volume 5, #19, Summer, 1958). Reprinted by permission.

Playboy Enterprises: Excerpts from the article "Mason Hoffenberg Gets in a Few Licks: An Eight-Martini Chat with the Co-author of 'Candy,' Who Reminisces About William Burroughs, Terry Southern, Bob Dylan—and the Night He Didn't Get Raped by Eleven Faggots," by Sam Merrill, which originally appeared in *Playboy* magazine (November 1973). Attempts were made to contact the author of the article, Sam Merrill, without success.

George Plimpton: Excerpts from letters. Reproduced by permission of Russell & Volkening. Copyright George Plimpton.

Random House, Inc.: Excerpts from *Venus Bound: The Erotic Voyage of the Olympia Press and Its Writers,* by John de St. Jorre, copyright © 1996 by John de St. Jorre. Reprinted by permission.

Seven Stories Press: Excerpts from *Paul Krassner's Impolite Interviews,* ed. Paul Krassner. Copyright © 1999. Reprinted by permission of Paul Krassner.

William Styron: Extracts from "Transcontinental with Tex" reprinted by permission of the author and Don Congdon Associates. © 1996 by William Styron, first published in *The Paris Review,* issue 138.

Notes

xi The Krassner exchange: "An Impolite Interview with Terry Southern," *The Realist no. 50*, ed. Paul Krassner.

xi *"Its as if you vomit"* Sam Merrill, "Mason Hoffenberg Gets in a Few Licks: An Eight-Martini Chat with the Co-author of 'Candy,' Who Reminisces About William Burroughs, Terry Southern, Bob Dylan—and the Night He Didn't Get Raped by Eleven Faggots," *Playboy*, November 1973.

xvii *"the connecting link"* Patrick J. Kearney, *The Paris Olympia Press: An Annotated Bibliography* (London: Black Spring Press, 1987), p. 7.

xvii *"a day out of court"* Couquite Hoffenberg, letter to author, 2003.

xx Girodias often maintained that between thirteen and fifteen million copies of *Candy* were sold in unauthorized editions, vaguely citing *Publishers Weekly*. Putnam's announced (on the cover of its 1975 edition) that it had by then sold three million copies.

1. Paris: 1947–1953

3 *"When people saw him"* John de St. Jorre, *Venus Bound: The Erotic Voyage of the Olympia Press and Its Writers* (New York: Random House, 1994), p. 160.

4 *"From '48 to '52"* Mike Golden, "Now Dig This: Interview with Terry Southern," *Reflex*, no. 27 (September 1992).

5 *"I don't think intentions"* Krassner, "Impolite Interview."

5 *"silent, inscrutable presence"* Avakian and Southern made an impression, especially on Marquand, whom Hill interviewed. Lee Hill, *A Grand Guy: The Art and Life of Terry Southern* (New York: HarperCollins, 2000), p. 36.

5 *"where the whole point"* Terry Southern, "I Am Mike Hammer" (New York: Kensington Publishing, 1990), p. 176.

5 *"It was sort of an embarrassment"* Lee Hill, *A Grand Guy: The Art and Life of Terry Southern* (New York: HarperCollins, 2000), p. 36.

6 *"The essence of hip"* Henry Allen, "Terry Southern's School of Satire," *Washington Post*, 1 November 1995.

6 *"Back in the late Forties"* Michael Perkins, "An Interview with Terry Southern," *Screw*, 26 October 1970.

7 *"1) pay a French person"* Lee Server, "An Interview with Terry

Southern," *Now Dig This: The Unspeakable Writings of Terry Southern 1950–1995* (New York: Grove/Atlantic, 2000), p. 4.

7 Couquite Hoffenberg's recollections of her first encounters with Mason are based on a phone interview with her in the Dordogne and her letter to the author, December 2003.

8 *"I was living"* William Styron, "Transcontinental with Tex," *The Paris Review,* no. 138 (1996): 215.

9: *"It was a time"* Couquite Hoffenberg, interview with author, Paris, 2003.

9 *"He was really Mr. Soun"* De St. Jorre, *Venus Bound,* p. 164.

9 *"Get up, no matter what"* Carol Southern, interview with author, New York, 2003.

10 *"In the early stages"* George Plimpton, "Terry Southern: Introduction," *The Paris Review,* no. 138 (1996).

2. A Booklegger's Son

14 *"spice between the covers"* De St. Jorre, *Venus Bound,* p. 6.

14–17 *"These were the novels"* Maurice Girodias, *The Frog Prince* (New York: Crown, 1980), p. 113; Girodias describes his early days and style, p. 315; describes Mr. Bogous, p. 241.

18 *"I published a pamphlet"* Mike Golden, "Chez Lolita: Candy and the Ginger Man Make Too," *New York Writer,* Spring 1989.

18 *"These people"* Ibid.

19 *"One evening, Maurice"* De St. Jorre, *Venus Bound,* p. 57.

19 *"I usually printed"* Golden, "Chez Lolita."

19 *"Afterward, we talked"* De St. Jorre, *Venus Bound,* pp. 57–58.

20 *"Girodias of Olympia Press"* Bill Morgan, *An Accidental Autobiography: Selected Letters of Gregory Corso* (New York: New Directions, 2003), p. 240.

20: *"Our backgrounds"* Marilyn Meeske, interview with author, New York, 2003.

20 *"With most of the writers"* Mike Golden, "Chez Lolita."

21: *"Twice I was caught"* Ibid.

21 *"The anti-censorship aspect"* Marilyn Meeske, interview with author, New York City, 2003.

21 *"Aside from her Junoesque beauty"* Terry Southern, "Flashing on Gid," *Grand Street* (1991), ed. Jean Stein.

21 *"We were natural DB writers"* De St. Jorre, *Venus Bound,* p. 84.

22 *"He seemed to fancy himself"* Southern, "Flashing on Gid."

3. Greenwich Village: 1952–1955

23 *"I'm walking home"* Sam Merrill, "Mason Hoffenberg Gets in a Few Licks: An Eight-Martini Chat with the Co-Author of 'Candy,' Who Remi-

nisces About William Burroughs, Terry Southern, Bob Dylan—and the Night He Didn't Get Raped by Eleven Faggots," *Playboy,* November 1973.

25 *"This was the first wave"* Marilyn Meeske, interview with author, New York, 2003.

4. Enter Candy Christian

29 *"Everyone who read the story"* Southern, "Flashing on Gid."

31 *"You could stroll"* William Styron, "Transcontinental with Tex," *The Paris Review,* no. 138 (Spring 1996): 215.

5. Giving the Old Head a Breather

36 *"They were sitting together"* Carol Southern, interview with author, New York, 2003.

38 *"Sinbad Vail at the time"* Couquite Hoffenberg, letter to author, December 2003.

41 *"I first went to Europe with Nori"* Marilyn Meeske, interview with author, New York, 2003.

42 *"We were Barge Captains"* Golden, "Now Dig This: Interview with Terry Southern," p. 49.

44 Nelson Algren's letter is in The Terry Southern Archive, Henry W. and Albert A. Berg Collection of English and American Literature, New York Public Library.

6. Our Poets Love It So

45 *"The publication of Lolita"* Golden, "Chez Lolita."

45 *"[Trocchi] was going to collect some money"* Terry Southern, deposition, 30 April 1975, Terry Southern Archive, Berg Collection, New York Public Library.

46 *"It was one of those"* Southern, "Flashing on Gid."

50 *"The job was fun"* Carol Southern, interview with author, New York, 2003.

52 Lee Hill writes about Terry's relationship with Henry Green in *A Grand Guy: The Art and Life of Terry Southern* (New York: HarperCollins, 2000).

7. A Clean, Well-Lighted Place: Geneva, 1956–1958

56–57 Girodias's stormy relationship with J. P. Donleavy is documented in de St. Jorre's *Venus Bound,* p. 92

57 *"Those were the days"* De St. Jorre, *Venus Bound,* p. 96.

57 *"The soirée itself proved"* Terry Southern, "Flashing on Gid," *Grand Street* (1991), ed. Jean Stein.

58 *"This was the lowest point"* De St. Jorre, *Venus Bound,* p. 104.

8. Publishers and Other Criminals

62 *"One day a police inspector"* Golden, "Chez Lolita."

65 *"I think the idea of Candy"* Carol Southern, interview with author, New York, 2003.

65 *"When Mason first came in, he wrote a scene"* De St. Jorre, *Venus Bound,* p. 159.

9. Essentially More Warm Than You

68 Mordechai Richler's telegram is in the Terry Southern Archive, Berg Collection, NYPL.

69 *"Driving Henry on to the airport"* Carol Southern, interview with author, New York, 2003.

10. I to the Hunchback, and Thou Therefrom

78 *"[Ted] Kotcheff recalls Hoffenberg"* Hill, *A Grand Guy,* p. 36.

12. This Souped-Up Correspondence

99–100 Alston Anderson's letters are in the Terry Southern Archive, Berg Collection, NYPL.

13. ". . . 3 . . . 2 . . . 1 . . . Jack Off!"

101 *"Mason and Couquite were away"* Carol Southern, interview with author, New York, 2003.

101 *"Our most frequented"* Terry Southern, "Flashing on Gid," *Grand Street* (1991), ed. Jean Stein.

103 John Marquand's letter is in the Terry Southern Archive, Berg Collection, NYPL.

14. Flashpoint: 1958

113 The BBC interview transcript is in the Terry Southern Archive, Berg Collection, NYPL.

113 Allen Ginsberg's letter is in the Terry Southern Archive, Berg Collection, NYPL.

114 Michael McClure's letter of March 26, 1958, is in the Terry Southern Archive, Berg Collection, NYPL.

15. A House O' Porn Extraordinaire

123 Donleavy's and Terry's comments on the publishing industry are from the piece written by Elaine Dundy, "The Off-Beat Americans" New Writers in Search of Peace Away From Home," *Harper's Bazaar*, August 1958.

124 *"He and Vera were absolutely convinced"* De St. Jorre, *Venus Bound*, p. 144.

16. Just Call Me Lollipop

130 *"Whether the title changes were obvious"* Kearney, *The Paris Olympia Press*, p. 32.

17. New Life, New England

139 On the opening and history of the Grande Séverine, de St. Jorre, *Venus Bound*, p. 259.

139 *"On the ground floor"* Thomas Quinn Curtiss, *New York Herald Tribune*, 7 August 1960.

140 *"He thought he would* get *to Paris"* Marilyn Meeske, interview with author, New York, 2003.

140 *"At its height"* De St. Jorre, *Venus Bound*, p. 259.

140 Eric Kahane and Miriam Worms on the Gallimard party, de St. Jorre, *Venus Bound*, p. 151.

141 *"He was a genius as a publisher"* Walter Zacharius, interview with author, New York, 2003.

141 *"A girlfriend and myself"* De St. Jorre, *Venus Bound*, p. 261.

142 *"Lou said"* Zacharius interview.

142 *"My friends from the vice squad"* Maurice Girodias, introduction, in Kearney's *The Paris Olympia Press*, p. 9.

144 *"American critics—and this is true"* Terry Southern, "William Gaddis," in *Writers in Revolt*, ed. Richard Seaver, Terry Southern, Alex Trocchi (New York: Viking, 1962).

144 *"What all this assorted dada"* Martin Levin, "A Panther in the Kennel Show," *New York Times*, 21 February 1960.

147 *"They emerge, they hold him he stays"* R. F. Fortune, "Arapesh: Folktale 32," American Ethnological Society, vol. 19 (New York: J. J. Augustin, 1942).

18. *Candy* Goes to Italy, Mason Gets Nervous

150 *"We wondered"* De St. Jorre, *Venus Bound*, p. 261.

20. The *Olympia Review*

168 *"I was surprised"* Marilyn Meeske, interview with author, New York, 2003.

21. sHit Habit (#6)

177 *"Terry came to me"* Sterling Lord, interview with author, New York, 2003.

22. The Naked and the Sucked

188 Terry's interview with Kubrick, translated into French, was published shortly after Kubrick's death in *Les Inrockuptibles.* Portions of it, which Terry worked into a piece on *Strangelove,* will appear for the first time in English in David Wallis's book *Killed: True Stories You Were Never Meant to Read,* forthcoming from Nation Books.

189 The phrase "A Kafkaesque nightmare comedy" appears in Terry's unpublished interview with Kubrick. Terry attributes the phrase to Kubrick.

23. Fuzz Against Junk

192 *"It was extremely staid"* De St. Jorre, Venus Bound, p. 272.

194 *"That summer"* Carol Southern, interview with author, Boulder, CO, 2003.

194 *"Girodias didn't pay us"* De St. Jorre, *Venus Bound,* p. 167.

194 *"None of them had applied"* Ibid.

25. The *Candy* Wars

219 *"I had this fantastic nightclub"* Golden, "Chez Lolita."

26. Something Worth Blasting

221 *"it's a scandal" Newsweek,* 20 April, 1964.

224–225 The exchange with Krassner appears in "An Impolite Interview with Terry Southern" *The Realist,* Krassner, ed.

27. A Suitable Vehicle for Prosecution

230 *"What is rare"* Terry Southern, "Miller, Only the Beginning" *The Nation,* 18 November, 1961.

231 The FBI memos on Terry are in his archive in the Berg Collection, NYPL.

232 *"It is a devastating ridicule"* Terry Southern, "Rolling Over Our Nerve Endings," *Book Week,* 8 November 1964.

233 Attorney Edward de Grazia quotes the Burroughs letter and recalls Ginsberg's testimony in his article entitled "Allen Ginsberg, Norman Mailer, Barney Rosset: Their Struggles Against Censorship Recalled," originally published in *Cardozo Life,* Fall 1998, a publication of Benjamin N. Cardozo

School of Law and Jacob Burns Institute for Advanced Legal Studies, Yeshiva University, New York.

28. *Candy* Does America

236 *"Your article 'Creeping Censorship'"* Maurice Girodias, *Newsweek,* 11 May 1964.

239 *"Unavailable in all [Northern Illinois] libraries"* Richard Schwarze, "Want to Read 'Candy'?, Don't Go to the Library," *Berwyn Life*, 7 August 1964.

239 *"Official United States, or Texas"* Alfred Chester, "A Sugar-Coated Purgative," *New York Herald Tribune,* 17 May 1964.

240 The letter from the "Holy Warrior" is in the Terry Southern Archive, Berg Collection, NYPL.

241 *"AN UN-AMERICAN IDEA"* Nelson Algren, *Life*, 8 May 1964.

242 *"pits the bachelor trainee ('you')"* William Styron, "Tootsie Rolls," *New York Review of Books,* 14 May 1964.

243 *"sex in this country has been"* Nelson Algren, "Donkey Man by Twilight: The Talents of Terry Southern," 18 May 1964.

243 *"Dig a thing like this"* Sam Merrill, "Mason Hoffenberg Gets in a Few Licks" *Playboy,* November 1973.

245 *"Terry Southern is a new kind"* Mel Gussow (uncredited), "No Limits," *Newsweek,* 22 June 1964.

29. Going Hollywood

250 *"it was my fault"* Merrill, "Mason Hoffenberg Gets in a Few Licks."

250 *"Mason swore to me many times"* Walter Minton, letter to author, 10 March 2002.

251 Walter Minton's letter is in the Terry Southern Archive, Berg Collection, NYPL.

255 *"When I heard they had been kidnapped"* De St. Jorre, *Venus Bound,* p. 170.

256 *"With the publication of Candy"* Jack Hunvaldo, "Terry Southern: The Man Who Made Candy Quicker Than Liquor" *Ace,* Vol. 8, No. 4, (New York, January 1965), ed. Tom Lasswell.

30. Enter the Pirates

257 *"I never heard that Girodias"* De St. Jorre, *Venus Bound,* p. 171.

258–259 Walter Zacharius described Girodias's presentation of *Candy,* Minton's involvement, and the Lancer edition cover in an interview by the author, New York, 2003.

259 *"A lot of legal people at Putnam"* Walter Minton, interview with author, New York, 2003.

259 *"I don't know why Terry"* De St. Jorre, *Venus Bound,* p. 180.

260–264 John de St. Jorre interviewed Walter Minton about getting the paperback out and captured Leon Friedman's assessment of the ill-fated Rosset deal (p. 263) and Williams' account of the New York operation (p. 264), as well as Nabokov's assessment of Girodias in *Venus Bound,* pp. 180, 171, 270, 139.

261 Girodias on "porno-gangsters" in Kearney's *The Paris Olympia Press,* p.10.

261–263 The FBI memos on Terry are in his archive in the Berg Collection, NYPL.

31. *"Good Grief, Me a Movie?"*

270 *"The first time Dylan"* Merrill, "Mason Hoffenberg Gets in a Few Licks."

270 *"Mason was quite manic"* D. A. Pennebaker, interview with author, New York, 2003.

271 *"He was writing the script"* Hill, *A Grand Guy,* p. 133.

272 Terry's *Candy* screenplay is in his archive in the Berg Collection, NYPL.

274 *"What with the Big Lettuce"* George Plimpton's undated letter is in Terry's archive in the Berg Collection, NYPL.

275–276 De St. Jorre sums up the stalemate, as well as the Copyright Office's position in *Venus Bound,* pp. 173, 174.

32. Half of Paris for the Rights

280 *"I remember being"* Walter Zacharius, interview with author, New York, 2003.

33. Bedlam Was Never So Hectic

290 Sy Litvinoff's letter is in Terry's archive, Berg Collection, NYPL.

291 *"I told myself"* Mason Hoffenberg, "Notes from the Sixties," unpublished journal.

291 *"I got very depressed"* Hill, *A Grand Guy,* p. 184.

34. Tangled Up in Gid

292 *"He was desperate and contrite"* De St. Jorre, *Venus Bound,* p. 185.

292 *"If you want to talk about a pirate"* Walter Zacharius, interview with author, New York, 2003.

293 *"Mason was, as usual"* De St. Jorre, *Venus Bound,* p. 189.

301 *"Putnam and the authors"* De St. Jorre, *Venus Bound,* 196.

304 *"Within the last couple of weeks"* Paul Nathan, "Rights and Permissions" *Publishers Weekly,* 8 May 1967, Vol. 191, No. 19.

305 *"It is a sad fact"* Paul Nathan, "Rights and Permissions" *Publishers Weekly,* 22 May 1967, Vol. 191 No. 21.

306 *"I liked the book"* Robert Haggiag, interview with author, New York, 2003.

35. With the Spring Comes Mason and Brando

306 *"Ultimately what persuaded ABC was"* Sy Litvinoff, interview with author, Los Angeles, 2003.

311 *"The* [ABC] *producers asked me to go"* De St. Jorre, *Venus Bound,* p. 197.

311 *"They thought it couldn't be done"* Robert Haggiag, interview with author, New York, 2003.

312 *"When Christian Marquand"* De St. Jorre, *Venus Bound,* p. 197.

312 *"She had made a picture"* Robert Haggiag, interview with author, New York, 2003.

312 Haggiag recalled the terms with Brando in an interview with the author, New York, 2003.

313 *"We're going to throw the book away" Candy* DVD, Anchor Bay Entertainment.

313 *"We were all kind of gathered"* Peter Manso, *Brando: The Biography* (New York: Hyperion, 1994), p. 636.

314 The unsigned review of *Candy* appeared in the *Times Literary Supplement,* Sept. 26, 1968, p. 1069. A week prior, an editorial had appeared concerning the appearance of NEL's censored edition.

315 Holly Hutchins on the closing of Olympia Press, de St. Jorre, *Venus Bound.*

36. Scrawlings on a Cave Wall

318 *"It was like a coffee table book"* Robert Haggiag, interview with the author, New York, 2003.

320 Girodias's strange involvement with Valerie Solanas is recounted in de St. Jorre's *Venus Bound,* pp. 276–278.

321 *"Lamy has now"* De St. Jorre, *Venus Bound,* p. 280.

321 *"I am now winning"* Ibid., p. 281.

37. Weird Scenes Inside the Big Pink

325 *"Girodias would never admit"* De St. Jorre, *Venus Bound,* p. 108.

326 *"Since I was unable"* De St. Jorre, *Venus Bound,* 281.

326 *"I could then"* Ibid, 282.

326 *"I bribed the receiver"* Ibid.

326 Girodias described the auction of Olympia in Golden, "Chez Lolita."

327 *"I heard that he suspected Mason"* De St. Jorre, *Venus Bound,* p. 286.

327 *"At some point Alex and I"* Ibid., p. 77.

328 *"I regarded him as a bully"* Ibid., p. 114.

329 *"I found this a tasteless"* David Dempsey, "Stupefying Peep Show," *New York Times,* 13 September 1970.

331 *"That place was"* D. A. Pennebaker, interview with author, New York, 2003.

331–334 Mason's recollections of his time in Woodstock, as well as the Burnett incident, are taken from Sam Merrill's *Playboy* interview, "Mason Hoffenberg Gets In a Few Licks," November 1973.

332 *"What's up?"* Recalled by Tim Keenan, who was a teen when he met Mason in Woodstock.

332 *"We had many visits from Dylan"* Letter from Couquite Hoffenberg to author, December 2003.

333 *"Now, secretly, the important revelation"* Mason Hoffenberg, "Notes from the Sixties," unpublished journal.

335 Girodias writes of *President Kissinger* and his arrest in his introduction to Kearney, *The Paris Olympia Press,* p. 11.

336 *"I am paying a heavy karma"* Girodias letter cited in de St. Jorre, *Venus Bound,* p. 297.

38. Mason Licks Terry

337 *"Levon's a redneck"* Merrill, "Mason Hoffenberg Gets In a Few Licks."

339 Terry's deposition for the *Playboy* suit is in his archive in the Berg Collection, NYPL.

341 Stuart Cornfeld reflected on Mason's party tricks and Mel Brooks in an interview with the author, Los Angeles, 2003.

342 *"I noticed quickly"* Mason Hoffenberg, "Notes from the Sixties," unpublished journal.

345 *"Late that night"* Mason Hoffenberg, "Notes from the Sixties," unpublished journal.

346 *"People were pitching these ideas"* Hill, *A Grand Guy,* p. 246.

346 *"I think NBC was just a weird"* Ibid., p. 247.

347 *"We went out with Anita"* Eric Michelson, interview with author, Los Angeles, 2003.

39. The Refreshing Ambiguity of the *Déjà Vu*

349 *"There are too many stories"* Patrick J. Kearney, email to author, September, 2003.

349–350 For Girodias's quote about his book, *The Frog Prince,* and Rosset's assessment of Girodias, see de St. Jorre, *Venus Bound,* p. 298.

350–351 The narrative is from "The Refreshing Ambiguity of the Déjà Vu," *Grand Street* (1992), ed. Jean Stein.

350 *"If this Arab thing"* Merrill, "Mason Hoffenberg Gets In a Few Licks."

352 *"In appearance he is rumpled"* George Plimpton, introduction to Terry Southern's *Red Dirt Marijuana, and Other Tastes* (New York: Kensington Publishing, 1990).

Appendix A: Selected Interviews with Terry Southern Concerning *Candy* and "Pornography"

357 Albert Goldman's interview with Terry is in Terry's archive in the Berg Collection, NYPL.

Appendix B: Anatomy of a Pornectomy

362 The du Cann letter is in Terry's archive in the Berg Collection, NYPL.

For additional *Candy Men* material, visit www.terrysouthern.com/candymen.

Index